Preaching the Gospel of Matthew

Also available from Westminster John Knox Press

Dawn Ottoni Wilhelm, *Preaching the Gospel of Mark: Proclaiming the Power of God*
Keith F. Nickle, *Preaching the Gospel of Luke: Proclaiming God's Royal Rule*
Lamar Williamson Jr, *Preaching the Gospel of John: Proclaiming the Living Word*

Preaching the Gospel of Matthew

Proclaiming God's Presence

Stanley P. Saunders

WESTMINSTER
JOHN KNOX PRESS
LOUISVILLE • KENTUCKY

First edition
Published by Westminster John Knox Press
Louisville, Kentucky

10 11 12 13 14 15 16 17 18 19–10 9 8 7 6 5 4 3 2 1

Unless otherwise indicated, Scripture quotations are from the New Revised Standard Version of the Bible, copyright © 1989 by the Division of Christian Education of the National Council of the Churches of Christ in the U.S.A., and are used by permission.

Book design by Sharon Adams
Cover design by Kevin Darst & Jennifer K. Cox

Library of Congress Cataloging-in-Publication Data

Saunders, Stanley P.
    Preaching the Gospel of Matthew : proclaiming God's presence / Stanley P. Saunders.
      p. cm.
    Includes bibliographical references.
    ISBN 978-0-664-22920-7 (alk. paper)
    1. Bible. N.T. Matthew–Homiletical use.   2. Bible. N.T. Matthew–Commentaries. I. Title.

BS2575.55.S38 2010
226.2'06–dc22

2010017843

PRINTED IN THE UNITED STATES OF AMERICA

♾ The paper used in this publication meets the minimum requirements of the American National Standard for Information Sciences–Permanence of Paper for Printed Library Materials, ANSI Z39.48-1992.

Westminster John Knox Press advocates the responsible use of our natural resources. The text paper of this book is made from 30% post-consumer waste.

*In memory
of Max and
Evilo Saunders*

CONTENTS

INTRODUCTION

"All authority in heaven and on earth has been given to me. . . .
And remember, I am with you always, to the end of the age."
Matthew 28:18, 20

The two assertions above, which frame the Great Commission, articulate the goal of Matthew's Gospel. From beginning to end, Matthew is the story of how Jesus is "God with us." A necessary corollary to this focus on the nature of divine presence is Matthew's relentless attention to the differences between human powers and God's power at work to redeem the world from bondage to death. The power at work in Jesus reveals the immediate, effective dimensions of God's presence in human experience. As the story of Jesus unfolds, Matthew uncovers the curse of violence, distrust, and alienation that has stalked humankind, including Israel, under the power of death. This curse is overcome only when death itself is vanquished and God dwells again with the people. Matthew promises that God is present with Jesus among the "least ones," wherever even two or three gather in Jesus' name and even in the face of apparently overwhelming human forces. God's power brings healing, gathers the lost, forgives, restores, and challenges all our assumptions about the way the world must be. In a world beset by daily violence, economic exploitation, alienation and distrust, and the collapse of cherished institutions—our world as well as Matthew's—the gospel continues to offer the only real "good news." When we hear this story and become immersed in Jesus' teaching and way, we become witnesses, like Jesus' disciples, who carry the good news to all the world.

Matthew's claim that Jesus is the defining expression of God's presence and power among us arises both from early Christian convictions about Jesus and from the historical circumstances of the day. When the Romans destroyed Jerusalem and the temple in 70 CE, the people of God, including followers of Christ's way, had to face hard questions. Was God punishing Israel again for her sins? Had God abandoned God's people? Would the prophetic vision of restoration and liberation ever be fulfilled? Was the hope for a messiah and king mistaken? Was Caesar, in fact, the "savior" and "**son of God**"? [A glossary of key words, concepts, and groups in Matthew is provided at the end of this volume. In each section of the commentary, the first occurrence of terms included in the glossary is marked in boldface type.] Did the empire of Rome really embody divine will and order, and offer "salvation" and "peace," as it claimed? These questions compelled all those who identified themselves with Israel's story to reexamine the institutions that had defined them as a people and to search the Scriptures with new eyes. For Christians like Matthew, the story of Jesus, not Caesar, was the real "good news." Jesus had announced and inaugurated God's "empire," where divine power is displayed in mercy and healing, not in exploitation and violence. Matthew's story calls forth and trains a community of interns and agents who live in the transformed time and space that is the "**empire of heaven**," bearing witness to God's presence and power among the nations. Wherever these witnesses go, the one to whom all power has been given goes with them.

PERFORMING THE GOSPEL

The nature, cast, and power of Matthew's story become most evident to those who experience the story as the first Christians did: performed aloud as a whole in the worshiping assembly. Oral performance, like a radio drama, engages the audience more completely and powerfully than mere words on a page. When we hear the Gospel performed as a whole, we join emotionally as well as intellectually in the interpretive process. As we bring our own creative energy to bear, we become part of the story. Our written Gospels are transcripts of performances that had been presented again and again in congregations across the Mediterranean world, usually without needing script in hand. Just as modern Americans often allude in conversation to well-known stories, lines, and images from television and movies, the evangelists could rely on people to know the media of their day: everything from Genesis to Isaiah to the stories about Caesar. They could quote Scripture with the certainty that their audiences knew it by heart, even the larger contexts from which the quotations came. Our modern approach to the Gospels as collections of discrete stories and teachings, usually read in pieces and snippets from the page, makes it much harder for us to "hear," "see," and "understand" (cf. Matt. 13:10–17) them. In order to hear Matthew's Gospel well, we must learn how to perform it as a living community. As we preach and teach from Matthew, we should also consider occasions in which congregations might hear it again as a whole. As we work with individual stories and passages, we need to attend constantly to the larger story. What are some of its most important features?

GENRES AND STRUCTURES

Matthew was an accomplished storyteller working with astute audiences, who would hear the Gospel more than once. In order to provide that kind of audience with a rich story to engage, Matthew intentionally mixes the generic conventions associated with Greek and Roman biography, Jewish history, and "apocalypses." Biographies usually focused on the lives of philosophers or kings, whose life and teaching formed a coherent whole that was worthy of emulation. History writers, on the other hand, were more interested in the themes, movements, conflicts, meaning, and destiny of peoples. Matthew's story of Jesus combines both of these agendas into one. As a teacher, Jesus' teachings and deeds form a consistent, compelling whole that coheres with his calling and destiny. But he is more than just a teacher. Jesus is the culmination and fulfillment of Israel's history, and he changes the course and destiny of the whole world. Already in the genealogy (a form found in both Jewish histories and pagan biographies), Matthew is identifying Jesus' biographical origins and locating him at the turn of Israel's history. Jesus is also a revelatory (**apocalyptic**) figure, whose life and ministry show us God's presence and power. Matthew emphasizes the ways Jesus crosses the boundaries between the human and the divine, between earth and heaven, and invites his followers to do so too.

Because the Gospel would be heard more than once, the evangelist provides more than one way to hear it. Matthew incorporates multiple, overlapping structural patterns. Five times the formula "and when Jesus had finished these sayings . . ." signals the transition from one of Jesus' major speeches to a narrative section that recounts his ministry (7:28–29; 11:1; 13:53; 19:1; and 26:1). This helps the audience identify the most obvious of Matthew's structural schemes: the alternation of narrative and discourse (which resembles the Deuteronomistic History). Matthew suggests another structural pattern by the use of the formula "from that time Jesus began to . . . ," at the beginning of Jesus' ministry (4:17) and when he turns toward Jerusalem, where he will be crucified (16:21). Other readers note the presence of recurrent themes and motifs, arranged as a series of parallels that fold back on themselves (a "chiasm"), with the parables of chapter 13 as the center point. Still others organize the Gospel into narrative blocks, each focused on key incidents. Together these diverse ways of perceiving the Gospel's structure help us hear it better. For simplicity's sake, in laying out this commentary, I have followed primarily Matthew's

scheme of alternating narratives and discourses, while reminding readers
here and there of other structural factors at work.

RIDDLES, IRONY, DOUBLE ENTENDRE, AND OXYMORON: MATTHEW TRAINS THE AUDIENCE TO LISTEN

Matthew's canonical location at the head of the New Testament, the
first of the Gospels, may be an indication of its popularity among the earliest generations of Christians, part of which was due to the abundance
of teaching materials intermingled with stories about Jesus. Matthew's
Gospel may also have been appealing because of the evangelist's penchant for riddles, irony, double entendre, and oxymoron. This may be
most evident in Jesus' **parables**, which often feature images that may be
understood in multiple ways. Matthew wants us not to settle on just one
of these as the "right way" to hear the parables, but to grapple with the
parables' many facets and discover the diverse ways they may speak to
or even entrap us. Even Matthew's **fulfillment quotations**, which seem
superficially straightforward, usually carry dimensions that create ambiguity and ambivalence, forcing us to grapple with what they really mean.
From the very beginning of the Gospel, in fact, Matthew is training the
audience to struggle with interpretive problems for which no clear solution is provided. How will Jesus "save his people from their sins," and who
are "his people" (1:21)? Why does Jesus ride two animals into Jerusalem
at his "triumphal entry" (21:2, 5, 7)? How does Jesus fulfill the law and
the prophets (5:17)? More broadly, how is **judgment** related to **salvation**, especially for Israel? How is Jesus at once both **Son of God** and
Son of Humanity? Matthew provides clues along the way that may help
us settle some of these questions, but in the end we must formulate our
own answers. By posing riddles and presenting us with unresolved (and
sometimes unresolvable) tensions, the evangelist calls forth a community
of active interpreters. Faith is nurtured in the tensions, not the certainties.
The best answers are discovered in the life of the community in mission.

RAISING QUESTIONS FOR THE CHURCH'S PERFORMANCE OF THE GOSPEL

Matthew's proclivity for raising questions has shaped my own approach
in writing this commentary. We usually think that the goal of exegesis is
to uncover the meaning(s) in a text. But "meaning" is discovered more in
the dialogues that transpire between interpreters, their communities and
worlds, the text, the worlds of the text, and the tradition. Making meaning
is always messy. The goal of exegesis is not only to sort through alternative

possibilities for what the text might mean, but to raise and clarify the questions with which Christians and congregations must struggle in order to find their way faithfully between "earth" and "heaven." Each discussion in this commentary includes an "exploration" of the main features and issues in the passage, followed by suggestions about how to engage it for preaching and teaching. Usually, "Preaching and teaching the Word" entails identifying important topics, themes, and especially questions. The questions I have identified are certainly not the only ones the text may raise. They are meant primarily to challenge and annoy us. Always the answers must be worked out within the life of the community.

QUESTIONS ABOUT POWER

The most irritating of these questions, for me at least, concern issues of power in the life of the church and the world. Matthew correlates the claim that Jesus is "God with us" directly with the assertion that he also embodies divine power. In story after story, Matthew explores the nature and effects of this divine power among humans, often in direct contrast to the kind of power exercised by Israel's leaders, especially the **Pharisees, scribes, chief priests,** and **elders**. Matthew's interest in power and authority replicates that of Mark, which is not surprising given the fact that the two Gospels share roughly 90 percent of the material found in Mark's Gospel. The persistently negative, even mocking caricatures of the Jewish authorities in Matthew have over the centuries fed the flames of anti-Jewish sentiments and actions among Christians. But the Jewish leaders do not represent Judaism or all Jewish people. They stand, rather, for any exercise of human power that gives rise to injustice, exploitation, violence, and death. Matthew's Jewish leaders represent those who have baptized merely human ways and institutions with an aura of divine legitimacy and power. The evangelist's running polemic against human power locates both Jesus and Matthew within the streams of Israelite prophetic tradition. Matthew resonates with the imagery especially of Isaiah, Jeremiah, Zechariah, and Daniel, and mixes in frequent allusions to the exodus of God's people from slavery in Egypt and the later experience of exile in Babylon. The dangers of abusive human power lie not only outside the community of disciples, however, but within. What Jesus says about God's judgment of the Jewish authorities and other imperial powers is directed ultimately to the Christian community itself, especially its leaders. This may make Matthew a hard word for pastors and other leaders to hear.

Although the Jewish leaders are much more prominent in Matthew as the opponents of God's rule, the Roman Empire is also a target. The "**kingdom of heaven**" is God's alternative to the empire of Rome. The fact that we translate the Greek word *basileia* in one instance as "kingdom" and in the other as "empire" obscures Matthew's anti-imperial thrust, which Warren Carter has brilliantly illuminated over the last two decades. The chief priests, elders, and other leaders of the people in Jerusalem exercise their power in collaboration with Roman rule. Rome's control of land, political and religious office, military authority, taxation, legal systems, economic structures, and even religion generated widespread poverty, alienation, humiliation, and suffering. Caesar was hailed as king, "Lord," "savior," and even "son of God." Announcements of his deeds and edicts were called "good news" ("gospel"). Rome demanded "faith" from its subjects, to whom it promised "**justice**" ("**righteousness**") and "salvation." Matthew's story of Jesus thus contests Rome's exercise of power and construction of reality, including its imperial theology and eschatology.

THE DEFEAT OF DEATH AT THE CROSS

The difference between imperial power and God's rule comes to definitive expression over the meaning of Jesus' death on the cross. For Rome and the Jewish leaders, the crucifixion of Jesus restores order and reasserts the power of death to control the living. For Matthew the cross is the turning point of history, the perfect expression of God's love for and identification with the victims of human domination, and the definitive revelation of God's true identity and character. Because the crucified and resurrected Jesus is present in power on earth as well as in heaven, the earthly realm itself is being transformed. Matthew's story invites its audience into this new world, where death is no longer the ultimate barrier and where divine power is accessible to humans in the authority to forgive sins, to cast out unclean spirits, heal disease, cleanse lepers, and even raise the dead. Disciples are not to use this power for their own sake. They are not to be called "master" or to exalt themselves as human rulers do (20:25–28; 23:2–12). Instead, divine power is expressed in servanthood, identification with the humiliated ones, and in becoming slaves of one another (20:26–28; 23:11–12). God's power gathers, heals, restores, overwhelms death itself, and creates communities of equality, mutual service, sharing, reconciliation, and restored relationships. Matthew's Gospel was produced in a time when cherished institutions were under attack and lives were being uprooted. We, too, live in a time when people trust the powers of violence and death more than the mercy and love of God. For people such as us, Matthew brings a word of both judgment and hope.

PART ONE

The Beginnings of "God with Us"
1:1–4:25

Roots

Exploring the text

While many people today have taken renewed interest in genealogies, most readers still skip quickly past the genealogies found within the pages of the Bible. The names are unfamiliar and difficult to pronounce and, after all, it's not our family. Or is it? Matthew's genealogy of "**Jesus Christ, Son of David** and son of Abraham," sets forth the lineage not only of Jesus himself, but of those who call themselves his disciples. Still more important, the genealogy names the new time and new world in which the risen Jesus and his disciples live. Finally, Matthew uses the genealogy to begin training the audience for what they will experience throughout the Gospel. Matthew will continually surprise us and compel us to become active interpreters.

Matthew's first line functions as a title for the whole Gospel as well as the opening section. "Origins" (or "genesis" or "genealogy") names the literary form that follows, a genealogy, but also hints that the whole Gospel is the story of a new beginning, a new creation like that described in Genesis (cf. Gen. 2:4, "the generations of the heavens and the earth"). Matthew uses the genealogy to establish two seemingly contradictory impulses: the story of Jesus is both the continuation of Israel's story and, at the same time, something definitively new. The genealogy locates its auditors in the stream of Israel's history, yet dislocates them from their ordinary expectations. Throughout the Gospel, Matthew highlights elements of both continuity and discontinuity, treasures "new" and "old" (cf. 13:52), and the fulfillment and re-formation of Israel's expectations in Jesus Christ. Matthew thus locates the audience at the edge of history and prepares them for life between the empires of this world and the **empire of God**.

Jesus is the "Christ" and also the Son of David, Israel's royal **Messiah**, and the son of Abraham, who fulfills God's promises to the patriarch. Jesus the Son of David seeks the restoration of God's people. Matthew's narrative will define this title with images of Jesus as a merciful healer rather than merely a political leader. It is the "little people"–the blind (12:22–23; 20:30–31), the Canaanite woman (15:22), the little children in the temple (21:15)–who perceive most clearly the meaning of Jesus' identity as Son of David. As son of Abraham, Jesus embodies God's blessings not only to Israel, but to all of the world's peoples (Gen. 12:1–3), bringing righteousness and justice as well as material abundance–food (Matt. 14:13–21; 15:32–39), healing, and the forgiveness of debt (6:12; 18:23–35)–to the whole earth.

Matthew may have used the genealogical lists in Ruth 4:18–22 and 1 Chronicles 2:10–15 as primary sources for this genealogy, but the final product displays the evangelist's bent in both style and content. Matthew directs the audience's attention in 1:17 to the fact that the genealogy has been carefully crafted into three segments, each corresponding to a historical epoch in Israel's life. The first (1:2–6a) runs from Abraham to the establishment of the monarchy under "David the king." The second begins with Solomon and ends with the deportation to Babylon (1:6b–11). The last segment runs from the return from exile to Christ. Jesus brings the last epoch to an end and begins a new era. The Gospel thus traces the temporal transition from one **time** to another, to a time that is both continuous with and unlike what has preceded.

Matthew's careful, even monotonous, structuring serves to highlight departures from the norm. When read aloud, breaks in the repetitive structure announce a particularly important generation or, more often, an anomaly that Matthew wants to underline. At the end of 1:2, for example, Jacob is named as the father of "Judah and his brothers" (the twelve tribes), and at 1:11 "Jechoniah and his brothers" designates the generation that was taken into exile in Babylon. The more arresting departures from the normal structure, however, involve women: Tamar (1:3; cf. Gen. 38), Rahab and Ruth (1:5; cf. Josh. 2:1–21; 6:22–25; and Ruth 2–4) and "the wife of Uriah," i.e., Bathsheba (1:6b, cf. 2 Sam. 11–12). These names recall moments in Israel's history when God's purposes were achieved through the agency of women who were outsiders (non-Israelites). Each of these stories also involves some kind of sexual impropriety. Matthew goes out of his way to suggest this especially in the case of Bathsheba, where, rather than using her name, the evangelist designates her "the wife of Uriah," thereby highlighting David's covetousness and deceit in arranging the death of Bathsheba's husband. These women all set the stage for Mary, whose conception of Jesus also raised questions of impropriety, both for Joseph and for Christians of later eras. God works not only through the patriarchs and kings, but through women, outsiders, Gentiles, and even by means of situations of intrigue and compromise. The prominence Matthew grants to these women subverts the patriarchal world inscribed in the rest of the genealogy. The Messiah's lineage reaches back to David and Abraham, but also to Tamar, Rahab, Ruth, and Bathsheba. It includes both the righteous and the wicked, the powerful and the lowly.

When Matthew finally introduces Jesus himself at the end of the genealogy, several details suggest a sense of discontinuity from what has preceded. Matthew uses a passive voice construction to break the heretofore consistent use of the active voice of the verb "to beget": "Jacob begot Joseph, the husband of Mary, from whom was begotten Jesus, the one called Christ" (Matt. 1:16). The shift to the passive voice signals that Jesus breaks the mold and suggests God's agency in Jesus' birth. His birth marks the culmination of the lineage that stretches (through Joseph) back to Abraham, and also the genesis of a new world and a new time.

The summary in 1:17 has at least three purposes. First, it makes explicit the historical structuring of the whole genealogy; Matthew's goal is not merely to name Jesus' ancestors, but to locate him in Israel's story and within the larger history of creation and new creation. Second, Matthew's use of the number fourteen in each segment lends the genealogy an apocalyptic flavor (cf. 2 Baruch 53–74, "The Messiah Apocalypse"). Third, when Matthew repeatedly names "fourteen generations," he issues an engraved invitation to go back and count. When one does so, however, it becomes clear that the last segment, which runs from Shealtiel to Jesus, is defective, yielding but thirteen generations.

Did Matthew make a mistake? If so, it is likely an intentional "mistake." Throughout the genealogy Matthew has included surprises, incongruities, and broken patterns. Matthew is training us to attend to the details. Here he creates a puzzle for us to grapple with. Is Jesus to be counted twice, once as Jesus and again as the Christ? Or does Matthew understand Jesus as the one who simultaneously stands as the sole survivor of his generation (cf. 2:16–18) and again as the firstfruits of the time of resurrection (cf. 27:51–54). Is he both the "**Son of Humanity**" (or "the human one" or "**Son of Man**") and **Son of God**, the representative of both God and humankind? Does the Holy Spirit (cf. 1:20) represent the thirteenth generation, and Jesus the fourteenth? Matthew does not resolve the puzzle, but compels us to become active interpreters who, in the light of the larger story, must sort out for ourselves who Jesus is. By the end of the genealogy we already know that we should expect the unexpected, look for God's agents among the vulnerable and powerless, and learn how Jesus fulfills Israel's history while radically disrupting it.

Preaching and teaching the Word

The genealogy is not included in the lectionary and is rarely used for preaching today–both to our loss. Many churches today find themselves in times of transition, in crises of identity and vocation, and in thrall of conventional notions of power and status. Matthew's genealogy provides rich resources for addressing these concerns. First, with its careful structuring and intentional disruptions and its focus on disorientation and reorientation, the genealogy suggests ways in which we might understand the task of preaching itself. Matthew's Gospel dislocates its auditors from the assumptions and perspectives of the old creation and then moves them toward a place where they can perceive, experience, and name the power of God in their midst. Faithful preaching cannot leave the world's assumptions unchallenged. The Gospel challenges the root assumptions upon which we make meaning, construct our societies, and transmit "culture." Preaching should "move" us, and not just emotionally, by dislocating us from our ordinary sense of time and location and then reorienting us so that we gain fresh perception of God's ways.

Second, the genealogy provides roots for those who have none. While modern readers may not see this genealogy as their own, Matthew understands that Jesus' identity is the foundation for Christian identity even today. The genealogy is the "beginning" of the story of God's new creation coming into being. Jesus embodies God's presence and power among us. As disciples, we live in the time of Jesus Christ, when God is restoring and healing the creation, gathering the lost, and overwhelming the powers of violence and death. Discerning and living faithfully into this new time and space is at the heart of Matthew's vision of discipleship.

Modern Christians live amidst constant change. We are witnessing the diminishment and marginalization of traditional forms of religion. It feels as if the world we have known is slipping rapidly from our grasp. Matthew was produced in a time of great upheaval for Jews and Christians, who lived under the domination of Roman imperial rule, in the wake of the destruction of the temple and Jerusalem, and in a time of intense social and political conflict and economic hardship. Matthew does not offer easy answers, but affirms that disciples of Jesus Christ live most faithfully at the edge of history, between epochs, in a time of both continuity and radical discontinuity. Disciples trace their lineage to patriarchs and kings, the mighty and the humiliated, men of power and women from the margins. Matthew does not locate security or stability in what humans produce or control, but in God's merciful rule, where the powerful are brought low and the lowly are lifted up, and where even the boundaries between earth and heaven are blurred. Matthew's whole Gospel explores and maps these "in-between" times and places for subsequent generations of disciples. The genealogy reminds us that God works through those we least expect (cf. 25:31–46) and in situations that bend the rules of this world. God's power constantly challenges the structures we create and our perceptions of what is firm, real, and secure (cf. 27:51–53). We also begin to see what the gospel is, as Matthew understands it: a story of disruption and fulfillment, danger and blessing, upheaval and hope. It is precisely in times like these that we should expect to see God.

The Origins of Jesus

Matthew 1:18–25

Exploring the text

Jesus has two fathers, so Matthew now explores the implications of Jesus' dual "origins." The Greek word "genesis" in 1:18 (cf. 1:1) may be translated as "the birth" of Jesus Christ (as in most English translations) or as "origin" or "genesis." Matthew here aims to define who Jesus is in relation to both of his fathers. In doing so, Matthew addresses an anomaly raised by the genealogy, which runs through Joseph, yet abruptly dissociates Jesus from Joseph in 1:16, where Joseph is described only as "the husband of Mary, of whom Jesus was born." Whose son is Jesus? Whose identity and power is in his blood?

Jesus' divine origins are "from the Holy Spirit" (1:18; the same grammatical structure used in reference to Tamar, Rahab, Ruth, and the wife of Uriah in the genealogy). Later in the passage Matthew confirms Jesus' divine identity by designating him "God with us" (1:23). Because Jesus is "from the Holy Spirit" (1:18, 20), he is also the true "**Son of God**." As soon as Matthew has named the Holy Spirit's agency in Jesus' birth, the spotlight shifts to Joseph. Even though Matthew first mentions Joseph (1:16) in a way that distances him from Jesus, his relationship to Jesus is still important. It is Joseph, not Mary, who stands in the line of David (1:20) and Abraham. Jesus is the **Son of David** by means of Joseph's legal paternity, which Joseph signals according to custom by publicly announcing Jesus' name, as the angel has commanded him (1:21, 25). Matthew then carefully develops Joseph's image, emphasizing his **righteousness**, obedience, and chastity (cf. Gen. 37–50). Matthew's portrayal of Joseph owes much to images of Joseph's namesake in Genesis 37–50 and in *The Testament of the Twelve Patriarchs*, especially the *Testament of Joseph,* which was popular in the first century. Like the Joseph of Genesis, Matthew's Joseph is morally upright, caring for the preservation of life and relationships above all. Joseph refuses to put Mary to shame, although it would be within his rights, but seeks rather to end the relationship quietly (Matt. 1:19). Both Josephs have dreams that shape the subsequent course of their lives. And both find refuge in Egypt (cf. Matt. 2:13–15). Matthew's portrayal of Joseph thus affirms a link between Jesus and the Old Testament stories of brotherly jealousy, betrayal, enslavement, and finally the redemption and restoration of Jacob's family.

The angelic dream vision (1:20–21) first reassures Joseph and then affirms his responsibility for naming the child. Joseph is to name the child Jesus because "he will save his people from their sins." "Jesus" is the Greek version of the Hebrew name Joshua, the one who brought to completion the redemption of the people from Egypt and their conquest of the Canaanites. The naming of Jesus in 1:21 also sets forth another interpretive puzzle, which will come to the fore as the Gospel unfolds: who are "his people," and in what sense does Jesus save them from their sins? Does "his people" refer to Israel, to the followers of Jesus, to the church, or to all people? Does Jesus save his people Israel despite their rejection of him (27:22–25)? The relationship between the saving activity of Jesus and the people of Israel is one of the central interpretive puzzles that Matthew's audience must resolve. But the resolution of this puzzle must await the end of the Gospel and the audience's own interpretive choices along the way.

Especially in the early chapters of the Gospel, Matthew often cites Old Testament passages that interpret events described in the narrative and affirm aspects of Jesus' life and ministry as the realization of God's will. An introductory formula similar to what we find in 1:22 typically introduces these **"fulfillment quotations"** (1:22–23; 2:5–6; 2:15; 2:17–18; 2:23; 4:14–16; 8:17; 12:17–21; 13:35; 21:4–5; 26:54; 26:56; 27:9–10). The first fulfillment quotation in Matthew (1:22–23) cites Isaiah 7:14, which presents a rich, ambiguous array of interpretive possibilities. The word "virgin" or "young woman" in this quotation has generated a great deal of attention over the years, in some ways distracting readers from other important implications of the citation. Isaiah 7 describes both God's promise of deliverance and the threat of judgment if the promise is refused. Isaiah addresses King Ahaz of Judah in order to affirm God's faithfulness in the midst of impending defeat at the hands of Syria and Israel (the Northern Kingdom). The birth of the child from a "young woman" is to be a sign that during the baby's lifetime both Syria and Israel will be deserted (Isa. 7:16), while Judah experiences a time of abundance. Ahaz, however, refuses to heed this prophetic vision, refuses to trust God, and suffers God's punishment from the Assyrians. The child born of the "virgin" becomes a sign of judgment rather than hope of salvation. For the first time, we hear a hint of Matthew's interest in the juxtaposition of **judgment** with **salvation**.

The citation is also the second instance in which Jesus is named and his name explained (1:23; cf. 1:21). Jesus is "God with us." Matthew develops this designation throughout the Gospel, climaxing at the very end, when the risen Jesus commissions his disciples for mission to the ends of the world, supported with the promise that "I will be with you to the end of the days." The designation of Jesus as "God with us" in 1:23 and 28:20 (cf. also 18:20) frames the whole Gospel as an exploration of what it means for Christians to claim that Jesus is "God with us." In a context where Caesar was hailed as "savior" and "son of God," and perceived as the mediator of divine power, will, and salvation, the claim that Jesus is God with us represents a challenge to the dominion of human empires. Wherever empires dress their goals and actions in the clothing of divine will, God brings judgment. Matthew confesses that there is but one true Lord, only one who is God with us, the one who was crucified by Rome and raised from the dead by God.

Preaching and teaching the Word

In this passage Matthew begins to develop an image of the dual nature of Jesus' identity–both human and divine–that will run throughout the Gospel. The two elements of Jesus' nature do not temporarily cohabit the same space as separable entities. In him the human and the divine merge into an integral whole. The boundaries between divine and human blur and mingle in Jesus, just as they will in his ministry and even among his disciples (cf. 14:22–33). Matthew locates the **empire of heaven** on the borders of human perception and experience, where new assumptions, new ways of seeing, and new relationships are possible. Jesus leads his disciples safely from one world to another. This in turn becomes the vocation of the disciples, and then of the church. Faithful discipleship flourishes among those who are convinced of how the world is being transformed, down to its very foundations, in the presence of "God with us."

The account of Jesus' origins and birth makes clear that the story of Jesus is Matthew's way of talking about God (cf. 10:40; 11:27).[1] The designations of Jesus as savior (1:21) and "God with us" (1:23) challenge some of our most basic assumptions about the nature of this world and God's presence. Popular forms of spirituality often presume God's distance from us. We imagine that prayer, for example, is like calling "long distance." In contrast, Matthew locates the risen Jesus here with us, wherever even two or three are gathered in his name (18:20; 28:20). This has both ecclesiological and soteriological implications. Matthew's **church** is not a sect waiting for the end, but a community of "watchers" (24:42–44) invoking his presence and discerning signs of his redemptive power. For Matthew,

salvation does not mean removal from this world, nor is it something reserved for the end of the world or the next life. Salvation is already taking place in the recognition of the living Christ in our midst. One of the church's tasks is to create social spaces where disciples can discern and name God's saving presence and power among us.

Joseph is a righteous and caring person who quietly fulfills his role as the link between Jesus and David. He is also the figure responsible for protecting and nurturing Jesus' life. He obeys God's direction even when his own righteous inclinations run in another direction. Joseph takes his place alongside the women mentioned in the genealogy, reminding us that God's will comes to fruition through the faithful actions of individuals whose obedience may hardly be noticed by others, sometimes even in actions that strike others as odd or incongruous.

Joseph's "righteousness" encompasses at least three dimensions. First, when confronted with Mary's pregnancy, he follows the law in determining to end the relationship. Second, even though affronted, he has compassion for the one who has apparently wronged him and chooses not to end the engagement publicly, but quietly for her sake. Third, when God directs him to marry her anyway, he does so even though this means placing his own honor and safety at risk. Confronted with a series of difficult personal and moral decisions, he places God's direction and his sense of compassion above what even the law dictates. In similar circumstances, many of us might choose a more conventional, even vengeful path. Joseph shows us what "righteousness" really means: attentiveness to God's will and compassion for others, even those who have wronged us.

Israel's Ruler

Matthew 2:1–12*

Exploring the text

Most of us imagine the Christmas story in terms of mangers, magi, shepherds, and a sweet, newborn baby–images of joy, peace, and hope.

*The Revised Common Lectionary uses this in Years A, B, C: Epiphany of the Lord, or Sunday before Epiphany.

Given this, Matthew's dark, foreboding story of the political intrigue and violence that attends the birth of Jesus may cause dismay. Israel's rulers take center stage alongside "wise men from the East," but it is God, not humans, who control this story. God is at work in each scene to direct the various characters, to guide the travels of the magi, to secure Jesus' life from Herod, and to bring the family back from Egypt after the death of Herod. The **fulfillment quotations** that Matthew introduces in each section of chapter 2 affirm God's direction of the larger story even in the midst of flight and exile.

The innocent-sounding reference to time and location, "Jesus was born in Bethlehem of Judea in the days of Herod the king," pits Herod's **time**, an era of violence and exploitation, against the messianic time that is now beginning, a time associated in Matthew with healing, inclusion, restoration, gathering, and new kinds of power loose in the world. Just as time is shifting, so too the geographical centers of power are suddenly sent reeling (2:3). The announcement that the magi have come to worship the newborn "king of the Jews" (2:2; cf. 27:11, 37) "troubles" King Herod. The same sensation is mentioned in Daniel 5:9, when King Belshazzar's advisers are unable to decipher the writing–a word of judgment–on the wall. Later in Matthew, the disciples are troubled–panicky–when they see Jesus walking toward them on the sea in the midst of a great storm (14:26). Not only is Herod stirred up and set off balance, but "all Jerusalem with him," for the new king does not come from and is not controlled by the Jerusalem establishment, and so threatens the religious, social, economic, and political arrangements in which "all Jerusalem" is so heavily invested. Matthew thus identifies the forces and interests that will oppose Jesus throughout his ministry and eventually seek his death. When the new king finally comes to town, Herod the Great will be dead, but by then the religious authorities, here the **"chief priests and scribes"** (2:4), will have emerged as Jesus' primary adversaries. The deceit and murderous ambition that Matthew here associates more with Herod will thoroughly infect the **religious leaders** too.

The chief priests and scribes are "gathered"–the religious elites will "gather" repeatedly against Jesus throughout the Gospel–to tell Herod where the new king is to be found. They appeal to Scripture for the answer. The composite quotation in 2:6 is drawn from Micah 5:2 and 2 Samuel 5:2. The new ruler will come from little Bethlehem in Judea, just a few miles south of Jerusalem, where David was anointed by Samuel (1 Sam. 16:1–13). The last portion of the quotation comes from 2 Samuel 5:2, where all the tribes of Israel confirm the shepherd David's kingship. The shepherd king who is born in Bethlehem, who brings an end to the time of exile (cf. 1:12–16), will also bring about the realization of Micah's vision of peace not only for Israel, but for all people (Mic. 4:3–4). The image of a king who is a shepherd also resonates with Ezekiel's critique of Israel's leaders as false shepherds (Ezek. 34). The chief priests and scribes who here speak of the coming Messiah as a shepherd seem unaware of the implications of this tradition for their own leadership. Matthew will return both to the image of Jesus as shepherd (9:36) and repeatedly to the criticism of Israel's leaders, who fail to produce "fruit" from the vineyard (Israel) that has been entrusted to them (cf. 3:7–10; 21:43).

When Herod learns from the religious rulers where the Christ is to be born, he implements a plan to snuff out the threat. He summons the magi secretly to learn when the star first appeared, and assures them that he too will come to worship the king when they find him (2:7–8). Herod's performance here embodies the self-serving hypocrisy that Matthew will associate again and again with Israel's leaders. Herod knows that knowledge is power. He gathers information from diverse sources while keeping his informants isolated from one another.[1] He then manipulates the wise men for his own purposes. God thwarts Herod's plan, of course, but the king's rage will cost the lives of the male children under the age of two in the region around Bethlehem (2:16–18).

Micah's vision of the nations coming to God's house to worship is first realized in Matthew in the visit of the magi to the home (not a stable or manger as in Luke) of Joseph and Mary. The wise men have followed a star–apparently unnoticed by the inhabitants of Jerusalem itself–from the east all the way to Jerusalem. After naively alerting Herod of the new king's birth, they resume their journey, with the star once more before them (2:9). The reappearance of the star is a turning point in the story, signaled by Matthew's use of the word "behold" (2:9, an "archaism" deleted from most modern English versions) to mark significant moments. The magi have sought directions for their quest from Israel's political and religious leaders, but now it is the star, which comes to rest over the very place where the child is, that actually leads them to their destination and, according to Matthew, incites their intense jubilation (2:10). Much ink has been spent identifying the magi and interpreting the meaning of their various gifts, but Matthew's focus is on the recognition and honor implied in the Gentiles' actions toward Jesus, whose birth is of cosmic importance. Their gifts recall the offerings of Gentile kings mentioned in Isaiah 60 (vv. 6, 9), where the prophet sets forth a vision of salvation, restoration, and justice for the whole earth. The worship of the magi only partly fulfills the eschatological vision of the prophets (cf. Ps. 72:10–11; Isa. 2:1–4; 45:22–23; Mic. 4:1–2), however, for while Gentiles worship the newborn king, they are not joined by Herod or the other Jewish leaders. God warns the magi in a dream not to return to Herod, but to go home by another route, thereby frustrating Herod's plot to eliminate the true king.

Preaching and teaching the Word

In American society the celebration of Christmas has become a blurry amalgam of images of the baby Jesus, Santa Claus, and, most of all, the renewal of the economic order. The current celebration of Christmas is the product of urbane, nineteenth-century, upper-class interests, which transformed a European holiday associated with social inversion, carnality, and the mockery of established authority into a domestic rite focused on the private exchange of gifts among family members. Christmas was once such an unruly holiday that New England Puritans outlawed it.[2] The carnivalesque excesses of Christmases past have been supplanted by material excess and a high incidence of depression and suicide. Matthew's Christmas story, in contrast, unveils the inner workings and motivations of human empires and provides the foil against which the new king's displays of power—gathering, healing, and redeeming his people—will be set. Matthew here articulates the conflict between human power and Jesus' vocation that will run throughout the Gospel. Some may find Matthew's Christmas story unsettling, even offensive. Our European ancestors, in their rough way, had a clearer sense than do we that the birth of Jesus signals the undoing of the established order.

This passage is the Gospel reading for Epiphany, the celebration of God's glory revealed in the world. Matthew does not think of this revelation in terms of God coming from somewhere else (heaven), being present for a while, and then leaving again. God has been here with us all along. The birth, life, death, and resurrection of Jesus is the clearest and most revealing expression of God's presence and power. Matthew uses this story especially to illustrate the promise of God's presence in the form of deliverance from evil and violence. Throughout Matthew's account God is the invisible (except for the star), quiet (except for the angels), yet all-powerful presence guiding the characters and the story. It is God's hand that turns a story of manipulation and threat into a story of ebullient joy and hope. God's presence and power always surprise us, turning danger to deliverance and despair to hope. Disciples live in the confident conviction that the alternatives set before us by the world do not begin to exhaust what is possible in God's power.

The pilgrimage of the wise men anticipates the eschatological gathering of the nations before God. We often envision this merely as the extension of **salvation** beyond Israel to non-Israelites, and this in largely individualistic terms. But Matthew, like the prophets, considers the gathering of the nations to worship God as the fulfillment of Israel's calling to be a witness of God's power and justice to the world. Salvation here means the realization of peace among the nations, in this world, not merely the rescue of individuals from the world. The gospel is good news for the nations, the realization within history of eschatological hope for peace and reconciliation.

Retracing Israel's Steps

Matthew 2:13–23*

Exploring the text

When the magi come to Herod the Great in search of the new "king of the Jews," they incite the first expression of human opposition to Jesus. In response to Herod's attempt to eradicate the child, God sends the family of Jesus to Egypt, the site of Israel's enslavement, and then, after Herod's death, to Galilee, where Jesus grows up in "exile." Matthew began the Gospel by identifying Jesus with David and Abraham and locating him in relation to Israel's history (1:1–17). Matthew now uses the story of what happens to Jesus and his family after his birth as an ironic retelling and reliving (or recapitulation) of Israel's story, embodied anew in Jesus. Matthew uses three **"fulfillment quotations"** (2:15, 17–18, 23) to draw out connections between Jesus' experiences and Israel's exodus and exile. As this reenactment of Israel's story unfolds, Matthew also begins to develop a typological relationship between the stories of Moses and Jesus, both of which involve an evil ruler who plots the slaughter of innocent male children (2:1–12, 16–18; Exod. 1:16, 22), flight to another land (2:13–15; Exod. 2:15), and return after the death of the ruler (2:19; Exod. 2:23). The language Matthew employs when Joseph is told that it is safe to return home, "for those who sought the child's life are dead" (2:20) recalls God's direction of Moses in Exodus 4:19. Moses and Jesus are both itinerant

---

*The Revised Common Lectionary uses this in Year A, First Sunday after Christmas Day.

leaders associated with wilderness and movement, rather than settled and centralized power.

"OUT OF EGYPT I HAVE CALLED MY SON" (2:13–15)

The story of the flight into Egypt focuses on Joseph. Again, dreams are the medium by which God directs the action (cf. 2:13; cf. 1:20; 2:12; 2:19; 2:22), and again Joseph faithfully follows God's instructions perfectly. Matthew's note that the family flees "by night" (2:14) suggests both Joseph's swift and certain obedience and the immediacy of the danger. The parallels between the flight of Joseph, Mary, and Jesus to Egypt and the stories of Moses in Exodus and Joseph in Genesis 37–50 also yield ironies. Gentiles come to worship Jesus, the new king, but his own people force him to flee to Egypt, back to the place where God's people had once been enslaved. The passage Matthew cites in relation to the flight to Egypt (Hos. 11:1: "Out of Egypt I have called my son") is itself a commentary on Israel's exodus from Pharaoh's oppression and enslavement of God's people. Just as God called Israel from slavery in Egypt, now God will call Jesus. Hosea 11 also describes the people's failure to obey God's call and their injustices toward one another. Matthew is interested in more than merely a superficial fulfillment of Scripture. The reference links the story of Jesus with Israel's judgment and liberation.

"A VOICE WAS HEARD IN RAMAH" (2:16–18)

In this portion of the story Matthew's attention turns to Herod, who, enraged that the magi have not played into his hands, orders the slaughter of Bethlehem's male children. Herod perceives he has been "mocked" or "tricked," a term also found in the exodus story, when God tells Moses how God has made fools of the Egyptians (Exod. 10:2). Like Pharaoh, Herod's power is rooted and finds expression in violence and death, while the rule of Jesus will focus on gathering, inclusion, restoration, and liberation. Matthew draws the fulfillment quotation in this portion of the story from Jeremiah 31:15. Ramah is the location of Rachel's tomb, near Bethlehem, and the place where the exiles on their way to Babylon gathered as they left the promised land (Gen. 35:16–19; 48:7). Jeremiah himself was carried away into exile in Egypt by another group of Judeans fleeing Babylonian rule (Jer. 43). In Jeremiah 31 the prophet expresses the people's grief, but also looks forward to the day when the exiles will return. The chapter is filled with images of **judgment** and lament, but also the vision of a "new covenant . . . written on their hearts" (Jer. 31:33). The citation is important not only for the place name Ramah, and for its expression of lament, but for its message of hope for return from exile and for a renewed relationship with God.

"HE SHALL BE CALLED A NAZARENE" (2:19–23)

Yet another angelic visit by dream informs Joseph that it is now safe to return with his family to Israel. The angel's message recalls the word of God to Moses after he had fled Pharaoh to Midian (2:20; Exod. 4:19). Again, Joseph obeys the angel's instructions without hesitation (cf. 1:24; 2:13–15). But upon the family's return, they learn of new dangers in Judea: Herod's son Archelaus, almost as famous as his father for his violence and corruption, now rules. Again God directs the family's movements by dreams, now toward Nazareth in Galilee, where Jesus will grow up.

Matthew asserts that the move to Nazareth fulfills "what was spoken by the prophets," but the fulfillment citation does not follow any known prophecy. What does the claim that Jesus will be called a "Nazarene" imply? On the one hand, the identification suggests that he is "from the sticks," i.e., from an insignificant place. Another possibility is that Jesus is a Nazirite, one set apart for holy service (cf. Num. 6; Judg. 13:5–7). Still another possibility links the place name to Isaiah 11:1, where a "branch" (*neser*) comes from the root of Jesse, that is, a king from the line of David. We need not choose any single association. The identification of Jesus as a Nazarene means that Israel's Messiah, the one who fulfills Israel's hope for a king in the line of David and for a liberator in the mold of Moses, has been pushed to the margins. That is where Jesus will conduct the most successful portions of his mission, among the poor, the sick, the humble, and the outcaste.

Preaching and teaching the Word

Matthew's careful, succinct account of the Holy Family's flight to Egypt, return, and subsequent "exile" in Galilee accomplishes many things at once. First and foremost, the story of Jesus is the recasting of Israel's history. In order to redeem Israel, Jesus must retrace her steps with new outcomes. God remains faithful to the one who is chosen, but Jesus will be obedient in ways that Israel was not (cf. 4:1–11). As Israel's representative, the new king will lead in the way of faithfulness toward God, bringing freedom, peace, and the end of exile. It's very hard to free people from the demonic grasp of their old stories. In order to set them in a new direction, you have to change their story. Matthew accomplishes this by both linking and contrasting Israel's stories with the story of Jesus.

Preaching that recasts our human stories in the light of God's faithfulness and mercy also leads toward the renewal of our perception and experience of salvation. Every congregation has its own stories, replete with tenacious demons. How does the story of Jesus meet and recast these crippling tales?

The story of the holy family's flight also demonstrates God's power to preserve the life of Jesus from all human threats, and graphically illustrates, in contrast, the violent nature of imperial power. Herod the king kills Israel's innocent children. Jesus the king will lift up children as model disciples (18:1–5; 19:13–15). Herod is Rome's minion, which means his power is by its nature insecure and he is likely to respond to threats with force. Jesus is a new Moses, who will lead his people to salvation (cf. 1:21) by enduring suffering and death. Herod and Jesus represent two "empires," two mutually exclusive embodiments of power. Matthew is utterly realistic about the nature of human power. Even when empires appear peaceful, benevolent, and divinely ordered, as Rome claimed of itself, violence may be only a stroke away. Fear, especially the fear of death itself, is the tyrant that rules all other tyrants. The gospel fundamentally challenges this tyranny, urging us to seek security in the God of Jesus, Mary, and Joseph, rather than in human pretenders. The true king manifests divine power by conquering death, not by dealing it.

What can we say in response to Herod's slaughter of innocent children? God does not make this happen in order to fulfill Scripture, but Scripture does prophesy that the victims of enslavement and exile will weep for the death of their children. God promises that the exile will end, but this does not mean that the children will return. In Jeremiah 15, Rachel's weeping is heard in the midst of a jubilant celebration of return from exile. Israel's hope and joy are thus mingled with the bitterness of loss. The way of Jesus embodies these same realities. God knows our suffering firsthand. Yet beyond Rachel's grief lies the hope of restoration and of life free from imperial violence and the tyranny of death. The creator of life itself now preserves Jesus' life, so that he may die to renew and sustain the life of the world.

John the Baptizer

Matthew 3:1–12

Exploring the text

John the Baptizer's ministry and proclamation builds the framework for Jesus' mission. Although the people of "Jerusalem, all Judea, and all the region along the Jordan" go out to the "wilderness" to hear him and to be baptized, it would be a mistake to think of John as a "popular" figure. His location in the wilderness, his baptism of repentance, his proclamation of the nearness of **God's empire**, and his conflict with the **Pharisees** and **Sadducees** all mark him as an outsider. He dresses in conscious imitation of the prophet Elijah (3:4; cf. 2 Kgs. 1:8), who also preached repentance, especially to kings and queens (cf. Matt. 14:3–4; cf. 1 Kgs. 18; 21) and religious leaders. John makes a point of eating what God supplies from the land. His ministry in the wilderness constitutes an alternative to the Jerusalem establishment and his baptism signals a vote of no-confidence in the redemptive power of the temple and the sacrificial system. John proclaims that God is "near," not within the temple, but with those at the margins.

Israelites understood the wilderness as a place of danger where demonic forces reside (cf. 4:1–11), but also as a locus of revelation (cf., e.g., Exod. 19:1–6) and redemption, where God led the people on their way from slavery in Egypt toward the promised land. In the wilderness, it is possible to see the rest of the world more clearly, and perhaps even turn in a new direction. John's preaching calls for just such a turning. "Repent, for the **kingdom of heaven** has come near" (Matt. 3:2) signals both temporal and spatial immediacy; God's empire is near, here and now. Jesus will use precisely these same words at the beginning of his own ministry (4:17). John and Jesus both call Israel to repent of its collusion with human empires and its exploitation of the marginal and defenseless ones, and to turn back to faithfulness, justice, and right relationship with God.

Why is repentance so closely associated with the immediacy of God's kingdom? God's presence and power fundamentally disrupt what we know as reality, especially what we as humans construct—whether houses, states, or religions—to secure our lives and keep death at bay. The coming of God's reign thus makes repentance both possible and necessary. In 3:3, the evangelist links John with Isaiah 40:3, which announces the end of Israel's punishment and exile in Babylon, and calls upon her to "prepare the way of the Lord" and make his paths straight. This citation describes not only the nature and purpose of John's ministry, but also the goal of Israel's repentance: turning back toward God prepares the way of the Lord.

Many from Jerusalem and Judea confess their sins and are baptized by John in the Jordan River. It is not clear whether the Pharisees and Sadducees come to be baptized by John or to observe and oppose him. When John recognizes Pharisees and Sadducees among those coming, he launches a sharp challenge that anticipates Jesus' conflicts with these same leaders in Jerusalem (cf. 21:23–22:14), which will focus on their rejection of John's ministry and baptism (21:24–27) and on the leaders' failure to "produce fruit" (3:8; cf. 21:43; 12:33–37). In any case, John wonders aloud who warned them to flee from God's coming wrath (3:7), wrath that Jesus will describe in the final discourse of the Gospel (chaps. 23–25), where Jesus follows his own blistering critique of the religious leaders (chap. 23) with predictions of the **judgment** against Jerusalem and the fall of the temple (cf. 23:37–24:2).

"Bearing fruit worthy of repentance" denotes behavior that embodies God's will as manifested in the already-here-and-coming empire of God, especially the restoration, gathering, healing, and redemption of Israel (cf. Matt. 5–7; 25:31–46). John knows that the Pharisees and Sadducees would lay claim to their pedigrees—"we have Abraham as our ancestor"—in support of their inclusion in God's saving activity. But marking exclusive distinctions and status is a function of the current order, not of God's reign. John mocks them: God could use stones in the wilderness to raise up children for Abraham. The issue, John reiterates, is producing fruit (cf. 7:16–20; 12:33; 21:43). In prophetic writings the tree is an image for Israel, from which fruit is expected (Hos. 9:16; Isa. 27:6; Jer. 12:2; 17:8; Ezek. 17:8–9, 23). John warns that trees not producing fruit will be cut down and thrown into the fire. The image of the ax already lying at the root of the trees indicates that judgment is imminent. The shock for the Pharisees and Sadducees would be that they, the pious whom God supposedly blesses, would be the focus of judgment, rather than outsiders or the "unrighteous." The judgment is not merely a phenomenon of the "end of history," but is present already in John's proclamation and Jesus' messianic ministry, which expose the hollowness of human religiosity and inaugurate God's end-time rule.

In the next breath, John turns back to the larger audience (3:10–12) and assumes more clearly his role as the one who prepares the way. John baptizes with water (symbolizing cleansing and repentance), but the one coming, who is stronger, will baptize with the Holy Spirit and with fire, both of which imply the eschatological tenor of Jesus' ministry. Both Holy

Spirit and fire also suggest that Jesus' ministry entails both **salvation** and judgment (each image carries both connotations). John then shifts metaphors, from baptism to the threshing floor, again emphasizing both judgment and salvation in the Messiah's mission: the winnowing fork is in his hand, he will clean the threshing floor and gather the wheat, but the chaff will be burned with unquenchable fire.

Preaching and teaching the Word

John's proclamation, including setting, costume, action, and word, speaks from the margins, points persistently toward God's power, names the new **time** and space in which the audience now lives, speaks truth to power (offending the rich patrons of Jerusalem), and affirms both judgment and salvation. These are still the reasons we preach today.

Salvation and judgment are integral aspects of Matthew's understanding of Jesus and the empire of heaven. Repentance necessarily implies on one hand God's judgment of the world and our lives within it and, on the other, the reorientation that is at the heart of salvation. While many of us find it difficult to hold these together in our preaching and teaching, faithful witness to God's presence in the world requires both. How do we nurture congregations and ministries that profess and embody the good news of God's empire without removing the hard edge and scandal of the gospel?

The "fruit worthy of repentance" is lived practice that bears witness to the reality of God's reign. For some, Matthew's attention to deeds teeters on the brink of "works righteousness." Much of this concern, however, is a product of modern distinctions between theory and practice, word and deed, theology and ethics, or faith and works. For Matthew, as for the apostle Paul (and James too, cf. Jas. 2:14–26), faith always entails lived practice. Repentance is not a one-time experience associated with conversion, but ongoing reformation of individuals and communities into the body of Christ, formed around the cross.

Here for the first time Matthew identifies representatives of the **Jewish leaders** as potential adversaries of God's rule and Jesus' mission. The treatment of these groups within the Gospels, which often resembles caricature, has too often bred distorted generalizations about "Judaism," or "Phariseeism," yielding the very self-righteous judgments among Christians that Matthew here attributes to John's opponents. The evangelists are artists painting pictures with words and stories, often with exaggerated, monotone characters. The Pharisees and Sadducees of history were more varied, more complex, more human, and more humane than the evangelist's images suggest. Many modern Christians would have found themselves at home with these groups. How can we talk about the adversaries of Jesus in ways that allow us to see ourselves among them?

The Revelation of God's Son

Matthew 3:13–17*

Exploring the text

In the preceding story, "the people of Jerusalem, all of Judea . . . , and all the region along the Jordan" came out to John (3:5). Now a Galilean comes to be baptized by him. Would a Galilean have as much to repent of as a Judean or a member of the Jerusalem elite? What if the Galilean were the Messiah in exile? The dialogue between Jesus and John regarding who should baptize whom emphasizes Jesus' humility and obedience to God. For the first time in Matthew, we hear Jesus speak: "Let it be so now, for it is proper for us in this way to fulfill all **righteousness**" (3:15). Jesus' first words concisely manifest his authority and name the time. "Now" is the right moment, the time when God is "fulfill[ing] all righteousness" (3:15). The **empire of heaven** has drawn near, and Jesus' participation in the baptism of repentance signals his identification with this reality (3:2 and 4:17). By submitting to John's baptism Jesus also signals the end of his obligations to Rome, Caesar, Herod, the temple, the chief priests, even his own family. Matthew, like the other evangelists when they tell this story, has no interest in whether Jesus needs baptism because he is a sinner. Jesus is "repenting" of the "sin" of a world that has turned away from God. He is declaring social, political, economic, and religious bankruptcy. In order to live for God and God's empire, he has to cut his ties with human powers. Jesus publicly commits his life to God alone, whose presence and power he will now manifest.

The baptism of Jesus is thus a "sacramental" moment, when human and divine wills and actions coincide. Immediately, as Jesus rises from the waters, the heavens are opened–the passive voice indicates God's action–and Jesus sees the Spirit of God descending as a dove and coming to him. Then a voice from the heavens announces to John and the crowds, "This is my beloved Son, with whom I am well pleased," declaring what was already true before the baptism. But now this reality is confirmed on earth from the heavens. The opening of the heavens displays the cosmic, tectonic shift taking place. God breaches the boundaries between heaven and earth. God's Spirit accompanies and accomplishes this transformation of the world, for, as in the first creation, God's breath or Spirit now animates

---

*The Revised Common Lectionary uses this in Year A, Baptism of the Lord.

the new creation. The Spirit's descent and God's words together recall Isaiah 42:1 (cf. Matt. 12:18–20; Ps. 2:7 may also be in Matthew's mind here), Isaiah's first "Servant Song." Isaiah announces that this chosen one, upon whom the Spirit falls, will bring forth justice to the nations. The fulfillment of all righteousness thus includes the realization of God's promises to Israel and the nations. The new creation involves the whole creation. The baptism confirms Jesus' submission to the will of God and his identification with God's mission of peace and reconciliation to the world.

Preaching and teaching the Word

The baptism of Jesus is an **"apocalyptic"** moment that unveils the reality of God's reign in Jesus. At Jesus' baptism, God crosses the border of earth and heaven in order to declare Jesus' identity as the **Son of God** and servant. Jesus' baptism also anticipates another apocalyptic moment, the death of Jesus, when he looses the Spirit, the temple veil is torn from top to bottom, the earth shakes, and even the dead are raised, and he is again named Son of God, this time by an agent of Rome (27:50–54). Baptism thus links God's power with servanthood, suffering, inheritance, the crucifixion, and the shattering of the walls between the human and the divine. Is this the same rite we know in the church? Christian baptism usually focuses on cleansing from sin and identification with Jesus in his death and resurrection. As this story makes clear, baptism also enacts identification with **God's empire** and will. This entails turning from sin, to be sure, but the real issue is what or whom we turn toward. In our baptisms we make the story of Jesus our own story, and we make public our submission to the authority of God and God's Son. We are named God's children and we become servants of God and one another (cf. 20:26–28). Our participation as individuals and communities in this ritual focuses our attention on Jesus and his story, trains our bodies and "the body" for discipleship, and transforms us from bondage to the life of this world into participants in the life of God's world.

Ritual is foundational for the formation of culture and the social organization of life, as well as for "meaning making" and "practice." The stories and rituals around which we construct our lives make sense when they cohere. Twenty-first-century North Americans shape their identities through rituals of consumption, domination, and violence. We are "somebody" when we consume the appropriate material goods, whether cars, clothing, houses, guns, electronics, or food. The goods we purchase tell others who we are, our status, and our allegiances. We use ritualized forms of violence, including war, torture, and executions, in order to project a sense of order, to distinguish friends from enemies, and to "preserve our way of life." We seek meaning and identity by conforming ourselves to the pictures beamed into our homes on flat-screened altars. These rites and ritual objects shape our daily imagination and practice. How do Christian rituals, primarily baptism and the Eucharist, challenge what we learn from and practice in the world? How do our baptisms mark a real shift—our repentance—from the ways of the world? What other religious or secular rituals today compete with baptism in shaping Christian imagination and practice, and to what ends?

Jesus' baptism declares the beginning of his active participation in God's empire. John's preparation of the way, his ministry of baptism, the baptism of Jesus, and Jesus' subsequent ministry all participate in God's realization (or fulfillment) of the world made right (cf. 5:7). It is our participation in this same mission of God, through our own baptisms, our identification with God's reign, and our continuing participation in the story of Jesus that also "fulfills all righteousness."

Retaking Israel's Tests

Matthew 4:1–11*

Exploring the text

Immediately after the baptismal revelation of Jesus' identity as servant and **Son of God**, Jesus is tested. From the River Jordan, the Spirit leads Jesus into the wilderness. The temptations themselves will move from wilderness to Jerusalem and finally to a very high mountain. Each location draws upon Israel's memories and hopes while also contesting the assumptions and social arrangements that determine Israelite life and identity. The wilderness conveys chaos and danger, but also recalls Israel's pilgrimage from Egypt to the land promised by God. The "holy city" (4:5) is in Matthew an ironic designation. Jerusalem is the focus of Israelite hope for national redemption and honor and the locus of God's presence, yet also the embodiment of elite interests and power, the setting where the symbol systems and trappings of priestly and Herodian power are manifest. It is the place where Jesus will be crucified. Matthew associates mountains with divine presence and authority (cf. 5:1; 8:1; 14:23;

---

*The Revised Common Lectionary uses this in Year A, The First Sunday in Lent.

15:29; 17:1; 21:1; and 28:16). In these verses Matthew moves us, with Jesus, across the landscapes of Israel's hopes and frustrations and through the spaces of God's power and presence.

After the Spirit leads him from the Jordan "up" to the wilderness to be tested, Jesus fasts for forty days and forty nights. Jesus disciplines himself for his mission. The setting and duration of his fast again establish connections between Jesus and Moses and Elijah. Moses was twice on Mount Sinai "forty days and forty nights" (cf. Exod. 24:18 and 34:28), and the second time neither ate nor drank. Elijah walked "forty days and forty nights" to Mount Horeb (1 Kgs. 19:8). Forty days was also the length of Noah's flood (Gen. 7:4, 12, 17), which signified both judgment and new creation, and Israel wandered for forty years in the wilderness (Exod. 16:35), being led by God (Deut. 2:7) and tested (Deut. 8:2–3).The setting and background of Jesus' testing thus resonates richly with the stories of Israel and its seminal figures.

The "devil" is known to the audience as an accuser who entices humans to sin and frustrates God's designs. In Job 1 and 2, Satan is a member of the heavenly court, given the task of testing Job's faithfulness. The devil also represents the cosmic forces that are arrayed against God and God's will. The devil's tools include the empires of this world (Matt. 4:8). Matthew thus connects the devil with human rulers such as Herod, the forces of Rome, and even the **religious leaders** who will come to see Jesus as a threat to their own power. For Matthew, temptation and sin are not merely matters of personal choice, but forces lodged in the social, economic, and political constructions of human life.

The first temptation sets the agenda for the whole series of tests: "If you are the Son of God . . ." (4:3, 6). The question concerns what Jesus understands by this identity and vocation and whether and how he will faithfully embody it. The invitation to turn stones into bread arises from the fact that Jesus is famished (4:2) after forty days and nights of fasting. The devil does not question whether Jesus has power to command stones to become bread, but whether he will put this power to use to satisfy his own needs. Jesus' answer draws upon Deuteronomy 8:3 (cf. Exod 16), where Moses reminds the people of Israel that God let them experience hunger so that God might feed them with manna and they might learn to trust God's word. Jesus has learned Israel's lessons well. His trust in God to provide what is needed represents faithful Israel.

From the marginal and desolate space of the wilderness where Israel was tested, the devil now takes Jesus to the developed space of the Holy City, where Israel's hopes were realized and then so often dashed. For Israel, Jerusalem was the geographical center of the world, the location of political, economic, and religious power. The city was understood to be more holy, more filled with God's presence, than any of the other walled cities in Israel. It was the seat of the kings and the focus of messianic hopes and expectations. The devil places Jesus on the very pinnacle of the temple, the highest point in the city, where the powers of heaven and earth intersect.

This time the devil's challenge focuses on whether Jesus' God will intervene to preserve his life: "If you are the Son of God, throw yourself down." Then the devil quotes Psalm 91:11–12, as if to suggest that this action would be the fulfillment of divine will. This is a more stringent test of Jesus' trust in God and God's promise to preserve life, but also a test of Jesus' willingness to reveal his power publicly in association with the Holy City, holy temple, and Holy Scripture. But God's power is not beholden or limited to any human institution, not even Jerusalem or the temple. Jesus' answer comes from Deuteronomy 6:16, which affirms God's good and sovereign faithfulness in providing the people of Israel with everything they needed to take possession of the land. Jesus will not test God's faithfulness, as Israel had at Massah (Exod. 17:1–7), but will trust God in the realization of his own vocation and mission. This temptation also anticipates the passion account, where Jesus the Son of God will refuse both the aid of angels to escape the cross (Matt. 26:53) and calls to come down from the cross and save himself (27:40).

The third test again challenges Jesus' faithful trust in God's power. Each temptation moves higher: first the Spirit led Jesus "up" to the wilderness (4:1), then the devil took him to the pinnacle of the temple (4:5), and now they go to a very high mountain, from which Jesus can see all the empires of the world and their glory (4:8). Each new vista represents a higher, broader perspective, and an elevation of the level of power offered. The devil offers Jesus all the kingdoms of the world if he will but fall down and worship the devil. The offer implies that the devil controls the whole world by means of such empires–they are his to give. By accepting this offer, Jesus can achieve control of the world without the necessity of the cross. But this would subsume God's power in Jesus to the power of death and Satan. The kind of power the devil offers is the power of domination, exploitation, and manipulation. This kind of power divides and destroys, does not care about healing, and is ultimately violent rather than merciful. God's power, as Jesus' ministry will reveal, is inclusive, restorative, healing, and merciful.

Rome sought to unite the world under its supposedly benevolent and divinely ordered rule. All empires see their dominion over others as just and good and as the embodiment of divine will. The devil proposes to let Jesus rule in this way too, as a benevolent, religious king. Perhaps such a king could even eliminate poverty and injustice. But to worship the devil and rule over kingdoms in fact means that Jesus would perpetuate the same systems of hierarchy, domination, and violence by which the empires of this world operate. **God's empire,** on the other hand, is constituted around service, justice, mutuality, sharing, and right relationships. God's reign is realized among those who follow in the path of Jesus, who risk becoming fully human by giving their lives for the sake of others. The final temptation thus articulates the fundamentally different notions of power that are at work in the world and in Jesus' ministry. This test foreshadows the clash of powers on Jesus' way to the cross. God's power will prevail over the world's violent, life-taking power. On a mountain in Galilee, Jesus will receive "all power in heaven and on earth" (28:18), not merely the derivative power offered to Jesus by Satan. Jesus now dismisses "Satan" with the citation of Deuteronomy 6:13, affirming that he will worship and serve God alone. The devil immediately departs, and the angels, whom Jesus earlier refused to invoke, minister to his needs.

Preaching and teaching the Word

Jesus fulfills and rewrites Israel's story. Jesus carries with him into the wilderness the story of Israel's own testing and accomplishes what Israel could not. He demonstrates complete trust in God and remains faithful to God's call. Just as the tests put before Jesus recall the testing of Israel in the wilderness, so also his tests embody the temptations that every human, every Christian, and every human society, including the church, will face. Will we trust God, as Jesus did, to supply our every need (cf. 6:25–33; 14:13–21; 15:32–39)? Will we serve ourselves first? Will we use God's power for our own self-aggrandizement? Will we trust humans and human institutions to bring justice and peace and to supply our needs? Whose power and what kind of power will we seek to realize in our own lives? These are ultimate questions that face every Christian and every congregation in every generation. Our answers to these questions determine how we will live in the world and whether we will discern and bear witness to God's presence and power among us.

The temptation story also demonstrates Jesus' understanding and acceptance of his identity and mission. At the end of this episode, Jesus begins his way to the cross. His refusal to worship Satan and rejection of worldly forms of power mean that they must now defeat and destroy him. Turning away from worldly power constitutes a rebellion of the most radical kind. The church is tested as Jesus was, and as Israel was before him. Passing these tests leads necessarily to confrontation with the world and ultimately to the cross. We can follow Jesus' way with confidence because we know that Jesus has already conquered the powers of death.

We often locate sin within the individual and make ethics a matter of personal choices. Satan represents evil greater than our own personal inclinations. The writers of the New Testament, including Matthew, rightly perceive evil as a cosmic power that holds even the righteous in its grasp. Jesus duels the devil over ultimate power that transcends even the power granted to emperors and empires. Our decisions and actions are a part of this cosmic battle. Knowing this may also help us see our enemies as pawns and victims—as we are—of Satan's power.[1]

A Light in the Darkness

Matthew 4:12–25*

Exploring the text

The three episodes in this section succinctly describe Jesus' mission: he brings light to those in darkness, announcing the advent of God's reign and calling to repentance (4:12–17); he calls disciples from their families and vocations to follow him in mission (4:18–22); and he gathers people from across the region—both Jewish and Gentile territories—to participate in **God's empire** (4:23–25). God's empire does not come by force or violence, but by calling and gathering for the sake of healing and restoration. Into these scenes of light and restoration, Matthew also weaves threads of danger and foreboding. As soon as Satan departs, having failed to divert Jesus from his mission, Jesus hears that John the Baptizer has been arrested (4:12). John's proclamation of God's reign and call to repentance, which have drawn crowds even from Jerusalem (3:5), prove too threatening to the ruling powers. The dangers posed by the rulers have already led the magi (2:12–13) and Joseph (2:14, 22) to flee, and now Jesus withdraws to Galilee. But "Galilee of the Gentiles" (4:15) itself is not free of dangers. Jesus locates his ministry not in the regional centers of power (Sepphoris or Tiberias), but in the fishing village of Capernaum, among common folk whose lives and livelihood were often threatened by imperial politics.

Jesus does not hide out, however, but goes where he is likely to find receptive audiences for his proclamation of **good news** and ministry of healing. If John's "success" in ministry brought his arrest, Jesus is still

*The Revised Common Lectionary uses this in Year A, The 3rd Sunday in Ordinary Time: Matthew 4:12–23.

more successful, drawing even larger crowds from a wider area (4:25). The content of Jesus' proclamation replicates John's exactly (3:2; 4:17), but with a different temporal nuance. When John says that God's reign is at hand, he names a reality that for him is still on the horizon. When Jesus says the same thing, "at hand" conveys greater immediacy, because Jesus' ministry of gathering and healing already manifests, while it works toward, the reality of God's power and rule.

The **fulfillment quotation** from Isaiah 9:2 in Matt. 4:15–16 sets forth yet another interpretive lens through which to make sense of Jesus' ministry. Isaiah 8 describes the Assyrian occupation of Samaria and Judah in 722 BCE, a context all too similar to the occupation and exploitation of Israel by the Romans and Israel's own ruling elite in Jesus' day. Isaiah contrasts the "former **time**," when the land of Zebulun and Naphtali (i.e., Galilee) experienced "contempt," with the "latter time" when God "will make glorious the way of the sea" (Isa. 9:1). The prophet then describes the time when the yoke of their burden and the rod of their oppressor will be broken (Isa. 9:4; cf. Matt. 11:28–30). Isaiah celebrates the coming of the messianic king, a child whose power brings peace, justice, and righteousness (Isa. 9:6–7). While Matthew quotes only the portion of this context that names "Galilee of the Gentiles" as those "in darkness" for whom "light has dawned," the larger passage would have been well known to first-century audiences and would have resonated deeply with the promise of Jesus' mission. God's reign, long awaited, is indeed at hand (4:17).

As Jesus walks by the Sea of Galilee, now the locus of messianic promise, he calls two sets of brothers, first Simon Peter and Andrew, then James and John, the sons of Zebedee (4:18–22). The first are casting their nets, the latter are mending theirs while in the boat with their father. Lured by the promise that Jesus will teach them how to fish for people, both sets of brothers immediately leave everything behind. The scene is both curious and shocking. Jesus' call is like a tsunami that suddenly reshapes their world. Why else would these fishermen suddenly disrupt their families and livelihoods to embark on such a path? The force of Jesus' call implies once again his astonishing authority, which gathers everyday people from everyday lives, to make of them a new family and empire.

Jesus continues to transform the landscape as he pursues his ministry of healing, preaching, and teaching (4:23–25), all of which point to the reality of God's heavenly reign on earth. Matthew lists the healings in detail in order to emphasize the comprehensive scope of Jesus' power. Healing carried social as well as physical consequences, for those healed were restored to their places within their households. Demoniacs, epileptics (lit., the "moonstruck"), and paralytics will all feature prominently in later stories. Demon possession and paralysis name conditions that are common even today in situations of imperial domination and violence. Jesus' power already overwhelms the forces that oppose God and seek to oppress and destroy humankind.

Preaching and teaching the Word

John and Jesus both preach the same word: "Repent, for the kingdom of heaven is at hand." The healing and gathering that accompany Jesus' words signify that the realization of this message is already under way. Although this message is featured in countless cartoons and jokes, and provokes embarrassment among some Christians today, it still describes the situation announced and embodied in Jesus' ministry and that of the church. The vocation of the **church** is to be a repentant and repenting body, a witness to the presence of God's reign, especially in the face of human empires and systems of domination. In Jesus, God's kingdom is close enough to touch.

Matthew again underlines the marginal location of Jesus' ministry. His message and presence have never been good news for those who are deeply invested in the preservation of the current order, or who benefit from the imbalances of human social, political, and economic arrangements. For those who suffer under these systems, however, the message of the Gospel generates hope, vision, and renewed life, which in turn fuel their participation in and realization of God's rule. One of the tasks of the church today is to learn how to listen to those on the margins of the world's power. Encouraging and drawing forth the perspectives of those on the edges of congregations–artists, children, the humble and humiliated ones–is still a foundational agenda for pastoral ministry. How do we locate congregations so that we can hear more clearly the voices of those at the margins?

Jesus' call to the first disciples displays the disruptive, world-shaking character of discipleship. God calls us from our families and everyday vocations, regardless of whether these are humble or high-powered. Even for those of us whose calls do not seem so dramatic, the demands of God's call are no less disruptive. The kingdom of heaven does not exist for the sake of our families or careers, which may distract us or even choke our commitment to God (see 13:5–7, 20–22). Our families and vocations exist, rather, for the sake of God's mission in the world; they are venues where the reality of God's power and presence will be made manifest and where we give witness to what God is doing among us. When we respond to God's call we can no longer go back to the way things were, for the foundational reorientation implied in call and repentance means that even what once was familiar will now appear in a new light (4:16). The church's vocation is to enable hearing and nurture faithful responses to God's call.

PART TWO

The Announcement of God's Empire: The Sermon on the Mount

5:1–7:29

Preliminary Remarks

Few passages in the New Testament have exercised more power in shaping Christian imagination than the Sermon on the Mount, Matthew's classic compilation of the core of Jesus' teaching. The sermon is a manifesto, constitution, and working manual for "the **heavenly empire**" (4:17; 4:23; 5:3; 5:10; 5:19; 5:20; 6:10; 6:33; 7:21) and the first of five great discourses in Matthew (Matthew 5–7; 10; 13; 18; 23–25). The five discourses suggest a typological correlation with the Pentateuch. The fact that Jesus goes up a mountain to deliver the sermon also links Jesus with Moses, who went up a mountain to receive the Commandments from God. Matthew's Jesus thus continues to fulfill the patterns and typologies of the Old Testament, but he will also break the molds, both in his call to surpassing **righteousness** and in his convictions about how God is at work in the world. Unlike the commandments Moses received, Jesus' sermon is not so much a rule book as a series of images and case studies that describe the nature of God's reign. Jesus, the poet laureate of God's empire, imparts impressions and images that point the way for those who seek God's will and ways in the world.

Many interpreters rightly speak of the **"eschatological"** character of the sermon, but this should not be taken to mean that Jesus' teaching is inappropriate for this world except as an "interim ethic" for those who live at the end of human history. The sermon addresses real people in the real world, in Jesus' day and Matthew's day and our day. The sermon's eschatological character lies in its power to free its auditors' imaginations from the limitations of their everyday assumptions about the world and to open eyes and ears to the reality and nature of God's reign. Because Jesus presumes the perspectives and practices of the empire of heaven, his teaching often sounds "crazy" or "impossible" to people whose "common sense" is conditioned by earthly assumptions. We should resist any attempt to diminish or domesticate these expressions of divine lunacy.

The Sermon on the Mount is directed first to the disciples (5:1), second to the crowds that have been following Jesus (see 4:25; 7:28), and finally to the churches that hear the performance of Matthew's Gospel. We are expected to locate ourselves among the potential disciples eavesdropping as Jesus speaks to the Twelve. More important still, the audience Matthew has in mind for this sermon is not merely individual Christians, nor even an aggregate of individuals, but disciplined communities of disciples. The sermon calls forth the kind of community that sustains the vision and practices described in these chapters. In fact, the images found within the sermon may only be realized–or even understood–within such sustaining communities. When read, heard, experienced, performed, ingested, studied, and lived within the context of faith communities, the sermon has been powerful indeed, even serving as the "center of the canon" for many intentional communities of discipleship.

Modern readers may first perceive only a loose collection of topics and sayings, but the sermon is artfully constructed around recurrent themes. Some readers discern a series of concentric, thematic brackets, with the Lord's Prayer at the center (6:9–13),[1] while others identify 5:17–48 as the "nucleus." The sermon does not proceed in a linear fashion but, like poetry, employs a variety of forms and devices to move the audience toward a place where it is possible to participate in the world the sermon describes and to discover the God who creates and shapes this space.

The Subjects of God's Rule

Matthew 5:1–12[*]

Exploring the text

When Jesus sees the crowds pressing about him, bringing to him the sick and afflicted for healing (4:23–25), he goes up the mountain (a locus of divine power and revelation in Matthew, cf. 14:23; 15:29–31; 17:1; 28:16–20), sits down with his disciples, and begins teaching. The crowds are also listening (cf. 7:28). They have witnessed God's healing power in Jesus' ministry, and Jesus now names for them the transformative, but disorienting and potentially misunderstood, power that they have observed. Jesus' first act of naming takes form in nine pronouncements of blessing, each introduced by the word *makarios* ("blessed"), which are similar to pronouncements of divine favor in the Wisdom literature and apocalyptic works (e.g., 1 Enoch 58:2–3; Pss. Sol. 17:44). Jesus here describes the subjects of God's empire, their experiences and stations in life, and the

---

[*]The Revised Common Lectionary uses this in Year A, The 4th Sunday in Ordinary Time and All Saints' Day.

ways they are affected by and engage the broken world around them. In many ways these subjects resemble the people Jesus has been healing and calling. He articulates the fundamental values and practices that God seeks from the subjects of the **empire of heaven**. The first four beatitudes (5:3–6) have their roots in the language and imagery of Isaiah 61, which both envisions the character of God's eschatological rule and describes situations of distress or injustice that God reverses. The next five (5:7–12) describe the actions of those whose lives conform already to the values and ethos of God's reign.

Blessed are the poor in spirit, for theirs is the kingdom of heaven (5:3). Matthew's phrase "the poor in spirit" is often seen as a "spiritualized," watered-down version of the parallel saying in Luke 6:20. But, as in Luke, those named here include real poor people, but without idealizing "the poor" as an abstract social or religious category ("the poor" was one of Israel's self-designations). Those who for the sake of the kingdom of heaven trust God to supply what they need each day (cf. 6:19–34; 19:16–30) most clearly embody this designation. This includes those who sustain hope and trust in the midst of economic injustice and crushing circumstances, as well as those who because of their vulnerability are despised by those who dominate them. It is these who belong to, and to whom belong, "God's empire."

Blessed are those who mourn, for they will be comforted (5:4). The damage the world inflicts–whether through experiences of alienation, oppression, loss, or violence–cannot be repaired. But Jesus promises the comfort of God's presence, the transformation of sorrow to joy (Isa. 61:1–3), and the hope of restoration and redemption. God's presence does not erase the causes of lament and mourning, but transforms and redeems the suffering of the world through the cross of Christ.

Blessed are the meek, for they will inherit the earth (5:5). Jesus invokes Psalm 37 (esp. 37:11, 22, 29), which invites the powerless and downtrodden to trust God for their salvation. The term "meek" does not imply passivity in the face of exploitation, but affirms those who trust in God to redeem them and restore their relationships rather than their seeking vengeance. Jesus offers examples of such practices in the "antitheses" later in the sermon (5:38–42; cf. Rom. 12:14–21). God overthrows all systems of oppression, exploitation, and injustice. The earth will be returned to all the people, as in the visions of the "year of jubilee" in Leviticus 25 and in Isaiah 61 and 60:1–2. When humans seek their own solutions to oppression and injustice, too often they merely meet violence with violence. Only God's action holds the promise of genuine transformation, justice, and the restoration of broken relationships.

Blessed are those who hunger and thirst for righteousness, for they will be filled (5:6). Those who hunger and thirst for righteousness are neither "do-gooders" seeking to establish their own rightness before God and humans, nor even those who work for "social justice," worthy as their causes may be, for both activities too often lead to further division and to the self-righteousness that destroys the integrity of human community. Hungering and thirsting for righteousness describes those who yearn for the full restoration of broken relationships, who feel the ache and frustration of aloneness in the world, and who are willing to make themselves vulnerable to those who are enemies and strangers. Jesus promises that this hope will be satisfied in God's reign.

Blessed are the merciful, for they will receive mercy (5:7). The merciful forgive (18:10–35), love enemies and strangers (5:38–48), and care for the "least ones" (25:31–46). Mercy is one of Matthew's signature themes, which the evangelist sets in contrast to the sacrificial system (cf. 9:13; 12:7, both citing Hos. 6:6). Mercy consists of acts that create space for those who have none, space to turn around, to be forgiven, reconciled, and restored to full humanity. Actions that create dependency do not constitute mercy. Mercy is, rather, a reciprocal experience, a reality that must be mutually shared in order to be realized. Jesus promises that those who practice mercy will receive it themselves.

Blessed are the pure in heart, for they will see God (5:8). Jewish people understood the heart to be the locus of perception, knowledge, will, and action, in short as the center of the whole person. "Purity in heart" refers to inner and outer integrity of thought, emotion, and action. Purity in heart excludes hypocrisy and self-serving behavior. In Matthew's story of the judgment of the "sheep and the goats" (25:31–46), the actions of the righteous sheep toward the sick, the hungry and thirsty, the naked, and prisoners apparently arises without any expectation of receiving something in return, and without awareness that the "king" is among those who are served. The sheep embody what it means to be "pure in heart," and they will see God, perhaps even among the least ones.

Blessed are the peacemakers, for they will be called children of God (5:9). Peace is not calm, inner detachment or tranquillity, but relationships restored and made whole. Rome's empire claimed to offer peace to those it had conquered, even to embody divine peace in the world. But those at the bottom of the empire experienced the Pax Romana much differently than those who had access to land, resources, and power. Jesus calls upon disciples to love their enemies and pray for those who persecute them (5:44) and in this way to "be perfect" or "whole," as God is (5:48). Those who root their identities and practices in the wholeness of this heavenly father become God's children. Enmity, violence, and war all arise from our alienation from one another and from God. The peace achieved through violence is always ephemeral; where God's power, presence, and mercy are not named, peace is false and fleeting. Peace begins with the recognition of God's merciful presence in the world and the realization of our common humanity before God.

Blessed are those who are persecuted for righteousness' sake, for theirs is the kingdom of heaven (5:10). For the second time Jesus speaks of righteousness (cf. 5:6), but here in association with persecution. Why does persecution accompany the quest for righteousness and justice? Restored relationships are too threatening to those who benefit from the current ordering of the world. The kind of righteousness and justice that Jesus envisions radically undermines the hierarchies of class, race, and even religion that are deemed normal or inevitable in our world. Social, economic, and political systems that breed or depend upon such distinctions will not long tolerate those who name the presence of a merciful and forgiving God in our midst.

Blessed are you when people revile you and persecute you and utter all kinds of evil against you falsely on my account. Rejoice and be glad, for your reward is great in heaven, for in the same way they persecuted the prophets who were before you (5:11–12). The final beatitude focuses the discussion of persecution squarely on "you," the disciples. Jesus' disciples can anticipate a hostile reaction from the world, including slander, persecution, and attacks upon their person (cf. 10:16–25). Jesus links their behavior and fate with that of the prophets. Disciples should "rejoice and be glad," not only because of their great reward in heaven, but because their suffering conforms to the model of the one who is revealing God's power and presence.

Preaching and teaching the Word

Even people in churches will regard the Beatitudes as impossible, impractical, and foolish. The key to preaching and teaching these verses is to discern what kind of community these blessings call into being, for the vision they invoke can only be sustained by communities of discipleship. What does a congregation that identifies with the poor in spirit, those who mourn, the meek, and those who hunger and thirst for righteousness look like? Where would it be located? How would its gatherings and worship services be distinctive? How might a community focused on mercy, purity of heart, peacemaking, and the restoration of right relationships relate to the great issues and controversies that face the church today? Would such a congregation face persecution and derision, as Matthew's community may have?

The Beatitudes dislocate and disorient us because they are rooted in a radically different perception of the world. The myths moderns live by derive from the perception of a broken and hostile creation and a distant, angry God, and thus give rise to greed, alienation, and violence. They teach us that this is just "the way the world is." The Beatitudes take us into a different world, with different assumptions, values, and practices. Preaching the Beatitudes entails throwing light on this disturbing world of God, painting pictures of the nature of God's power and presence, and inviting audiences to begin living out of this fresh imagination of the world. The Beatitudes do not portray "pie-in-the-sky by-and-by," but provide a realistic picture of the nature and character of God's reign, with all its attendant risks and rewards.

Surpassingly Salty Righteousness

Matthew 5:13–20*

Exploring the text

The Beatitudes have highlighted the ways of life that God blesses. Do disciples pursue these practices for the sake of the heavenly rewards they bring? Jesus now makes clear that the people and practices named in the Beatitudes serve as salt and light in the world (5:13–16). The **righteousness** they embody fulfills the intention of the law and the prophets (5:17–20), i.e., to create a people who bear witness to God's faithfulness, mercy, and power. The **church** is a "contrast community," called to stand out from the world, not only so that others might see the disciples' good works, but so that together they might give glory to "your Father in heaven" (5:16). The work of the community is not for self-gratification, but always to glorify God. We would not be far from the mark in claiming that the peculiar practices of the community of disciples constitute its mission, witness, and worship.

The emphatic "you" (plural) in 5:13 and 14 binds these sayings to the final beatitude (5:11–12), which describes the persecution and insults that will come on account of the disciples' identification with Jesus. "You" who

*The Revised Common Lectionary uses this in Year A, The 5th Sunday in Ordinary Time.

are slandered and persecuted "for my sake" are the salt of the earth. Just as the prophets gave witness to God amidst persecution, so, too, the community of disciples will give witness–crucially–in situations of opposition. In these situations the disciples' salt is saltiest and their light brightest.

Salt can be used to despoil the earth, but in its more common, daily applications it serves as an indispensable preservative, an agent of purification (cf. 2 Kgs. 2:19–22) and sacrifice (Lev. 2:13; Ezek. 43:24), and as seasoning. In each case, salt permeates and alters that which it touches. The phrase "If salt has lost its taste" literally speaks of salt becoming "dumb" or "foolish," that is, no longer able to fulfill its purpose or essence. Technically, salt cannot lose its saltiness; if it does, it is no longer salt. Unsalty salt might as well be thrown out and trampled underfoot. How and when is the community of disciples "salt"? Always, and by its very essence. Jesus' claim is not that the community ought to be salty some of the time, but that "You! You are salt!" When they cease to bear witness to the reality of God's reign, the disciples become something other than salty disciples. When their witness in situations of conflict and oppression leads others to glorify God, the disciples demonstrate their saltiness. When the community functions in the world to preserve, purify, and season, when it permeates the world as salt permeates and flavors food, it is a salty community.

A second cluster of sayings focuses on visual imagery (5:14–16). Matthew has already described Jesus' ministry as "a great light" shining in darkness and light dawning "in the region and shadow of death" (4:16). The light here is the means by which people navigate upon the seas or through life (cf. Phil. 3:15). The Christian community provides both illumination and a point of reference. Likewise, a city set on a hill is hard to miss; its activity is plain for all to see. Like salt, light spreads; a small candle can illuminate a whole room (5:15). Light belongs on a lampstand, where it can serve its intended purpose, like a city on a hill.

In the light of the Beatitudes, does Jesus' proclamation and ministry "destroy" or fulfill the law and the prophets? The repeated assertion "I have come [not] to abolish the law or the prophets," coupled with the affirmation "but to fulfill [them]" (5:17), underlines resolutely and powerfully Jesus' positive relationship with the tradition. Jesus affirms this claim yet again in 5:18: "Not one letter, not one stroke of a letter, will pass from the law." Jesus fulfills the law and the prophets in three ways: (1) by continuing to teach and uphold their commandments and instruction; (2) by recasting in his own life the story of Israel; and (3) by embodying in his ministry and person the realization of God's will for the redemption and salvation of Israel and the nations. Two temporal clauses–"until heaven and earth pass away" (cf. Isa. 65:17; Rev. 21:1) and "until all is accomplished"–frame and qualify the central assertion of verse 18. Both clauses carry an eschatological ring, yet Jesus' ministry already bears God's presence and power, fulfilling "all things" that the prophets had envisioned. His ministry blurs the boundaries between "heaven and earth" (e.g., 6:9–10; 28:18) in anticipation of the time when heaven and earth pass away and God dwells with us (cf. 28:20).

Jesus' affirmation of the abiding authority of the law and the prophets has implications for the disciples. Those who loose even the smallest commandment and teach others to do so will be least in the **empire of heaven**, but those who "do and teach" the commandments will be great in the heavenly empire. Here again, Jesus' formulation confirms the importance of integrity of word and deed, teaching and doing. The final verse in the section intensifies this call: "unless your righteousness [or justice] exceeds that of the **scribes** [teachers of the law] and **Pharisees**, you will never enter the kingdom of heaven" (5:20). Taken out of context, this statement could be seen as a call for a stringent, personal righteousness, perhaps focused on purity issues (like the Pharisees) or casuistry (following the scribes). But within Matthew it is clear what fulfills this call to exceptional "righteousness": following in the path of Jesus himself, whose righteousness is embodied in proclamation of God's empire, in table fellowship with strangers, in healing and restoring the sick and unclean, and especially in his crucifixion and resurrection, in order to redeem the very ones who call for his death.

Preaching and teaching the Word

The mission of the church is not to preserve itself, but to preserve the world, not to point to itself, but to illuminate the way and bring glory to God. The church has always been challenged to realize these goals, but perhaps no more than today, when many congregations may function as semiprivate organizations with little or no appreciable impact on their surrounding communities. Such congregations may be salty, but the salt is still in the box. There may be light, but it's under the basket. How can and does the church today shine as light in the world? How does it function to illuminate reality, to uncover the world's deceptions, and especially to reveal and clarify–powerfully and brilliantly–what God is doing in the world? How do we shine so as to bring glory to God, especially in situations of conflict and opposition, when the church's witness is neither popular nor in the majority?

Jesus' authoritative claim to fulfill the traditions of Israel is an invitation to explore again the continuity between Jesus and the story of Israel. We are also invited to consider how the church continues to honor and embody Israel's story and calling, especially in a time when the story of Jesus itself is often eclipsed in the church by other agendas? The strong christological assertions in this section make him, not just his teachings about the law and the prophets, the link between Israel's story and the church's witness.

Matthew does not advocate in these verses a position contrary to Paul's conceptions about righteousness based on works. Both Paul and Matthew affirm the importance of what we do, not merely what we think or believe. For both, Christian faith is about real practice in the world. Jesus' focus in this passage is on the living fulfillment of God's will, which is articulated both through the law and the prophets and through Jesus, and brought to fruition among those who repent of this world and follow Jesus to the cross.

Pursuit of a "surpassing righteousness" has led at times to sectarianism and withdrawal from the world. Yet nothing in the passage would suggest that such withdrawal is Jesus' intention, especially when we recall Jesus' vision of the disciples as salt and light in the world. The kind of righteousness Jesus advocates and embodies is focused on redeeming and restoring this world, on love of strangers and enemies (5:43–48), and on the realization of God's reign on earth! Jesus' kind of righteousness is "this-worldly" or it is not God's righteousness at all.

Case Studies for the Empire of Heaven

Matthew 5:21–37*

Exploring the text

Six "case studies" (four treated in this section, two in the next) develop Jesus' claim to fulfill rather than tear down the law (5:17–20). Each case study juxtaposes an element of traditional teaching with instructions for the new reality of God's reign. Do the "antitheses" (the conventional designation of these teachings) imply that Jesus is overturning rather than fulfilling the law? It is not the law itself, but conventional interpretations

*The Revised Common Lectionary uses this in Year A, The 6th Sunday in Ordinary Time.

of it that Jesus challenges, usually recasting and intensifying the tradition in light of his sense of God's will for the world. Each antithesis focuses on some dimension of human relationships. Jesus' starting point is not the brokenness, violence, and alienation of creation, although he is well aware of these, but the reality of God's empire, where restoration, inclusion, healing, abundance, and true peace are the norm. His conviction that God's rule is already a reality in his own ministry overturns the false premises that guide conventional human interactions.

Jesus' authority as a teacher is also on display in this section. "You have heard it said . . . , but I say to you" expresses his certitude about the true nature of the **times** and the character of God's relationship with humankind. Because Jesus' teachings arise from his relationship with God rather than from worldly commonplaces, his words ring with a different kind of authority (cf. 7:28–29). Jesus' own ministry will provide further "authorization" for his teachings; his deeds will be completely consistent with his words.

ON ANGER AND MURDER (5:21–26)

The fifth commandment of the Decalogue (cf. Exod. 20:13; Deut. 5:17) prohibits killing. The clause "whoever kills shall be liable to judgment" is not found in either version of the Decalogue, but may be based on Deuteronomy 17:8–13, which envisions diverse kinds of cases, including killing, and the courts in which they are judged. Jesus' antithesis also presumes different kinds or levels of courts ("judgment," "the council," and the "hell of fire," Matt. 5:22). He broadens and intensifies the tradition by indicating that continuing anger, insults, and calling someone a "fool" (or perhaps "godless") are also liable to judgment. Jesus thus associates killing with apparently more mundane offenses. In each case the offender deprives the other of full humanity and usurps God's role as judge. Such actions arise from alienation and yield dehumanization. The following verses assert the alternative: whether on the way to the altar or the courts, disciples must attend first to reconciliation with those who have something against them (5:23–26). True worship and justice presuppose restored relationships. God's righteousness is not satisfied until broken relationships are healed. Jesus imagines a world of restorative rather than retributive justice.[1]

ADULTERY AND LUST (5:27–30)

Again Jesus radicalizes the conventional teaching, this time by insisting that looking at a woman lustfully is already an expression of adultery.

This case presupposes the male-oriented world of the first century, in which adultery was considered a form of theft, an attack on another man's property and honor.[2] Jesus, in contrast, recognizes that this world makes women objects to be possessed. To look at a woman lustfully is already to rob her of her humanity. The hyperboles in 5:29–30 underscore the importance of attending to the wholeness and justice of our relationships. Even if your right eye, usually understood as the dominant one, causes you to sin, you should pluck it out and throw it away. So, too, if your right hand, the strong one and the one with which you make contracts, causes you to sin, cut it off and throw it away. It is not, however, the eye or the hand that causes us to sin, but our imagination of the world as a place full of things, including people, to be consumed and exploited. God's reign, in contrast, is built on the realization of our full, common humanity, which lust denies.

DIVORCE (5:31–32)

The third case presumes the regulations found in Deuteronomy 24:1–4, which aimed at preventing a woman from remarrying her first husband after she had married a second. Interpretations of the law typically presupposed that men had virtually limitless power over their wives, including the right to initiate divorce proceedings if they found something "indecent" or "immodest" about her. The rabbis of Jesus' day debated over what these terms really meant, but did not challenge the tradition's orientation toward the male's interests. Jesus, on the other hand, refuses to accept the assumptions that lie beneath the surface of these disputes. As in the similar discussion in Matt. 19:3–9, he claims that God's intention was for union and for recognition of the full humanity of both male and female. While the law makes concessions for a broken world, Jesus articulates God's will for a restored and reconciled world. The reign of God thus does not treat divorce as a normative occurrence. Jesus makes an exception for "unchastity" (probably adultery), in which case the relationship is already broken. In any other circumstance, a man's decision to divorce his wife leads inevitably toward adultery (5:32). Divorced women often faced the prospect of prostitution in order to support themselves. Men who marry divorced women participate in the brokenness of the first relationship. Jesus' teaching addresses a tension within the law itself between the commandments, on the one hand, that describe the circumstances under which a man may divorce his wife and those, on the other hand, that prohibit adultery and affirm the sanctity of human relationships. Jesus confirms God's primordial will for union and lasting relationships.

ON OATHS AND INTEGRITY (5:33–37)

On the face of it, the fourth set of teachings appears to challenge a commandment of the law, Leviticus 19:12: "You shall not swear falsely, but shall perform to the Lord what you have sworn" (cf. also Exod. 20:7; Num. 30:3–15; Deut. 5:20; 23:22–24). Oath-taking was common in antiquity, not only in legal settings such as the courts and civic administration, but in social settings such as guilds, clubs, or other voluntary associations. Swearing an oath presupposes that the oath taker's word is untrustworthy and so must be buttressed by a higher authority. The Jewish tradition tended to stipulate the precise circumstances under which various oaths might be taken. But Jesus dismisses the entire practice. He lists and dismisses the powers–from heaven to one's own head–by which people were likely to swear an oath. Disciples are not to swear "by heaven, for it is the throne of God, or by the earth, for it is [God's] footstool, or by Jerusalem, for it is the city of the great King" (5:34–35). God does not act according to human prescription (5:36). Even swearing by one's own head is an empty gesture, for humans are unable even to control whether the hairs on their own head are black or white. Oath-taking is thus "from the evil one" (5:37). Jesus calls upon disciples to let their word be simply "yes" or "no," that is, to let their actions and words so confirm one another that no further demonstrations of or claims for one's integrity are necessary. It is the simplicity and directness of "yes" and "no," and the performance in deed of what one has said, that nurtures a world of trust and integrity.

Preaching and teaching the Word

Jesus' proclamation of God's rule focuses on the nature of our relationships, both with God and with our fellow human beings. Each of these cases is meant to be illustrative, to paint a picture rather than codify a law. While Jesus fulfills and affirms God's law, he also understands that where laws implicitly or explicitly confirm the existing, broken order, they may be abandoned in favor of reconciliation, restoration of relationship, and wholeness. Jesus' teachings in this section cover a range of social, familial, and intrapersonal relationships. Jesus' use of these case studies allows us room to explore the many ways that our own presuppositions, even among Christians, lead not to wholeness but to division and hatred. How do our economic and political arrangements inscribe and affirm differentiations of status and power? Do we affirm that some have the right to lord it over others, or to gain massive wealth at the expense of others? How do our own allegiances to family, party, class, race, or even denomination hinder our realization of and participation in God's wholeness? How do we, whether by social convention or personal choice, turn other human beings into objects or commodities?

Most of us will find Jesus' teachings daunting. Adultery and divorce are at least as common today as they were in Jesus' day. Few of us are practiced in the arts of reconciliation, or even inclined to use them in relationships that bring us the most pain. We live in a world filled with alienation and distrust. But this is precisely the kind of world in which the antitheses offer a vision of hope. The antitheses are not laws but illustrations that reveal **God's empire**, where different relationships and assumptions are possible. They point us toward a world where reconciliation is the norm rather than the exception, where the broken places in our lives are restored and we, together, are made whole. This is not the world we know on a daily basis, but it is the vision under which the church lives. The antitheses show us how the church might be a city on the hill, or salt and light in a decaying and dark world. The church is not a place where there is no conflict, or where there are only perfect marriages. But it can be the place where God's reconciling power is on display.

The Way of Wholeness

Matthew 5:38–48*

Exploring the text

Domination, exploitation, and injustice were everyday experiences for the people to whom Jesus proclaimed the **good news** of the **kingdom of heaven**. The powerless had little choice but to accept the abuse of the powerful, but among parties of relatively equal status retribution was considered a matter of honor. Jesus, on the other hand, accepts neither passivity nor violence as appropriate responses to injustice. Instead he calls disciples to transform relationships of domination and subordination, victimizer and victim, into relationships that embody reconciliation and restoration.

In a world of retributive justice, "an eye for an eye and a tooth for a tooth" was an attempt to moderate responses in proportion to the offense,

* The Revised Common Lectionary uses this in Year A, The 7th Sunday in Ordinary Time.

so as to limit the spread of violence (cf. Exod. 21:23–25; Lev. 24:20; Deut. 19:21). But retributive, response-in-kind "justice" still preserves the fundamentally violent character of human interaction. As the saying goes, "'an eye for an eye and a tooth for a tooth' leaves everyone blind and toothless" and, even more important, still alienated and angry. Jesus' teaching offers a "third way."[1] "Do not resist one who is evil" is not a counsel of passivity, as often presumed, but Jesus' foundational principle of nonviolent engagement. Jesus' first concrete illustration (5:39) involves situations of insult and provocation, in which the initial blow—probably a slap—conveys the subordination and dishonoring of the one who is struck. "Turning the other cheek" reclaims the dignity and honor of the victim without resorting to violence. The intent is not to imply that the blow did not hurt, but to refuse to play the role of victim, thereby disrupting the powerful meanings associated with the roles of victim and victimizer. The instruction to carry a soldier's pack twice as far as required has a similar goal (5:41). A soldier's right to conscript and compel subject citizens to carry their provisions asserted Rome's imperial authority. The same verb is used when Simon of Cyrene is compelled to carry Jesus' cross (27:32). Again Jesus does not advocate passivity. "Going the second mile" reclaims the conscript's self-determination and dignity and surprises the soldier. In this new, unexpected space, where the power imbalances of the world are undone, the possibility emerges for a new order of relationships.

The second and fourth illustrations (5:40, 42) involve economic relations. Outer garments served as a poor person's pledge of payment for a loan (cf. Exod. 22:25–26). Giving the accuser one's undergarments exposes, literally and figuratively, the stripping of land and property that attended ancient usury and exploitation. Giving one's undergarments is a **prophetic-symbolic action** that displays the true nature of the economic system at the same time it actively reclaims, ironically, the dignity of the accused. In the fourth admonition Jesus calls his disciples to share what they have, apparently without expectation of either repayment or deference from those with whom they share. Here the goal is to overturn the "normal" order of domination and dependence.

Jesus' final antithesis focuses on the boundaries between enemies and allies, strangers and friends. "You shall love your neighbor" comes from Leviticus 19:18b, but the next phrase, "and hate your enemy," is not a citation of the law, but a commonly presumed implication of the first claim. "Neighbors" presupposes the existence of "not-neighbors," i.e., enemies and strangers. Ancient and modern people alike express their identities around the articulation of such "in-group"/"out-group"

distinctions, usually based on ethnic, racial, social, economic, or political differences. We know who we are because we can articulate who we
are not. But this nearly universal approach to identity formation carries
within it the seeds of violence and alienation. In contrast, extending
the love usually reserved for "neighbors" to enemies as well effectively
obliterates the distinction between them. "Love" is not merely cordiality
or niceness, but committed compassion, worked out in real relationships
across time and through the challenges and conflicts that beset every
relationship. Continuing prayer, even for one's persecutors, is a powerful
expression of this love.

Jesus supplies a series of rationales in support of the radical and risky
life to which he calls his disciples in these verses. The familial resemblance
between God and God's children (5:45) means that they will treat friends
and enemies alike, just as God makes the sun to rise and rain to fall upon
the just and the unjust alike (cf. Rom. 2:11). Creative, nonviolent love of
enemies distinguishes God's heavenly children from the rest of the world.
Loving those who love you is typical of most people, even Gentiles and the
reviled tax collectors (5:46–47). Loving one's enemies, on the other hand,
embodies the "perfection" or "wholeness" (cf. 19:21) that is one of God's
distinguishing characteristics (5:48). The assertion of God's wholeness
may have roots in the Septuagint version of Leviticus 19:2: "You shall be
holy, because I the Lord your God am holy." But "holiness" often signified separation by means of purity distinctions, whereas for Jesus it means
inclusive wholeness, or "perfection," completion rather than separation.

Preaching and teaching the Word

In these final illustrations of the way Jesus fulfills the law, Matthew continues to describe a world where creative, surprising, sometimes even risky
patterns of interaction open the door for relationships that would otherwise
have been unimaginable. The heart of the law is to be like God, to love
our enemies, and to risk even our lives, as Jesus will, for the sake of God's
kingdom. Each of Jesus' illustrations here describes a situation of injustice
or domination, and imagines a response that refuses to accept the terms,
the roles, and the common patterns of response–whether passivity or
retaliation–that leave the system intact and hinder the reconciliation of the
contending parties. Jesus cuts to the heart of the matter: restoring right relationships requires creative actions and responses that do not accept alienation, violence, and exploitation as the normative reality. In the empire of
heaven, we love our enemies and pray for those who persecute us.

At its heart, all Christian practice is concerned with making room for
others, especially strangers and enemies, as God has made room for us.[2]
Jesus calls on his disciples to make space for the full humanity and dignity

of those we might otherwise despise or denigrate. Making room for those who are different from or even threats to us requires risk and vulnerability; it is costly and dangerous. But making space for others embodies the way of our heavenly Father, who in the ministry of God's Son has made space for all of us. Preaching these illustrations of Jesus' approach to the law can invite audiences to explore the ways our ordinary social arrangements, even in the church itself, exclude others or limit space for transformation. Jesus' teachings here invite us to think critically about our own social and economic arrangements and to consider surprising actions that overturn the conventional wisdom and hidden assumptions of the world and that make room for renewed, reconciled relationships. Discipleship requires "working the cracks" to transform especially the situations of oppression and injustice that disciples will encounter in the world.

The practices Jesus illustrates here are not best undertaken by solitary individuals. They require the support of sustaining communities to nurture vision and strategic perspective, to monitor situations of intentional engagement, and to intervene as needed in support of the vulnerable. Without such support, "turning the other cheek," for example, only exposes the vulnerable to continued harm without hope of transformation. When we preach and teach the antitheses, our primary objective is always to create and preserve space for reconciliation and whole relationships.

Public Piety and Hidden Righteousness

Matthew 6:1–18[*]

Exploring the text

Jesus' call to be salt and light (5:13–16) and to practice a surpassing **righteousness** (5:17–48) carries certain risks in societies, like the ancient Mediterranean world, where public displays of beneficence or patronage advance one's status. Do one's "righteous" deeds really lead to restored,

---

[*] The Revised Common Lectionary uses this in Year A, B, and C, Ash Wednesday: Matthew 6:1–6, 16–21.

whole relationships, or to prestige and power among humans? Jesus explores these questions through the lens of three common acts of righteousness (or "**justice**"; the NRSV's "piety" obscures the fact that Jesus is still addressing a continuing topic: "righteousness/justice"): almsgiving (6:2–4), prayer (6:5–15), and fasting (6:16–18). Matthew 6:1 articulates the governing principle for Jesus' approach: "Beware of practicing your righteousness so as to be seen by other people, for then you have no reward from your Father in heaven" (cf. 6:2; 6:5; 6:16).

ALMSGIVING (6:2–4)

In Jesus' day, giving and receiving "gifts" was the ritual framework in which relationships were negotiated and status was displayed and advanced. Almsgiving was an aspect of the **patronage** system, which generated and preserved the steep social and economic hierarchies of ancient Mediterranean society. "Being seen by others" while giving gifts and receiving honor was precisely what one wanted to have happen. If no one was watching, acts of benevolence and piety were wasted. The word we translate as "almsgiving" is a cognate of the word for "mercy" in 5:7, but almsgiving with the strings of patronage attached is anything but merciful. Jesus' teaching seeks to address precisely these dynamics by removing acts of righteousness and justice from the playing field of human self-interest. He warns the disciples not to sound any trumpets in order to gain notice and praise when engaging in acts of mercy. The "hypocrites" (i.e., people who play parts in a theatrical production), who act out their "righteousness" in the synagogues and streets (6:2), have already received whatever reward they will get. In contrast, disciples are to give without letting the left hand know what the right hand is doing (6:3), so that the gift will be in "secret" (or "hidden")–known only to the Father, who sees in secret (6:4). Acting in secrecy, so that only God sees, becomes the refrain for all three topics in this section (6:4; 6:6; 6:18).

PRAYER (6:5–15)

The "hypocrites" (6:5) also like to pray in synagogues and on street corners so that other people will notice them. Again Jesus claims that "they have received their reward," attention and honor from other people. Disciples, however, are to go into their storeroom (or closet, or a hidden room), close the door, and pray. The God the disciples seek in prayer is found in the secret places, where there is no need for pretense and where no one else is watching. Those who approach God in this way will be rewarded with what they are seeking–no honor among humans, but right relationship with God. Nor is God impressed by the "empty phrases" and "many words" of the Gentiles' prayers (6:7), for God "knows what you need before you ask" (6:8). The focus here is not primarily on divine omniscience, but on God's trustworthiness and closeness with those who pray in simplicity and honesty.

The Lord's Prayer (6:9–13) stands at the center of the Sermon on the Mount. Matthew's version lacks the concluding formula of the traditional prayer ("for thine is the kingdom . . . glory forever"), which comes from Didache 8:2. We have heard this prayer so often, we may no longer really hear it. And while we often recite it, we may not really perform or live it. In contrast to the prayers of the hypocrites and the Gentiles, the community of disciples (the command to pray in 6:9 is plural) is to pray "in this way." "This way" affirms God's rule and invokes relationships of trust, grace, and security in the presence of the "Father [who] knows what you need before you ask" (6:8). The address "Our Father, the one who is in heaven," suggests God's immediate presence and care for the members of God's family, not a distant god or a god who needs to be appeased. God's being transcends but is not removed from earthly space and human experience. Hallowing (or setting apart) God's name expresses the disciples' recognition of God's holiness and heavenliness, that is, God's differentness. Prayer springs from the recognition of God's presence among us, where even "two or three are gathered" in Jesus' name (18:20).

The first petition (6:10) invokes **God's empire** and will, rather than the empire and will of Caesar, Herod, or the gods of the Greco-Roman pantheon. God's empire is coextensive with the realization of God's will, and is a direct alternative–not merely a spiritual corollary–to the kingdoms of this world. The phrase "on earth as it is in heaven" expresses Matthew's sense that God's presence and power blur the boundaries between the perfect and whole space of heaven and the broken, violent, and alienated space of the world. Jesus himself continually breaches the boundaries between heaven and earth. Praying in this way focuses the disciples' vision on the discernment of this reality.

The next three petitions explore the implications of God's reign for humankind. The first calls upon God to supply the bread that is needed each day. The adjective usually rendered "daily" may refer to what is "necessary for existence," is "coming soon," or "belongs to" or is appropriate for this day. The petition recalls God's supply of manna to Israel in the wilderness (Exod. 16) and foreshadows Jesus' feedings of the crowds gathered in the wilderness (Matt. 14:15–21; 15:32–39). The story of manna reveals both God's care for Israel and God's judgment against those who grumble or hoard. So, too, Jesus here offers hope for those who hunger and thirst every day and judgment against those who keep more than they need or who do not trust God to supply what is needed each day. God supplies what is needed, when it is needed.

"Forgive us our debts as we forgive our debtors" is often reduced to a request for forgiveness of "transgressions" or "sins" (cf. below, 6:14–15; Luke 11:4). But Matthew's use of "debts" here designates not only religious, spiritual, or interpersonal forgiveness, but the cancellation of all debts, as in the jubilee year described in Leviticus 25:8–17–a **time** when hoarding, inequality, and social and economic stratifications are erased. The practice of forgiving debts brings into being a community of sharing and mutual dependence on God, a real alternative to the system of patronage, which generated unceasing debt and dependence on wealthy elites. This petition also poses a radical alternative to modern economic systems that generate wide discrepancies of income and access to resources.

The final petition takes up the language of testing (or temptation), including both the world's tests of the disciples and the disciples' own tests of God's power. In either case, testing concerns the certainty of the disciples' relationship with God. Ultimately, this petition looks toward the consummation of God's rule, when evil is banished and God's perfect presence and power are evident to all.

As soon as the prayer is ended, Jesus returns to the theme of forgiveness (6:14–15). Here, however, Jesus speaks of "transgressions" or "trespasses," rather than "debts" as in 6:12. The shift marks a clearer focus on interpersonal, rather than economic, relationships, although the two realms overlap. The experience of divine forgiveness is embodied horizontally among humans who practice forgiveness toward each other. Forgiveness implies the realization of our common humanity and dependence on God. Failure to practice forgiveness presupposes the continuing reality of a broken creation and imperils our capacity to discern and experience God's forgiveness of us, thus placing us on the pathway of evil that leads to testing and temptation (6:13). The teaching on forgiveness is thus not a loose, independent appendage to the prayer, but an elaboration of the foundational power of forgiveness, one of the constitutive powers and practices of God's empire.

FASTING (6:16–18)

The practice of fasting was associated among Jewish people with penitence, atonement, and health. Fasting is still widely practiced today in many cultures and religions, but is a neglected discipline in many churches. Jesus presumes that his disciples have practiced fasting in the past and will continue to do so in the future. As in the discussions of alms-giving (6:2–4) and prayer (6:5–15), Jesus contrasts fasting in order to "be seen . . . by others" with fasting in order to be seen by "your Father who sees in secret." Jesus highlights the ways people "dress up" their spiritual-ity in order to draw attention. But fasting as theater is fasting perverted. Because it is aimed at self-aggrandizement and marking distinctions, it is not an expression of real repentance or atonement and, thus, is incongru-ent with God's call to righteousness, which gathers, restores, reconciles, and loves. The right approach to fasting, according to Jesus, is to put oil on the head and wash the face–that is, to dress as normal–so that the effects of one's fasting remain hidden, except to "your Father who is in secret." This kind of spirituality preserves its focus on the real object of devotion and does not foster distinctions of religious or spiritual status. Our rela-tionships with God and other people remain the focus of Jesus' concern.

Preaching and teaching the Word

Jesus recognizes that even acts of "**mercy**" may be deeply embedded within cultural scripts that twist and pervert our piety from its intended focus on God. So he makes certain his disciples know that they are no longer playing the games of human self-interest and honor. What we do in "secret," hidden from public awareness, reveals where our true heart may be found. Jesus unveils and dismisses the scripts in which acts of mercy and righteousness are usually motivated and judged by the world. Do our actions toward God and others lead to self-righteousness? Do they take down the walls between ourselves and others, or build them higher?

Although the particulars of Jesus' teachings are rooted in cultural insti-tutions of the ancient Mediterranean world, the concerns articulated in this passage are still relevant today. Patronage is still the norm in some realms of business and politics. Our concern with who gives what, at what cost, on birthdays or at Christmas is but one indication that gift-giving is still a means of organizing and regulating relationships. People still give to organizations with an eye to what they get in return. While most North American Christians do not often fast, we do find other ways to parade our religiosity before others. Cultural values still play powerful roles in shaping our benevolence and piety. North Americans like to fix things; we prefer giving to charities, for example, that have a positive "success rate." Yet "fixing things" often does not include reconciling and restoring the relationships involved, which requires long-term commitment and is harder to quantify. How do our cultural values and assumptions shape and limit our actions? How does our concern for what others see impact our engagement with them?

The Lord's Prayer invokes the disruptive and transformative reality of God's reign on earth, but the repetitive, rote use of the prayer in worship may also rob it of its power. Christians are called not only to recite the prayer, but, still more important, to live it, to embody the reality it invokes. The prayer is an **eschatological** bombshell, meant to be perpetually reloaded and detonated among complacent, world-wearied disciples. It calls forth dependence upon God alone, generates fresh and just economic arrangements, and affirms the intimate, merciful presence of God among Jesus' disciples. Each petition names God's presence and power, working to restore broken relationships and engender new forms of community. The Lord's Prayer, like the sermon as a whole, can only be understood and realized within the context of communities of faithful disciples. Whether we focus on the images of God the Lord's Prayer invokes or the images of discipleship it calls forth, the prayer requires a community with distinctive vision and practices to embody its meanings. What kind of community can pray this prayer with integrity? How does our public recitation of Jesus' prayer implicate us in the realities the prayer invokes?

The instructions about almsgiving and prayer (6:1–6, 16–21) constitute the heart of the Gospel lesson for Ash Wednesday, matched with Paul's discussion of reconciliation, and how we "become the righteousness of God," and his catalog of the travails he has suffered for the sake of Jesus Christ (2 Cor. 5:20b–6:10). These texts, together with the Old Testament lessons for the day (Joel 2:1–2, 12–17 or Isa. 58:1–12; Ps. 51:1–17), present a rich array of images focusing especially on righteousness and relationship with God. Seeking God's righteousness in our lives requires repentance, a turning away from the world's ways toward God "who is in secret" and sees in secret. How might the principle of acting in hiddenness, seen only by God, shape our religious practices today, especially in conjunction with Jesus' earlier call to be salt and light in the world? Can our practices be at once both hidden and revealing? Jesus' concern throughout this section is for practice that represents the truth about God and God's righteous reign, for practice that realizes the vision of restored, whole relationships. This vision should lie at the heart of all Christian spirituality.

God's Justice and Materialism

Matthew 6:19–34*

Exploring the text

God's reign encompasses the whole of life, not just its religious or spiritual dimensions. Our relationship with God is revealed in our relationships not only with other people but with creation and the material world, so Jesus continues his sermon on **righteousness** with a discussion of food, clothing, and possessions. Jesus' radical teaching here strikes many readers as irresponsible, or out of touch with reality. To be sure, Jesus is not articulating an economic program that is congruent with human economic systems or assumptions, which presume the necessity of competition for scarce goods and resources, economic hierarchies, and a hostile environment. Jesus' foundational message here is that God can be trusted to supply what we need to live. God's reign is about shared abundance, trust, and transformed life together. God's empire is, without question, out of touch with our "reality."

Matthew 6:19–34 may be broken into four subunits, focusing on "storing up treasure" (6:19–21); the eye as the lamp of the body (6:22–23); serving God or mammon (6:24); and "worrying about life or trusting God" (6:25–34). The discussion of "treasure" addresses human insecurity and greed, both of which cause people to amass and hoard wealth. In most societies wealth is also closely associated with power and status. Pursuit of wealth can be blinding, causing the one who treasures things to lose sight not only of God but of the humanity of other people. In the ancient household, slaves, children, even wives were considered property. But earthly treasures, whether human or material, are ephemeral and subject to decay and theft (6:19). Earthly treasures do not satisfy the basic needs for security, meaning, and self-esteem that we rely on them to fulfill. As we know in our world of superheated consumption, there is no end of new models, new toys, and new programs shouting out the promise of satisfaction—but never delivering. Jesus' call to "store up . . . treasures in heaven" refers not so much to "**salvation**" (which we often treat as a commodity) or to future, otherworldly rewards, but to the transformed relationships that attend the "**reign of heaven**." These treasures last, and they satisfy

*The Revised Common Lectionary uses this in Year A, The 8th Sunday in Ordinary Time: Matthew 6:24–34.

our foundational human needs. The goods we treasure—whether material possessions, financial security, power, or right relationships—reveal where our "heart" is (6:21), the core of our identity. A heart attuned to heavenly treasure stores up—and shares—mercy, grace, and justice.

Jesus then turns from the heart to the eye, the "lamp of the body." Ancient people understood the eye as a lamp that admits light within the person (perception) and transmits the light within the body outward (radiance). The eye thus reflects one's character and orientation toward the world. An "evil eye" represents greed, envy, conniving, or hexing. A good or "simple" eye means honesty, integrity, and generosity. The envious eye fills the whole body with darkness, shrouding even the light of the body (6:23), while the eye that is not envious fills the body with and transmits light to others.

The saying in 6:24 again expresses the stark, exclusive contrasts in Jesus' teaching: just as you cannot have your heart in two places, nor have both a greedy, envious eye and a generous eye full of light, nor can you serve two masters, both God and "mammon." "Mammon" (NRSV: wealth) involves what is counted, abundant, concealed or laid up, and what one trusts. Mammon is what you "take to the bank" or put your confidence in.[1] In Jesus' day, "mammon" included the land, wealth, and produce that were gobbled up and hoarded by the wealthy, while the vast majority of the population struggled to gather enough to live. The saying thus points to a real conflict—one that had its costs in human life—between serving the master that is greed, self-interest, and possessions, or serving God.

"Do not worry" (6:25, 31, 34) is the refrain that runs through the final portion of this passage. Here the focus is not on bank accounts, financial transactions, security, or the market, but on the basics of life: what you will eat and drink, your body, or what you will wear (6:25, 31). The audience Jesus has in mind is not made up primarily of rich people, but of those who live on the edge, who are the object of God's special care and mercy. The images of God's care for "the birds of the air," the lilies, and the grass (6:26, 28, 30) emphasize God's role as the Creator and sustainer of all of life. If God cares for these, even though they do nothing to prepare for their future, God also cares for us. God knows what people need, especially those who live with daily concerns for food and clothing. Making such concerns the focus of attention, however, adds nothing to our lives (6:28a) and merely replicates the striving of the "Gentiles" who live apart from God (6:32). The climax of Jesus' argument is in 6:33: "Strive first for the kingdom of God and [God's] righteousness, and all these things will be given to you as well." This means making God's empire and rule the focus of our preoccupation, the thing we "worry about," the master we serve, the light in our eye, and the place where our heart is. We strive first for God's kingdom by being people of justice, peacemakers, humble and humiliated, by looking for signs of and giving witness to God's power and presence, day in and day out.

Preaching and teaching the Word

Because God has drawn near, the world is fundamentally reordered. Jesus here promises God's care for humankind, care that is discovered only by those who have turned away from greed and exploitation and from the presuppositions that drive them. Jesus' teaching will always sound foolish to those who still presume a world where God is absent or who limit God's reign to only the "spiritual" realm. Jesus is not advocating economic irresponsibility, but rather responsiveness to the reality of God's reign, from which mercy, justice, and true economic responsibility will spring. How do those of us who live with middle-class (or higher) assumptions and values reorient our hearts and practices toward this reality? The church's tendency to pursue its mission primarily as a religious institution, operating alongside existing economic and social structures, means that we offer no real alternative to the world around us. We trust our financial energies and resources to economic systems that are rooted in the assumptions of fallen humanity. How can the church faithfully conform its practices to God's economy?

Like our ancient brothers and sisters, we are easily tempted to place our trust in material things, which we use to articulate our identities and to communicate status and power. Our materialism and consumption of resources outstrips anything seen before in human history, even that of the empire of Rome. More than ever before, members of our society turn to material goods, rather than relationships, to meet both real and market-generated "needs." These economic practices are tied to the displacement of populations, economic exploitation, and our rapid destruction of the earth's resources and habitats. Our sense that Jesus' teaching is unrealistic overlooks the destructiveness and futility of our striving after material possessions. It is not possible to understand or sustain Jesus' teaching on the economics of God's reign without committed, supporting communities. Communities made up of those who are committed to current economic paradigms, whether patronage, socialism, or capitalism, will find it impossible to embrace Jesus' teachings here. Preaching must expose the reality of our economic idolatries, while also pointing to God's mercy and promise of care.

Jesus' teaching in this section addresses both those who had the means to lay aside earthly treasures and those who had to worry about basic necessities of food and clothing. Matthew's audiences included both.

Most of our congregations tend rather to draw from one or another social and economic segment. How can our congregations become settings where we gather to share stories and perspectives and seek community with those who are unlike us? How can we encourage one another to share the resources God gives us more openly with one another, trusting that God will always supply what we really need? What shape might a congregation committed to exploring alternative economic practices in the name of God's righteous empire take? Where would we locate ourselves, and with whom, in order to discern more clearly God's power to transform the world's economics?

The Accountable, Compassionate Community

Matthew 7:1–12

Exploring the text

The community of disciples bears witness to God's righteousness and faithful care of creation. This portion of Jesus' sermon addresses potential threats to the life of the community, affirms God's accountability to God's "children," and calls the disciples toward mutual accountability to one another. The final saying in this section, the "golden rule" (7:12), is the capstone for this passage and for the whole central section of the sermon (5:17–7:12).

Judgment is one of the trickiest aspects of community life (7:1–5). When members of the church stand in judgment of one another, they usurp God's authority and rupture the fabric of the community. At the other end of the spectrum, the failure to exercise appropriate discernment and to call members to accountability threatens the integrity of the church's witness. The opening prohibition against judging is not meant to cut short either the disciples' exercise of discernment or their care for and accountability to one another (cf. Jesus' discourse on community care and discipline in chap. 18). The sayings about logs and specks in the eye (7:3–5) indicate that Jesus is thinking more about those who stand in self-righteous condemnation of others, especially while failing to attend to their own offenses (cf. also Rom. 1–3, especially 2:1–11). To assert one's own **righteousness** before God and superiority over others is to deny both our common humanity and God's own righteous judgment and salvation. Matthew's Jesus (like Paul in Rom. 2:1–4) asserts that those who judge will be held accountable to the same standards by which they condemn others (7:2).

The images of the log and the speck anticipate Jesus' story about the servant who is forgiven an exorbitant debt, only to condemn another servant for a tiny obligation (18:23–35). Both passages revolve around a failure to perceive clearly the implications of mercy, resulting in distorted images of both oneself and others. Those who notice their neighbor's specks often do, in fact, overlook their own logs. Jesus does not tell the disciples to ignore the specks in their neighbor's eye, but first to remove their own logs. This is a call to self-awareness and compassion. The community of disciples is built upon relationships made right and preserved in sharing, mutual care, and compassion, and always attendant to God's mercy toward all.

The line about casting pearls before swine in verse 6 has enjoyed a rich life of its own in popular culture, but it is not clear how either of the sayings in verse 6 is related to the immediate context. This verse seems to warn against the dangers (trampling or mauling) of sharing with others what they cannot appreciate or understand. These images convey a sense of misunderstanding, risk, and frustrated hope. They heighten our sense of the fragility of community, and thereby may steer us toward greater attention to compassion and mutual accountability.

The saying on "ask . . . seek . . . and knock" is widely seen as another teaching on prayer. While this connection makes good sense, nothing in 7:7–11 speaks directly of prayer. The focus more clearly is upon the heavenly Father's compassion and care for the children. Jesus encourages his disciples (together and as individuals) to be aggressive in their asking, searching, and knocking. And Jesus promises results, for God is more trustworthy than humans. If even humans, who are "evil" (or "unsound," or "unhealthy," as 6:23, where the same adjective is used to refer to the eye), give good gifts–bread and fish rather than stones and snakes–to their children who ask, won't God do so all the more certainly? At the heart of the community of disciples is the promise of God's faithful attentiveness, compassion, and provision (cf. also 6:25–34)–precisely what the disciples in turn are to seek in their relationships of justice and solidarity with one another.

In 7:12 Jesus articulates the summary principle for this portion of the sermon, the famous "Golden Rule." God's faithful care (7:7–11) is the presupposition of the "rule." Because God is loving and full of mercy, humans do not need to attend first of all to their own interests, but are free to "do to others as you would have them do to you." Jesus claims that "this is the law and the prophets" (cf. also 5:17; 22:34–40), i.e., their essence and fulfillment. Doing to others as you would have them do to you generates a community of care, compassion, and mutual account-ability (removing both one's own logs and others' specks!), a community that embodies God's justice and mercy. The Golden Rule does not stop at the boundaries of the community, but makes God's good and righteous power contagious.

Preaching and teaching the Word

Jesus ties **justice** within the community to God's presence in the world. The realization of our common humanity before God and God's good and merciful care for us is the foundation for unity. How much pain and suffering in the world results from distinctions of status and from misun-derstanding or hurt borne of self-aggrandizement and posturing? How much violence has human insecurity generated? How would the world be different if we rejoiced together in our common humanity and in God's grace? How can the church be a crucible for such rejoicing, and for nur-turing the convictions that challenge our fallen, human presuppositions?

The community of disciples is the locus of God's re-creation of human life, the setting where disciples explore the goodness, mercy, and compas-sion of God. Jesus' encouragement to "ask, seek, and knock" is an invita-tion to dream boldly about what the world might be. Jesus' assurances in these verses and throughout the sermon point to a world where alienation, injustice, and violence are no longer normative. The realization of **God's** righteous **empire** in Jesus Christ is not merely a solution to the religious needs of humankind, but a radical reordering of reality that brings with it our only real hope of peace, freedom, and justice.

The Two Ways

Matthew 7:13–29*

Exploring the text

Jesus' sermon closes with a series of exhortations that place in sharp relief the way of the world and the way of God's reign. Each subsection

---

*The Revised Common Lectionary uses this in Year A, The 9th Sunday in Ordi-nary Time: Matthew 7:21–29.

in this unit (two gates/two roads, 7:13–14; false prophets/trees and fruit, 7:15–23; and the wise/foolish builders, 7:24–27) provides both warning and encouragement. Matthew's Jesus eliminates the middle ground and encourages the choice for God's rule and **righteousness**. The opening teaching about gates and roads emphasizes the difficulty of the path that lies before those who choose discipleship. The contrasts play on the terms "wide" and "narrow," "easy" and "hard," and "many" and "few." The disciples are among the few who may find the narrow and hard road. Their way is inevitably the minority position, the path of greatest resistance, the more treacherous route.

The second subsection begins with a warning against false prophets. The image of ravenous wolves in sheep's clothing suggests the "hypocrisy" Matthew's Jesus repeatedly speaks against. The sheeplike wolves may be outsiders who come to the community, or simply those who appear to be what they are not, but whose ravenous actions bring destruction (7:15). Matthew underlines by repetition the saying "You will know them by their fruits" (7:16, 20). Figs (cf. 21:18–22) and grapes signify God's blessing; thorns and thistles the curse under which humanity lives. The latter cannot produce the former. In 7:17–20, Jesus returns to the images of trees and fruit first heard in the preaching of John the Baptizer (3:8–10). The adjective here translated "bad" (e.g., bad fruit, 7:17, 18) was used earlier of those with an "evil" or "unsound" eye (6:23), and of humankind in general (7:11). By now it is clearly connected with those who oppose God's righteousness.

Matthew's Jesus persistently emphasizes what we do as the basis for knowing what is in the heart. While words can deceive, what we do as we perform the gospel conveys what we truly believe. Saying, "Lord, Lord" does not guarantee entry into **God's** heavenly **empire**, nor does prophesying, casting out demons, or performing deeds of power in Jesus' name (7:21–22), all of which may affirm and demonstrate God's power, but say little about the heart of the one who makes such displays. Those whose lives conform with the will of God—as manifested in the Beatitudes (5:3–12), the antitheses (5:21–48), and in acts of genuine compassion and forgiveness—manifest God's righteousness.

The third subsection contrasts one whose house withstands the storms, floods, and winds with one whose house does not. The rock upon which the wise one builds is apparently the teaching of Jesus (7:24), but not his words alone. The contrast is not between hearing and not hearing, but between those who hear and do, on the one hand, and those who hear but do not do, on the other. The last words of the sermon focus on the house built on sand, whose "fall" was "great" (7:27). The audience is left to ponder, with the disciples, which road they will take, which fruit they will produce, and which house they will build.

Matthew closes the account of the sermon with the report that the crowds were astounded by the authority of Jesus. The crowds discern a different kind of power than they detect among the interpreters of the law. The crowds may not yet be able to define it, but they are beginning to discern in both Jesus' teachings and his actions the power of God. Jesus' power will also be revealed in the healings and miracles that follow. The Jewish leaders will make the source and nature of Jesus' power the focus of their resistance (9:32–34; 12:24; 21:23–27). The conflict over power will climax at the cross.

Preaching and teaching the Word

Triumphalist attitudes remain widespread among Christians today. The Christian way is presented as a better, more positive, more successful way through life. While these perceptions may be true at some level, the witness of the New Testament writers is that the reign of God most often brings conflict, disruption, violence, and death. Coming to grips with this reality may be difficult for congregations and even pastors, for our culture trains us deeply to prefer growth, effectiveness, and success. Our calling, rather, is to the narrow and difficult way. As Paul reminds us repeatedly in his letters, Christian "success" is measured in arrests, beatings, and shipwrecks–in conforming ourselves to the shape of the cross.

The subsection that focuses on false prophets (7:15–23) teaches the need for careful discernment, on the basis of the "fruit" produced, within the community of disciples. Charlatans still dress themselves up as super-Christians, making displays of their power, charisma, and rhetoric. Matthew's Jesus calls on the disciples to develop critical discernment so as not to be fooled by such people. Do our leaders call attention to themselves, are they building their own empires, or do they manifest humility, meekness, and solidarity with the "little ones"? Are they peacemakers? Do they yearn for God's rule of justice? What applies to leaders also applies *mutatis mutandis* to the church itself. Every congregation is a living performance of what it really believes and values.

PART THREE

Gathering and Healing the Lost Sheep of the House of Israel

8:1–9:34

Preliminary Remarks

The stories in chapters 8 and 9 belong together with the Sermon, demonstrating the dimensions of Jesus' power and the integrity of his speech and action (cf. 7:28–29). Jesus embodies his vocation as God's Son (3:17) by healing, liberating, and restoring Israel (cf. 9:36–38; 10:6). The summary at the close of this section (9:35–36) corresponds to the summary that precedes the Sermon (4:23–25), binding the material between into a whole. Matthew intersperses three clusters of "miracle stories" (8:1–17; 8:23–9:8; 9:18–34) with smaller blocks of material focused on discipleship (8:18–22 and 9:9–17). The miracles are evidence of God's extraordinary power irrupting according to the promises set forth in the prophets, especially Isaiah (see, e.g., 8:17). The first "irruptions" (8:1–17) display Jesus' power to heal by both word and touch. In the first two stories the supplicants must cross prevailing social barriers to make their requests of Jesus, who in turn transgresses boundaries in order to address their needs. Jesus' demonstrations of divine power and the related boundary transgressions signal that a new "space," God's empire, is now real. God's power and presence alter the fabric of time and space, compelling the actors in the stories and the listening audience to reconsider the assumptions that shape their lives.

Breaching the Boundaries of Uncleanness

Matthew 8:1–4

Exploring the text

The crowds who have been listening over the disciples' shoulders to Jesus' sermon follow him down the mountain. Mention of his having "come down from the mountain" and "the crowds" forms the back end of a bracket around the Sermon on the Mount (cf. 5:1) and underlines the continuity between Jesus' teaching and the actions he will now undertake

60

among the crowds in chapters 8 and 9. Jesus resembles Moses descending from Sinai (Exod. 34:29), revealing God's will and continuing God's work of liberation.

Jesus' first encounter is with a leper. "Leprosy" covered a variety of skin disorders that rendered the person ritually unclean and forced social isolation (cf. Lev. 13–14). Ancient people viewed the body as a microcosm for the community; a breach in the skin thus threatened the integrity and boundaries of both the group and the person, requiring the latter's removal, leaving the person socially isolated and without identity. Some Old Testament texts treat leprosy as punishment for sin (cf. Deut. 24:8–9; 2 Kgs. 5:25–27; 15:4–5; 2 Chron. 26:16–21).

The leper's approach to Jesus, "kneeling" and addressing him as "Lord," suggests acts of worship (cf. 4:9–11; 2:11). In Matthew only the disciples and people of great faith call Jesus "Lord." The leper's words, "Lord, if you choose, you can make me clean," confirm his faith and demonstrate his humility before Jesus. In order to reach Jesus, the leper has breached powerful social and religious barriers, rendering unclean all those who might touch him, including Jesus (Lev. 5:1–3). But here Jesus' healing and cleansing power is even more contagious. Jesus stretches out his hand, an expression of salvation (cf. 14:31), and touches the leper (cf. 9:25, 29), affirming at the same moment his willingness to respond to the leper's faith: "I do choose. Be made clean!" This word accomplishes the healing, but Jesus nonetheless initiates physical contact with the leper, thereby demonstrating his own willingness to cross the social barriers as well as his power over uncleanness. Boundary crossing faith unites the healer with the healed.

While the healing is instantaneous, additional requirements must be met in order to complete the cleansing and restore the leper to the community. Jesus thus commands the leper to speak to no one, but first to go and show himself to the priest and offer the proper gift to confirm his healing (and forgiveness) and complete his reintegration into the community (cf. Lev. 14:4, 10). The leper's witness (or testimony) to the priests–the first persons to whom he is to speak–would signal to them that the time of God's healing presence among the people has come.

Preaching and teaching the Word

Faith crosses all boundaries, whether physical, social, political, or religious. All boundaries! The leper's worshipful faith is exemplary. But Jesus' own faithfulness also crosses social barriers (cf. 8:17: "He took our infirmities and bore our diseases."). Does God continue to cross boundaries to bring healing and restoration? How do our social, economic, political, or religious boundaries hinder our access to God's presence and power? What boundaries do we refuse to cross, and why? Can we imagine God's power still at work to heal and restore?

Who are the "unclean" among us today? Whom do we avoid, shun, or refuse to touch? We are often content to give our money and let others do the touching. But full restoration and right relationship—real justice—require face-to-face, hand-to-hand contact, transforming both parties. Those in need must cross the boundaries imposed by the world, but so too all those who join them in God's empire.

Jesus' purity is contagious, sweeping away all the demarcations of clean and unclean, the marking of social boundaries on the basis of disease or other defilements, and the resulting disruptions of family and community life. Jesus demonstrates the power of God, not only over physical infirmities, but power to restore and make whole both the person and the community. Jesus has announced the coming of **God's empire** and the time of repentance (4:17; 5–7). The manifestation of God's power makes repentance even more urgent.

Patronage, Power, and Faith

Matthew 8:5–13

Exploring the text

The story of the healing of the centurion's servant overturns foundational elements of first-century systems of power, status, and social identity. A Roman centurion, the local embodiment of imperial domination, becomes a model of faith. Jesus, for his part, demonstrates power to heal from afar, by means of a word, and to heal even a member of an oppressor's household. Capernaum, Jesus' mission base (cf. 4:13), is also part of Roman-occupied Galilee. The centurion "comes to" Jesus (8:5; cf. also 8:2) and "begs" him, both suggesting the centurion's deference toward Jesus. In the cultural ethos of first-century Mediterranean life, where economic **patronage** and social hierarchy were the norm, the centurion's actions locate him as a client seeking Jesus' patronage. The centurion calls Jesus "Lord" (8:6, 8) and claims not to be worthy to have Jesus come under his roof (8:8), further confirming his extraordinary humility. Members of the Roman power structure did not bow before those whose lands they occupied, especially not to peasants.

The centurion's request carries another surprise: he lowers himself before Jesus for the sake of a subservient member of his household. His "*pais*," a term usually translated as a "servant" or "child," but also used in Greco-Roman literature for sexual slaves, lies within the centurion's house, paralyzed and terribly tormented. Centurions were not permitted to marry, and often took girls or young boys as sexual slaves, for whom they sometimes developed great affection. In any case, the person for whom the centurion seeks help is in a subordinate–probably exploited– role within the centurion's household. Matthew describes the *pais* as paralyzed and tormented, terms that further enhance the imperial flavor of the story. Paralysis is sometimes a somatic, psychosocial response to imperial control.[1] The term here translated as "tormented" is used repeatedly in 2 and 4 Maccabees in reference to Antiochus Epiphanes' torture of Jews who resisted his occupation of Israel. Matthew's scene thus suggests the ambiguous and conflicted power dynamics at work in situations of imperial occupation and domination. Jesus' syntactically ambiguous initial response to the centurion adds to the mystery. It may be read either as a clear, forceful affirmation, "Yes, *I* will come and cure him," or as a question expressing resistance, e.g., "You want *me* to come and cure him?" Is Jesus asserting his willingness to come to the centurion's aid or his reluctance to be distracted from his mission to the people of Israel (cf. 10:5–6)? In either case, the emphatic "I" suggests that Jesus' identity and vocation are here on display.

The centurion is quick with a response. He asserts that he is not worthy to have Jesus come into his house, but seeks only to have Jesus accomplish the healing, literally, by means of a "word." The centurion then launches into an extended description of his understanding of the nature of power (8:9). He knows that he can make things happen by means of a word. Whatever he commands, whether to soldiers or slaves, happens. So Jesus need not "come" to his house; all that is required is Jesus' commanding word. The centurion then argues that he, also, is not only in authority, but under authority. For the centurion, power functions hierarchically. The realm in which Jesus exercises power (healing those who are paralyzed and tormented) is analogous to the realm where the centurion's own power (to control social disorder) is operative.

Jesus first responds not to the centurion, but to his own followers, with a strong affirmation of the "faith" he has just observed (8:10). "Faith" in Matthew is often associated with those who cross strong social barriers to entreat Jesus for healing (cf. 9:20–22; 15:21–28; 21:14–17), as the centurion has just done. This kind of faith defines those who "will come from east and west and will eat with Abraham and Isaac and Jacob in the

heavenly empire." In contrast, "the heirs of the empire will be thrown into the outer darkness, where there will be weeping and gnashing of teeth" (8:11–12). This portion of Jesus' response reverberates with **eschatological** imagery, including darkness (cf. 4:15–16; 27:45), weeping and gnashing of teeth (cf. 13:42, 50; 22:13; 24:51; 25:30), and the image of the "eschatological banquet" (cf. 22:2–14). The reference to those who come "from east and west" may signify diaspora Jews, in contrast to those in Israel who resist and finally crucify Jesus, but since the passage focuses on a Gentile's faith, it is likely that the reference is more inclusive, signifying all those who respond to the **gospel** message and are incorporated among those who, whether Jew or Gentile, gather to worship God (cf. Isa. 2:2–4; 25:1–9; Mic. 4:1–8; Zech. 2:11–12; 8:20–23). Jesus' word to the centurion, "Go," echoes what the centurion says to his subordinates, with an added note: it is not hierarchical power that accomplishes the healing, but the centurion's faith. Matthew records that the *pais* was cured in that very hour.

Preaching and teaching the Word

Matthew locates the most powerful demonstrations of faith among the least likely people. Faith is not intellectual assent to confessions or ideals, but a way of life centered on trust in God's power to bring a new reality–God's reign–into being. Such faith is not willing to submit to the terms and conditions of the world as it is, but crosses social taboos and boundaries to discover God's power to restore and renew the whole creation.

Matthew's stories carefully juxtapose such themes as faith, power, healing, judgment, restoration, and social reordering. In this story all of these elements are at work together. What, then, is the relationship between, for example, faith, healing, and social transformation? How does this story challenge our contemporary notions of faith, which often permit us to continue on in the world as usual, whereas the faith demonstrated by the centurion challenges conventional social structures and interpersonal power dynamics? While the centurion returns to his household and Jesus continues on his way, their encounter nonetheless transforms both. Is there such a thing as faith that does not challenge the social structures of our world? Why, in contrast to those who come from east and west, will the "heirs" experience judgment? Do they presume too much about their place, and God's place, in the world as it is?

Does the centurion's situation aptly describe the ambiguous and confusing consequences of imperial power, where domination and exploitation may mingle with affection, insight, and even faith? Whereas imperial dynamics in our own experience are often accompanied by black/white ways of thinking, Matthew's story makes us more aware of the complexity of such situations. Matthew also calls us toward the rejection of domination and subordination, away from reliance on violence and exploitation and toward the embrace of inclusive and restorative expressions of power. Our capacity to perceive and participate in such power may have much to do with whether our faith allows us to cross the social barriers of our own world.

"He Took Our Infirmities and Bore Our Diseases"

Matthew 8:14–17

Exploring the text

The third episode in a sequence of three healings (cf. 8:1–4 and 5–13) takes place in the household of Peter. Peter's mother-in-law represents another group of marginalized people: she is a female, possibly a widow, and on fire with a fever (fevers were sometimes seen as the work of demons). Jesus sees her and takes the initiative to heal her—this time without a word—by touching her hand, signaling both his power over her illness and his active inclusion of her in **God's reign**. Matthew carefully structures the clauses in 8:14b–15 as a chiasm[1] centered on the moment when Jesus touches her hand. Touching her makes space for her and others like her in God's liberating and healing work. As in the healing of the leper (8:1–4), Jesus touches someone others would have probably avoided. After the healing, she serves him, as disciples serve their lord.

The summary of Jesus' healing activity in 8:16 speaks of Jesus' ministry to a still wider group (cf. 4:23–24; 9:35). The temporal notation that it was evening will recur in settings where Jesus' divine power is revealed: when he feeds the five thousand in the wilderness (14:15), on the mountain before walking on the water (14:23), and at the Last Supper (26:20). Matthew's note that Jesus casts out demonic spirits with a "word" (8:8; cf. 8:3) balances his touch of the fevered woman's hand in 8:15.

The episode closes with another **fulfillment quotation**, this time a line from the last of Isaiah's "Suffering Servant" songs (cf. Isa. 53:4). Isaiah 40–55 envisions the return of the exiles in Babylon through the agency of a suffering, battered, disfigured servant (Isa. 52:13–53:12; the servant is often understood as Israel herself), rather than a heroic military leader. The citation provides an interpretive lens through which to understand Jesus' ministry of healing and exorcism. He not only brings physical healing and liberation to individuals, but is gathering, restoring, and setting them free from imperial domination. This particular song emphasizes the servant's vicarious suffering for others, as well as the surprise his exaltation generates among the kings of nations. Jesus' ministry of healing also entails suffering and rejection. Even in a time when the crowds are celebrating Jesus' work among them, the cross is not far from sight. The reference to the Suffering Servant reminds us to hold these seemingly disparate dimensions of Jesus' vocation together as one.

Preaching and teaching the Word

The healing of Peter's mother-in-law highlights the power of Jesus' touch. Touch is important for healing in Matthew (cf. 8:3, 15) because it enacts the crossing of social boundaries and disrupts the conventions of social order, thereby redefining identities and relationships. Today we are wary of touch, for we know that hands, especially, carry germs, bacteria, and viruses. For some, human touch represents a threat to their very life. But can we then neglect the importance of touch? How do we reach out to those who are sick or burdened, and knit them once more into the fabric of our discipleship communities without also threatening them?

Modern people understand healing through the lens of medical and technical approaches to physical disorders. Ancient notions of both disease and healing were more encompassing. Jesus heals and liberates the whole person, not just the body, and restores to wholeness within the community. Jesus' healings thus alter the social system as well as the person. When and where might our touch cross social barriers for the sake of restoration, liberation, and healing, to remake the world in God's presence and power?

The citation of Isaiah 53:4 roots Jesus' ministry within the prophetic vision of God's people (cf. 1:22–23; 2:5–6; 2:15; 2:18; 4:15–16). We are accustomed to thinking of Jesus' suffering as taking away our sins, but how does he also "take our infirmities" and "bear our diseases"? And how does the community of disciples, with whom Jesus is present with power in the world (28:18–20), continue to participate in and enact its role in God's mission, giving witness to God, bearing sins, taking away infirmities, and liberating from bondage? These are matters that point to the profound power and mystery of our life and witness in **God's empire**.

The Demands of Discipleship

Matthew 8:18–22

Exploring the text

Matthew turns the focus momentarily from Jesus' demonstrations of God's power to the demands of discipleship. Jesus, noting the crowd around him, orders his disciples to "go over to the other side" (of the Sea of Galilee). But the movement across the lake does not happen immediately. Each of the stories that follow marks a step in the movement toward "the other side" (cf. 8:23, where they get into the boat, and 8:28, when they arrive in the country of the Gadarenes).

The events that immediately follow Jesus' command to cross over create tension, for two different people hinder the realization of Jesus' intention. Both encounters are ironic. The first involves a scribe, who proclaims that he will follow Jesus wherever he goes. On the one hand, this assertion makes him sound like an ideal disciple. But he addresses Jesus as "teacher," an address used in Matthew by those who challenge Jesus (12:38; 17:24; 19:16; 22:16). Does he really intend to follow Jesus wherever he goes, even now across the Sea of Galilee and beyond that to Jerusalem and the cross? And why? Unlike the fishermen (4:18–22) or the tax collector (9:9), he is not responding to Jesus' bidding. He has an agenda; he will follow, but for his own reasons. "Follow," on the lips of the scribe, may be an expression of his desire to have Jesus as his "teacher," for students "followed" their "teachers." Jesus is not for hire. Not all of those who claim to follow, even those who call "Lord, Lord" (7:21), will find their way into the **empire of heaven**.

Jesus then names the itinerant lifestyle that he and the disciples will pursue. Both foxes and birds bring to mind an image of itinerancy, yet by comparison to the "**Son of Humanity**" they are homebodies. Having a home suggests being settled, perhaps even owning land or property. Jesus has nothing to do with such human forms of security and power. He and his disciples will be utterly dependent on God for what they need (cf. 10:9–10). Jesus refuses to stay at home and become the scribe's teacher.

"Son of Humanity," used here for the first time in Matthew, is Jesus' self-designation of choice throughout the Gospel. The title is multivalent: in some contexts it suggests Jesus' full participation in and identification with common humanity, especially with humans who serve God (used so in Ezekiel); in others, an identification with the heavenly figure who comes as judge, à la Daniel 7:13 (cf. also 1 Enoch 37–71; 4 Ezra 13). As part of Jesus' response to the scribe, the designation here carries an ironic twist: the Human One who comes as judge is a vagabond, moving with the vast sea of dispossessed and marginal people in the hinterlands of the Roman Empire. Does the scribe really want to follow this one?

The second person who interrupts Jesus before he can "cross over" is a "disciple." It is not clear if this is one of the Twelve or a member of the broader group of disciples, but the designation clearly distinguishes him from the scribe: the disciple has been called. Furthermore, the "disciple" calls Jesus "Lord" (8:21) and articulates his desire as a request, thereby affirming Jesus' authority. Ironically, the disciple-already-called wants to stay home to take care of his family obligations: "First let me go and bury my father." He is willing to pursue his calling to discipleship, but after or alongside his other concerns. He must meet his household obligations if he is to inherit, as well as obligations to his parents under the Torah. Like the scribe, he envisions a more stable life than that which discipleship demands.

Jesus' answer–"Follow me!"–reiterates his call and claim on the life of this disciple. Jesus' rationale is shocking. "Let the dead bury their own dead." Perhaps this means "Let the (spiritually) dead bury the (physically) dead," or, based on an Aramaic reconstruction, "Let the gravediggers bury the dead."[1] In any case, the saying strongly, even harshly, implies the priority of Jesus' call to discipleship. No other obligation, no matter how reasonable, takes precedence. Discipleship demands radical rending from the fabric of this world.

Preaching and teaching the Word

Jesus will not be distracted from his own call or allow his disciples to be distracted. So he leaves a would-be disciple on the shore, and not so gently wrenches an already-called disciple into the boat that is about to leave. Both individuals may seem quite reasonable to us; we may more easily identify favorably with them than with Jesus in this instance. Those feelings dramatize the demanding character of Jesus' call. Are we like the scribe? Do we seek Jesus for our own purposes? Do we domesticate him? Real discipleship is a disciplined response to God's call, neither a reasoned nor a reasonable choice. Discipleship is not about our agenda, but God's.

Jesus' call preempts every obligation we have to this world–whether nets, boats, or family. This call requires a radical reorientation of our self-understanding and commitments for the sake of God's kingdom. Every action rooted in the world that is passing away poses a threat to our capacity or willingness to follow. We live today in an age of distractions that dull our hearing, distort our vision, and deaden our hearts. Careers, sports, the media, e-mail, television, getting the kids through college, even the church itself may provide distractions. The call to follow Jesus in discipleship for God's reign is quite different from joining the church and continuing on with the rest of our lives. What good and important tasks distract and divert us from God's reign? Are we willing to follow Jesus into the boat and on to the "other side"?

Jesus persistently calls those he has chosen as disciples toward a life of itinerancy, poverty, homelessness, and dependence upon God (cf. 6:25–34; 10:9–10; 19:16–30). We are not to romanticize, idealize, or concretize these conditions, for they are not ends in their own right. Jesus' call to such a life is rather for the sake of witness. The disciples' daily dependence on God is an embodied alternative to the politics and economics of the world. This witness must be clear for others to see and hear (and even taste, cf. 5:13–16). All too often, the church has been content to issue opinions or take sides on various hot-button issues, all the while comfortably ensconced in the prevailing social, political, and economic structures. Discipleship is not about opinions, but about following Jesus in witness to God's power and presence. Where and how does the church demonstrate its participation in God's reign, standing forth clearly from the world?

Saving "Little-Faiths" from the Tsunami

Matthew 8:23–27

Exploring the text

Jesus and the disciples finally get under way in their attempt to "cross over" (cf. 8:18). Heeding Jesus' reissued call to the reluctant disciple of 8:21–22, his disciples "follow" (4:18–22; 8:23) him into the boat. The crossing proves both challenging and enlightening for the disciples. The "windstorm" (NRSV) is literally a great shaking in the sea, or an "earthquake" (in 27:54 and 28:2, the NRSV renders the same Greek words as "a great earthquake"). In Jewish **apocalyptic** texts, earthquakes symbolize God's **eschatological** shaking of the world, the end of the age and the beginning of a new **time** (cf. 24:7; Zech. 14:4–5; 4 Ezra 6:13–16), as well as **judgment** (Isa. 29:6; Ezek. 38:19). The story juxtaposes danger with deliverance, chaos with Jesus' authority to subdue, and powers that resist God's reign with the shaking that signifies God's re-creation of the world. The disciples' "crossing over" with Jesus represents a seismic shift in creation, like Noah's passage through the floods, another story concerned with judgment and new creation (Gen. 6–10). Commentators customarily turn toward allegorical readings of these multivalent images. Does the quaking storm that threatens to cover the boat represent the chaotic forces that rebel against God's rule, forces that God subdues (Pss. 89:8–11; 107:23–30)? Has Jesus' ministry stirred up these powers?

Regardless of whether the tsunami is an eschatological sign or the work of malevolent forces, its life-threatening tenor aggravates the disciples' fears, while Jesus sleeps. He may be tired, but the point is that his demeanor stands (or in this case, reclines) in sharp relief to that of his disciples. They awaken him, saying, "Lord, save us! We are perishing!" Again the language works at multiple levels. Certainly they seek deliverance from the storm, but "save" can also mean deliverance from eschatological "destruction," a cognate of the word they use to indicate that they are "sinking" or "perishing." Jesus' response continues to manifest a very different perception of the circumstances. He addresses them as "little-faiths" (cf. 6:30; 14:31, another storm on the sea; 16:8), and asks why they are afraid (8:26). Have the disciples misperceived the nature of the storm? Have they not yet realized the extent of Jesus' authority? Or both?

Jesus arises to "rebuke" the wind and the sea. He has a personal relationship with these forces; he speaks to the wind and sea as he would to a demonic power (17:18), or as Peter speaks to Jesus himself in 16:22. The ensuing "great calm" corresponds to the great shaking in the sea of 8:24a. The forces of sea, wind, waves, earthquake, and tsunami are all in submission to Jesus' authority. The "people" (specifically the disciples) marvel at this demonstration of power: "What sort of being is this, that even the winds and the sea obey him?" In this one, God's powers are present in abundance.

Preaching and teaching the Word

From the early church until today, readers have approached this story allegorically: the boat is "the little ship of the church," threatened by demonic forces and compelled to cry out to Jesus for deliverance. This reading focuses primarily on disciples (i.e., the church) and the storms of life, and implicitly on the faith that allows the church to weather such storms. While this approach presents good possibilities for preaching and teaching, there is a risk of overshadowing Matthew's focus on Jesus' divine power, which extends over sickness, sin, demons, death, and here over creation itself. We hear these claims so often, however, that they become banal. In many churches concerns about the trials of life or the future of the church itself indeed threaten to swamp the boat in which Jesus is present, seemingly asleep. Is Jesus now a problem for the church, as he was for his disciples? Without Jesus, without his embodiment and exercise of God's power, there is no boat, no crossing, no reason for faith, not even any disciples—nothing but storms. Are we, like the disciples, more cognizant of the storms than we are of the Lord with us in the boat?

It may be difficult even for disciples to determine whether the trials and seemingly chaotic experiences we encounter while following Jesus are signs of rebellion against God's purposes or manifestations of God's own shaking of earth and sea for the sake of a new creation (or both). The important thing is for us to trust God's saving power. God is at work in the chaos and the shaking, hearing the cries of terror of the "little-faiths." We are more likely to discern God's power and presence in the stormy crossings than we are back home on stable ground.

The Conqueror Comes to Gadara

Matthew 8:28–34

Exploring the text

Jesus and his disciples finally come to "the other side" (8:28; cf. 8:18), to Gadara, one of the cities of the "Decapolis" within the province of Syria, which were Hellenistic in culture and religion. Roman presence was evident in economic, political, social, and architectural features, but also in the form of military forces. Jesus' visit to Gadara represents an incursion of God's power into an area that was largely unfamiliar with Jewish tradition and messianic expectation. This trip to "the other side" is an early warning of the irruption of God's power among "the nations." The story presupposes conventions associated with the arrival of a military conqueror, when villagers would come out to meet the conqueror and sue for peace before he reached their gates.

Even though Jesus speaks but one word in the whole episode, all of the action and dialogue swirl about him. Matthew exercises his penchant for doubled characters (cf. 9:27–31 and 20:29–34): not one, but two demoniacs come from the tombs to "meet" him. They are so fierce that no one is able to pass that way–until Jesus arrives. They apparently perceive, without Jesus saying or doing a thing, that he is more powerful. They name Jesus as "**Son of God**," the first in the Gospel beside God (3:17) to do so. Their questions suggest that they regard him as out of proper space and **time**. "What have you to do with us?" is a spatial or relational question, as if to say, "You are from a different world, not ours; what are you doing here?" The second question, "Have you come here to torment us before the time?" indicates that they think there is a time for their judgment (or "torment"), but this moment is not it. Perhaps they understand that Jesus' mission is to "the lost sheep of the house of Israel" (10:5–6) and not yet to the nations (cf. 28:18–20). Clearly they recognize who Jesus is and what his presence means for them.

The demoniacs begin to negotiate, making the kind of offer that befits those in a weak position–a plea bargain, as it were. They "beg" Jesus, if he does cast them out, to send them into the herd of swine that is feeding some distance from them. He grants their request with a word, "Go!" But whatever gain the demons hoped to realize from this maneuver dissolves in the sea, where the herd of swine rushes as soon as the demons enter them (8:32). Upon hearing the swineherds' report, all of Gadara comes out to meet Jesus, as they would a conquering general about to subdue them. The key words "meet" and "beg" align this encounter between Jesus and the townsfolk (8:34) with that between Jesus and the demoniacs (8:28, 31). This delegation, however, neither names nor honors Jesus, nor sues for peace. Instead they beg Jesus to leave their region. Perhaps the people of Gadara do not understand the nature of Jesus' power, which they find more threatening than liberating. God's freedom can be terrifying.

Preaching and teaching the Word

The townspeople apparently find their life under Roman domination preferable to liberation from demonic oppression. The demoniacs may represent the chaos, fear, rage, and violence associated with Roman occupation and domination of the region. Jesus' visit foreshadows God's destruction of the powers of empire. Jesus, not Rome, will possess "all power in heaven and on earth" (28:18). Jesus, not Caesar, is Son of God, as the demons themselves recognize. The story thus uncovers some of the psychosocial dynamics of empire, including the preference of subjected people for Rome's way, even when a greater, liberating power is present. God's power stands in judgment of and will ultimately destroy all human empires, no matter how blessed or benevolent they think themselves.

Once again Matthew's primary focus is Jesus' power. He demonstrates authority over the demonic world, even beyond the borders of Galilee and Israel. He takes his disciples across the sea in a terrifying storm, arrives on "the other side," says one word, and alters both time and space for the people of the region, although they refuse to accept him. While the modern, Western worldview has little room for demons, the forces that oppose God's way are nonetheless well and active, however we name them. But so, too, is the One whose power is here so simple and effective.

Many people today, even in the churches, believe, like the demons, that God's power and presence are reserved for another place and time, that in this world the powers of human empires hold sway. Jesus continues to surprise us, as he did the people of Gadara and his own disciples, by allowing God's power to irrupt in the least likely places, even amidst the tombs, the pigs, and the demoniacs. The church waits, to be sure, for the manifestation of God's full presence and power, but for Matthew that power and presence are already here, now, waiting to be named by those who hunger and thirst for God's righteous presence. God's power is here to be seen and experienced in the risen Christ in our midst. So we wait and we watch, knowing that the One we wait and watch for is already among us in power.

God's Power to Forgive

Matthew 9:1–8

Exploring the text

Jesus crosses back over to his home base, Capernaum (9:1; cf. 4:13; 8:23; 14:22), where he had healed many before (cf. 8:5–17). Matthew associates Capernaum with both hope (4:13–16) and **judgment** (11:23–24). For the second time in Capernaum, Jesus deals with a case of paralysis (cf. 8:5–13). Does paralysis symbolize Capernaum's life amidst the trappings of empire? The "healing of the paralytic" is a hybrid story, combining a healing, which provides the frame (9:2, 6b–8), with a "**controversy**" (9:3–6a), in which Jesus must defend his words and actions. This story and the two controversies that follow (9:9–13, 14–17) signal the beginning of formal opposition to Jesus and his ministry.

Matthew leaves out the dramatic highlight of the story told by Mark and Luke: the moment when the supplicants dig down through the roof of the house where Jesus is teaching and lower the paralytic into Jesus' presence. Some commentators accuse Matthew of ruining a good story by removing the basis for Jesus' recognition of the supplicants' faith. But Matthew's version is carefully structured so as to shift the focus from the supplicants' faith to Jesus' insight and authority and to highlight Jesus' dual identity as **Son of God** and **Son of Humanity**. Matthew locates the heretofore divine authority to forgive sins firmly within the human realm.

Matthew introduces two character groups, the supplicants and the **scribes**, each time using the introductory phrase "and behold" (NRSV: "and just then," 9:2; "then," 9:3). Jesus "sees" the supplicants' faith (9:2), just as he "sees" (NRSV: "perceiving") the scribes' thoughts (9:4). Matthew thus sets the two character groups in contrast and demonstrates another dimension of Jesus' power as Son of God. In Greco-Roman thought, the capacity to read the hearts and minds of others was one of the characteristics associated with "son of God" figures. Matthew does not need the account of the supplicants' dramatic effort to reach Jesus, thereby demonstrating their faith, because the "Son of God" doesn't require hard evidence to see into hearts. Matthew's streamlined version of the story thus yields a stronger assertion of Jesus' identity as Son of God.

Upon seeing the supplicants' faith, Jesus first offers encouragement to the paralytic. "Take heart, son" (cf. 9:2; 14:27) echoes what Moses says to the Israelites as they escape through the sea before the Egyptians (Exod. 14:13) and when they first hear the Ten Commandments (Exod. 20:20). Jesus' word to the paralytic thus hints of both liberation and divine authority. But why does Jesus offer forgiveness of sins, rather than simply heal the man? Perhaps he presumes a causal link between sin and sickness. In any case, he offers the paralytic something different from and more than what he sought.

The scribes who begin to say among themselves that Jesus is blaspheming presume that forgiveness of sin is a divine prerogative, not something that humans can mediate or declare apart from atoning sacrifice and the temple cult. They think Jesus is usurping God's authority, and also their own, as defenders of the temple system. Jesus does not dispute the divine character of forgiveness, but suggests rather that this power is now at work among humans apart from the temple. His question to the scribes, "Why do you think evil in your hearts?" suggests that their concern is rooted not in an attempt to defend God, but in the rejection of what is good. Before they can answer, he challenges them with a riddle: Which is easier to say? "Your sins are forgiven" or "rise and walk"? The question effectively equates the two sayings and their associated actions. The two actions are not the same, but both are rooted in his person. He can as easily say and accomplish one as the other. But forgiving sins has no obvious physical consequences. Healing does. Jesus uses the demonstration of his power to heal to authenticate his authority to forgive sin. The two words and two actions stand or fall together, as the last portion of Jesus' discourse makes clear. Jesus turns back to the paralytic to offer healing, asserting that this action is a public demonstration that "the Son of Man has authority on earth to forgive sins" (9:6). Here the title "Son of Humanity" designates Jesus' full humanity. The "human one" has divine power on earth, not only to heal, but now also to forgive sins. Both healed and forgiven, the man gets up, takes his bed, and goes home. The healing is complete when the man is restored to full membership within his "house" (9:6–7).

When the crowds see what has happened, they respond first with fear or awe, the classic human response to divine presence (cf. 14:26; 17:6; 28:4–5; 28:10). Then they give glory to God, "who has given this kind of authority to human beings" (9:8). The crowd that witnesses Jesus' healing of the paralytic understands Jesus' actions not only as demonstrating his own power, but as a sign that God's power to heal and forgive is now loose in the world among human beings. Matthew thus "democratizes" the divine power of the Son of God and Son of Humanity. As the Gospel unfolds, Jesus and his disciples will slip again and again across the threshold between earth and heaven, revealing God's power among humans.

Preaching and teaching the Word

Matthew presents Jesus implicitly as "Son of God" and explicitly as "Son of Man" (the human one). Jesus' ministry blurs the boundaries between divine and human, heaven and earth. Divine power to heal and to forgive is now loose in the world among humans. For Jewish audiences this would have signified God's presence and power again among the people of Israel. Is God's power still loose in the world, blurring the boundaries between heaven and earth? Where do we see signs of this power around us? What difference does God's presence and power make for us? Are there ways in which we, like the scribes, deny or resist evidence of God's presence and power?

We may be more impressed today with a clear demonstration of miraculous healing, whereas for the audience in Jesus' day forgiveness of sins was the more significant claim. Forgiveness of sins was tied up with the sacrificial system and the temple. Jesus' offer to forgive the paralytic's sin bypasses these institutions, implying their end. Many people, even in the church today, desire to serve as God's gatekeepers, to determine who is in and who is out, as priests and temple authorities did in the first century. Forgiveness is not something that humans can limit or control, but is rather experienced, discerned, and named among those who know firsthand the grace and mercy of God. God's forgiveness brings an end to the human quest to establish our **righteousness** before God, transforming not only the individual, but also the social, political, and economic systems of the world.

Healing is not complete until restoration within families and social networks is also accomplished. If God healed only our bodies, the world would remain trapped in brokenness. The healing the church seeks in the world should focus not least on the restoration of our relationships. God's healing is not merely about physical bodies, but especially about social transformation and restoration.

"Mercy, Not Sacrifice"

Matthew 9:9–13*

Exploring the text

The call of Matthew the tax collector follows a pattern already established in the earlier calls of the fishermen (4:18–22). Jesus calls disciples as they pursue their daily work, and they follow without hesitation, discussion, or explanation. These spare, abrupt accounts emphasize Jesus' singular authority and the decisive, disruptive call to God's empire from the imperial order in which the disciples have been laboring. Matthew the tax collector would have been despised and mistrusted by almost everyone around him, both those from whom and those for whom he collected taxes. "Tax farmers" collected tolls on transported goods—such as the fish caught by Peter, Andrew, James, and John. Matthew is thus part of a system that milked the "little people" dry for the sake of the imperial order. As a collaborator with the Romans, the tax collector falls lower in

---

*The Revised Common Lectionary uses this in Year A, The 10th Sunday in Ordinary Time: Matthew 9:9–13, 18–26.

the social and moral order than even lepers (8:1–4), Gentile centurions (8:5–13), or women (8:14–15). He is less threatening, perhaps, than the demoniacs (8:28–34), but no less loathed. Jesus intentionally forms his inner circle of disciples as a diverse group, drawn from across the spectrum of first-century Jewish life. Jesus calls these disciples not because they are righteous or from good families, nor because they hold the same opinions he does or have already committed themselves to doing good, nor even because they have shown any particular interest in his teachings (cf. 8:18–22) or healings. Jesus calls disciples who together embody the restorative, reconciling, and righteous **reign of God**. Together as one body, not merely as a collection of individuals, this group manifests God's inclusive mercy (9:13).

The evangelist has no interest in the motivations that would lead people like Matthew, or the fishermen before him, to abruptly leave their positions. The call to discipleship does not follow conventional logic, and those who answer the call do not respond on the basis of any identifiable personal motive or inclination, including self-interest. Jesus' call simply arrests them and wrests them from whatever they have been doing. When Jesus calls, there is no time to mull things over, to consider the cost-benefit ratio, or weigh the options. His words "Follow me" have performative power. Whether he is teaching (Matt. 5–7; cf. 7:28–29), healing (8:3; 8:5–13; 8:32; 9:1–8), or calling (4:18–22), Jesus' words accomplish what he utters.

After calling Matthew, Jesus continues his open association with people like him at dinner "in the house" (9:10). Perhaps this is again Peter's house (8:14), but the hospitality, inclusion, and intimacy conveyed by sharing meals in the household space is more important than the address. Eating with tax collectors and sinners, whose lives do not conform to the dominant codes and values, is important for the sake of the individuals involved, but at the same time represents a "symbolic action" against the dominant social configurations. Ancient meals were a form of social theater, where honor and wealth were put on display for all to see. Quality and quantity of food, location, and the status of those invited served to inscribe the hierarchies and values of the society deeply into the minds of both participants and observers. By dining with those who would ordinarily be excluded, or invited only to be shamed, Jesus disrupts the social scripts of everyday life and challenges the social, political, economic, and religious assumptions they embody. Sharing household space and food with the unclean, the marginal, and outcasts reclaims such people in God's mercy. The fundamental expression of Christian discipleship is making space for people like these.

Jesus' wanton conviviality offends the **Pharisees**, for whom table fellowship was a means of preserving and displaying social boundaries, status, purity, and religious devotion. They ask Jesus' disciples why "your teacher" (cf. 8:19) eats with "tax collectors and sinners" (9:11). Jesus' response consists first of a health-care proverb (9:12), then a defining, prophetic statement of the nature of Jesus' ministry (9:13ab), and finally a summary claim about the focus of Jesus' ministry—sinners, rather than the righteous (9:13c). In the first saying, Jesus implicitly claims the mantle of "physician." Here the physician's "healing" is clearly about social inclusion, not just physical healing. "Well" and "sick" in the first statement (9:12) parallel "righteous" and "sinners" in the third (9:13c). While the first saying would not be thought offensive, the third saying scandalizes: God's anointed comes not to gather the righteous and judge the sinners, as expected (cf., e.g., Pss. 1:5; 45:7), but to gather the sinners and the sick and to challenge the well and the righteous.

"I desire mercy, not sacrifice," is from Hosea 6:6, where the prophet portrays God as the one who heals Israel. This statement is programmatic for Matthew's vision of Jesus' ministry (cf. 12:7). "Mercy" is the expression of God's forgiveness, compassion, justice, and inclusion. Sacrifice, on the other hand, here designates religious observance that seeks not the welfare of people, but the establishment of one's own **righteousness** before God. The introductory clause "Go and learn" (or "as you go, learn . . .") anticipates the resurrected Christ's commission to his disciples in 28:19–20: "As you go, teach . . ." The same root word for learning or teaching occurs in both cases, as well as the participle for "going." Jesus will call his disciples to teach the nations, while the Pharisees—the well and righteous—still have things to learn about God's mercy.

Preaching and teaching the Word

Jesus' call to discipleship uproots people like Matthew from the very soil that has nurtured and sustained their lives. Discipleship is a "radical" transformation, reaching to the roots—a "repotting," as it were, that moves disciples from the soil of this world to the new soil that is God's reign, to be nurtured in justice and mercy (9:13). Jesus does not call the disciples toward "the rewards of the life to come" or any other form of enlightened self-interest, but to the difficult ways that shine God's light into the world (cf. 5:14–16).

Meals remain, as in Jesus' day, a form of social theater, in which we act out the primary stories and values of the culture in which we live. North Americans thus eat ever more frequently alone, or while rushing out the door to the next activity, or obsessively. What stories and values do our meals and our ways of eating inscribe? What social and economic arrangements do we assume? Do we know where our food comes from? Do we know those with whom we eat? What does Jesus' practice of inclusive table fellowship say to the life of our congregations, especially about the meals we share together? Whom do we invite to our tables as we celebrate and bear witness to God's rule and power?

The Pharisees here represent religious people whose piety upholds the existing social system rather than God's reign. The Pharisees are "well" and "righteous" (9:12–13), but precisely this wellness and righteousness, which depends on marking difference and inscribes division and hierarchy, separates them from those Jesus is calling and restoring in God's name. Without the poor, the unclean, and the marginal at their tables—without the tax collectors and sinners—the Pharisees eat their way toward judgment rather than mercy. In what ways do our religious pursuits, whether at table or elsewhere, serve further to inscribe patterns of division and alienation? James 1:27 claims that "religion that is pure and undefiled" before God is this: "to visit orphans and widows in their affliction, and to keep oneself unstained by the world." The seeming paradox in this saying, as in Matthew's story, is that visiting orphans and widows, or tax collectors and sinners, is precisely what "the righteous" think will stain them. In fact, it is precisely the failure to make space for these that sets the stain of the world upon our souls.

Again we see Jesus crossing and undermining social boundaries in pursuit of God's reign. With this comes increasing resistance from those who benefit from the current order. Jesus' actions symbolize the end of the rules and boundaries that keep the system in place. Why else would the Pharisees challenge him? It is in the nature of human religions, including Christianity, to erect and impose boundaries. It is in the nature of God's reign to transgress and tear down all barriers that hinder God's inclusion and restoration of the "sick" and "unrighteous," and that deny God's mercy and forgiveness toward all. Does being a good person, a religious person, hinder our realization of God's grace and mercy?

Actions That Fit the Times

Matthew 9:14–17

Exploring the text

Jesus may still be at table (9:10) when disciples of John the Baptizer, who remains in prison (3:12; 14:1–12), raise questions concerning the fact that Jesus and his disciples apparently do not fast. The Pharisees had challenged Jesus' choice of dining companions, but John's disciples wonder if he should be eating at all. They presume that fasting–an act associated with contrition, repentance, and forgiveness of sins–is appropriate for the **time** of repentance when the **empire of heaven** has drawn near (3:2; 4:17). John's disciples align themselves with the **Pharisees** as those who "fast often," in distinction to Jesus and his disciples, who fast little or not at all. While the preceding story about eating with tax collectors and sinners (9:14–17) focused on Jesus' reconstruction of the relationships and social configurations appropriate for God's empire, John's disciples challenge whether Jesus understands what time it is and why he eats as he does.

In Jesus' day (and in many parts of the world today), people reckoned time not as an abstract, linear, measurable commodity, as North Americans do, but in terms of "what kind of time" (Gk: *kairos*) it was and what actions, behaviors, experiences, and relationships were expected or appropriate. The *kairos* when God's reign draws near is associated with perspectives and actions such as repentance. Jesus does not disagree with John or John's disciples about what kind of time it is, but he offers two analogies that suggest he understands the practical implications of the "time" differently than they do. First, mourning in the presence of the bridegroom would be inexplicable, a denial of the kind of time it is and the behavior appropriate to it. Fasting is appropriate when the bridegroom is gone. This image lends itself nicely to allegorization: Jesus is the bridegroom, his ministry is a time of celebration, but he will be "taken away" (crucified). The bridegroom image also foreshadows Jesus' parables about the "wedding banquet" (cf. 22:1–14) and the age of watchfulness just before the bridegroom comes (25:1–13). But it is not necessary to allegorize the image for it to work. The analogy simply affirms that fasting is not appropriate for the *kairos* in which Jesus and his disciples now minister. God's reign is not only near, as it was during John's ministry, but already present in Jesus as light for those in darkness (cf. 4:12–25). The greatest party ever has begun and everybody's invited–but no mourning or fasting allowed.

Two more sayings (9:16–17) affirm Jesus' line of reasoning. Sowing an unshrunk patch on an old garment would be silly, creating a worse tear when the patch shrinks. Likewise, putting new wine in old skins results in the loss of both. New wine must be put into new wineskins. Both sayings concern what fits a given container or setting. Jesus thus clarifies why he and his disciples do not fast. Between John and Jesus a corner has been turned: fasting that was appropriate for John's time is no longer fitting for Jesus' ministry. Jesus' ministry, in other words, does not fit the container that was John's mission, or the container that is the world of the Pharisees. It's a question of knowing what time it is and conforming one's behavior rightly.

Preaching and teaching the Word

Our modern notions of time are so deeply rooted in capitalism, industrialization, and technology that we can scarcely make sense of what is at stake in the discussion between Jesus and John's disciples. But discerning "the times" rightly still makes all the difference in our relationships with God and each other. If indeed God's reign has come among us in Jesus, who continues with us in power (28:18–20), then conformity to the world is no longer fitting. Even religious behavior, if it wrongly presumes God's absence or sees God's power as functioning only beyond this world, in the "spiritual" realm, for example, will yield consequences that do not fit the container that is the empire of the heavens. What kind of time is it? Whose time is it? Is God's time merely another line on the daily schedule? Or does time itself belong to God?

Jesus presumes his disciples will fast (cf. 6:16–18), but in this story he does not set forth a definitive teaching concerning Christian fasting. Matthew has other skins to fill. Jesus claims once more the radical newness of his calling and God's empire. From lepers to paralytics, centurions to demoniacs, and from women to tax collectors, Jesus' ministry is bursting the containers of imperial life. The new container for God's power is the community of disciples, not the temple system or the empire of Caesar. Nor does the life of discipleship fit today in the containers of American culture, economics, and politics. Where the church does seek to make the gospel fit these garments and skins, there will inevitably be tearing, spilling, and destruction. What garments and skins are we using to contain the gospel?

Faith, Touch, and Healing

Matthew 9:18–26[*]

Exploring the text

Matthew here tells a story within a story. Both episodes feature inter-actions with females, one a woman who has been suffering from hemor-rhages for twelve years and the other a young girl who has died. In both stories the healing involves touch: first the woman touching the hem of Jesus' clothes (9:20), and then Jesus taking the little girl by the hand (9:25). Both situations suggest a risk of defilement, the woman because of her flow of blood and the girl because she is "dead." Jesus' willingness to touch and be touched by women demonstrates how God's power pushes back the barriers that divide male from female. The wineskin of God's empire includes women and men alike.

These stories also lift up the ruler (surprise!) and the woman as mod-els of faith. The ruler "comes to" Jesus and kneels (cf. 2:2, 11; 8:2). His posture denotes his humility before Jesus. In Matthew's account the girl is already dead when the ruler approaches Jesus. The ruler's faith is such that he believes Jesus can make her live again, if he will only lay his hand on her. Perhaps this faith is why Jesus then "follows" the ruler (9:19)–the same word Matthew uses persistently with reference to discipleship. The story features unusual reversals of authority; the ruler and Jesus take turns placing themselves in submission to one another. The hemorrhaging woman also manifests exemplary faith. She believes that touching even the fringe of Jesus' cloak will bring "**salvation**" (9:21; 9:22 [twice]; NRSV reads "made well"). Her touch causes Jesus to turn around and announce that her own faith is the primary force in her "salvation." She, too, models faith that crosses boundaries.

The exemplary faith of the ruler and the woman has a foil in the crowds gathered at the ruler's house. Jesus first tells them to "go away," that the girl is "not dead but sleeping." This claim elicits derisive laughter. In the next line, the crowd is "cast out," the same word used elsewhere to refer to exorcisms (e.g., 8:16; 9:33; 9:34) and in announcements of judgment (8:12; 22:13; 25:30). They are unable to transcend the imagination of life and death mediated to them by their "wineskin," at least not until they

[*] The Revised Common Lectionary uses this in Year A, The 10th Sunday in Ordi-nary Time: Matthew 9:9–13, 18–26.

witness the girl, raised, led before them by the hand of Jesus. Then they report this event throughout the region (9:25–26).

Preaching and teaching the Word

The story of the woman reveals faith that is willing to take leaps, even just to touch the fringe of Jesus' cloak. The ruler's faith recognizes in Jesus what no one else yet has, the power to overcome death. Jesus, in turn, is willing to "follow" this ruler to his house. Jesus then affirms the authority of their faith. In these episodes Jesus displays his willingness to be led by others and his use of touch to topple the social barriers that constitute the wineskin of the world. How might we recognize and respond to such powerful expressions of faith?

Whether touching or being touched, Jesus transmits power to heal and restore. Faith crosses all human boundaries. Jesus shatters even the barrier of death. His touch redefines the world, redraws inclusive boundaries, and reveals the limitless power of God. How do we extend God's touch to others around us and thereby redraw the boundaries of the world?

Seeing and Believing

Matthew 9:27–34

Exploring the text

As Jesus leaves the ruler's house, two blind people "follow him," hail him as **"Son of David,"** and beg for **"mercy."** The audience already is learning that "mercy" is a foundational practice for those who follow Jesus into **God's empire** (5:7; 9:13; cf. 12:7), as God's own mercy makes room for, forgives, and restores those in need. This story links mercy and faith with both physical sight and, metaphorically, the capacity to "see" God's presence and power. Jesus is able to restore sight for all but the "blind" leaders of Israel (13:13–15; 23:16–28), who continue to turn away from the "light" that Jesus brings (cf. 4:16).

Matthew's succinct account includes a number of verbal echoes that bind it together with earlier episodes, especially the calling of Matthew and Jesus' table fellowship with tax collectors and sinners (9:9–13). As is Matthew's custom, the number of supplicants is doubled. Like the two demoniacs in 8:28–29, the two blind men "cry out loudly." As so often in earlier stories, the healing employs both faith (9:28–29; cf. 9:18, 22) and

touch (9:29; cf. 8:3; 8:15; 9:20; 9:25). One new feature is Matthew's identification of Jesus as "Son of David" (cf. 1:1; 1:6; 20:30–31; 12:23; 15:22;
21:15), which carries with it messianic and kingly associations. When the
blind hail Jesus loudly as "Son of David," they risk provoking the authorities, for they are naming Jesus aloud as Israel's rightful king. Matthew also
understands the Son of David as a healer who manifests his authority, not
in the mold of a tyrant, nor by violence and exploitation of God's people,
but as the one who heals and restores Israel. In this instance, however,
the Son of David does not immediately respond to the pleas of the blind.
They must "follow him," then "come to him" (a gesture of respect) when
he has entered the house (9:28). Perhaps their loud identification of the
Son of David compels this movement inside the house, possibly the same
house where Jesus ate with tax collectors and sinners (cf. 9:10). By now
the "house" designates not just the physical space Jesus inhabits, but the
social space in which Jesus exercises his authority on behalf of those under
his care.

Jesus tests the blind supplicants' faith and commitment with a simple
question that is nonetheless laden with associations. "Do you believe that
I am able to do this?" juxtaposes the words for faith, (miraculous) power,
and doing. Their even simpler response, "Yes, Lord," effectively functions as a confession. As in the story of the woman with the flow of blood
(9:20–22), Jesus touches the supplicants as he affirms that the healing happens "according to their faith." His touch and their faith combine to open
their eyes. Although he warns them not to tell anyone what has happened,
after they leave they spread the news of him "throughout that district."

As "they" (probably the blind men) are leaving the house, others
arrive with a mute (Greek implies he may have been both deaf and
mute) demoniac. Just as blindness symbolizes the inability to see what
God is doing in the world, so also the loss of hearing and speech suggest
diminished capacity, either to hear (and obey) or to give witness to God's
presence and call. Isaiah uses deafness and muteness alongside blindness
as metaphors for Israel's condition (cf. Isa. 29:18–20; 35:5–6; 42:18–19;
43:8). The affliction in this case does not arise from "natural" causes, but
is a manifestation of the demonic. Silence or speechlessness is a common
response to terror and domination. Rome used crucifixion to induce such
speechlessness among subject populations. As soon as the demon has
been cast out, the man is able to speak.

The exorcism yields two immediate and strongly contrasting responses.
The first witness comes from the crowd, which "marvels" (like the disciples, after Jesus has "saved" them from the storm at sea, 8:23–27; cf. also
7:28–29): "Never was anything like this seen in Israel." God is restoring

sight, hearing, and speech, freeing the senses and loosing the tongues of those who had been bound by demonic power. The Pharisees also recognize Jesus' power, but offer an alternative appraisal of the source of Jesus' power: "He casts out demons by the prince of demons" (9:34; cf. 12:24). They are more willing to admit the reality of demonic power in the world than God's power, even when the results are liberative. We are left wondering who is really deaf and dumb.

Preaching and teaching the Word

Healing the blind is both another demonstration of God's power to heal and restore and a metaphor for Jesus' unveiling of the light of God's reign where darkness has held sway. Israelite tradition held that when humankind turned from God to idols, the light of God that had reflected from their eyes faded away. Paul, too, regards the darkening of human imagination as a symptom of our idolatry (cf. Rom. 1:21; 13:11–12; Eph. 5:8–14). We who now live in a world full of electric lights may find it even more difficult to discern God's light, for the artificial brightness of human creation dulls our senses and occludes our sight. Turning away from the world, toward God, restores sight. The blind are the first in Matthew to name Jesus as Son of David. How do the blind see in Jesus what his own disciples have not yet seen? Does their physical blindness engender a more discerning faith? What can we in the church learn from those who "see" the world differently?

God's power liberates us from the demonic, restoring sight, hearing, and speech. Those who study the effects of abuse or trauma note that the capacity to bring events to speech is crucial to healing and restoration. The inability to speak, to name the truth around us, or to give witness to what God is doing in the world, is indicative of the presence of demonic power at work in the human community. The witness of the Christian community depends on the capacity of disciples to see, hear, and name aloud what God is doing. The church gives witness to God's power and presence in the world both by creating space for victims of trauma to regain their hearing and speech, and by itself, as a witnessing community, bringing truth to speech and speaking truth to power.

This story also speaks to the power of naming. The crowds name Jesus' actions in terms of Israel's story, perhaps with her history of domination by foreign powers in mind. The Pharisees also name Jesus' power, but in terms of demonic forces. Jesus' ministry is engendering a clash of cultures and powers. The crowds remain open to the possibility that Jesus' power is from God and is meant for the good of Israel, while the **Pharisees** are slowly hardening their opposition to Jesus and the power he represents. The contrasting ways of naming what both the crowds and the Pharisees see distinguish divergent ways of seeing the world and God. Naming rightly what we see and hear remains a central discipline of the church. Today we are accustomed to events' being "spun" by politicians and the media, as well as by religious leaders. The exercise of physical violence, for example, may alternatively be named as "terror" or "justice," as serving "freedom" or "tyranny." By means of such naming, the powers of this world control our imagination, shape our perspectives on what is real or possible, and tell us who we are. Christians are called upon to discern the powers critically, in light of the power of the cross. The blind people disobey Jesus' command not to tell anyone what has happened to them. Perhaps they are living illustrations of the light that cannot be hidden under a bushel (5:15–16). God's power is not meant to be hidden. The church's proclamation and life together lifts up and names what God is doing. This witness requires clear sight, faithful hearing, and bold speech.

PART FOUR

The Mission to the Lost Sheep of the House of Israel

9:35–11:1

The Call to Mission

Matthew 9:35–10:4*

Exploring the text

Matthew's introduction to the second lengthy discourse in this Gospel echoes the first. Matthew 9:35 recalls almost verbatim the summary of 4:23. Both stress Jesus' announcement of the **heavenly empire** and his healing power. Again Jesus sees the crowds (9:36, as in 5:1) and responds by offering instruction to his disciples. The differences between the two introductions allow Matthew's audience to discern how the story has moved since the first sermon. This time Matthew notes that as Jesus sees the crowds, he has compassion for them because of their "harassed and helpless" condition as "sheep without a shepherd," an image with roots in Ezekiel 34, where it describes the effects of Israel's exploitative leadership, which deprives the people of what they need. The sickness, the demonic possessions, the paralysis, the blindness–all the disorders Jesus has addressed in his preaching and healing–are symptoms of the failure of Israel's leaders who neither heal the sick and injured nor seek the lost (Ezek. 34:2–4; cf. Num. 27:17; 2 Chron. 18:16; Ps. 100:3; Isa. 53:6; Jer. 23:1–4; Zech. 11:16–17). More than just a summary of Jesus' activities, then, Matthew is here presenting a scathing social critique of leadership that uses its power to exploit ("harass" or "torment") and disempower, rather than to heal, gather, and nurture.

Jesus too is a leader, a king dispossessed of his rule. But Jesus has been ministering among the people of Galilee to meet the very needs the leaders of Israel and Rome have created. Now, using yet another image with deep roots in the Scriptures, Jesus calls his disciples to join him in ministry: "The harvest is plentiful, but the laborers are few" (9:37). The harvest image was also used in prophetic literature, usually in association with God's **judgment** (cf. 3:12; 13:39–42; Isa. 18:4–5; 27:12–13; Joel 3:13). In the current context, "harvesting" also aptly describes the ministry of Jesus as he gathers the marginal, scattered people of Israel (cf. 9:13). Jesus' kingly rule focuses on the restoration of Israel, rather than his own

---

*The Revised Common Lectionary uses this in Year A, The 11th Sunday in Ordinary Time: Matthew 9:35–10:8 (9–23).

aggrandizement. He is the "ruler who will shepherd my people Israel" (2:6, citing Mic. 5:2). The image of the harvest also confirms the "**eschatological**" character of Jesus' mission (cf. 3:12; 13:39), for the gathering of Israel, and subsequently "the nations," was a staple of popular Jewish expectation for the "last days."

While the harvest is great and there are few workers, Jesus affirms his trust in God's power to provide what is needed. Before he commissions his disciples for their role in gathering the harvest, he first calls them to join him in asking the Lord of the harvest (i.e., God; cf. 1:22; 2:15) to send out workers. As in the Sermon on the Mount, prayer is the heartbeat of God's mission. The work of harvesting will entail announcing both God's mercy and God's judgment. The disciples' commission is based on the need, not their own personal qualifications. Their number, twelve, underlines the eschatological nature of their mission: the twelve disciples stand for the twelve tribes of Israel (cf. 19:28). The gathering of the Twelve already prefigures the restoration of Israel. Together they bear witness to God's mercy and the reality of God's empire. Jesus grants the Twelve the same powers he has been demonstrating in his ministry. They too now have authority to cast out "unclean spirits" and "to heal every disease and every sickness" (agreeing exactly with the language of 4:23 and 9:35). Matthew's Jesus "democratizes" his divine authority, not keeping it for his exclusive use but sharing it with the twelve disciples and, by implication, with the whole of Israel.

In 10:2–4, Matthew names the twelve as "apostles," i.e., as those who are "sent out." The designations "disciple" and "apostle" do not imply standing offices, but relationships and tasks. Disciples are "learners" or interns who are schooled or "disciplined" in the ways of Jesus' calling and mission. So, too, apostles are sent for specific tasks, in this case, to gather the lost sheep of the house of Israel (10:6) by proclaiming the **good news** of God's empire. While the focus in chapter 10 is on the twelve named disciples/apostles, Matthew always has in mind those who continue to eavesdrop on the story, the audience that hears the performance of Matthew's Gospel. The **church** is called and empowered to pursue the same mission of restoration, proclamation, teaching, and healing, albeit in an expanded form, for by the end of the Gospel the mission will explicitly include the nations as well.

Matthew names the first four disciples in the same order they were called in 4:18–22, again providing Simon with a second name, Peter, which anticipates his confession and special commissioning in 16:16–19. Simon Peter is "first" (10:2) not in terms of his authority or office, nor his rank among the disciples, but as a representative figure (both positively and negatively) of discipleship. Matthew will develop Peter's character more thoroughly than the other disciples, who remain for the most part "faceless" as individual characters. The mixed, ambiguous character of Jesus' disciples is also suggested in the naming of "Matthew, the tax collector" (cf. 9:9–13) and Judas Iscariot, "the one who betrayed" Jesus. Simon "the Cananaean" likely refers not to a place of origin, but to Simon's "zealousness," or possibly a background among the "Zealots," loose bands of pious, refugee resisters and brigands who eventually had a hand in overthrowing the Jerusalem aristocracy in 68 CE. As a group, the disciples seem not to be upstanding leaders of their communities; rather, they embody a remarkable diversity, including common folk from across the spectrum of Israelite society.

Preaching and teaching the Word

The summary of Jesus' mission with which this section begins provides the foundation for the disciples' mission and for the mission of Christian disciples in all times and places. The disciples exist not as a self-perpetuating social institution, nor as the founders of a particular organization, but as representatives of Israel as a whole and as those called especially to give witness to God's power and presence in the world, teaching and proclaiming the reign of God and healing all the people. Today many congregations and denominations struggle to identify their mission and calling. When mission devolves into forms of institutional self-preservation or self–aggrandizement, Matthew's summary of the nature of Christian mission cuts to the core. How would churches organize themselves if they understood their calling primarily in terms of naming and giving witness to God's empire, and healing all those who suffer from the afflictions of a broken creation? How would we gather together? With whom? What would we do in our time together as a body of disciples? In what ways might we understand our gathering and practices of discipleship as symbolic actions, pointing to the realization of God's eschatological power and presence already among us?

Mission emerges from Jesus' authoritative call, from the perception of need, and from prayer for God to send forth workers for the mission. The mission is also rooted in the perception that the **time** for harvest has arrived, the eschatological time and space embodied already in Jesus' own ministry. The disciples' mission clearly continues Jesus' own, manifesting the same powers to heal and to cast out demonic powers, as well as to teach and proclaim the good news. For congregations at the beginning of the twenty-first century, the sense of God's eschatological presence and power may have grown dim or dull. Are we "seeing" the crowds, as Jesus did? Are we praying for discernment of God's call and power? Have we lost touch with the reality of God's presence and power in our midst? Do we embody the kind of diversity present among Jesus' own disciples?

Here, as throughout the Gospel, Matthew carefully juxtaposes and interweaves images of God's mercy and God's judgment. How do we make sense of the singular image of Jesus as both merciful shepherd and eschatological judge? How does the church itself continue faithfully to embody this dual identity and calling? What kind of leadership—what kind of church—is required in order to realize at once both mercy and judgment? Another way to ask this question is to focus on the nature of Jesus' own leadership, especially his embodiment of what it means to be "king," which stands in marked contrast to the kind of leadership provided by the Roman and Jewish authorities of his day. The leadership patterns we take for granted in our day, even in the church, also stand in contrast to the kind of power—and its effects—that Jesus demonstrates and here shares with his disciples. How do we best nurture "disciple" leaders for God's empire and mission? How do such leaders faithfully demonstrate God's mercy for the "harassed" and "tormented" while also announcing God's judgment against those who wield self-serving power, in their own interests?

The Terms of Call

Matthew 10:5–15*

Exploring the text

Jesus' preparation of his disciples for mission now focuses on the recipients, the content, and the manner of engagement. The mission is not to "go out into the way of the nations" (or "Gentiles"), nor to any city of the Samaritans (10:5). At the end of the Gospel the call to go to the nations (28:18–20) will supercede the mission that is here so carefully limited. The focus on "the lost sheep of the house of Israel" corresponds with Jesus' identity as the one who "will save his people from their sins" (1:21). Popular Jewish expectation for the last days anticipated the restoration

---

*The Revised Common Lectionary uses this in Year A, The 11th Sunday in Ordinary Time: Matthew 9:35–10:8 (9–23).

of Israel prior to the gathering of the nations.[1] Matthew's presentation of Jesus' mission here follows that scenario: first Israel will be restored, then the nations (Gentiles) will gather. At this stage in the Gospel, the mission of Jesus and his disciples is clearly focused on the realization of God's faithfulness to the "house of Israel," the "lost sheep."

The disciples' primary task is to proclaim and demonstrate that **God's empire** has drawn near (10:7–8; cf. 3:2; 4:17). The kingdom's proximity is sometimes given a primarily temporal cast, as if the hour of its coming is near, but it is not yet present. Jesus may, rather, be saying that the empire of the heavens is spatially within grasp of the audience, having already drawn near (past tense, suggesting something already accomplished), alongside the disciples and those to whom they will preach, jostling with and displacing the reality they have known. The four imperatives that follow in quick succession—heal the sick, raise the dead, cleanse lepers, and cast out demons—link the disciples' mission with that of Jesus (4:23–24; 8:1–4; 8:16; 8:28–34; 9:32–34). The power he has demonstrated so far, even power to raise the dead, is also available to the disciples.

The disciples should pursue their mission expecting nothing in return except hospitality (10:8b, 11). Like laborers, the disciples deserve to be fed (10:10), but they will be dependent on others for sustenance. Abraham offered hospitality to the strangers and messengers of God at Mamre (Gen. 18:1–21); the disciples will be like any stranger or traveler to whom hospitality is given. As they journey the disciples are to carry no symbols of material wealth, no gold or silver, not even the smallest copper coin or an extra tunic, sandals for their feet, or a staff for protection. Their mission is to be conducted in complete dependence on God to provide them with security, food, and other needs for each day. This lifestyle is an integral element of their proclamation of God's faithfulness (cf. Matt. 6:25–34). The means and message of the kingdom are one. The disciples' poverty, defenselessness, and utter dependence on God are "**prophetic-symbolic actions**,"[2] enactments of the empire of heaven that challenge the existing order, point toward God's power and presence, and subvert the presuppositions and values associated with imperial systems of power.

This mission will engender diverse and potentially violent responses. So, whenever they enter a new setting, the disciples should discover who is "worthy" and stay with them. The "worthy" include those who offer hospitality to strangers, including strangers who have nothing to offer in return (cf. 25:31–46), and those who are receptive to the proclamation itself. The disciples' "salute" or greeting of peace upon the houses they enter (10:12) may be the promise of God's **salvation** for all those within the house. When the disciples encounter a house that does not receive them or accept their proclamation, they are to "shake the dust off their feet." This symbolic statement of judgment imitates the ritual performed by Jewish travelers to rid themselves of Gentile contamination upon reentering Israel (cf. also Neh. 5:13).[3] On the day of judgment, those who have rejected Jesus and his disciples will face a threat more devastating even than the fate suffered by Sodom and Gomorrah, prototypically wicked cities that were destroyed by God for their sinfulness (10:15; cf. Gen. 18:20; Deut. 29:23; Jer. 49:18). It is hard to imagine a judgment more terrifying than this utter destruction; Jesus' warning thus works rhetorically at the limits of human imagination.

Preaching and teaching the Word

Jesus entrusts to his disciples his power to heal, to liberate, and to overcome death, his proclamation of God's reign, and his lifestyle and fate. The disciples' mission employs intentional poverty, defenselessness, and dependence on God in order to illustrate the true source, nature, and power of the empire they proclaim. This mission, including both its content and the manner in which it is conducted, is for all who identify themselves as disciples of Jesus, not only for the Twelve. This is a hard word for prosperous Christians in the modern world, where we are accustomed to stable, secure, even endowed religious institutions. We hear many sermons about depending on God, but when we go home we find many other things to depend on. Jesus' instructions here call us to embrace actions and lifestyles that are congruent with the gospel itself, to look for material ways to embody–individually and communally–the reality that we preach when we give witness to God's reign among us. What kind of lifestyle demonstrates our conviction that the gospel is true? What are the prophetic-symbolic actions that today proclaim our dependence on God? The church's real leaders are those who embody the gospel in intentional actions that demonstrate this trust and dependence on God. On a broader scale, how might congregations nurture individuals and groups who will embody for the whole church the poverty, dependence, and integrity of proclamation and action that Jesus here advocates for his disciples?

Jesus shares his divine powers with his disciples. Discipleship is not merely a matter of obedience to Jesus' commands, but entails both empowerment and accountability. The empowerment includes gifts that bend and burst the world's rules for what is possible. This power is not meant for the aggrandizement of the individual, but to address the needs of "lost sheep" and to manifest God's reign. The disciples' accountability thus has a dual focus, both giving witness to God's presence and power and reaching out to the harassed and helpless. As in the world, so in the churches: power exercised without accountability leads to abuse. Without divine empowerment coupled with accountability to God and human need, discipleship and mission inevitably devolve into institution-building and self-preservation. Self-sufficiency is a strong cultural value. Depending on God, curing the sick, raising the dead, cleansing lepers, and casting out demons are countercultural signs of divine grace and power.

The Risks of Mission

Matthew 10:16–23*

Exploring the text

What happens when the disciples of Christ turn away from the social, economic, and political conventions of this world in favor of poverty, defenselessness, and radical dependence on God? Jesus now paints pictures of sheep amidst wolves, of antagonistic and violent legal actions, and of families torn apart by hatred and violence. With each scenario Jesus describes, the antagonism becomes more immediate and intimate, and more deadly. Yet each occasion of risk, opposition, and rejection also brings with it new opportunities for those who continue to witness faithfully.

Like the Sermon on the Mount, this discourse is delivered "out the window," to all who hear the Gospel performed, whether in Matthew's day or today. Matthew intentionally winds together material that speaks to Jesus' disciples as they begin their mission; to the events of Jesus' own ministry, especially his passion; and to the situation of Matthew's audience at the end of the first century. This mixture of sayings correlates the mission of the disciples, in all times, with the mission of Jesus himself. The fate Jesus faces is the same as his disciples will confront in mission. The opposition and suffering he will endure is their model.

Jesus has earlier described the people of Israel as sheep without a shepherd (9:36; 10:6), but now it is the disciples of Jesus who are like sheep surrounded by wolves (10:16). For Jesus, "wolves" denotes primarily

*The Revised Common Lectionary uses this in Year A, The 11th Sunday in Ordinary Time: Matthew 9:35–10:8 (9–23).

the leaders of Israel and the Gentiles (10:17–18), but in the time of mission even one's family members may reveal lupine tendencies (10:21). Jesus' advice to his disciple-sheep is paradoxical: they are to combine the cunning of serpents with the purity and innocence of doves. Subtlety, prudence, clear thinking, and practical wisdom here join with purity, vulnerability, and transparency.[1] The goal is not merely to elude opposition, but to nurture faithful, creative, enduring witness in the face of inevitable opposition.

Is the opposition really inevitable? Jesus' blanket warning in 10:17– "Beware of [people]"–says it all. The disciples will be "handed over," just as Jesus is "handed over" to those who will kill him (17:22; 26:24; 27:2, 18, 26). They can expect trials in local courts and beatings in the synagogues (perhaps a reference to the thirty-nine lashes imposed, according to the Mishnah, on those who committed serious transgressions of the Law, including Paul; cf. 2 Cor. 11:24). Actions by the Jewish authorities lead to trials before Gentile (Roman) authorities. But here Jesus mixes a hint of opportunity into his warning: being dragged before governors and kings–as Jesus himself will be–provides an occasion for testimony. Opposition and persecution are inevitable, but they also provide new opportunities for faithful witness.[2] Just as the disciples are to be defenseless against attacks and dependent on God's care (10:9–10), when they stand before the legal authorities they are not to worry about what to say. "The Spirit of your Father" will provide the words at the very moment they are needed (10:19–20). God's presence is powerful, especially in times of conflict and threat.

The conflict the mission provokes is most poignant, and lethal, among the disciples' own family members (10:21–22). The fact that Jesus will soon speak again of conflict amidst families (10:34–36) underlines the importance of this concern for the evangelist. The threat may come from any quarter, even from brother, parent, or child. The disciples "will be hated by everyone" on account of Jesus' name (10:22; cf. 5:11). But again, Jesus ends this unit with a note of promise: "the one who endures to the end will be saved." Jesus requires of his disciples neither eloquence nor charisma, but a capacity for enduring, steadfast resistance. Because opposition and persecution are permanent fixtures in the disciples' mission, their long-term faithfulness is of highest importance. The church that faces opposition may burn out quickly if it thinks the opposition will eventually go away. But Jesus is preparing disciples of all ages for the reality of a gospel that generates not success, but constant opposition and even violence. In some cases, flight may be necessary (10:23; cf. 24:15–20), but this too will bring opportunities for witness in new locations.

The last portion of verse 23–"you will not have gone through all the towns of Israel before the **Son of Man** comes"–has generated a tangled history of interpretation. The saying about the coming of the Son of Humanity has an eschatological ring. Is Jesus implying the return of the Son of Humanity in the near future? Was he mistaken about this? The issue is complicated also by Matthew's larger claim that Jesus is "with us" in mission–having been given all power in heaven and on earth–until the end of the age. If Jesus is already present, what does his "coming" as Son of Humanity imply? Matthew persistently uses references to the coming of the Son of Man as reassurance in the face of opposition, conflict, and suffering and as a promise of judgment against those who oppose God's way (cf. 16:28; 24:27; 24:30; 26:64). This will be the reality until the time of final **judgment**, when the Son of Humanity will redeem his disciples from suffering and vindicate their ministries. The saying, therefore, is a promise of grace in the face of a harsh, relentless reality. Jesus has in view not only the mission of the disciples to the lost sheep of the house of Israel, but the continuing mission of all disciples in a world that resists the gospel with violence.

Preaching and teaching the Word

Where the gospel is associated with worldly success or Christian triumphalism, Jesus' characterization of the disciples' mission will convey a harsh, unwelcome, even shocking reality. The New Testament authors–from the evangelists to Paul to John's Revelation–are consistent in describing the hostility and resistance the **gospel** generates. Disciples who know the true nature of the gospel will proclaim and embody it with the full expectation that they will meet resistance more often than success. The church in mission is not a church in triumph, but a church living in the shadow of the cross.

Suffering, even death, is the order of the day for disciples in mission. Yet opposition and suffering for the sake of Christ are also full of promise. Whether disciples are witnessing to rulers and authorities or fleeing to the next town, God provides new opportunities, words to say, and the assurance of vindication. This hope is made more certain not by indications of "success" or apparent "progress" in the proclamation of the gospel, but by the knowledge that Jesus' own mission, to which the disciples' mission corresponds, met both death and resurrection. Both the presence of the Spirit in times of trial and the clear-eyed conviction that God's power is manifested definitively in the suffering, death, and resurrection of Jesus are crucial for the steadfast endurance of the disciples.

Jesus' teaching here raises a host of questions. Is it possible to pursue mission without the risk of opposition and persecution? Do we understand suffering as an essential component of the missionary experience? What has God's mission to do with our notions–so pervasive in the current context–of success and prosperity? How can we nourish the complete trust and dependence on God that attends Matthew's sense of mission? How do disciples learn not to flinch at the prospect of suffering and death, yet know when to flee to the next town? What does God's mission, finally, have to do with the growth and success of the church, or with the preservation of its institutional structures? What are we to make of mission in a culture where the gospel message increasingly seems to generate indifference rather than opposition?

Jesus' Representatives in Mission

Matthew 10:24–11:1*

Exploring the text

Jesus has described the means by which the disciples are to carry out their mission (10:5–15) and the opposition they will encounter along the way (10:16–23). Now he redevelops many of the topics from those earlier discussions: opposition (10:24–25), witness (26–27, 32–33), division (34–36), and hospitality (40–42). In the midst of these he addresses the problem of fear (26–31). Again the dangers and divisions that attend the mission are prominent, but also a sense of assurance that their mission is integrally related to his own and to the promise of "finding life" with God.

Mediterranean people articulated their identities in relationship to their masters, patrons, or teachers. Jesus' assertion that the same fate awaits disciples as their teacher and master (10:24–25) corresponds to this cultural perspective. If Israel's leaders call Jesus "Beelzebul" (cf. 9:34; 12:24), his disciples can expect worse. The disciples represent and "acknowledge" Jesus publicly (10:32–33), as he will acknowledge them before God. The integral connection between Jesus and his disciples means that the same fate–opposition, persecution, suffering, and

---

*The Revised Common Lectionary uses this in Year A, The 12th Sunday in Ordinary Time: Matthew 10:24–39; Year A, The 13th Sunday in Ordinary Time: Matthew 10:40–42.

death–will overtake them both. God's empire brings peace to the world, but not before the sword that is the **gospel** brings lethal division between disciples and those who live in thrall of death, cleaving even the disciples' own households (vv. 34–36). The sayings about the divisions the gospel produces in households (10:35–37) offer a surprising twist on Micah 7:6, where the prophet laments the turmoil and disruption of households as a symptom of faithlessness. For Jesus, the disruption of households is an inevitable consequence of the disciples' proclamation of the gospel. The call to follow Jesus renders secondary all other claims upon one's identity and allegiance, even those of family (cf. Matt. 8:21–22; 12:46–50).

With good reason "fear" is the organizing motif for the sayings at the center of this passage (10:26–31). By naming openly the suffering to be endured and its causes, Jesus has already taken the first step toward freeing the disciples from the grasp of terror (thus the phrase, "So have no fear of them . . ." at the beginning of 10:26). Jesus entrusts his disciples with being agents of truth. Worldly power depends on facades, half-truths, and the fear that silences those who glimpse the truth. The greatest threat to the truth of the gospel is Christian accommodation to these false powers.[1] Revealing the truth of God's presence and power exposes the cracked foundations and the props that pass for hard reality. Although the disciples know it will bring suffering, their most powerful tool against the forces of death is the gospel, heretofore whispered in darkness, but now to be announced "in the light" and "from the housetops" (10:27). The continuing proclamation of the gospel–democratizing the knowledge of God's power and presence–is itself the most powerful defense at the disciples' disposal.

The disciples can take comfort in the knowledge that God alone, who can destroy both soul and body in hell, is the one whom they should fear, not those who have only the power to destroy the body (10:28). The coming crucifixion of Jesus will reveal that the power to kill the body is only the main prop among the facades of human power. Jesus wants his disciples to know that the threat of violence and death is real, but death is no longer the determining reality of their lives, for the "Father" who has power over both body and soul is among them with mercy and love, transforming and renewing the creation, and gathering those who have been pushed aside by Israel's leaders. God knows even the number of hairs on our heads (10:29–31).

Jesus began this sermon by sending the disciples out, vulnerable and dependent on hospitality, which he equated with "worthiness" (10:11–15). He closes by returning to the theme of "welcoming." Welcoming others in the name of Jesus is both the foundational practice of disciple-ship and a primary means of discovering and maintaining familial bonds with the members of God's household (10:40–42). The spacious heart required for welcoming is largest among those who "take up the cross" and follow Jesus (10:38–39), embracing the humiliation, suffering, shame, opposition, and death that Jesus' adversaries seek to avoid. "Taking up the cross" designates identification with those who live at the margins of the world's power, who do not trust or offer obeisance to such power. The promise is that those who "lose their life" in this way will in fact "find it" in Jesus and the familial relationships of God's house (10:39). These are the prophets and righteous persons whom God rewards. Their life is described succinctly in the image of one who offers cold water to the "little ones" (10:42; cf. 18:5–6; 18:10; 25:31–46).

Preaching and teaching the Word

Matthew includes no report of the success or failure of the disciples' mission, but keeps the focus on Jesus' own continuing mission "in their cities" (11:1; cf. 4:12–16). We know the outcome of the disciples' mission—our mission—because we know the outcome of his. Everything Jesus warns his disciples about in this sermon happens also to him. He is preparing his interns for what both he and they will encounter as they announce and incarnate **God's empire**. We pursue his mission because it is the only way to life. We study his life so that we will know how to be faithful in the face of inevitable opposition, suffering, and death. This is the way we bear witness to the power and presence of God.

Fear is a primary cause for the failure of discipleship. Fear is also the primary motivation for our obeisance to human powers and our conformity to the structures and assumptions of a fallen world. Faithful proclamation of the gospel puts disciples on a collision course with the very powers that foment this fear. The primary tools at the disciples' disposal include knowledge of God's loving and merciful presence in the world, recognition of the facades of human power that are rooted in fear of death, awareness that the gospel produces division, and ongoing practices of hospitality and welcoming, especially with those at the margins of this world. These constitute both the mission itself and the means of persevering in mission.

In what ways do fear and the threat of death still hold us captive? How do political and social powers continue to exploit violence and fear of death for their own purposes? What does it mean to "take up the cross" and to "lose one's life" for Jesus' sake in a world that trades on the fear of death while anesthetizing us with endless distractions? In a world full of false promises of **salvation**, how might we cast light upon a gospel that creates division and embraces suffering, yet endures even through death?

PART FIVE

Israel's Crisis of Faith
11:2–12:50

Preliminary Remarks

Jesus' Mission Discourse makes clear that **God's empire** brings both healing and division within Israel. Now Matthew presents more and more warnings about blindness, violence, division, and **judgment** alongside images of **salvation** and healing. God's judgment of Israel begins to take a larger role in the story. Jesus' conflicts with the **Pharisees** become more pointed and hostile. Jesus is gathering the harvest (cf. 9:37–38), but this very ministry is also the point of crisis and division around which judgment will turn. The stories in these chapters clarify the basis on which the wheat is separated from the chaff (cf. 3:12; 13:24–30; 13:36–43; 13:47–50).

The Sign Bearer's Question

Matthew 11:2–15*

Exploring the text

Who and what are we looking for as we await the coming Messiah? Does he fit our hopes and expectations? Will we even recognize him when he comes? John the Baptizer's disciples have already expressed some doubts about Jesus' piety (cf. 9:14), and now John's patience may be waning as he sits in Herod's prison, facing eventual death (14:1–12). Is Jesus really the **Christ**, the one who will set the captives free? The designation "[he] who is to come" (11:3) echoes John's own proclamation concerning "the one coming after," who uses his winnowing fork to "gather his wheat into the granary" and will "burn" the chaff "with unquenchable fire" (3:11–12). John may be looking for the fire, while Jesus seems more clearly focused on gathering. But Jesus' ministry actually accomplishes

---

*The Revised Common Lectionary uses this in Year A, The 3rd Sunday of Advent: Matthew 11:2–11.

both tasks at once; the acts by which Jesus gathers also generate resistance and **judgment**.

Jesus invites the audience to focus on the concrete signs of God's power at work among them, signs that will tell them what **time** it is and whether Jesus is the one coming: the blind see, the lame walk, lepers are cleansed, the deaf hear, the dead are raised up, and good news is proclaimed to the poor (11:5). These signs correspond to Isaiah's vision of the time when God redeems and restores Israel (e.g., Isa. 29:18–19; 35:5–6; 42:18; 61:1). Blessing comes to those who do not stumble (or take offense) over these irruptions of divine power (cf. 16:17, 23), but judgment to those who turn away.

John himself is a sign of God's presence and power (11:7–15). He is a prophet who, like Elijah, announces judgment against the king and his advocates. Jesus describes John in terms that also mock Herod, who minted coins bearing the image of reeds (11:7) and dressed in the soft clothes of the elite (11:8). Herod is indeed violent and fearsome, but in the end really more like a reed in the wind, or a dandy (cf. 14:1–12). The people have come to the wilderness, recalling the exodus from Egypt, to be set free from slavery to rulers like Herod. The image of reeds blowing in the wind also evokes the memory of Israel crossing the Sea of Reeds as God delivered them from Pharaoh's hand (Exod. 13:18). Just as the images Jesus uses mean more than one thing, so too John himself, though bound in Herod's prison, is more than he seems. He is the prophetic forerunner, come to announce liberation, judgment, and the advent of **God's empire** (11:10; cf. Mal. 3:1; Exod. 23:20; Isa. 40:3). John is, in fact, the greatest of those yet born, greater even than his captor. He is overshadowed only by the least one—the servant—in God's empire (11:11).

Jesus' comments in 11:11–12 subtly distinguish three eras: the time until John, the time from John until "now" (a time when the violent attempt to seize the rule of God by force), and the time when one greater than John is present. Reading the signs rightly helps one know what time it is, just as knowing what time it is helps us know what the signs mean. The latter two "times" are not ordered in linear sequence, but overlap, for this is both the time when the signs of God's presence and power are abundant, the time of repentance, and the time when the violent seek to turn God's power to their own will. This is the time of **salvation** and of judgment.

John's ministry, like Jesus' own, is not violent, but nonetheless generates violent responses (cf. 14:1–12). Herod Antipas is one of the political and religious leaders who employ violence to seize the empire of heaven (11:12), as the prophets before John had warned (11:13). The powers of this world seek to bend religion to their own purposes, to baptize their violence in the language of divine will, destiny, and holy order, or to destroy it. God's rule suffers these attacks no less than any other.

Preaching and teaching the Word

Advent texts more often than not carry a strong element of judgment in concert with the hope of God's coming. Throughout Matthew, God's judgment and blessing go hand in hand, two sides of a single reality. God's coming is good news, but not for everyone. The **gospel** raises defining questions: Will we turn from the idols we have made to protect us from a harsh world? Will we follow a **Messiah** who suffers the ways of violence? The key question is not whether God is present in the world, but whether we will experience God's presence and power as redemptive or as judgment.

For John, Jesus is a problem. He does not quite seem to fit John's hopes and expectations. The modern church also has problems with Jesus. We may regard him as our "personal savior" ("he died for me"), a divine "friend," or a glorified "life coach" who conveys wisdom. Each of these identifications says more about what we want him to be than about who he is. Our popular notions about Jesus do not come close to the richness, power, or confounding character of Jesus in the Gospels. Jesus is always more and other than we expect. He bursts all the boxes, stretches the definitions, and reorders the questions. "Blessed are those who take no offense at me" (11:6), but Jesus is always an offense.

We may be confused or offended, as John was, by Jesus' mission of healing, restoration, gathering, and raising the dead. Does he also bring salvation, **justice**, and judgment? Jesus' acts of healing, restoration, and gathering mean salvation for Israel, and at the same time are completely consistent with his role as judge. For some the harvest means gathering, for others division and destruction. Judgment always turns on what people make of Jesus—on whether they will see, hear, understand, and respond to his ministry. So Matthew reminds us of the signs to look for (11:4–5). The blind, the lame, lepers, the deaf, and the poor are not people of worldly status, accomplishment, or honor. It is likely that none of them enjoyed financial success or religious esteem. But if we would see God, our attention should be focused on people like these, not on the Herods of the world.

Advent is both a time of hope and anticipation and the time when we hone our skills of resistance to the powers. Do our leaders wed religion and violence? Is our faith in those who call for violence to secure the peace? Are we in thrall of those who dress in fine clothes? The prophets who make known God's ways are not concerned with appearances, do not ride the political tides, and will not employ the world's power for their own interests. We are more likely to find such prophets in the wilderness, among those who suffer, than in the halls of power.

The Judgment of This Generation

Matthew 11:16–30*

Exploring the text

Jesus continues to instruct the crowds about the division within Israel generated by the arrival of **God's empire**. First he compares those who are rejecting his and John's proclamation to street urchins sitting in the marketplace and refusing to play each other's games (11:16–19). In the next unit (11:20–24), Jesus issues not just a warning, but the first direct declaration of judgment against the cities where he has ministered. Against this background of harsh judgment, Jesus' tender prayer of thanksgiving for God's revelation of the kingdom to "infants" (11:25–30) seems discordant. Together, however, these three units highlight Jesus' dual role as savior and judge and the sharply divergent responses his ministry elicits. For those who are committed to the present, human order of things, he is the agent of judgment. But for those who hear God's call even amidst the burdens of oppression, he is the Gentle One who brings rest (vv. 28–29). Jesus will continue to speak and act in ways that clarify and deepen the chasm.

"This generation" is like children sitting in the marketplace, unable to play together (11:16–17). "This generation" does not refer to Jesus' contemporaries alone, but to those in any time who are unfaithful and unrepentant (cf. 12:39–45; 16:4; 17:17; 23:36). They are the same "generation" as those who mocked Noah's preparations for the flood, and wandered in the wilderness, not trusting God's deliverance from slavery in Egypt. How is "this generation" like children? One group wants to play "wedding," but the others won't dance. They want to play "funeral," but no one will mourn with them. Whatever the game, no one joins, so they

*The Revised Common Lectionary uses this in Year A, The 14th Sunday in Ordinary Time: Matthew 11:16–19, 25–30.

all just sit, like judges, issuing bitter recriminations against the others. This is their real game. Mourning and dancing, of course, also represent the distinctive cast of John's and Jesus' ministries. John's asceticism fit well his call to repentance, while Jesus, the bridegroom, feasts with sinners and tax collectors (cf. 9:10–13, 14–15). But the "children" refuse in each case to recognize and conform to what God is doing. They did not repent when called to do so by John, nor will they celebrate with the **Son of Humanity**, whom they regard as "a man" (Greek), a glutton and a drunkard. The phrase "wisdom is vindicated by her deeds" means that actions and outcomes reveal, confirm, and vindicate what counts for wisdom, i.e., God's will and way. Jesus has just recounted the deeds that define his messianic identity and reveal the power of God (11:4–5). Are these really just the work of a carouser bent on breaking social mores, or do they demonstrate divine power and express the intimate connection between Jesus and the Father (cf. 11:25–27)?

The refusal to respond rightly to Jesus' "mighty deeds" (11:20, 21, 23) forms the basis for his pronouncement of judgment against the cities where he has ministered (11:20–24). Jesus' statement reminds us that resistance to Jesus and John is communal as well as individual. Cities create and maintain systems of meaning, order, and purpose that often distract us from what really matters. Tyre and Sidon were renowned for their economic injustice, excesses, and arrogance (cf. Isa. 23; Ezek. 27–28), but their citizens undoubtedly conducted themselves with pride and thanked their gods for richly blessing them. Then judgment came. Yet these cities will have it better on the day of judgment than the Galilean cities of Chorazin and Bethsaida. Jesus reserves his most solemn judgment for Capernaum, the home base of his ministry. If the people of Capernaum imagine that the divine power manifested among them implies that they don't need to repent, they are mistaken. The powers that Jesus has demonstrated are not meant to elicit a sense of triumph or complacency; they are a call to discern the **time**, to repent of the ways that enslave, and turn toward God. Every generation that witnesses the signs of God's presence and power but continues on its way joins the ranks of "this generation."

Jesus' abrupt shift to the prayer of thanksgiving in 11:25–30 reminds the audience that the Son of Humanity is not only judge, but savior. The prayer echoes the Lord's Prayer (6:9–13) and, like it, turns the focus on God, the source of rest and well-being. It begins, however, by mocking the leaders and the elite, who consider themselves "wise" and "intelligent." Their "wisdom" has blinded them to what God is really doing. The vulnerability and humility of the "infants" (or "simpleminded," "stupid"), in contrast, make it possible for them both to see and to respond faithfully to the power of God among them. Jesus reveals the Father not to the powerful, but to the beaten, the weary, and the burdened (11:28). They will find rest that would never be possible under the "yoke" of the wise and intelligent. To take Jesus' yoke and learn from him (11:29) means to live under God's rule and by God's way, neither accepting oppression as the way things must be nor returning violence for violence. Their model is Jesus himself, who is gentle with those who labor, "humble in heart," and counted among the humiliated.

The prayer also makes an emphatic identification between Jesus and God. Jesus is the Son through whom the Father is made known (11:27). All things have been handed to him by the Father (anticipating 28:18). To know the Father one must know the Son, who chooses those ("infants") to whom he will reveal the Father. Matthew is reasserting a central claim of the Gospel: Jesus is God with us. He is the focal point of revelation and of relationship with God. The chapter that began with John the Baptizer questioning whether Jesus was really "the one who is to come" (11:3) now ends with the open assertion that Jesus is God's son, the one through whom God is made known. Jesus' own obedient relationship with God (11:25–27) corresponds directly with his call to take on the yoke he offers (11:28–30). Matthew here ties Christology directly to the way of repentance and discipleship.

Preaching and teaching the Word

The Revised Common Lectionary removes some teeth from this section by omitting the second of the three units in this passage, where Jesus issues his statement of **judgment** against the cities of Galilee where he has ministered. We are often inclined to separate Jesus' identity as savior from his role as judge. But Jesus is at once both savior and judge. The **good news** of God among us always entails judgment. When we hold our lives up against the light of God's presence, we are always found wanting. God's coming means the end–judgment–of prior ways of living. Whether it is the prophets, John, or Jesus speaking, judgment is always meant to bring repentance, to turn us around toward God, the source of our life. Those who turn away condemn themselves. Jesus' statements of woe are the public recognition of decisions already made. The **church** itself is no less subject to the judgment of God than any other body, perhaps even more so, because we, like the cities of Galilee, have witnessed the powerful acts of God among us. Judgment is a tool God uses to reveal our hardness, to open our eyes and ears to discern another way. Judgment is necessary not to induce brokenness, but to draw us toward repentance, to uncover and heal what is broken.

No one escapes the necessity of deciding what to make of Jesus. To sit on the sidelines is already to make a choice for the current order. Much of American political and social life, in fact, seems to be a game of reducing life to abstractions, picking sides, adopting critical distance and, increasingly, yelling at one another. The Protestant tradition has been particularly guilty of this. Like the children in the marketplace, we are often tempted to reduce even the gospel to ideas and ideals over which we argue and posture, failing to realize that in this posturing we have left the real game. What is that game? For Jesus it focuses on recognizing the work of God in the world, naming it rightly, and then turning ourselves so that we continue to bear witness to God's presence and power.

We are likely to find evidence of God's presence and power, according to Jesus, among the infants, the "stupid" people, and those who bear heavy burdens. This may not be good news for congregations full of powerful, finely dressed people. We must make persistent, conscious efforts to identify and listen to the poets, artists, children, strangers, dancers, fools, and "outsiders." These are the people who perceive what others do not, and thus help the rest of us cope with our arrogance, distance, and blindness. The gospel is meant to make all of us "infants," dependent on God for all of life. When we trust God, many of the ideas and ideals over which we argue and divide, which usually entail distinctions of status, will be rendered irrelevant. The empire of heaven is not an idea or an ideal, but a reality made known through real acts and experiences of redemption and judgment. Where do we experience that reality most powerfully?

Always, whether by God's judgment or mercy, we are called to repent. Repentance is hard because it requires us to relinquish our role as judges. Instead, we are called to prayer and advocacy. Like Jesus, the humble, gentle, repentant person prays. Do we know enough real people—not just abstractions—who carry heavy burdens, are oppressed by the powers of this world, or cast aside by the economic engines of the day to fill our prayers? Are we on intimate terms with the One who is redeeming them?

The Lord of the Sabbath

Matthew 12:1–21

Exploring the text

What **time** is it, and whose world is it?[1] The advent of **God's empire** inaugurates a new kind of time and a reordering of the world. In the prayer that ends chapter 11, Jesus has offered an easy yoke and rest for the burdened and weary, signs of this new order. The two Sabbath **controversies** (12:1–8 and 9–14) follow naturally upon this announcement, for the Sabbath is about the reordering of time and relationships. These stories cast more light on the altered terrain of divine and human relationships; at the same time they clarify the **religious leaders'** deepening opposition to Jesus' ministry. Many others, however, respond positively to Jesus. He heals all who follow him, but warns them to keep silent (12:15–16). A long **fulfillment quotation** (12:18–21) drawn from Isaiah 42 emphasizes the merciful and gentle character of God's servant. The primary focus throughout these episodes is on Jesus' identity, the congruence of his words, actions, and mission, and the irony that his manifestation of God's mercy generates such resolute and violent resistance.

The opening phrase of the chapter, "At that time . . . ," links these stories (12:1–8) to the preceding discussions of division, **judgment**, and **salvation**. "That time" is marked by hunger and conflict, by the death throes of the old order and birth pangs of the empire of heaven. Because Jesus is the defining figure of this transition, the story begins and ends with him. The Lord of the Sabbath (12:8), followed by his disciples, goes through the grainfields—a symbol of harvest and of God's provision—on the Sabbath (12:1). The master-disciple relationship is an important element in the story. The disciples, not Jesus, are hungry. When they pluck grain to eat, an action that is considered a form of harvesting, they violate the Sabbath prohibitions against labor, which leads the **Pharisees** to challenge the master to account for his interns' behavior. Jesus' **honor** is under attack.

The Pharisees presume to have Scripture on their side, but Jesus challenges how well they can read (12:3, 5, 7). His response draws first from Israel's history (12:3–4; 1 Sam. 21:1–6), then from the Law (12:5; Num. 28:9–10; Lev. 24:5–9), and finally from the Prophets (12:7; Hos. 6:6). The story of David requisitioning the bread of the Presence (1 Sam. 21:1–6) is not a Sabbath story, but an example of responsible leadership. In a time of need David dispensed with standard procedure in order to provide for those under his care. Jesus defends his followers, and supplies what they need. At the same time, Jesus establishes a precedent for the right of those who are hungry to eat, thereby fulfilling the real intent of the Sabbath. God provides, David provides, Jesus provides.

Jesus then reminds the Pharisees that when the priests offer sacrifice on the Sabbath in fulfillment of biblical commandments (12:5) they profane the Sabbath, but are guiltless. Obligations associated with certain kinds of time—the offering of sacrifices in the temple, for example—thus require the suspension of Sabbath law. The Pharisees might reply that Jesus' disciples are not priests offering sacrifice in the temple. Jesus anticipates this objection with the claim that "something greater than the temple is here" (12:6). What is that "something"? There are three obvious answers: the empire of heaven, Jesus himself, and the time of mercy—each integrally related to the other and each an aspect of the new order.

Jesus' third reference to Scripture (12:7; Hos. 6:6) confirms that **mercy** is more important than the sacrifices of the temple. Jesus had already reminded the Pharisees of this passage when they had challenged his choice of dining companions (9:10–13). Then he used the phrase "Go and learn what this means . . ." (9:13) to introduce the quotation. Now the phrase "If you had known what this means" makes clear that they have not learned the lesson. Mercy is a preeminent expression of God's will. If the time of temple sacrifice permits the priests to displace the strict requirements of the Sabbath law, should not the practice of mercy, which God desires more than sacrifice, do so too? Mercy requires that the hungry eat, even if they must harvest on the Sabbath to do so. Finally, Jesus argues that he, the **Son of Man**, has greater authority than the temple, for the Son of Humanity is Lord of the Sabbath. Earlier, Matthew associated the Son of Humanity with the divine authority to forgive sins (9:8), and now with the authority to fulfill the Sabbath. Jesus is Lord of the Sabbath because he offers mercy and rest (11:28–29) to the hungry and burdened, as well as healing and wholeness for those who are broken (11:5).

The second Sabbath controversy (12:9–14) demonstrates the nature of Jesus' Lordship of the Sabbath by focusing on healing. In contrast to the parallel stories in Mark 3:1–6 and Luke 6:6–11, Matthew's Pharisees clearly intend to present a direct challenge to Jesus' authority and honor, which he defends by means of an analogy drawn from shared, common experience and by demonstrating his power to heal. Matthew arranges the story in chiastic parallels (12:9//14, 12:10//13) centered around the story of a man whose sheep falls into a pit (12:11–12). The first parallel concerns "their synagogue" (12:9), which the Pharisees leave in a murderous rage after the healing (12:14). Sacred space has changed hands. In Matthew, the synagogue is a setting where Jesus pursues his mission of healing and restoration (4:23; 9:35; 13:54) and sometimes encounters opposition and rejection (10:17; 13:57–58; 23:34). This story incorporates both healing and rejection. The second set of parallels focuses on the man with a withered hand (12:10, 13). In biblical tradition, the arm and hand symbolize strength, whereas a withered arm signifies divine punishment (1 Kgs. 13:4–6; Isa. 37:27). The climax of the healing occurs when Jesus commands the man to stretch out his hand, which is restored (12:13). The Pharisees use the man's presence in the synagogue on the Sabbath for their own self-interest, as a means to challenge Jesus' authority and thereby secure their own status and power. Jesus restores the man to wholeness, affirms that it is "lawful to do good on the sabbath," and reasserts the connections between healing, restoration, and the Sabbath. The analogy of a man whose sheep has fallen into a pit on the Sabbath is the focal point of the story (12:11–12). The man is poor; he has but one sheep, whose survival is crucial for the life of the man and those dependent on him. "What would you do in such circumstances?" Jesus asks. The answer would be clear. The word translated "lawful" (12:12) implies not just that rescuing the sheep is permitted, but that it is "proper." It is, thus, proper to do good on the Sabbath, especially for the Lord of the Sabbath, who is entrusted with the care of humankind and the fulfillment of the Sabbath.

Because he is aware of the Pharisees' murderous intent, Jesus withdraws but heals all who follow him. "Withdrawal" in Matthew is nearly always followed by healing (4:12, 23–25; 14:13–14; 15:21–31). Jesus' flight and subsequent admonition to his followers not to make him known (12:15–16) do not signal fear. His calling is to bring healing, not to become captive to the conflicts the healing generates. Matthew uses the withdrawal and call to silence to make a christological assertion, by means of a fulfillment citation based on Isaiah 42:1–4, the opening portion of the first of Isaiah's "Servant Songs" (Isa. 42:1–9; 49:1–7; 50:4–11; 52:13–53:12). Isaiah 40–55 concerns God's promise to return the exiles from Babylon. God has chosen a servant, either an individual or Israel itself, to bear witness, to be a light to the nations. In contrast to the force and violence of the powers that have enslaved Israel, this witness demonstrates God's power through care and healing for the people. The analogy between Jesus' ministry and God's servant is clear, not only here in Matthew 11–12, but throughout the Gospel. The citation recalls language from Jesus' baptism (12:18; cf. 3:16–17): Jesus is God's chosen one, upon whom God pours the Spirit. He will announce **justice**, or judgment, to the nations (perhaps anticipating 28:18–20). The remaining clauses of the citation emphasize the gentle, merciful character of the servant's work: he does not quarrel or shout, and preserves both the damaged and worthless reed and the light of a flickering lamp until God's justice is victorious (12:19–20). The assertion in 12:19b, "nor will anyone hear his voice in the streets," is ambiguous. Does it refer to Jesus' withdrawal and the silence he has invoked, or does it mean that no one is listening? In either case it is hyperbole, for Jesus himself has not been silent and, while many now refuse to listen, others still follow and are healed (12:15, 22).

Preaching and teaching the Word

Sabbath is a *kairos*, a kind of time that evokes an alternative reality and orders the rest of the week. Sabbath has profound spiritual, economic, political, and ecological implications. The modern experience of time as a tyrant arises in large part in concert with the deterioration of Sabbath practice. While modern life has pushed Sabbath keeping to the margins of Christian practice, it would be hard to overstate the importance of the Sabbath for Jesus and the people of Israel. The Fourth Commandment calls us to keep the Sabbath holy by ceasing from the labors of the other six days (Exod. 20:8–11; Deut. 5:12–15). On the Sabbath we remember our dependence on and renew our relationship with God. Sabbath practice thus reorients our everyday economic assumptions and activities. Where its practice is diminished or lacking, humans come to imagine themselves as alone in the world, captains of their own ship, fending for their own interests and needs. The Sabbath truth is that all of creation, together, is dependent on God for life. The Sabbath thus levels the playing field before God and offers resistance to exploitive and rapacious economic relationships.

Deuteronomy emphasizes the connection between the Sabbath and God's deliverance of the people from slavery in Egypt (Deut. 5:15), while Exodus interprets the commandment within the framework of God's creation of the earth (Exod. 20:11). Both associations are appropriate in light of Jesus' prayer at the end of chapter 11: the empire of heaven brings liberation from slavery and the fulfillment of God's will for the creation. In the first creation account, the Sabbath is the climax of all of God's creative activity (Gen. 2:2–3). The goal and pinnacle of creation is not humankind, as we often think, but rather the state of rest and right relationship embodied in the Sabbath. For Jesus, the Sabbath is a celebration of God's provision, not a time of limitation and restriction. The intention of the Sabbath is met in the restoration of wholeness. Matthew's Sabbath stories call us to a renewal of Sabbath practice as a communal, spiritual discipline, and to the practice of an alternative social life, committed to healing and wholeness. Have we lost a grip on time? Are we connected to God and to each other in the quest for wholeness and healing?

Reclaiming the Sabbath entails renewing our sense of what it means to be disciples of the Lord of the Sabbath. The Sabbath stories are profound illustrations of Jesus' identity and authority. The fulfillment citation from Isaiah 42 (12:18–21) provides not only an effective summary of the character of Jesus' ministry but an excellent paradigm for Christian ministry. Jesus is the master who cares for and defends his disciples. He calls for and embodies both mercy and healing. Modern people often draw a sense of purpose and identity from the conflicts in which they engage. Jesus too is engaged in conflict, one that will lead to his death, but he is careful to keep his focus on his ministry of healing and restoration. He is not defined by the conflict his ministry generates, but by his obedience to God's call and will. He is the servant. Amidst the many conflicts that dominate American political and religious life, it is important for us to remember that we are, above all else, servants of the Lord of the Sabbath, who does not break a bruised reed or extinguish a flickering flame.

Whose Son Is Jesus?

Matthew 12:22–50

Exploring the text

The religious elites perceive the divine power that attends Jesus' ministry—mercy, restoration, rest, gentleness, humility, and healing (11:28–29; 12:7, 19–20)—as a powerful threat. The **Pharisees** from whom Jesus has withdrawn (12:15–16) now challenge the nature and source of his power. The cure of a blind and mute demoniac generates a spasm of conflicting "spins" concerning Jesus' identity. Is he the **Son of David**, as the crowds wonder, or the minion of Beelzebul, as the Pharisees contend (12:22–24)? Jesus' reply (12:25–37) exposes the Pharisees' contradictory and self-incriminating logic, as well as their hypocrisy. He refuses to provide them with a sign of his authority, offering instead a riddle and warnings of **judgment** (12:38–45). The arrival of his family prompts him to redefine the nature of kinship in the empire of heaven (12:46–50). The question that runs through these episodes is "Whose son is Jesus?"

Matthew's introduction to the healing of the blind and mute man is spare but suggestive. Anthropological studies have drawn a connection between demon possession and situations of imperial oppression.[1] Blindness, deafness, and muteness are symptoms of imperial control. They manifest the success of the Roman Empire and its regional agents, the Jewish leaders, in convincing people that the current state of affairs, however unjust, is inevitable, divinely ordained, and in their best interest. The Pharisees themselves are like the demoniac: effectively blind, mute, and unable—or unwilling—to resist an occupying power. The crowd's question, "Can this be the Son of David?" suggests, in contrast, that the cure of the demoniac has ignited a spark of political hope. The Pharisees know that renaming potential threats—in this case, "demonizing" Jesus—is an effective tool of social and ideological control. But naming the "prince of demons" as the source of Jesus' power is blasphemy (12:31–32) that demands a compelling response.

The language of power suffuses Jesus' response: "kingdom" or "empire" (12:25, 26, 28); "city" or "house" (possibly references to Jerusalem and the temple system, 12:25, 29); "strong man" (12:29); and "plundering" and "binding" (12:29). Jesus first contends that an empire or house divided against itself will not stand (12:25–26). If Jesus exorcises demons by the power of the ruler of the demons, then Satan's house is evidently divided against itself. Then Jesus tars the Pharisees with their own brush: if Jesus' power to exorcise is by Beelzebul, then what about the exorcisms conducted by the Pharisees' "sons" (12:27)? Surely their own sons will stand in judgment against them. Apparently, the Pharisees' own house is divided. Next Jesus explores the alternative to the Pharisees' charge: if Jesus does not cast out demons by Beelzebul, then he must cast them out by the Spirit of God, which means that the empire of God has come "to you" (12:28). The details are important. The verb Jesus uses suggests that the empire of heaven has "already" come to them, for all to see. Matthew's use of "empire of God" in place of the usual "empire of heaven" underlines the divine source of this power. Finally, the preposition translated by the NRSV as "to [you]" might also mean "upon," "toward," or even "against." The Pharisees' response determines whether God's empire comes to, upon, or against them.

The image of someone entering a strong man's house, tying him up, and plundering his property (12:29) is a riddle for the Pharisees to resolve. Is Jesus the thief who enters the strong man's (Satan) house, ties him up, and plunders the house? Or are the Pharisees the thieves, seeking to enter God's "house," bind the strong man (God or Jesus?), and plunder what does not belong to them? The riddle forces a choice, either to join Jesus in gathering the harvest or to scatter (12:30).

The warning about "blasphemy against the Spirit" (12:31–32) has generated centuries of speculation and introspective hand-wringing. What does it mean to blaspheme against the Spirit? The saying is a clear response to the Pharisees' charge that Jesus' power comes from Beelzebul. Those who openly resist God's Spirit-inspired mission (12:28) of mercy, forgiveness, and healing necessarily close themselves off from the possibility of mercy, forgiveness, and healing. The most remarkable thing Jesus says is often overlooked: every sin and blasphemy will be forgiven (12:31a). Even those who speak a word against the **Son of Humanity** will be forgiven (12:32a). Jesus is not concerned about the Pharisees' resistance to him personally (12:32a), but about their resistance to the clear evidence of God's Spirit in their midst. Jesus' prophetic warning is meant to induce the repentance the Pharisees have thus far resisted.

The statement about trees and their fruit (12:33–37; cf. 7:16–20) draws upon an ancient tradition concerned with the integrity of word and deed. You identify a tree by the fruit it produces, not by the noises it makes. Jesus does not mean to suggest that our words do not matter, but actions speak louder than words (12:33c). Adopting John the Baptizer's epithet (cf. 3:7), Jesus calls the Pharisees "a brood of vipers" (cf. 23:33). Like the serpent in the garden, they are cunning orators, but their words deceive and destroy. They may sound "wise" and "intelligent" (cf. 11:25), but they will be held to account for their "useless," "fruitless" words, uttered in order to discredit Jesus and deny God's power. Whether by their actions or their words, the Pharisees demonstrate what tree they have fallen from.

The next story might have elicited peals of laughter from Matthew's audiences. Astonishingly, some of the scribes and Pharisees ask Jesus for a sign to authenticate his authority. Hasn't the whole argument been about how to account for the wonders that Jesus performs? Apparently the Sabbath healings and the exorcism of the blind and mute demoniac were insufficient or ambiguous signs. What kind of sign would they find convincing? But Jesus is not interested in additional authentications of his authority. His response begins and ends with the designation his adversaries have earned, "an evil and adulterous generation" (12:39; cf. 12:45). Earlier Jesus had compared "this generation" to children sitting in the marketplace hurling complaints at one another (11:16–19). He will give "this generation" no material sign, only a riddle: like Jonah in the belly of the sea monster, the Son of Humanity will be three days and three nights in the heart of the earth (12:40). The image of Jonah in the sea monster symbolizes death. According to Jewish tradition, God will not leave a righteous person in distress more than three days.[2] The only sign that matters, the only sign that truly and fully reveals the source and nature of Jesus' power, is Jesus' crucifixion and resurrection. That sign too the Pharisees will deny, and so it will become a sign against them and the other leaders. The people of Nineveh–like so many other outsiders and no-accounts in the Gospel–will rise up in judgment against "this generation" (12:41), as will the queen of the South, who sought out Solomon for his wisdom (1 Kgs. 10:1–13). Because these Gentiles demonstrated humility and repentance when they heard about and saw signs of God's presence and power, they will stand in judgment and condemn "this generation," for something greater than Jonah (who came back from death) and greater than Solomon (the preeminent representative of wisdom) has come.

Yet another warning completes Jesus' response to the request for a sign. Drawn from the traditions of exorcism, it is the story of an unclean spirit that leaves a person and wanders for a time looking for rest (12:43–45). When it finds no rest (cf. 11:29d) it decides to return to its "house," which has in the meantime been thoroughly cleaned and ordered, and is still vacant. So the unclean spirit goes and gathers a full complement of still more evil spirits, who also take up residence there. While the story follows the unclean spirit, the person who provides the "house" is the target of the analogy: "the last state of that person is worse than the first" (12:45). The person is scrupulous about cleanliness (like the Pharisees?), but exercises no control over what kind of spirits live in the house. Have the Pharisees cleaned house, as they await the coming of the Messiah, but put nothing good back in place? What demons have taken up residence with them?

The final unit in the chapter (12:46–50) is a bittersweet assessment of Jesus' true kin. Unlike Mark nothing in Matthew's account suggests that Jesus' family visits him out of concern (cf. Mark 3:21; 3:31–35). Jesus redefines the bonds of kinship around the paternity of God, manifested among those who do God's will. Matthew 11–12 has focused on the nature of Jesus' relationship with God and the importance of deeds that bear witness to God's merciful and healing power. Amidst the conflicts with the Pharisees, a community of followers (not just the Twelve) who do the Father's will has endured with Jesus. Some seed has fallen on good soil (cf. 13:1, 3–9).

Preaching and teaching the Word

One of Matthew's primary goals in this section has been to clarify the nature of the conflict between Jesus and the Pharisees, whose social and religious commitments make them resistant to the message and evidence of God's presence in Jesus. Because the sharp polemic between Jesus and the Pharisees can easily give rise to anti-Semitic readings of the Gospel, some caveats are warranted. The Pharisees do not represent "Judaism";

they are a specific strand within first-century Judaism that competed and conflicted with early Christians, especially after the destruction of Jerusalem in 70 CE. We should not label and dismiss them as "legalists." They were deeply committed to their understanding of the nature of God's covenant with Israel. Matthew's depiction of them reveals how God's presence and power can threaten "good," religious people. When they see signs of God's power, they misidentify or resist what they see. The Pharisees represent tendencies that were at work within the church itself in Matthew's day and are still at work today. The stories about them ought to lead Christians to consider the ways our quest for status and security, our worldviews, and even our sense of religious justification may blind us to God's presence. What values and commitments do we hold that prevent us from attending to, discerning, and responding to God's persistent mercy? Do we see signs of God's power among us, yet refuse, like the cities of Galilee, to repent? Are our "houses" swept clean, but vacant and ready for whatever spirit may come?

Are you a liberal or a conservative? A Republican or a Democrat? Pro-life or Pro-choice? A Boomer or Gen X? A (you name it) believer or a skeptic? Christians today, like the culture around us, easily slip into name-calling. Politicians and the popular media thrive on "spinning" events and people in partisan ways. Such tactics are always dehumanizing and, as Matthew warns, may prevent us from seeing God's work in the world. When we put people in boxes we deny their humanity, and we may in fact blaspheme God's own name. Who, then, are the people we label and dismiss? Do we treat our opponents as people of dignity and integrity, regardless of the issue, while also representing our own convictions faithfully? Do our own actions and speech condemn us? Most important, how can the church, in both word and deed, bear witness to God's will and work, in proclaiming both good news and judgment, even when we are under attack?

Word and deed together manifest what is in our hearts. God holds us accountable not simply for our religious beliefs and sentiments, but for what we say and do. Especially in our culture of individualism, we may think that the only thing that matters is what's going on inside our heads. But our lives–both as individuals and as communities–consist of stories performed. Especially as Christians, we are part of a family–Jesus' family–that has a distinctive story, a peculiar understanding of who we are, where we have come from, and where we are heading. The church as a gathered community offers living testimony of what its members truly believe and value. What kind of tree does our fruit fall from? Is our story clear, coherent, and evident in our speech and actions? Is our story one of fear and insecurity, or of faith and hope?

PART SIX

Jesus Speaks in Parables
(13:1–52)

Preliminary Remarks

Delivered in the face of growing obduracy and resistance, the **parable** discourse represents a turning point in the Gospel story. Until now, Jesus' presentation of God's rule has been relatively straightforward. He has taught in synagogues, delivered a manifesto on the mountain, and offered diverse, compelling demonstrations of God's power on earth. The responses have been disparate, from wondering crowds that follow him seeking healing to the now murderous hostility of the **Pharisees**. In response to this growing division and rejection, Jesus begins speaking in parables, a form of teaching that at once reveals and conceals. Israel's prophets had used dramatic **sign-acts**–signs that perform what they signify–to convey their messages forcefully. Jesus' parables also are sign-acts, in that they both describe and intensify the growing division in Jesus' audience. His parables beget crisis, forcing the hearer either to embrace or to turn away from God's empire. The parables close the door, on the one hand, on those who see and hear but do not understand or obey. But for others the parables open a door to another world.

Modern audiences tend to read the discourse as a loose collection of stories delivered to a general audience, but Matthew has carefully ordered the parables and identified discrete settings and audiences throughout the chapter. The parables are arranged into two chiastic, parallel panels, with the story of the sower and the concluding statement about the householder's treasure providing the bookends:

I   Sower, Seeds, and Soil (13:4–9)
        Wheat and Weeds (division at the final judgment) (13:24–30)
            Paired Parables (mustard seed/leaven) (13:31–32, 33)
II   Paired Parables (treasure/pearl) (13:44, 45–46)
        Fishnet (division at the final judgment) (13:47–48)
    The Householder's Treasure (13:51–52)

Jesus delivers the first four parables (sower, weeds, mustard, and leaven) to the crowds as they stand beside the sea, but the last four (treasure, pearl, fishnet, treasures) only to his disciples, who are with Jesus in an unnamed "house" (13:36). Into this structure Matthew weaves three allegorical interpretations, addressed only to the disciples (13:18–23, 36–43, and 49–50). Matthew also includes two extended statements about Jesus' teaching in parables, the first (13:10–17) directed to the disciples alone, the only occasion in the first half of the discourse in which Jesus clearly excludes the crowds, and the second to the Gospel audience (13:34–35).

The chapter begins with Jesus departing the house where he has just instructed the disciples about membership in his true family (12:46–50). After concluding the parable discourse, he will go to his hometown, where he experiences the rejection typical of prophets (13:53–58). The parables invite those who will listen to join the family that does the will of the Father (12:50). The "house" (13:1, 36) represents a space of relative safety and privacy for Jesus and his "family." When Jesus leaves the house and large crowds "gather around him" (13:2; cf. 12:30!), Matthew establishes distance by putting Jesus in a boat while the crowds remain standing on the shore. When Jesus' disciples "come to him" (did they swim or wade out, or were they with him in the boat?) to ask why he speaks in parables (13:10), Jesus responds as if the crowds are no longer present. Moreover, the content of his explanation establishes a sharp distinction between the disciples and "them" (13:10, 11, 13, 14), i.e., the crowds to whom the next three parables are addressed (13:24, 31, 33). The disciples have access to the mystery of the **empire of the heavens** in ways the crowds do not. For the disciples, parables are revelatory, even if they sometimes require explanation (13:10–17, 36–43). For the crowds they may reveal "what has been hidden from the foundation of the world" (13:35) or may further conceal the reality of God's reign from those who have hardened their hearts against God's rule (13:10–17).

Jesus' explanation for why he speaks in parables (13:10–17) and Matthew's aside to the audience (13:34–35) both underline the distinction between the disciples, his newly defined "family," and the crowds (13:11). Jesus appeals to Isaiah 6, where God calls Isaiah to go to the leaders of Judah and Jerusalem and "make the mind of this people dull" (Isa. 6:10; Matt. 13:15), to explain why he now speaks in parables. In the face of Judah's rejection of clear demonstrations of God's power and presence, Isaiah's God determines to give the people, especially their leaders, over to their own blindness and deafness, with the certainty that **judgment** will come (Isa. 6:11–13). If the people will not heed God's prophets, perhaps judgment will turn them around–judgment that God decrees will last until everything is gone but the last burnt stump. But Isaiah also hints that from the stump of judgment comes a holy seed (Isa. 6:13). In the most unlikely place, God plants a sign of hope.

Jesus' parables at once both explore and create these dynamics of judgment and grace. The story of the sower (13:3–8) contrasts the failure of much seed–seed snatched by the evil one, scorched by distress, or choked by the world–with the astonishing production of seed that falls on good soil, a harvest of God's **justice**. The explanation of the parable of the sower in 13:18–23 develops more clearly the reasons for the failure of some seed and the success of the good seed. Jesus also explains that in God's kingdom weeds sown by the enemy are allowed to grow up amidst the wheat, so that the wheat will not be uprooted until the harvest (13:24–30, 36–43; cf. also vv. 47–50, the harvest of fish).

Recurrent images, topics, and themes that run throughout the parables in this chapter include sowing and seeds (13:3–9, 18–23, 24–30, 31–32, 37–40), the threats posed by invasive forces (13:4, 7, 19–22, 25–30, 31–32), "hiddenness" (13:33, 44), the surprising abundance or value of what seems small or insignificant (13:31–33, 45–46), and the harvest (a Jewish symbol for restoration and judgment). All of these are in some way related to Matthew's most prominent concerns: the "kingdom of heaven" (ten times in 13:3–52) and the hope and judgment it generates (13:1–30, 36–43, 47–50). All of these stories require the hearer to make a leap of faith and obedience in order to "understand." The harvest is certain and will be abundant, but it also brings separation and judgment.

The Sower, the Seeds, the Field, and the Harvest

Matthew 13:1–23*

Exploring the text

The multivalence of Jesus' **parables** is prominently displayed in this parable about parables, which supplies a stock of images to which the other parables of this chapter will return. Is this parable about the sower (a farmer? God? Jesus? the disciples? the **church**?)? Is it about the seeds (the gospel word? the **kingdom of heaven**? the parables themselves?)? Is it about the field (the audience? Israel? the world?)? Or is it about the harvest (the restoration of Israel? the final judgment?)? The ways we make

---

*The Revised Common Lectionary uses this in Year A, The 15th Sunday in Ordinary Time: Matthew 13:1–9, 18–23.

sense of the parable depend on where we stand, what we hear, see, and understand, and how we respond.

Sowing seeds is a stock figure in the Mediterranean world for teaching or training that prepares one for participation in the culture. Sowers are teachers, seeds are the instruction, and the soil is the students. Both "field" (a common image for Israel in the prophetic writings) and "harvest" (which concerns both **judgment** and Jesus' mission of gathering Israel, cf. 9:37–38) would also lie close at hand in this field of metaphors, even though neither is mentioned explicitly in the parable. Matthew has emphasized harvest and division in the preceding chapters. The simplest reading of the parable, then, is that it describes a mixed harvest, including reasons for the failure of some seeds to produce fruit. The seeds that fall on the path are snapped up by birds before ever taking root. The rocky soil receives the most attention of the four different soils or fates that await the various seeds. Three times Jesus describes the problems the rocky soil creates: "they did not have much soil" (13:5), "they had no depth of soil" (13:5), and "they had no root" (13:6). At first the lack of soil causes the plants to spring up quickly (13:5), probably because the shallow soil is warmer, but as the sun rises they are scorched and, lacking soil and root, they wither away (13:6). Other seeds fall among thorns that choke them (13:7). But finally some seeds fall onto good soil and produce a bountiful harvest (13:8). Scholars debate what the yields—hundredfold, sixtyfold, and thirtyfold—actually measure, and whether the crop is thus within reasonable expectations or an astounding harvest that defies all expectations. In either case, the yield of the good seed, while inconsistent, stands in sharp contrast to the failure of the others.

Even this simple reading of the story leaves many unresolved puzzles. Is it important that the failures outweigh the success stories three to one? Does it matter that the farmer appears to be profligate in scattering seeds and apparently does not cultivate or tend the crop until it is time for the harvest? Is the emphasis more on the success that occurs despite the obstacles and hazards, or on the plight of the seeds that do not produce as they should? Is success merely an outcome of location? What makes some soil good?

"Let anyone who has ears, listen" (Matt. 13:9) suggests that a literal hearing of the parable is not the same as listening in order to understand (cf. 13:13–17; Isa. 6:9–10; Ezek. 3:4–11, 27; 12:2). If we presume that Jesus' audience was aware that seeds, fields, and harvests were common images associated with God's blessing and judgment of Israel and that Jesus understood his own ministry as being about gathering and harvest (9:38–39), then the story would surely have resonated as more than a simple description of the vagaries of agrarian life. An astute audience might also recall Deuteronomy 11:13–19, where Moses, after receiving the commandments on two tablets and reminding Israel of God's deeds in liberating them from slavery, employs images of agricultural blessing and disaster in order to induce the people to heed God's commandments and to love and serve God with all their heart and soul. Or they might recall Isaiah 55:9–13, where God's word is compared to the waters that bring forth seed for the sower and bread for the eater (55:10–11). The most earful hearing of the story, of course, would also note its resonance with Jesus' own ministry, especially the division caused by his proclamation of God's rule and demonstrations of God's power. Jesus has sown the seeds broadly, like the sower, in both word and deed. Among some the harvest has been abundant, but elsewhere a disaster.

The parable may have left the disciples feeling ambivalent, both about its meaning and their own place within it. Yet they do not ask about the story itself, but about why Jesus speaks "to them" in parables. Their question already presupposes a division between "them" (the crowds) and "us" (the disciples). Jesus' response intensifies this sense of division. Knowledge of the mysteries of the kingdom of heaven has been given to the disciples, but not to "them" (13:11). Those who have (the disciples) will be given more, an abundance. But those who have nothing, those among whom the seed did not come to fruition, will lose even what they have (13:12). The heart of Jesus' response centers on Isaiah's account of his prophetic call (Isa. 6:8–13). God calls Isaiah to prevent understanding, lest the people really see, listen, understand, and turn and be healed. All means of communication must be blocked. When Isaiah asks God how long he must pursue this dark calling, God tells him that he must persist until all–cities, houses, and land–is empty and desolate (Isa. 6:11–12). If even a tenth is left, even the stump of a tree that has already been felled, it will be burned again (6:13). But the last burnt stump is the "holy seed" from which the promise of restoration springs. The symbol of total devastation thus carries the seed of hope, just as the cross of Jesus will bear both judgment and redemption.

Jesus' extensive citation of Isaiah 6 underlines his identification with Isaiah's vocation and prophetic project. Jesus speaks in parables because his audience, like Isaiah's, sees but does not perceive, hears but does not listen (viz., obey), and does not understand (13:13). Yet Jesus is not only responding to the reality of blindness and disobedience but, like Isaiah, causing it. As **prophetic sign-acts**, the parables both bring understanding and generate the blindness, deafness, and lack of understanding that attend the failure to bear fruit. Judgment is God's last-ditch effort, short of the cross, to induce repentance. But from the smoldering stump of judgment springs a seed, the word of promised restoration. One can listen, then, to Jesus' explanation of the parables and hear only judgment, or one can listen and hear hope.

The allegorical explanation of the parable (13:18–23) that Jesus supplies for his disciples associates the seed with the "word of the kingdom" (13:19), but Jesus' focus is almost wholly on the nature of the differing soils. No attention is given to the identity of the sower or to any of his other activities other than sowing and reaping. The soils correspond to responses to the "word of the kingdom." The differences have to do with what happens after that: the word is heard but not understood (13:19), received but unable to endure troubles (13:21), heard but choked by worldly cares and wealth (13:22), or heard, understood, and empowered to bear fruit (13:23). For the disciples, then, the parable of the sower becomes the parable of the soils.

Preaching and teaching the Word

It's often said that good preaching should comfort the afflicted and afflict the comfortable. Citizens of the empire of heaven see the world differently than other people. When the world trumpets progress and human triumph, Christians may be called to bring a word of judgment. And where troubles and despair fill the air, Christians look amidst the rubble for signs of hope. The parable of the sower/seed/soil/harvest presents enough diverse facets to address a wide variety of situations. For the church grown complacent, it provides a sharp warning of the dangers of rootlessness and the distractions of wealth and worldly cares. For the church awash in discouragement and despair, on the other hand, it provides a promise of God's abundant harvest. For the church constricted with narrow boundaries, it presents the image of a profligate sower, tossing seed wherever it will go. For churches locked in pathologies of exclusive judgment or easy, universal grace, this parable binds warning with promise. For churches focused on the responsibilities of the Christian calling, there is a reminder that the disciples' relationship with God comes as a gift. For churches that stress the gift of God's calling, there is also a clear call to nourish the roots, pull the weeds, and bring that calling to life by bearing fruit.

While there are many different possible messages in this complex of material for the church, its primary focus is still Jesus and the good news of God's kingdom that he proclaims and embodies. Jesus is both sower and the seed of the kingdom. He is the parable, bearing both mercy and judgment. The parable of the sower thus distills the Gospel as a whole. The differing fates that await the seeds cast here and there mirror the disparate responses of Israel, her leaders, and the disciples. Jesus is the bearer of both good news and judgment. Do we hear both words? Can we hear them together?

The church is often tempted to identify closely with the disciples in this story, for they are blessed as insiders, chosen by God to receive the mysteries. We are much less inclined to identify ourselves as the target of Jesus' judgment, even when we discern hints of correspondence between our world and the world of those who reject Jesus. Self-delusion is blindness that we choose. Jesus' warnings are no less appropriate for us than they were for the crowds that followed Jesus seeking healing. Problems with seeing, hearing, understanding, and bearing fruit are neither simply ancient maladies nor maladies of other religions, other churches, or even non-Christian people. In fact, the disorders Jesus here identifies are particularly viral among those who see themselves as blessed insiders. The thorns that choke the seeds have grown more numerous, refined, and powerful, not less. The noise of our world, the new gadgets and ever-evolving and ever more invasive forms of media, and our insatiable need to find new ways to numb ourselves and keep our growing list of insecurities at bay—all of these "necessities" of modern life make it nearly impossible for us to discern the signs of God's presence and power all around us. What blinds and deafens us? What are the things that keep us in thrall of the world, so that we are unable to see and hear? And when we do hear or see, what makes us unwilling to answer God's call?

Blindness, deafness, and the failure to understand what we hear and see are God's judgment on the church. The church in North America is rich, landed, and well-connected (even if we see ourselves increasingly in exile). That means we are also blind, hard of hearing, and unlikely to nurture strong roots or bear the fruit of repentance. Stanley Hauerwas expresses this concern provocatively:

> The church in America simply is not a soil capable of growing deep roots. It may seem odd that wealth makes it impossible to grow the word. Wealth, we assume, should create the power necessary to do much good. But wealth stills the imagination because we are not forced, as the disciples of Jesus were forced, to be an alternative to the world that only necessity can create. Possessed by possessions, we desire to act in the world, often on behalf of the poor, without having to lose our possessions.[1]

Does the situation of our churches reflect God's judgment? Are we a soil capable of growing deep roots?

Becoming a follower of Jesus entails embracing his way, whether it leads to success or to rejection. Those who preach and teach the word must anticipate the mixed responses–even "trouble and persecution"–the gospel is likely to generate. The Christian calling, in any case, is not to be "successful," unless casting the seeds of the gospel, tending the soil, and watching for signs of the harvest count for success. In a culture intolerant of apparent "failure" and a church grown comfortable with not being too objectionable, the scandal of the gospel may be an insurmountable stumbling block. Are we prepared to deal with the apparent failure of our efforts to proclaim the word and bear the fruit of justice? Are we willing to pursue this calling all the way to the cross?

Jesus' parable, his explanation of why he speaks in parables, and his interpretation of the parable all underline the importance of both understanding and bearing fruit as integral expressions of true discipleship. This too is a hard concept to master in a culture that customarily draws sharp distinctions between ideas and actions, knowledge and practice, and theology and ethics. But for Matthew there is no understanding apart from the harvest of fruitful actions, nor any good fruit that does not also bear witness to true knowledge of the mysteries of the kingdom. To put it in positive terms, understanding comes to those who bear fruit, and fruit gives body to mysteries revealed.

How, then, do we know if we have understood Jesus' parable rightly? Fruit is the answer. When we "see" the evidence of God's healing, mercy, gathering, and restoration and we "hear" the announcements of good news, we know that God has drawn near in power. The fruit of obedience grows when we conform our lives to the reality of God's presence. We may be tempted to construe knowledge of the kingdom's secrets as an absolute gift, always ours once given. But the fate of seeds that fall on the road, spring up in rocky soil, or are choked by thorns warns us that knowledge will wither and dissolve when it is not sustained in faithful practice. When Jesus blesses the disciples' "eyes that see" and "ears that hear" (13:16–17), he says nothing about their "understanding." Israel too has seen and heard, but not produced the fruit of understanding. The Gospel will continue to make clear that even the disciples' grasp on the reality of God's reign is tenuous and unfinished. Is God ever finished with us? Do we ever fully grasp the secrets of God's reign? Can we be patient with the pace of growth? Can we, together, nurture eyes that see, ears that hear, and hearts that turn in joy toward the perception of God's reign?

The Invasive Empire

Matthew 13:24–43*

Exploring the text

The three parables in this section of the discourse share motifs related to stealth, hiding, and invasion. In the parable of "weeds and wheat" (13:24–30), Jesus compares the **heavenly empire** to the story of an enemy who sows dangerous weeds among the good seeds the landowner has planted (13:24–25). The parable of the mustard seed (13:31–32) compares the kingdom with an invasive plant that grows beyond all expectation. In the final comparison, a woman "hides" yeast in a quantity of flour sufficient for a banquet, so that the whole amount is leavened (13:33). Each story contains an element of surprise or extravagance. And each leaves the audience wondering what Jesus means to say about the empire of heaven. The ambiguity and multivalence of these three parables admit diverse readings. Are they about the surprising nature and power of God's reign, or about invasion and contamination? Is the contamination a good or a bad thing? Does the growth each story depicts represent promise or threat? Again, where you stand in relation to God's rule determines what you see, hear, and understand.

Most modern readers are inclined to identify positively with the landowners, householders, fathers, kings, and other authority figures in Jesus' parables. Jesus' own interpretation of the parable of the weeds and wheat itself seems to confirm this approach (13:36–43). But we should not always presume that authority figures in Jesus' parables represent God. The crowds who listened to Jesus' parables may have included landowners, but even more smallholders, servants, and day laborers who did not necessarily hold the landowners in high esteem. The servants' question in 13:27 suggests, in fact, that they are afraid of being blamed by their "master" for the weeds now scattered among the good plants. The first ambiguity the parable presents, then, concerns whether we should take the side of the householder or the enemy, or either side at all. We should also note that Jesus supplies his allegorical interpretation for his disciples in particular, not for the crowds. The fact that Jesus' allegory is separated

---

*The Revised Common Lectionary uses this in Year A, The 16th Sunday in Ordinary Time: Matthew 13:24–30, 36–43; Year A, The 17th Sunday in Ordinary Time: Matthew 13:31–33, 44–52.

from the parable it interprets, and distinguished by setting and audience, should make us cautious about presuming that it is the only way to read the story. The allegory, moreover, says nothing about the main concern of the parable itself: letting the weeds and wheat grow up next to each other.

The enemy comes when everyone is sleeping and sows *zidzania* (Greek), usually identified as darnel, a ryegrass. Is the enemy a competing farmer? someone aiming to cut a powerful man down to size? At the allegorical level, does he represent the **Pharisees** or other opponents of Jesus who, threatened by the good seed he sows, attempt to spoil his harvest? Or might the enemy be Jesus himself, plundering the "strong man's house" (cf. 12:29)? The parable leaves room for differing assessments among the various members of Jesus' audience. Whoever he is, the enemy's action is stealthy and threatening. Darnel looks much like wheat but often carries a poisonous fungus that, when gathered with the wheat, can contaminate the whole harvest. The most common response in such circumstances is to pull the weeds before they mature, as the servants suggest (13:28). The surprise in the parable comes when the householder forbids them from doing so. He directs the servants to let the wheat and weeds grow up together until the harvest, when the weeds will be collected first, bundled, and burned, prior to gathering the wheat into the barn (13:30). Ancient audiences might well have wondered what kind of farmer this is and if this farmer knows what he's doing.

Ancient audiences also had an abundance of traditional associations that would tilt them toward understanding the story in metaphorical terms. In popular Jewish tradition, householders often represent God, the enemy the devil, and the servants the righteous. Wheat typically represents Israel and weeds the nations.[1] If we presume these equations, the parable would be a figurative story representing God's judgment of the Gentiles prior to the restoration of Israel. When Jesus supplies his own allegorical reading (13:36–43) for the disciples, however, he alters the traditional associations. His interpretation distinguishes "the children of the empire [of heaven]" from "the children of the evil one" (13:38), who cause sin and do evil (13:41). A parable that most would hear as an affirmation of Israel and a condemnation of Gentiles thus becomes a sign of judgment against the children of Satan, whom Matthew identifies as the Pharisees and Jewish leaders, the people of "this generation" (cf. 11:16–24; 12:22–32). The "children of the kingdom of the Father" (13:38, 43) follow the one who is the hope of the nations (12:18–21).

The story of the mustard seed is similarly ambiguous. Does the mustard seed represent something positive, such as faith (cf. 17:20), or is it an invasive, contaminating force? Mustard is a useful shrub, growing two to six feet tall, that was common along the shore of the Sea of Galilee. It was also regarded as a tenacious plant that could take over a garden. And here it is completely out of control, becoming as big as a tree—an image that would have sounded preposterous to ancient audiences—so that the birds build nests in its branches (13:31–32). Here again Jesus is improvising on prophetic traditions in a way that creates ambivalence. The image of birds nesting in the branches of a tree recalls three passages from the prophets. In Ezekiel 17:22–24, God takes a sprig from the top of a lofty cedar (probably a symbol for Babylon) and plants it on Zion (17:23), where it becomes a symbol for God's humbling of the nations. In Ezekiel 31 the cedar tree represents Assyria, another of Israel's enemies, which God cuts down so that the birds nest on its fallen trunk (Ezek. 31:13) rather than in its branches (31:6). Finally, in Daniel 4 the great tree represents Nebuchadnezzar. Again it is cut down, so that the animals and birds flee from its branches (cf. Dan. 4:12, 14). In two of these passages (Ezek. 31 and Dan. 4), the great tree in which the birds make a home is associated with the judgment of arrogant powers that enslave and oppress Israel, and once (Ezek. 17:22–24) with God's restoration of Israel itself. Why does Jesus replace the mighty cedar tree, a symbol of power, arrogance, and empire, with the invasive mustard plant, a weed? Would the crowds have understood God's mustard-seed empire to be like Jack's beanstalk, reaching, against all expectation, up to heaven and bringing the nations low? Or is it Israel's own leaders who would be brought low? Would the Pharisees or the landowners scattered among the crowds see the mustard as a weed, completely out of control and needing to be rooted out? Is the kingdom of heaven a surprise that brings redemption or a threat that must be eradicated, or both?

The image of the woman who, literally, "hides" leaven (Matt. 13:33) in the flour is also ambivalent. Hiddenness will again be featured in the fulfillment quotation in 13:36 and in the parable of treasure in the field (13:44). Is the leaven (fermented dough that was held back to start the fermentation of the next batch) like the treasure hidden in the field (13:44)? Is it like "what has been hidden from the foundation of the world," but is now made known (or hidden!) through the parables (13:35)? Leaven itself is a mixed image. It is essential, of course, for making bread. But Jewish households are required to remove it from their houses during Passover, when they eat only unleavened bread (Exod. 12:14–20; 23:18; 34:25; Lev. 2:11). Jesus himself warns his disciples that the corrupting teaching of the Pharisees is "leaven" (16:6, 11–12). So is the leaven in this case an agent of transformation or an invasive, corrupting power?

The woman hides the leaven in three measures of flour (about three gallons), enough to make bread for one hundred and fifty people. She is either ruining a lot of flour or preparing for a feast. The amount of flour corresponds to what Sarah baked for Abraham's three heavenly visitors (Gen. 18:6), to what Gideon used in preparation for an angel of God (Judg. 6:19), and what Hannah used to make an offering when Samuel was to be presented in the temple (1 Sam. 1:24). In each case this amount of bread is associated with a divine visitation. Perhaps, then, she is preparing for an epiphany.

Together the three parables in this portion of the discourse raise more questions than they answer. Each carries associations that may be taken either negatively or positively by Jesus' audience. Do they announce **judgment** (13:30, 32) or divine presence (13:32, 33)—or both? Does the empire of heaven set the world right, or is it, for some at least, invasive and corrupting? Any decision to limit the meaning of these parables to but one of these valences robs them of their power to evoke and compel choice. The decisions the audience makes about the meaning of these parables serve in turn to locate the listener in reference to the empire of heaven.

The brief aside that Matthew addresses to those who hear the Gospel (13:34–35) makes clear (1) that Jesus consistently speaks to the crowds in parables, that is, in indirect, enigmatic, yet revelatory figures; (2) that the parables express (lit., "belch," "bellow," or "roar") secrets that have heretofore been hidden; and (3) that this is the fulfillment of Psalm 78:2. Notably, the psalm recounts the long history of God's judgment and redemption of Israel and the people's persistent forgetfulness, stubbornness, and rebellion. Even the **fulfillment quotation**, in other words, subtly reminds the audience of the foundational issues of the discourse: Israel has been blind and faithless and God has responded with both judgment and mercy.

The movement back into "the house" signals an important shift of setting and audience (13:36). Jesus addresses the rest of the parables and explanations in the discourse to the disciples alone. They first ask him to explain the parable of the "weeds in the field," which may suggest that their question concerns particularly the identity and fate of the weeds. In contrast to what the crowds and the disciples might have first thought when they heard the parable, Jesus explains that the owner who sows good seed is not God, but the "**Son of Humanity**"; the field is not Israel but the world; and the weeds are not Gentiles but "children of the evil one." The allegory trades in sharply contrasting images of judgment (13:41–42) and blessing (13:43), thereby continuing the emphasis on division that has dominated chapters 11–13. Strikingly, Jesus' explanation leaves aside the element that had been central in the parable itself: the master's curious strategy of leaving the wheat and weeds to grow together until the harvest. Apparently Jesus' allegory is really aimed at answering the disciples' question. The interpretation Jesus offers is for the disciples and for their time. It is a word of certainty about what is coming, a warning about the judgment of the children of the devil, and, reassuringly, the redemption of the children of the heavenly empire.

Preaching and teaching the Word

The parable of the weeds among the wheat has typically been read as a warning to the **church**. The forces of the devil at work in the world seek to undermine the ministry of Jesus and the church. The church is a mixed body; it includes both saints and sinners. Members of the church are not to execute judgment on one another, but to wait for God's angels to sort the good from the bad at the final judgment. The farmer's unconventional practice of allowing the wheat and weeds to grow up together symbolizes God's grace for all. While these appropriations of the story have merit, they also miss some important dynamics. Within Matthew's larger story, all three of these parables point toward the mixed results that Jesus' sowing of the kingdom has produced. Each invites the audience to consider where they stand and how they read the signs as the harvest approaches. Each leaves the audience to grapple with ambivalent signs. And while Jesus' discourse has created a sharp sense of division between the disciples and the crowd, the multivalent metaphors at work in these parables also serve to inhibit the development of a clear sense of "insiders" (people who get the right meaning) and "outsiders." No one, not even the disciples, has a clear inside track that leads to the right interpretation. It is not right interpretation that distinguishes disciples, but enduring obedience, that is, steady, active, resilient witness in a world that does not clearly perceive the signs of God's power, that misidentifies the signs, and that refuses to admit or conform to the rule of God evident in Christ. How can the church bear witness to Christ's Lordship without arrogance or triumphalism? How does the church discern and name God's work in the world without standing in judgment of others?

Despite resistance and obstacles, the empire of heaven endures and even thrives. These parables suggest that things are not as they seem on the surface. God's reign is not present in these stories in ostentatious power or grandeur, but in subtleties, in a mixed field, in tiny seeds growing into towering trees, and in leaven quietly permeating everything it touches. Each of these images evokes a sense of promise and of threat. Bearing witness to this empire requires ongoing discernment and, most of all, patience. This is not merely patience to which we resign ourselves because we must, but patience born of faith; not silent endurance, but active, tenacious trust in the One who is coming. How does the church bear witness to the immanence and eminence of God's rule with humility and grace?

The Hidden Empire

Matthew 13:44–52[*]

Exploring the texts

TREASURE HIDDEN IN A FIELD (13:44)

In "the house" Jesus continues speaking in parables, but now exclusively to the disciples. He compares the **heavenly empire** to a treasure hidden in a field, which a man finds and then covers up. The nature of the treasure is not important; the activities of the finder are. The surpassing value of the treasure elicits a disruptive, "risk everything" response. The treasure is not visible to everyone, but "hidden" (13:33, 35) and accessible only to one who would risk everything else in life to possess it. Matthew's telling leaves some alternatives aside: the man does not simply steal the treasure, nor does he announce his discovery so that the rightful owner can be found. Instead he covers the treasure, then goes and sells everything he owns to buy the field. His decisive, radical, costly, and perhaps even shady action is the central factor in the story, as it will be in the parable of the pearl (13:45–46). If the treasure is like the kingdom of heaven, then the finder may be like the disciples, who are discovering "the secrets . . . hidden from the foundation of the world" (13:11, 35).

THE MERCHANT AND THE PEARL (13:45–46)

The story of the merchant and the pearl of surpassing merit again revolves around both the object of pursuit and the actions of the finder. Whereas the treasure in the field is discovered accidentally, the merchant in this story is actively engaged in searching, not necessarily for this one

[*] The Revised Common Lectionary uses this in Year A, The 17th Sunday in Ordinary Time: Matthew 13:31–33, 44–52.

pearl, but for "fine pearls" in general. The merchant has a trained eye, and discovers one pearl that transcends all the rest. Again, he knows something that no one else does. In Jewish usage, pearls represented an object of surpassing worth, as do diamonds today. "Pearl" was sometimes used to designate the Torah, Israel herself, a good thought, or God's reward for the righteous,[1] but for Matthew the most important quality of this pearl is its singularity. As in the story of the treasure in the field, the discovery generates extraordinary, even risky behavior. One who has spent his life trading pearls suddenly dispossesses himself of all that he has gathered. Again, the most important aspect of the story is the merchant's exchange of everything else for this one pearl.

The common points in both the treasure and the pearl stories include the discovery of an object of surpassing value, going away to sell everything the finder possesses, and the purchase of the field (treasure)/pearl. Both discoveries—one apparently accidental, the other part of an intentional search—yield knowledge that remains hidden or undisclosed to others. The two finders have been possessed, as it were, by the perception of something that the rest of the world does not see. The two finders are thus like those to whom "it has been given to know the secrets of the empire of the heavens" (13:11). Jesus' disciples have discovered "what has been hidden" (13:35) and what "many prophets and righteous ones have longed to see . . . and hear" but did not see or hear (13:17). When Jesus sent his disciples on mission to the "lost sheep of the house of Israel," he sent them without gold, silver, or copper, without bag, extra cloak, sandals, or staff (10:9–10). These parables suggest that claiming/being claimed by the kingdom of heaven induces risky, peculiar behavior, including dispossession of all that one has in this world. Are the protagonists resourceful and decisive, or just fools? How does their knowledge of what others cannot or will not see transform their lives? Does discipleship require a complete divestment of one's former life and goods?

THE DRAGNET (13:47–50)

The third parable in this series echoes the parable of the weeds (13:24–30). The language of "good" and "bad" recalls Jesus' teaching earlier in the Gospel about trees and their fruit (cf. 7:17–18; 12:33). Matthew establishes the most important associations, however, by means of verbal links with the introduction and setting of the parable chapter as a whole (cf. 13:1–2), where a large crowd "gathered" at the "shore" of the "sea," while Jesus "sat" in a boat to teach them by means of parables. The evangelist has carefully formulated this parable to remind the audience of that setting, even to comment on it. The empire of the heavens is like a net tossed into the sea, which catches every kind of fish. When it is drawn ashore, the fishermen sit down and separate the good from the bad. Just as Jesus separates himself from the crowds when he begins speaking in parables, and as the parables themselves cause separation between the disciples and the crowds, so now Jesus describes the moment at the close of the age (13:49; cf. 28:20) when angels separate the good from the rotten. "Throwing out" signals **judgment** (cf. 3:10; 5:13; 7:19; 8:12; 18:8; 22:13; 25:30), as the explicit description of judgment in verses 49–50 confirms. The sorting is swift and final. Those who are evil will be thrown into the fiery furnace, where they will weep and gnash their teeth (cf. 8:12; 13:42; 22:13; 25:30). As in the story of the weeds among the wheat, those who are evil are removed first. Judgment consists first of all in removal from the presence of God, in the loss of one's identity as a child of God.

TREASURES NEW AND OLD (13:51–52)

The parable discourse closes with a curious, even humorous, dialogue between Jesus and his disciples. The main topic, as throughout the chapter, is understanding, specifically the recognition of the reality and character of the empire of the heavens, which has been given to the disciples but not to "them" (13:10–17). Jesus asks his disciples if they have understood "all this." Their simple "Yes" affirms Jesus' authority as a teacher, but given what transpires in the subsequent narrative it seems that the disciples' understanding is less than complete or certain. Their "yes" seems almost too quick and too certain, as if they really mean, "Yes, but please don't ask us to explain it." If they say it strongly enough, maybe he won't call on them.

Jesus continues as if he accepts their answer, but offers a cryptic saying that itself is parabolic: "Therefore, every scribe who has been trained for the kingdom of heaven is like the master of a household who brings out of his treasure what is new and what is old." Who is this scribe/master? Does this refer to the disciples, to Jesus himself, to a special class in Matthew's **church**, or to all who are discipled in the ways of God's reign? As a rule, where the referent is not clear, we must be careful not to limit the range of possibilities unnecessarily.

The content of the saying is as ambiguous as the referent. What are the things new and old that the householder brings from his treasure? Are the old things the promises of the prophets, the law, or the tradition? Are the new things Jesus' teaching and healing? The only thing certain is that "things new and things old" mixes the categories, suggesting that Jesus is referring both to what is continuous with what came before (things old) and what is discontinuous (things new). Jesus himself embodies in his ministry both the fulfillment of Israel's story and its turn toward a new reality, the kingdom of heaven. Discerning and preserving the relationship between these two is especially important given the ruptures, dislocations, and separations that Jesus' ministry is generating, including the division his parables produce.

Preaching and teaching the Word

The parables of the treasure hidden in the field and the pearl of surpassing worth both describe the situation of the disciples themselves, who have received Jesus' teaching about the **reign of God**, the secret hidden from the foundation of the world (13:11, 35). These parables point to both the surpassing value of the empire of the heavens and the exclusive demands it makes upon our person and resources. God's reign is worth everything, but it is hard to see and harder to respond to, and thus generates both the great joy of discovery and the anguish of judgment. While Jesus focuses on gathering the lost sheep of the house of Israel, he also announces and effects their separation (cf. 25:31–46). Jesus' ministry is the occasion of both gathering and separation, of mercy and judgment, of restoration and definitive breach. With these images Jesus casts his notion of the empire of the heavens squarely within the **apocalyptic** traditions of Israel.

When God is present among us, division is certain. Some will recognize God's presence, others not at all. Some will conform to it, others will go back to the world. The gospel life and proclamation generate decision and division. The scandal of the gospel rightly proclaimed and embodied is that it will not bring comfort or joy to all who encounter it. Does the church understand all these things? Does it live faithfully on the cusp of what is old and what is new? Are we training ourselves to discover treasure and discern what is hidden to others? Does our life together embody the truth that has been shown to us?

PART SEVEN

Discipleship and Division

13:53–17:27

Preliminary Remarks

Announcements of **judgment** and images of division in Israel over Jesus' ministry have dominated Matthew's story since the latter part of the Mission Discourse (10:5–42). The narrative that now follows the **parables** of Matthew 13 continues to depict disparate responses to Jesus. The alienation between Jesus and the **scribes** and **Pharisees** deepens. As in the parable discourse, Jesus slowly turns his attention from the crowds and his adversaries toward his disciples. Matthew uses repetitive, parallel stories in this section to underline the conflict and mark narrative progress. Repeatedly Jesus withdraws from interactions with hostile authorities (14:13; 15:21; 16:4). Twice he miraculously provides food for large crowds (14:13–21; 15:32–39), and twice his disciples make the confession that he is God's Son (14:33; 16:16). With each story the lines of demarcation over Jesus grow clearer.

Hometown Blues

Matthew 13:53–58

Exploring the text

This brief story provides a transition between the parables discourse (13:1–52) and the narrative section that will end at 17:27. It explores yet another instance in which people discern Jesus' power but misunderstand and misname it (cf. 13:10–17). After Jesus finishes speaking in parables, he leaves "that place" (13:53), apparently "the house" (13:36; cf. 13:1) where he has been among his "brothers," and "sisters," and "mothers," those who do "the will of my Father" (12:50) and has taught them the secrets of the **heavenly empire** (13:11). He leaves this house for his hometown (it is not clear whether this is Capernaum or Nazareth), where people know him and his birth family. Together with the account of the visit of Jesus' own family members (12:46–50) this story forms a frame around the parables of chapter 13. The division that Jesus' ministry incites is at work even in his family and his hometown.

The setting in "their synagogue" (13:54) conveys mixed signals. In every prior instance this location is associated with healings (4:23; 9:35; 10:17; 12:9), but in 10:17 and 12:9 also with conflict (cf. also 23:34). The audience is meant to wonder what might happen this time, but not for long. Again Jesus meets rejection. His old neighbors are unable to get past their familiarity with him and his family. Why do the people of his hometown reject him? They are unwilling to accept that the one who demonstrates "this wisdom and these deeds of power" (13:54) is one of them. "Where did he get all this?" suggests that the box they have created for Jesus and his family is too small to contain him. Each of the questions they raise about Jesus carries potentially negative associations. A carpenter is a lower-class tradesman. The identification of Jesus as Mary's son suggests that Joseph has died or is gone, or even that there is some question about the legitimacy of his parentage. Perhaps they wonder why Jesus, the eldest son, has left his mother to fend for herself and his other brothers and sisters. All of these questions focus ultimately on the source of Jesus' power. Like the **Pharisees** (cf. 12:24, 38), the people of Jesus' hometown recognize his power but are unable rightly to identify its source. So they dismiss him.

The people of Jesus' hometown are not only dismissive, but "offended" at him (13:57, cf. 13:21, "falls away"; 15:12). They will not be counted among those who are "blessed" (cf. 11:6). What offense did they find in him? Perhaps it is hard to hear about repentance or God's kingdom from one of your own. The good news is good only for those who are willing to be transformed by it. Jesus himself attributes their rejection to the "prophet-not-accepted-in-his-hometown" syndrome (13:57). Their lack of faith means that any "deeds of power" he does among them would inevitably be misconstrued and dismissed (13:58). Faithlessness here implies misunderstanding, and thus blindness and deafness. Lack of faith does not mean that Jesus cannot do many powerful deeds among them, but that they will not accept them. Matthew gives no indication that Jesus ever again visits his hometown, nor even another synagogue.

Preaching and teaching the Word

Modern Christians often want to turn Jesus into our personal savior and friend, which the people of Jesus' hometown might also have been willing to do. But Jesus is no one's son but God's. He serves no city, no household, no master, no church—only the Father in heaven. Jesus is not our homeboy. Part of his offense lies in the fact that his mercy is not reserved just for insiders—whether they are Jesus' own kin and neighbors or the self-righteous. Are we willing to endure a prophet who is not impressed by our goodness and unwilling to be made our captive?

"Where did this man get this wisdom and these deeds of power?" is always the right question. The purpose of Jesus' mission is to point to God, not to himself. With regard to those who display various kinds of power, whether in the spheres of politics, the church, or the media, it is always important to discern the nature and source of their power. To whom do they bear witness and for what purpose? What God do they serve, not only in word but in deed?

Matthew uses this story to add another layer onto the canvas of opposition and judgment that Matthew has been accumulating. The tragedy of rejection goes deep; Jesus' new family may not include his own kin or neighbors. The story also foreshadows the rejection that is coming at the end of the Gospel story. How does the gospel relativize our various life commitments, even our commitments to family and friends? What is our true family, the place where we are at home? Is it among those who gather to discern and bear witness to God's presence and power?

The Haunting of Herod

Matthew 14:1–12

Exploring the text

The story of John the Baptizer's death is one of the few episodes in the Gospel in which Jesus is not the center of attention. Here Matthew's focus shifts from Jesus to the inner workings of Herod Antipas's household. Why? John's death foreshadows Jesus' fate. Matthew has also been exploring the constituency and nature of Jesus' family (12:46–50; 13:53–58). Now Matthew sets the disparate character of the two royal families—Jesus' and Herod's—vividly on display. Antipas's murder of John reminds us of his father's (Herod the Great's) murder of the innocent children in 2:16–18. Both Antipas and Jesus are their fathers' sons. One family holds political power by means of violence, while the other rules in gentleness and mercy. Both hold lavish banquets—one for the rulers, the other for the hungry masses (cf. 14:13–21). One is lord of the realm, the other is Lord of the Sabbath. Matthew thus invites us to consider closely the "fruit" that each family tree produces.

"At that time" links this episode with Jesus' rejection in his hometown. The people of Nazareth had wondered about the source of Jesus' wisdom and power (13:54). Herod thinks he knows: Jesus is John the Baptist raised from the dead (14:2). Herod is apparently haunted by his guilt for John's murder. When he sees and hears something similar to John, he thinks it must be John raised from the dead. Herod is on the right track, but it is not John's power at work in Jesus. The people of Nazareth could not get past the interpretive frame of their knowledge of Jesus and his family. Herod cannot get past the interpretive frame of his guilt. Matthew is giving us insight into the varying causes of blindness.

The account of John's death (14:3–12) is a tale of the buffoon who holds power but lacks the character for anything more than self-absorbed blundering and butchery. Herod comes across as a weakling leading a life of luxury, a reed blowing in the wind, and a dandy dressed in fancy clothes (11:7–8). He is unable to accomplish any of his purposes except as others dictate. He arrests John because John has told him his marriage to Herodias, his brother Philip's wife, is illegitimate. Herod would like simply to do away with John, but he is afraid of the popular sentiment of the people, who hold John to be a prophet (14:3–5). But when Herodias's daughter dances for him at his birthday party, he is sufficiently enamored to offer her a blank check (14:6–7). Is he trying to impress her, or is he just a fool who has lost his head? Or is this another expression of the stain of incest in Herod's family? The daughter is her mother's puppet, and what Herodias really wants most is John's head. The "king" (he is, in fact, not a king, but the "tetrarch" of Galilee and Perea) is "saddened" by this request—perhaps he is grieving his public stupidity or wondering what the masses will think. But his honor is at stake. And because his word, his honor, and his power are all of one piece, there is never any doubt that he will fulfill Herodias's request. Herod's honor is worth more to him than popular sentiment, and certainly more than John's own life. So he does what he had first wanted to do, kill John—but only because his own weaknesses have made him vulnerable to the manipulations of the women in his household. All of this, then, makes Herod into a joke. Like his father, he is dangerous and violent, but holds only illusory powers. The real power in the world is headed away to a place of solitude, followed by needy crowds (14:13).

Preaching and teaching the Word

Power corrupts. Every generation learns this painfully, through repeated demonstrations. This story is but one instance in Matthew's ongoing depiction of the corruption and violence of human rulers (cf. 2:3–18; 26:47, 59–68; 27:24–43; 27:62–66). Matthew holds up not just these particular rulers or this particular incident for critical scrutiny, but all rulers who are unrepentant before God's power. Nor is the polemic in which Matthew here engages merely the evangelist's own pet peeve. Biting criticism of human leaders is a rushing river in both Testaments. What symptoms of unrepentance do we see in our own rulers? How does our corruption and violence haunt us? How is Jesus' power and leadership different from the human political and social power we know so well?

Matthew persistently pulls back the curtain for us to see the true weakness of those who pretend that human power is in any way comparable to God's. Corruption, exploitation, and violence are the vapor trails of the blasphemous denial of God's presence and power in the world. Matthew here invites us to discern and resist the thrall of this world's powers. But this is no easy task when contemporary leaders customarily baptize their policies in the rhetoric of faith and divine will, or when the people merge and confuse the Christian story with the manifest destiny of any contemporary state. Just as Matthew here unmasks both the violence and folly of Herod Antipas, the church is called to pull the masks from this world's rulers. The rule of God is not the rule of the land or of any nation. The church cannot bear faithful witness to God's work in the world if our trust is finally in the forms of power and "salvation" offered by the rulers of this world. Where, on the other hand, do we see in our experience and in the broader Christian tradition examples of faithful, prophetic leadership? Can prophetic leadership ever be joined with the exercise of violence, even for the sake of "the greater good"?

The women in Herod's life have a prominent, but unflattering, role in this story. Matthew here trades in ancient stereotypes of the manipulative, scheming wife that we should not wish to perpetuate. The story also contains at least the scent of sexual impropriety. Already in the church fathers and later in Christian art, Herodias's daughter is lifted from this story, given the name Salome, and sometimes made the focus of eroticizing imagination.[1] But Matthew is barely suggestive about such matters. His focus is on the power dynamics at work in Herod's family. In Herod's house, power is not shared but contested, no one seems to wield power completely, and cunning and manipulation rule the day. The story thus reveals something of the conflicted, incestuous character of a family trapped in the quest for self-preservation and power. Trust dissolves where power has corrupted. Faith flourishes where truth is told and power is used to heal.

The Abundance of God's Empire

Matthew 14:13–21*

Exploring the text

The stories in Matthew 14 develop contrasting images of power and leadership. Matthew's account of the feeding of five thousand people (not counting the women and children, 14:21) provides the counterpoint to Herod's violence in the story of the death of John the Baptizer. The report of John's execution leads Jesus to withdraw by himself "to a deserted place" (14:13). Matthew typically uses the word for withdrawal in situations where flight from the violence of the powers is necessary (2:12–15; 2:22; 4:12; 12:14–15). Matthew has already indicated in 14:2 that Herod perceives Jesus as the reincarnation of John the Baptizer, so we can presume that Herod would have sought to kill Jesus too. Jesus is not the only one to perceive a threat; the crowds, too, follow him into the wilderness. They are looking to Jesus rather than to Herod for leadership and **salvation**. Matthew sets the mercy and abundance of God's rule in sharp relief to the terrifying and deadly character of "King" Herod's "traditional" family values.

The wilderness to which Jesus and the crowds now flee is not only a refuge, but a place apart from ordinary society. Matthew carefully constructs the clauses in 14:13 so that the "deserted place" stands in contrast to "the towns" from which the crowds follow him. In the wilderness, where God provided food for Israel, the assumptions and relationships that determine everyday life in the cities dissolve; here it is possible for Jesus, his disciples, and the crowds to rely on and experience God's merciful power. The crowds, who are traveling on foot, beat Jesus across the lake and are waiting for him when he arrives at the shore. As in 9:36, compassion (or mercy) determines Jesus' response; before he feeds the crowds, he heals the sick (or "weak," "powerless"). The subsequent feeding miracle often overshadows this notice of Jesus' healing activity. Both actions together demonstrate the nature of God's empire. Jesus is not only restoring the sick and powerless, but in this deserted place he is also laying the foundations for a new economic order, based on sharing and God's abundance.

*The Revised Common Lectionary uses this in Year A, The 18th Sunday in Ordinary Time.

Matthew uses the phrase "when it was evening" (14:15) in conjunction with manifestations of God's power and presence (e.g., 8:16–17; 14:23), with scenes of **judgment** (20:8; 26:20), and with discernment of signs of the **times** (16:2). The disciples, however, do not perceive evening as a time of **eschatological** fulfillment. They remind Jesus that they are in a wilderness place and the day is now nearly over. Their advice seems prudent given the circumstances, but this prudence reflects their everyday presuppositions about life, rather than the imagination and perception of **God's reign**. They want Jesus to send the crowds back to fend for themselves in the villages they had left behind to follow Jesus. For the disciples, the oppressive and alienating economic realities of life in the villages of Galilee seem a better alternative than night in the wilderness. But they have forgotten that God provides food in the wilderness, and that where God is present in power and mercy, human economic and social arrangements no longer hold sway. Scarcity and individual self-interest assume a fallen world. Jesus' response to the disciples' prudent advice yanks them back into God's reign: "They need not go away; you give them something to eat." Jesus had empowered his disciples to cast out unclean spirits, to heal, even to raise the dead, and to proclaim God's reign (10:1, 7–10), and he set them to their mission in complete dependence on God's care (10:8–10). Now he holds them accountable for the exercise of their power and responsibility as agents of God's reign.

But the disciples still can't connect the dots. "We have nothing here but five loaves and two fish," they protest. "Here" for the disciples is a "deserted place" with limited resources, a place of scarcity. Jesus' response redefines "here" as the place where God's power will be made manifest, a place determined by Jesus' presence. He commands the crowds to sit down on the grass–he is organizing a banquet–then takes the loaves and fish, looks up into heaven, blesses (God) and breaks the loaves, then gives them to the disciples for distribution to the crowds (14:19). These actions ring with eucharistic resonance (cf. 26:26–28), while also recalling Elisha's feeding of one hundred people (2 Kgs. 4:42–43). Just as God had fed Israel in the wilderness on her way to the realization of God's promised liberation, so now another wilderness feeding reveals a new power in the world and brings into being a new people. Unjust political, social, and economic arrangements produce scarcity, hunger, and violence, but God's reign brings both healing and the full satisfaction of everyone's hunger (14:20). The twelve baskets full of leftovers–enough for each of the disciples, or for the twelve tribes of Israel–underscore the reality of God's abundance, which will later be affirmed in Gentile territory as well (15:32–38).

Preaching and teaching the Word

The feeding of the five thousand has generated a rich history of interpretation. For some this episode is an allegory of God's merciful and abundant **salvation** for the world. Others discern not only an affirmation of salvation, but especially God's care for physical needs. Still others focus on the disciples' failure to embrace the social and economic implications of Jesus' ministry. The story also prefigures the church's eucharistic witness to God's abundance at the Lord's Table. We should resist any temptation to limit the story to but one or another of these possibilities.

In a day when starvation and hunger constantly afflict millions of people, some even in our own land, this story calls disciples to trust God to supply our needs, even in "deserted places." This is a recurrent message in Matthew (cf., e.g., 6:25–33) and the rest of the New Testament, but at the same time a message that is difficult for many of us to embrace, given the ways our own economic arrangements and our presuppositions of scarcity, independence, and the need to secure our own economic well-being dominate our imagination and practice. In cities and towns, where the symbols of this fallen world surround us, it is very difficult to discern and sustain an imagination suffused with the promise of God's care and abundance. At the margins and in the deserted places, where people necessarily live in dependence on God's mercy, one may just find the kind of faith that this story calls forth.

The eucharistic tones in this story also point us toward the economic and social implications of our practices at the Lord's Table. When the Lord's Table is "spiritualized" and disconnected from the daily realities of life, we will be unable to see in it the signs of God's abundance and power. Beyond the Eucharist itself, how do our own mealtime practices and assumptions manifest the reality of God's abundance? How do we move our congregations toward the kind of dependence on and sharing of God's gifts that this story demonstrates? How can our sermons and life together offer alternatives to the images of scarcity and self-interest that dominate our media, images that deny the reality of God's reign among us? What are the **prophetic-symbolic actions** that congregations can nurture in order to give faithful witness to the truth about God and the world?

Between Two Worlds

Matthew 14:22–36*

Exploring the text

The story of Jesus walking on the sea provides a prime example of Matthew's penchant for blurring the boundaries between the divine and the human. Matthew riddles this account with double entendre, much of which is lost in English translation and most of which focuses on the divine power of the human Jesus. Matthew develops two main claims in this story of divine power and presence: Jesus is again crossing the boundaries between the human and the divine, between earth and heaven; and the same powers Jesus demonstrates are also available to other humans, first of all to Jesus' disciples.

Like the feeding story that immediately precedes, this episode sets Jesus' power in contrast with Herod's murderous violence at the start of chapter 14. But as the story begins, Matthew uses language that would seem to fit Herod better. Jesus compels (or "forces"—the word is often softened in English translations) his disciples into a boat and sends them to "the other side" (14:22; cf. 8:18). He dismisses (or "divorces") the crowds. He acts decisively to put distance between himself and others. Then he prays by himself on the mountain. Both the mountain setting and the temporal reference to evening are linked in Matthew with the manifestation of divine power (cf. 5:1; 17:1; 28:16; 8:16–17; 14:15).

While Jesus is alone praying on the mountain, the disciples are caught in a storm in the middle of the sea. With a few choice words and images, Matthew paints a scene of extreme duress and conflict. The boat is being "battered" by the waves, and the wind is contrary. Matthew uses the term "battered" (literally, "tormented" or "tortured") elsewhere to depict extreme stress or conflict (cf. 8:6 and 8:29). The same term is used in the Maccabean literature to describe Antiochus Epiphanes's tortures of the Jewish people (e.g., 2 Macc. 7:1, 13, 17; 4 Macc. 6:5 al.). Sea, storm, and nighttime all carry a sense of chaos, risk, and even demonic threat in ancient Jewish imagination. The whole episode recalls their earlier adventure in a boat during a storm (8:23–27), after which the disciples had wondered, "What sort of human is this, that even the winds and the

---

*The Revised Common Lectionary uses this in Year A, The 19th Sunday in Ordinary Time.

sea obey him?" (8:27). Now their experience will again cause them to reconsider Jesus' identity, this time to confess that he is "**Son of God**" (14:33, the Greek here lacks the article "the," which leaves open the possibility that the disciples regard him either as "a" or "the" Son of God. See also 27:54).

Matthew makes this story drip with divinity. During the fourth watch, the darkest part of the night, Jesus comes to them, walking on the sea. The reference to early morning recalls God's deliverance of Israel from Pharaoh through the sea (Exod. 14:21–24). In the Old Testament, only God is able to walk on the sea (Ps. 77:19; Job 9:8; Isa. 43:16). The disciples are terrified, a common human response to divine presence in the Bible, and think they are seeing a "phantasm." Jesus' assurance, "Take heart, it is I; have no fear," is used elsewhere in Matthew in association with healings (9:2) and theophanies (17:7; 28:5, 10). The middle clause, "It is I," consists of the Greek words *ego eimi*, literally "I am," i.e., the Greek translation of YHWH, God's name. On the surface, Jesus' self-designation is meant to reassure: "Hey, guys, it's me!" But at the same time, it offers another indication of Jesus' divine nature and power. In the midst of the chaos and storm, "I am" is present.

The parallel versions in Mark and John end with Jesus' self-identification. Only Matthew expands the story to include Peter's walk with Jesus on the sea. In some circles Peter is castigated for brazenly thinking he can do what Jesus has done, but there is no hint in the narrative that Matthew regards Peter's request as inappropriate. Rather, Matthew is continuing not only to demonstrate the dimensions of Jesus' identity and divine power, but to suggest that the same power is available to other human beings as well. Peter's question to Jesus seems to recognize the divine power manifested in his human master. It's as if Peter is thinking, "OK, Jesus, if it is you, and you can walk on the water, can the rest of us humans do it too? Is divine power also available to people like me?" He turns Jesus' "I am" into the second person: "If 'you are' [i.e., if you are God], command me to come to you on the water." When Jesus immediately issues the command, he affirms that Peter's test is not inappropriate. Indeed, Peter gets out of the boat and walks on the water to Jesus. But then he "sees the wind." His human imagination once again asserts itself. He begins to sink and cries out to Jesus for salvation. Jesus "stretches out his hand," a typical gesture during healings (cf. 8:3; 8:15; 9:18; 9:25) and grabs him. God also stretches out the hand in order to save Israel (Exod. 3:20; 7:5; Ps. 144:7), as does Moses (Exod. 4:4; 8:5–6; 9:22). As Jesus reaches out to save Peter, he also calls Peter a "little-faith" and questions him about his doubting. The epithet "little-faith" both affirms the faith

Peter did exercise and rebukes him for his failure of nerve. The word Matthew uses for doubting (literally, "standing in two places" or "being of two minds") occurs in the New Testament only here and again in 28:17, where it describes the disciples when they first meet the resurrected Jesus on the mountain at the Great Commissioning. Jesus' question indicates not that Peter was mistaken to initiate his faith-adventure on the stormy sea, but that he was unable to sustain the imagination of God's new world. When Peter "sees the wind" he becomes trapped between his appropriation of divine power and his humanly trained perceptions. As they get back in the boat and the wind ceases, Jesus is worshiped by the disciples (see also 28:17), who confirm their recognition of Jesus' divine power with the confession, "Truly you are a [or "the"] **Son of God**."

The transitional summary of Jesus' healing activity (14:34–36; cf. 9:21) near Gennesaret after he and the disciples complete their voyage forms a bracket with the notice of his healing activity that introduces the feeding of the five thousand (cf. 14:14). Both the feeding and the walk with Peter on the sea reveal God's boundary-breaking power at work among humans through Jesus.

Preaching and teaching the Word

As in the case of the earlier story of deliverance from the storm on the sea (8:23–27), interpretation of this story has focused on the boat as a symbol of the **church** in a world of chaos, threat, and risk, while Peter stands for the representative Christian, who explores—with mixed results—the limits of faith and the boundaries of God's re-creation of the world. The parallels establish a link between these two stories of deliverance, but the differences help the audience discern how far Jesus and the disciples have come. The disciples' faith has grown to the point that Peter is willing to test the boundaries of heaven and earth for himself. The disciples are still little-faiths, but bigger little-faiths. How do we measure our maturation in faith, as individuals and especially as communities? Are we content to hold on to faith as if it were an inanimate object, a possession, or our entrance ticket to heaven, or does our faith live and grow at the borders between this world and **God's reign**?

The story raises questions about the nature of discipleship, about our perceptions of the world, even the physical world, and about our participation in God's divine power. Can we also traverse the boundaries between divine power and the human world? To what end? What factors cause us to be "little-faiths"? How does the world capture our attention, so that we too become caught between two minds, two ways of perceiving the world, ourselves, and God? Remember, this Gospel begins and ends with the claim that Jesus is "God with us." What difference does this claim make for us? Where do we perceive God's liberating power today, the power even to burst the limits of the physical world?

The Things That Defile

Matthew 15:1–20*

Exploring the text

The deteriorating relationship between Jesus and the religious elites now takes a more ominous turn. **Scribes** and **Pharisees** last joined forces to ask Jesus for a sign (12:38; cf. 16:1–4). The group that now challenges Jesus is from Jerusalem. Jesus has been ministering around Gennesaret, on the northwest shore of the Sea of Galilee (14:34–36), so the scribes and Pharisees of Jerusalem must come some distance for this encounter. Perhaps the Jerusalem leaders think that the locals are not up to dealing with Jesus, so they send their own people to put Jesus in his place. Jerusalem now looms on the horizon (cf. 16:21). In **controversies** such as this, Jesus' adversaries are hoping to assert their own status and diminish Jesus' authority with the crowds. The point of the attack is to discredit Jesus by demonstrating that he and his followers do not attain the high standards of purity required by tradition and practiced, presumably, by the Pharisees and scribes. Jesus' reply both defends his own honor and demonstrates the importance he places on the relationship he has with his disciples. For Jesus, purity consists of whole, integral relationships.

The charge that Jesus' disciples are not washing their hands before eating is less about hygiene than social purity, the ritual actions that establish social boundaries and hierarchies. Those who steadfastly wash their hands as an act of piety see themselves as surpassing the requirements of the Law, which requires hand washing only in situations involving priestly duties (Exod. 30:19–21), bodily discharges (Lev. 15:11), and as a declaration of innocence (Deut. 21:6).[1] The authority for the scribes' and Pharisees' challenge comes from the "tradition of the elders," the customs passed down from earlier generations but not accepted by everyone as

---

*The Revised Common Lectionary uses this in Year A, The 20th Sunday in Ordinary Time: Matthew 15:(10–20), 21–28.

binding. Jesus' counterquestion appeals to a higher authority, not just the Law, but the fifth of the Ten Commandments, the first that addresses human relationships. Jesus accuses his opponents of placing a higher priority on their traditions than on the Commandments (15:3–6). God wills faithful and responsible relationships, especially within the family. Service of God is rightly embodied in horizontal relationships among humans, not in actions that circumvent human relationships in favor of a direct relationship with God.[2] By excluding others, the Pharisees' pursuit of purity denies the importance of human relationships, thereby "making void the word of God" (15:6). Jesus buttresses his argument with an appeal to Isaiah 29:13. Because the scribes and Pharisees place a higher priority on outward piety ("this people honors me with their lips") than on the integrity of their relationships ("their hearts are far from me"), their worship is in vain and their teachings human rather than divine (15:8–9). Like their local counterparts, the scribes and Pharisees from Jerusalem demonstrate by the fruit of exclusion what tree they fall from (cf. 12:33–35).

The challengers offer no response, so Jesus calls the crowds to him, so that they might not only "hear" but "understand" (cf. 13:13–14) what the Pharisees and scribes will not. Purity is determined not by what comes into or touches a person, but by what comes from a person, that is, by the worthiness of their relationships. Jesus' many healings demonstrate that he is not rendered unclean when touched by others, for his own purity—manifested in healing and restoration—is itself highly contagious. Jesus' disciples note that the Pharisees were offended by (or "scandalized" by, or "stumbled over") what he had said to them. In reply, Jesus identifies the Pharisees as blind guides leading blind people into pits (where it's even harder to see!). Peter's request for clarification indicates that the disciples themselves have not yet "understood" (15:15–16). What comes into the mouth passes through the body, but what comes out of the mouth reveals the heart and core of a person. Jesus links defilement not with physical substances, but with actions that destroy human relationships: evil intentions, murder, adultery, fornication, theft, false witness, and slander—roughly the list of topics covered in the latter half of the Decalogue. Whole, restored relationships are the essence of purity. They fulfill the requirements of God's Law and manifest the integrity of our relationship with God.

Preaching and teaching the Word

The scribes' and Pharisees' piety is no doubt sincere, but also competitive, exclusive, self-serving, and ultimately destructive of relationships and community. Jesus, in contrast, emphasizes the relational character of true piety and devotion. What impact does our piety or spirituality have on the quality and integrity of our relationships? Contemplatives such as Thomas Merton provide excellent models of devotion that nurture relationship with God by attending to matters of human justice, peace, and right relationship. So, too, Jesus' relationship with the heavenly Father is dramatically demonstrated in his mission of restoration and life of solidarity with the marginal and broken people of first-century Galilee. Jesus did not appear to be very "pious" (11:19), but he shows us what kind of piety God desires. Jesus persistently crosses the boundaries of convention and social distinction. He models purity that is contagious. His spirituality transforms relationships and restores community.

Jesus does not disdain the Law or tradition. He is concerned, rather, with defining the criteria by which we evaluate the integrity of our interpretation of the Law and the legitimacy of our traditions. Tradition can be used to demarcate status and to build walls between people. The quest for "law and order" can often serve the interests of those who hold power at the expense of others. When we invest law, tradition, spirituality, or religion with essentialist values—claiming that whatever we understand by them is holy—we are likely replacing God's will with merely "human teachings." The culture wars of our own day spring from such ideals. What traditions do we uphold as inviolate? What forms of piety or spirituality do we consider essential? Do they lead us to whole, restored relationships, or do they exclude? Do they nurture our relationships with the least ones, or confirm our sense of superiority? Do they embody gentleness and humility (11:29) and nurture peace?

Jesus defends his followers and all of those who are burdened and crushed by the weight of social and religious conventions. He gives rest to those who are "weary and carrying heavy loads" (11:28). This is also the calling of those who follow Jesus in discipleship. Many North American Christians—whether "conservative" or "liberal"—believe it their obligation to defend "the tradition" tenaciously, even angrily. The tradition of Jesus is not to defend ideals, but to defend those who are hurting, whoever they might be, and to resist those who attack them, however "righteous" they might be.

Dogged Faith Gets the Crumbs

Matthew 15:21–28*

Exploring the text

Only one person ever gets the better of Jesus in a debate. She is a "Canaanite," the people dispossessed of their land when the Israelites came into the promised land under the leadership of Jesus' namesake, Joshua. A tenacious foe, she relentlessly pesters the disciples and then Jesus until she wins his admiration. She is one of two people—both Gentiles—whose faith Jesus praises (cf. 8:10).

Matthew begins the story by noting that Jesus "withdraws" or "flees" to Gentile territory after his confrontation with the **Pharisees** and **scribes** from Jerusalem. The same verb is used when the magi flee Herod after honoring the baby Jesus (2:12) and when Joseph, Mary, and the baby flee from Herod and his sons (2:13–14, 22). Matthew persistently uses the term in conjunction with the threat of death or strong conflict (4:12; 9:24; 12:15; 14:13; 27:5). Here, as in most instances, flight is followed by healings (cf. 4:23–25; 9:24–25; 12:15; 14:13–14). Tyre and Sidon are known in the prophetic writings (Ezek. 27–28; Isa. 23) for their economic disparities and arrogance. Yet Jesus has already said that these two cities will find more favor on the judgment day than the cities of Galilee, where he has ministered (11:22).

People living in the region of Tyre and Sidon at the time were no longer known as "Canaanites" (Mark 7:26 calls her "a Gentile, a Syrophoenecian"), so Matthew has probably chosen this designation to remind the audience of the ancient Israelite–Canaanite conflicts, dating from Noah's condemnation of the Canaanites, Ham's descendants, to slavery (cf. Gen. 9:20–27).[1] This biblical and historical context makes the woman's appearance before Jesus all the more remarkable. She shouts out to him, "Have mercy on me, Lord, Son of David," echoing the liturgical formula of the psalms (cf., e.g., Pss. 6:3; 9:14; 30:10; 109:26). The title "Son of David" means that she recognizes him as the legitimate heir, the King, Israel's Messiah. In Matthew this title is associated with healing, particularly with the recovery of sight (e.g., 9:27–29; 12:22–23; 20:30–34; 21:14–16). She already "sees" more than Jesus is ready to acknowledge. She names

---

*The Revised Common Lectionary uses this in Year A, The 20th Sunday in Ordinary Time: Matthew 15:(10–20), 21–28.

her daughter's affliction as a demonic possession, perhaps a symptom of imperial control (see on 8:28–33; 12:22–32). The story thus reminds us of Israel's own imperial reality, from which Jesus himself is now fleeing. Will this King behave differently than his predecessors?

Healing stories often contain obstacles that must be overcome by the supplicants or the healers. In this case, Jesus himself is the main obstacle. First he ignores her, but her continued shouting annoys the disciples, so he explains his position: "I was sent only to the lost sheep of the house of Israel" (15:24; cf. 10:5–6). The doctor is not taking new clients at this time. She fits neither his mission objective, restoring Israel, nor the demographic profile of his constituency. She ignores this rationale, falls before him, and pleads: "Lord, help me." He explains again the exclusive nature of his mission. The bread, a symbol of God's provision for God's people (cf. 14:13–21; 15:32–39), is for the children, not the dogs. The word "dogs" is sometimes used to refer to Gentiles, but here in its diminutive form it carries the particular connotation of household pets. Jesus has ignored her, rebuffed her, and now insulted her. Still she persists. She embraces the insult–implicitly acknowledging her people's servile relationship to Israel–and turns it to her advantage: "Yes, Lord, I am a dog, so treat me like one. Give me the crumbs." With this Jesus is beaten. He commends her great faith. The healing takes place at that very moment.

Preaching and teaching the Word

We may be offended by Jesus' callousness as he and his disciples repeatedly rebuff the Canaanite woman's entreaties. Yet Jesus has always been clear about the nature and focus of his mission (cf. 10:5–6). Matthew reminds us here that God is first of all faithful to the promises made to Israel, which in turn is to bear witness to the nations of God's faithfulness and redemptive power. At the end of the Gospel, when Jesus' death and resurrection have brought the divine plan for Israel's redemption to fruition, Jesus will extend the disciples' mission to all the nations (28:16–20). But not yet. Here Jesus will not be swayed–at least not easily–from his appointed calling. Jesus' response to the woman thus tells us more about the nature of his mission and his faithfulness to it than about his feelings toward women or Gentiles. Is the church actively attentive particularly to the voices–sometimes annoying–of those who are calling from the margins? Where do we need to locate ourselves so that we can hear their voices and see more clearly what they see?

From the woman's perspective, this is a story about walls, obstacles, persistence, ingenuity, and faith. The Gospels consistently associate strong demonstrations of faith with boundary crossings. In this story the woman scales the walls of race and gender, but she also must overcome

Jesus' own tenacious adherence to his mission. Three times Jesus seeks to turn her away, but she never quits. And while Matthew preserves the sense that Jesus remains undeterred from his calling, the story also suggests that she converts him. Faith not only brings healing, it transforms relationships. The woman's faith stands in sharp contrast to the dogged defense of the status quo, with all its walls and hierarchies, of the Pharisees and scribes (cf. 15:1–20). The church conducts its mission at the borders, wherever and whatever they might be. The church should expect to be transformed by the encounter.

The woman's tenacity and cunning are impressive. She models the kind of resilience and creativity necessary for social transformation and justice. She will turn whatever Jesus gives her, even insults, to her advantage, snatching a victory from apparent defeat. In this way she embodies the gospel story itself: God turns the world's rebelliousness, insults, and violence–even the death of God's Son–toward the realization of redemption. The woman defeats Jesus by means of his own insult. God defeats the powers of violence and death by means of the crucifixion itself.

Signs of the Time

Matthew 15:29–16:12

Since the moment that John the Baptist challenged Jesus to demonstrate whether he was really the "one coming" (11:2–6), Jesus has been providing various signs, both word and deed, for those with ears to hear and eyes to see, signs that reveal who he is and where his power comes from. The responses have been mixed. The crowds recognize the possibility that God's power is at work in Jesus, but they do not understand who he really is. The religious elites resist and reject him. The disciples have the potential to "understand" (cf. 13:11–15), but they struggle to keep their eyes and ears open (cf. 13:16–17) and their grasp is tenuous. Matthew's narrative will soon make a major turn. Peter will confess that Jesus is the **Messiah**, the **Son of God** (16:16), and Jesus will begin preparing his disciples more earnestly for what is coming in Jerusalem (16:21–28).

The four brief episodes in this unit prepare Matthew's audience for this transition by repeating and developing earlier material. Modern audiences accustomed to reading the Gospel on a page wonder why Matthew provides two very similar feeding stories (14:15–21//15:32–39) or two nearly identical accounts of Pharisees asking for a sign (12:38–42//16:1–4). In cultures oriented toward oral performance, however, repetition underlines the importance of material, solidifies key points, and prepares for transitions.

Exploring the texts

JESUS HEALS MANY ON THE MOUNTAIN (15:29–31)

Matthew again uses a summary of Jesus' healing ministry as a narrative transition (cf. 4:23–25; 9:35–38). Jesus, who has been temporarily sidetracked from his mission to the lost sheep of the house of Israel (15:24), now passes from the region of Tyre and Sidon (15:21) back along the Sea of Galilee to an unnamed mountain (15:29), where he sits down, as if to teach (cf. 5:1–2). It is not students who come to him, however, but "great crowds" bringing Israel's lame, maimed, blind, and mute for healing. Each of these conditions represents not only physical disorders that afflict individuals, but Israel's own maladies. These are the symptoms of oppression, exploitation, and rebellion against God. Whereas the **Pharisees** and **scribes** have challenged Jesus' authority and its source (12:1–14, 22–37; 15:1–9), the crowds rightly "see" the power of "the God of Israel" at work (15:31).

FOOD IN THE WILDERNESS AGAIN (15:32–39; cf. 14:15–21)

Matthew associates Jesus' power with compassion. In the first feeding story, the disciples noted the hunger of the crowds and suggested that Jesus send them away to buy food for themselves (14:15). In this instance, it is Jesus who is aware that the crowds are growing hungry, so hungry that if he were to send them away to get food for themselves they might faint on the way (15:32). The temporal note that the crowds have been with Jesus for three days, the same length of time Jesus will be in the tomb (cf. 16:21), helps connect this story of messianic feeding with God's vindication of the Messiah. God will not allow the righteous, either the Messiah or the people on the mountain who recognize God's power (15:31), to suffer more than three days (cf. Hos. 6:2). God's power will again be evident in the provision of food.

Jesus calls his disciples into service to provide food for the crowds (15:32), as he had also done in the first feeding story (14:16). Will they pass the test this time? No. They wonder where they can find enough food in the "wilderness" (Matthew intentionally juxtaposes mountain and wilderness settings in 15:29 and 33). The disciples have forgotten not only that God fed Israel in the wilderness (Exod. 16), but that Jesus himself, with their help, has just fed a crowd even larger than this one. Perhaps they think the prior feeding was a singular event: it won't happen again this time. But God's power is transforming "this **time**." The disciples do not yet clearly understand that they are living in messianic time. Jesus is indeed the "one coming" (11:2–3). Whatever provisions the disciples have with them will be enough. Again Jesus takes loaves and fish, gives thanks, breaks bread, and gives them to the disciples to distribute (15:36//14:19). Again there is an abundance left over (15:37//14:20). Again Jesus' words and actions carry a distinctly eucharistic tone. Jesus, his disciples, and the crowds are preparing for the messianic banquet. It is already beginning.

THE SIGN OF JONAH AGAIN (16:1–4; cf. 12:38–42)

Jesus leaves the crowds he has healed and fed, gets into a boat, and goes to the region of Magadan, which is now difficult to locate with certainty. His disciples have apparently not traveled with him (cf. 16:5). The Pharisees, this time with **Sadducees** in tow, again come seeking a heavenly sign. The effect of Matthew's placement of this episode after the stories of healing and feeding is almost comedic. A smashing great party has been going on in the mountains (15:29) and the wilderness (15:33), but the religious leaders have missed it. Would they have understood things differently had they witnessed the healings or the miraculous supply of food? Not likely, for the Pharisees and Sadducees have come, in fact, not to discern signs of God's power, but as adversaries, to "test" Jesus (cf. 4:1; 19:3; 22:18; 22:35).

Jesus focuses on their capacity to make sense of any signs they might observe. The sayings in 16:2–3b are not found in some of the best early manuscripts, but they nonetheless cohere with Jesus' reply. The familiar saying, "red sky at night, sailors delight; red sky at morning, sailors take warning," was apparently a piece of common wisdom even in Jesus' day. The Pharisees and Sadducees can read "heavenly signs" well enough to predict the weather, but are unable to read the heavenly signs of God's presence and power. Why? What are they looking for? Perhaps they are looking in the wrong places, for divine power coming from the sky rather than on the mountain or in the wilderness. The title "an evil and adulterous generation" (16:4), which has become Jesus' stock moniker for them (cf. 11:16–19; 12:39–42; 12:45; 17:17), identifies their blindness as a symptom of darkened hearts. They have become "adulterers" who are unable to connect religious insight and practice with the evidence of God's will and power.

Why does Jesus not just supply a dramatic, convincing sign? First, Jesus acts only in response to God's will, in compassion and mercy, not in response to the demands of blind leaders. Second, a dramatic sign would only further harden their hearts. So, the only sign he will supply is a riddle they have already heard, the sign of Jonah (16:4; 12:39–41). They do not understand this sign-riddle, but they will become participants in it; some of them have already begun making plans to destroy him (12:14; cf. 26:3–4). Even when they succeed in killing him, they will misunderstand the meaning and consequences of the sign that is Jesus' death and resurrection.

BREAD OF HEAVEN AND THE PHARISEES' LEAVEN (16:5–12)

The disciples now arrive from the other side of the sea. They are still thinking about the miraculous supply of bread, but with regret, because, although there were seven baskets of bread left over, they have forgotten to bring any of it with them. When Jesus, fresh from his conflict with the religious elites, warns them of the "leaven" (the dough set aside to permeate the next batch) of the Pharisees and Sadducees, the disciples immediately presume that he must be talking about the bread they left behind. Because they are forgetful and hungry, they misconstrue what Jesus is talking about. While Matthew intends us to take Jesus' warnings in this story seriously, he is also providing some comic relief, just before Peter's confession that Jesus is the Messiah and Jesus' predictions of his suffering and death (16:13–28).

As Jesus perceives their misunderstanding, he chides them: "Why are you mumbling to each other about the bread, little-faiths?" (16:8; cf. 6:30; 8:26; 14:31). Bread is not a problem! Remember how many thousands were fed by the five loaves (14:17, 19), and the seven loaves (15:34, 36), and how many baskets of leftovers you gathered? The troubling element in this episode is that the disciples are indeed still worrying about bread, when it should be clear to them by now that in the messianic time and in the presence of the Messiah himself, God will supply what they need. It's the leaven of the Pharisees and Sadducees they should be worrying about.

What then is this "leaven," and how might it permeate and corrupt the whole? Matthew identifies it as their "teaching" (16:12), without specifying its precise content. Pharisees and Sadducees held many positions contrary to one another, which makes it hard to identify any particular doctrines as leaven. If the leaven consisted of particular teaching, moreover, it would have been simple for Jesus, or Matthew, to identify the problematic teachings for us. Jesus may have in mind the elites' tendency to twist the Law to their own ends. Jesus also identifies the Pharisees' failure to align their actions with the intent of God's will as "adultery" (16:4; cf. 12:33–37; 23:3–7). What Jesus talks most about is "hypocrisy" (15:7; cf. 23:1–36). Perhaps the leaven, then, consists of those forces that impede or rupture the link between conviction and action, between sight and understanding (cf. 13:10–17). The Pharisees assert that Jesus' healings and exorcisms are signs of the power of Beelzebul (9:34; 12:24) rather than of God. In any case, Jesus does not tell his disciples to avoid the Pharisees and Sadducees themselves, as if the threat could be contained by quarantine, but to avoid the leaven that now controls his adversaries and renders their teachings both infectious and destructive of sight, hearing, and understanding. How then might the disciples recognize such leaven for what it really is? Jesus has already told them: study the fruit that falls from the tree (12:33–35).

The story names two dangers for the disciples: first, they may not realize what time it is and how the world is being transformed, and second, they may be susceptible to misidentifications of the nature of God's power and to teaching divorced from faithful practice. Matthew ends the narrative, however, with the assurance that the disciples finally do "understand" (16:12), thus setting the stage for Peter's confession.

Preaching and teaching the Word

These four brief stories confirm the major themes of chapters 11–16: God's power generates division, misunderstanding, and hostility. We should expect no different today. First-century Pharisees are not the only ones guilty of misunderstanding, blindness, and hostility. These stories are warnings to people of any day and any religion, including Christianity, and especially to those who consider themselves to be the righteous and leaders, who deny that God's power is at work among the lost and broken. Religious people, especially, are susceptible to misreading the signs, forcing God into boxes that will not fit, or denying God's power for the sake of our own.

What if the Messiah came, but we were all looking the wrong way? We are told in these stories to look in the wilderness and the mountains, among the maimed, the blind, the lame, the mute, and the hungry. Cities may also be "wilderness" places, but their tall buildings, stadiums, temples, and other human symbol systems often make it harder for people to discern the work of God. Like the Jerusalem elites, modern

Christians may look for dramatic signs of God's coming in the heavens, rather than in the wildernesses all around us. Will Christ's coming be different in kind from what it was in the ministry of Jesus? Where then should we be looking?

We live in a time filled with division, deceit, and death. These stories remind Jesus' disciples that, despite their stubborn perceptions to the contrary, they are in the time when God's Messiah comes in power—the time of resurrection, redemption, and reconciliation. The **church**'s calling entails not only discerning the times rightly, but living in them accordingly. We should regard with suspicion any supposed signs of divine power that do not require our repentance and transformation. We conform our lives to the sign of Jonah, the cross, which makes all of us missionaries. God's mission reveals light in the darkness, feeds the hungry, gives sight to the blind, and opens the mouths of the mute to sing God's praises. Disciples are expected to share the gifts of healing, food, sight, and understanding God has given us.

The Blessed Confession

Matthew 16:13–20*

Exploring the text

The disciples have had the secrets of the kingdom revealed to them (13:10–17) and they have repeatedly witnessed God's power at work in Jesus, but they continue to demonstrate that their understanding is incomplete and their faith immature (cf., e.g., 15:33; 16:8–12). Jesus' question about who "people" say he is forms a bookend with John the Baptizer's question in 11:2 about whether Jesus is "the one coming." Peter's answer marks a definitive turning point in Matthew's Gospel, alongside Jesus' announcement of his impending death and resurrection in Jerusalem (16:21–28). But few passages in Matthew pose more interpretive puzzles than this account. What does Peter's confession mean? Why does Jesus rename Peter? In what sense is Peter the "rock" upon which Jesus will

*The Revised Common Lectionary uses this in Year A, The 21st Sunday in Ordinary Time.

build his congregation? What are the keys given to Peter, and what is the power to bind and loose?

Matthew sets this story, significantly, in the region of Caesarea Philippi, where Herod the Great built a temple in honor of Caesar Augustus. Herod's son Philip later enlarged the city and renamed it Caesarea. Josephus reports that after the fall of Jerusalem in 70 CE, Jewish prisoners were thrown to the beasts in Caesarea Philippi (Josephus, *Jewish War*, 7:2:1 § 23–24).[1] The setting of this story thus provides a pointed reminder of the conflict between God and the powers of this world. As they draw near to Caesarea Philippi, Jesus asks the disciples, "Who do people say the Son of Man is?" The disciples' list includes prominent prophetic figures from Israel's history, including John the Baptizer, Elijah, and Jeremiah. To be sure, Jesus is a prophet. Even Herod Antipas thought Jesus might be John the Baptizer "redivivus" (14:2). When Jesus asks the disciples for their own perspective, Peter answers on their behalf: "You are the **Messiah**, the **Son of the living God**." Peter names Jesus as both the fulfillment of Israel's hope for a deliverer and the one who bears a unique and intimate relationship with God, God's very Son. This is a bold confession, especially in the shadow of Caesarea Philippi.

Jesus' beatitude, "Blessed are you, Simon son of Jonah!" (cf. 11:6; 5:3–11; on "Jonah," cf. 12:39; 16:4), links this story with his earlier blessing of those who do not "stumble" over him (11:6). Jesus identifies Peter's confession as a revelation from his Father in heaven (16:17; cf. 11:25–27; 13:11; 13:16–17). Peter's understanding is not something that could be accomplished by "flesh and blood" (e.g., by the crowds or the **Pharisees** and **scribes**, cf. 13:11–15), although his attention and obedience as he has followed Jesus has also contributed to his understanding. But as the next story will make clear (16:21–23), Peter's understanding is not yet complete, and won't be until he follows Jesus through his death and resurrection.

In the Old Testament, both Abram and Jacob received new names, and both were associated with the birth of a new people (Gen. 17; 32:22–32).[2] Peter now gets his name (cf. 4:18; 10:2). It is a play on the words for a round stone (*petros*) and a rock (*petra*). Peter himself, not just his confession, is the round stone that will serve as the foundation stone for the building that is Jesus' assembly. Matthew uses the word "**church**" (Gk.: *ekklēsia* = Heb.: *qahal*) here for the first time. In later usage, of course, *ekklēsia* becomes a primary designation for the community of disciples. But it was already used in the Greek Old Testament, especially to designate the Sinai "congregation of Israel" as it wandered in the wilderness after departing slavery in Egypt. Jesus' "church" is thus a "new exodus" from the powers of slavery at work in places like Caesarea Philippi,[3] and a seed for the restoration—not the replacement—of Israel.

The "gates of Hades" (16:18c) designates especially the powers of death. Because death is the chief power in Satan's arsenal, it is also the focus of Jesus' (and the church's) mission to liberate the creation from Satan's grip and reclaim it under the rule of God. For all its apparent power, death is not stronger than the assembly of those who follow Jesus. Peter's possession of the "keys of the **kingdom of heaven**" (16:19) implies the exercise of both authority and responsibility, more like a household servant who has the keys for all the master's rooms and buildings. Peter's responsibility may entail keeping the gates closed to the powers of death so that those who seek the living God may come in. "Binding" and "loosing" also suggest that Peter, and the church after him, bears a form of delegated authority and responsibility. The forces that Peter binds or looses on earth are in turn bound or loosed in heaven. It is often supposed that this authority pertains especially to establishing right interpretations of the Law, i.e., interpretations different from those of the Pharisees, who "shut people out of the kingdom of heaven" (23:13). But this would effectively turn Peter into a scribe. The Pharisees' interpretation of the Law, moreover, is only one of the forces that keep people from the kingdom of heaven. Jesus does not call Peter and the church merely to be faithful interpreters, but to continue to embody God's presence and power in healing, forgiveness, restoration, and the defeat of death, as Jesus himself frees people from possession and blindness.

Preaching and teaching the Word

This story draws together an array of christological strands that Matthew has developed in the preceding narratives. Jesus is here the **Son of Humanity**, both a child of this world and the one who will come finally as judge of the nations. He is also a **prophet** who speaks truth to power, in the mold of Elijah, Jeremiah, and John the Baptist. He is God's chosen servant, the **Messiah** sent by God to gather, redeem, and restore Israel, and to bring **salvation** to his people (1:21). Finally, he is the **Son of the living God**, the one, true God who has created and sustains all that lives. Jesus shows us who this God really is and what God desires in order that we too might live. Jesus is all that these titles say he is and still more. Is Jesus still the object of our wonder, as he was for the early Christians? Does he continue to defy our categories and definitions? Do our confessions of him still call into question all other allegiances and commitments?

This is a story about contesting the powers of this world. In the border region of an imperial stronghold, Jesus challenges his disciples to discern and name who he really is. Can they see beyond the monuments to Caesar and the ubiquitous reminders of the power of Herod the Great and his sons? Can they see not only the Messiah but the Son who reveals the Father? This confession is most meaningful and powerful when it is delivered in the face of the powers of this world, as, for example, the "confessing church" did, while so many other churches in Nazi Germany bound their proclamation to the interests of the powerful. Can we still speak Peter's confession today in the presence of the world's power? What powers does it contest?

Peter's confession relocates the disciples from the border regions of human empires to a space between earth and heaven itself, where the church proclaims the defeat of death and the powers that enslave humankind and the creation. With the confession that Jesus is both Messiah and Son of the living God comes discernment of the nature of the conflicts in which we are involved and the power to withstand even the forces of Hades. The church's calling thus entails locating ourselves at the border regions between life and death, between blindness and understanding, to make sure that the doors of the empire of heaven remain open to those who are burdened and enslaved (cf. 11:28–30), but shut to all that would distract, hinder, or restrain those who seek entry (cf. 13:3–9, 18–23).

This story has engendered much speculation and dispute about the exercise of power in and over the church. Is Peter the first pope? Does the church, whether Catholic or Protestant or Orthodox, always bear the right interpretation of the Law or of doctrine? Does the church have the authority to determine who is "in" and who is "out"? Is it our calling, as many Protestant churches have seemed to think, to issue judgments that determine what is right or wrong in any given dispute? Or does our confession that Jesus is Messiah and Son of the living God call us to bear witness to the One who sets the captives free, brings sight to the blind, humbles the rulers of this world, and defeats even death?

Gaining Life by Losing It

Matthew 16:21–28*

Exploring the text

Peter's confession (16:13–20) marks the beginning of the end of Jesus' campaign in Galilee. The phrase "from that **time** on . . ." (16:21; cf. 4:17) signals a moment of transition in Jesus' ministry. The king who has twice been forced to flee from his rightful kingdom in Judea (2:13–15; 2:21–23) now sets his sights on "coronation" in Jerusalem. His crown will consist of thorns (27:29) and his exaltation will coincide with his being lifted up on a cross. Jesus knows what is coming and now begins preparing his disciples. They have received and now confessed the "mystery of the kingdom" (cf. 13:11), but not yet plumbed its depths. He will lead them to the "gates of Hades" (16:18), where death stands ready to contest God's power.

Jesus has just renamed Peter as the foundation stone for the renewed gathering of the congregation of Israel. Now the foundation stone himself stumbles over Jesus' announcement that the **Messiah** will suffer and die and be raised on the third day in Jerusalem. Peter seems not to understand, if he has even heard, the last of part of this prediction. He cannot surmount the news that the Christ must endure suffering and death at the hands of the religious authorities. Confronted with the specter of the "gates of Hades," Peter, the keeper of the keys to God's kingdom, is blinded by fear and despair,[1] which leads in turn to bluster and a "rebuke" of Jesus. Peter's expression, "God forbid it, Lord!" (16:22) may more literally mean "May God be gracious." Surely a gracious God would not permit the suffering and death of the Messiah! Peter voices the common human conviction that divine powers, especially the Jewish messiah, do not endure suffering and death as humans do. At the gates of Hades, Peter confronts the deep mystery and scandal (stumbling stone) of the **gospel**. God's grace and power are revealed in suffering with and for us. God does not flee death nor rescue us from it, but endures it, conquers it, and renders its power void. The gospel promises not immortality, but life after death.

When Satan tested Jesus by inviting him to avoid suffering and death, Satan depicted death as a "stone" upon which Jesus might strike his foot

*The Revised Common Lectionary uses this in Year A, The 22nd Sunday in Ordinary Time.

(4:5–7, esp. 4:6). Jesus now hears in Peter's rebuke the voice of Satan once again. Peter has exchanged the revelation of God for merely human perception and values. Fear, self-interest, and perhaps even human devotion and love[2] choke the seed of understanding so recently sprung to life (cf. 13:20–22). As Peter stumbles, he becomes the stumbling stone that Satan employs to try to turn Jesus from his course. So Jesus turns to Peter and repeats the command he had issued to Satan at the end of the temptations (4:10): "Get behind me, Satan."

What does it mean to follow the Messiah, who must go to Jerusalem to suffer and die? Jesus is concerned less with his own fate than with preparing the disciples to bear witness to God's work through him. The sayings in 16:24–28 mingle images of loss with gain, demand with promise, and judgment with hope. Jesus draws from his earlier instructions to the disciples before their mission to the cities of Israel (16:24–25//10:38–39) and anticipates his final instructions to them (16:27// 24:30–31; cf. 25:31). Following Jesus means denying self-interest, taking up the cross, and embracing death as Jesus himself will. "The cross" was a symbol of Roman rule, a form of execution reserved for slaves and rebels against imperial authority. It was meant to bring extreme pain and suffering, shame and humiliation, and to assert Rome's power over life itself. "Taking up the cross" implies a call to martyrdom, as well as association with the most despised and powerless people. But losing life for Jesus' sake is, ironically, the only way to "save life." Satan had offered Jesus the power to rule the whole world in exchange for Jesus' worship (4:9–10). But what advantage would there be in gaining the whole world if it cost Jesus his life (16:26)? Now Jesus will die in order to gain life for others. One cannot preserve one's own life, nor gain sufficient wealth to redeem one's life (cf. Ps. 49:6–9). The only way to life is the cross. Taking up the cross runs contrary to all our human inclinations, but it is utterly consistent with the way God vanquishes the power of death.

For the first time, Jesus speaks of the **Son of Humanity** as the one who reveals God's glory and executes **judgment** at the end-time (16:27; cf. Dan. 7:13–14). The image of judgment here is meant to reassure the disciples, for judgment means the vindication of those who follow in Christ's way. Jesus' final saying, "Some of those standing here will not taste death before they see the Son of Humanity coming in his kingdom," is also meant as reassurance, but has generated mostly controversy. To what does the coming of the Son of Humanity in his kingdom refer? Is Jesus speaking of his transfiguration, the next story in the Gospel, when he is revealed gloriously to Peter, James, and John (17:1–8), or of his crucifixion and resurrection, when he is enthroned with power (cf. 28:18)?

Or does he refer, as many assume, to his final return as judge of the world (cf. 25:31)? Each of these solutions is at least partially right. The Son of Man comes in more than one way and is present even where two or three are gathered in his name (18:20). As with many other provocative but intentionally ambiguous statements in the Gospel, Matthew leaves the audience, including the disciples, to work out the riddle by following in his way.

Preaching and teaching the Word

Why is it necessary for God's chosen one to go the way of the cross? In part, Jesus' suffering and death is the inevitable outcome of the increasing hostility directed against him by the religious authorities. But human resistance to God's way is only part of the answer. Humans are not the primary drivers of Jesus' death. God is. Jesus' suffering and death at the hands of the **religious leaders** and on a Roman cross are necessary in order for God to shatter the power of death and free the creation from the grip of human empires, violence, and terror. The death of Jesus brings judgment on the worlds that humans construct in the shadow of death. The empires of this world offer the promise of **salvation** in many differing forms: security, pleasure, self-fulfillment, health, material possessions, constant distraction and isolation from the world around us. But this "salvation" is illusory. To "gain the world" this way requires, in fact, the loss of all life. In our denial that the living God is the source of all life, we fall prey to alienation, exploitation, violence, and the destruction of community and creation. We end up existing—not living—at odds with the world God created for us to live in. There is no solution to this but the conquest of death itself.

The cross of Jesus Christ bears ultimate witness to who God is—neither the god of the Jewish leaders demanding sacrifice nor the god of Caesar demanding order. The Romans see the cross as a public ritual that restores order. The religious leaders trust that the cross will remove a threat. But the cross turns out to be the perfect expression of God's own power to save and redeem. It is necessary for Jesus to suffer and die at human hands in order to demonstrate the depth of God's forgiveness, mercy, and love.

The suffering and martyrdom of those who follow in Jesus' way also bear witness to God's true identity and power. Jesus calls his disciples to suffering and death because those who "lose their life for my sake" (16:25) gain true life in God's presence, already in this life, where Jesus promises to be with us, and in the life to come. "For my sake" means that taking up the cross and following Jesus is the living embodiment of Peter's confession that Jesus of Nazareth is the Messiah and Son of the living

God (16:16). Martyrdom thus witnesses (martyr and witness are the same Greek word) to a truth that is bigger than oneself.[3] Martyrdom is very hard to understand or embrace for people who live in a culture where the self is the biggest truth, or the only truth, they can imagine. Not many of us in North American culture will feel called to suffer and die for the sake of Jesus Christ, in large part because our experience of Christian faith has become so deeply commingled with and compromised by the individualistic perspectives and self-serving values of the larger society. Where the pursuit of "personal salvation" replaces the community of discipleship, the call to deny self, take up the cross, and lose one's life for Jesus' sake will seem, at best, little more than an unpleasant means to an ultimately self-serving end, or perhaps no more than an abstract ideal. The question for disciples should never be "What will earn me salvation?" but "What bears faithful witness to God's power in the cross?"

This same question pertains to the life of the **church**. The confession that Jesus is the Christ gives rise in turn to communal practices shaped around and in the light of the cross. Confession without practice is empty, as practice without confession is aimless. The church lives toward the coming **empire of heaven** by joining confession and discipleship as an integral whole centered on Jesus the Christ. But neither the confession of Christ nor losing life for the sake of Christ can long be maintained by individuals alone. For this reason, Jesus calls his disciples into an organic community that bears witness in its cruciform life together. Whatever the church does—worship, education, stewardship, evangelism, social justice— must bear witness to the power of the cross or it will soon become self-serving banality. What story does our life together tell? What convictions do we embody as a people? Is the power of the cross the distinguishing mark of our communal life?

We are not required to be perfect disciples. Jesus' own disciples have the right confession, but not yet the right understanding. They are on the way, but still very much in the process of formation, and will be, through the experience of Jesus' death and resurrection and finally their own commissioning (28:16–20). None who have lived a long life deeply engaged in the Christian way will say that they fully understood what the call to discipleship meant when they first made their confession of faith. While the demands of discipleship are high and our practices timid and faltering, the Son of Humanity we meet as judge comes to us as the One who forgives and redeems. Discipleship is lived in the tension between demand and reality, judgment and forgiveness, heaven and earth.

The Transfiguration

Matthew 17:1–13*

Exploring the text

The way of suffering and glory—the way of the cross—lies before Jesus and his disciples. Jesus has just announced that suffering and death await him at the hands of Jerusalem's authorities, but he has also held forth the promise of resurrection (16:21), even the hope that some of those standing with him will not taste death before they see the **Son of Humanity** coming in glory (16:28). The transfiguration is not the only, but is the most immediate fulfillment of this promise. True to its **apocalyptic** nature, Jesus' transfiguration is enigmatic, symbolically dense, and resists singular interpretations. It both describes a transcendent glory and evokes transcending vision. The story leads Matthew's hearers into their own vision of Jesus' transcendent glory, a glory mediated through Jesus' suffering and death. Jesus the **Son of God** and Son of Humanity who manifests God's power will also submit his life to the authority of humans.

The story works by means of rich, multivalent associations with Old Testament passages, with apocalyptic traditions, and with other passages in Matthew, both recalling prior events and foreshadowing what is to come. The temporal notation "six days later" (17:1), the references to the mountain, the clouds, the shining face, the voice of God, and the fear of those who look on establish strong links between this story and the account of Moses receiving the Ten Commandments from God on Mount Sinai (cf. Exod. 24:16; 24:12; 24:15–18; 34:3; 34:5; 34:29–35). "Six days" may also carry **eschatological** significance, signifying the **time** just short of the seventh day, the end of the present age. In Matthew 27:45, the sixth hour coincides with the darkness that falls over all the land before Jesus dies on the cross. But at the transfiguration, it is light that is most prominent: Jesus' face shines like the sun (17:2; cf. 13:43), and his clothes become dazzling white (cf. Dan. 7:9; Rev. 3:5; 3:18; 4:4; 6:11; 7:9; 7:13). Images of dazzling light are common, especially in apocalyptic theophanies, and lend the scene an air of eschatological wonder.

Mountain settings carry a resonance of divine presence and power in Matthew (5:1; 14:23; 15:29–38; 28:16–20), but also hark back to the

---

*The Revised Common Lectionary uses this in Year A, The Transfiguration of the Lord: Matthew 17:1–9.

setting of the devil's invitation to Jesus to receive "all the empires of the world" in exchange for worshiping him (4:8–9). Rather than accept the devil's invitation to receive worldly power immediately, Jesus has obediently pursued his vocation as God's Son and now knows that the fulfillment of his mission leads through Jerusalem to the cross. "This is my Son, the Beloved one, with whom I am pleased" (17:5) echoes precisely God's words at Jesus' baptism (3:17), another apocalyptic moment. Now, however, God adds the command "Hear him!" which underlines especially what Jesus has just taught his disciples about the necessity of suffering and the way of the cross.

Jesus has taken with him to the mountain Peter, James, and John. These same three disciples will again be featured in Matthew's account of Jesus' preparation in Gethsemane for suffering and death. The disciples bring a decidedly human element to their role as witnesses of the transfiguration. Peter wants to build "huts" for Jesus, Moses, and Elijah. His offer seems like a foreign object in the scene; perhaps it is Peter's way of making his presence known or of seeming useful. God's voice simply overwhelms Peter's machinations. The disciples "fall on their faces," terrified (17:6). In Gethsemane, it will be Jesus himself who "falls to the ground" in prayer as he contemplates the suffering he is about to endure, while these same disciples fall asleep (26:39–40). The zenith the three disciples experience at the transfiguration thus stands as a foil for the nadir they will embody in Gethsemane. Their "great fear" in response to the divine voice anticipates yet another apocalyptic moment in the Gospel, when the centurion and his companions who will witness the events that coincide with the death of Jesus will also express "great fear," but nonetheless proclaim that "Truly, this was the Son of God!" (27:54). As soon as the disciples fall on their faces, Jesus comes to reassure them. Jesus' touch, his commandment, and his reassurance all recall scenes of healing or divine presence elsewhere in the Gospel (e.g., 8:3; 8:15; 9:6; 9:19; 14:27; 20:34). When they open their eyes, the disciples see only Jesus.

Why are Moses and Elijah with Jesus in this scene (17:3)? At the very least, their presence confirms Jesus' authority, as well as his faithfulness to the people and traditions of Israel. Possibly they signify the law and prophets, but they are also heavenly figures, representatives of God's will and authority. Both of them had mountaintop encounters with God, both struggled with human rulers, and both experienced rejection by humans (Exod. 34; 1 Kgs. 19). Their presence suggests typological associations with liberation from oppression. Jewish tradition also claimed that neither Moses nor Elijah experienced death. Jesus, of course, will face—and overwhelm—death.

Jesus commands the disciples to tell no one about the "vision" until after the Son of Humanity has been raised from the dead (17:9). The term "vision" underscores the apocalyptic (revelatory) character of the transfiguration. The transfiguration is no mere apparition, however, but a divinely granted revelation that, in contrast to the disciples' "everyday" perception of Jesus, pulls back the veil to make known the truth about Jesus as God sees him. The disciples are granted a pre-passion and -resurrection glimpse of the authority and glory of the Son of Humanity and Son of God. They are witnesses before the fact of the "Son of Humanity coming in his kingdom" (16:28), and thus must be warned not to speak of this reality until it comes to fruition. The disciples' question—"Why do the scribes say that Elijah must come first?" (13:10)—arises both from Elijah's presence in the transfiguration and from the sense, from Jesus' apocalypse in power and glory, that the manifestation of the Son of Humanity in his empire is already under way. Jesus affirms the scribes' teaching that Elijah will return for a second career of restoration before the coming of the Son of Humanity. He connects the figure of Elijah with one who has already come, not been recognized, and suffered at the hands of humans—John the Baptizer—as the disciples later infer (17:13). John's suffering and death inaugurate the eschatological *kairos* (time) and foreshadow the fate of the Son of Humanity (17:12). Matthew's story winds suffering and death inextricably with divine power, presence, and glory.

Preaching and teaching the Word

In the Eastern Church, the transfiguration is a central image for the way of discipleship, the hope-filled journey of the Christian community up the mountain to witness the revelation of Christ's true glory and back down the mountain to give witness to this glory amidst and through suffering and death for the sake of a lost world. Participation in this transfiguring journey means incorporation into the Body of the crucified and resurrected One. We dare not explain the transfiguration, but rather invite God's people continually to make the journey up the mountain to see the glorified Christ, then back down to the world, to join the suffering and crucified One in his mission.

From the paradoxical image of the suffering Son of Humanity, who is also the glorified, apocalyptic Lord, the authority and moral imperatives of the gospel arise, for the cross of Jesus Christ reveals both the nature of divine power and the nature of discipleship. It is from the confession that the crucified Jesus is indeed the resurrected Lord that all Christian ethics and all truly Christian community spring. Forgiveness, the love of enemies, the renunciation of status and wealth and privilege, hospitality without expectation of return, and practices of peacemaking and justice all have their roots in God's confirmation of the "way of the cross," which Jesus' transfiguration prefigures.

The transfiguration story combines a christological focus on the divine nature and glory of Jesus the Christ with the claim that the Son of Humanity must go on his way toward Jerusalem to suffer and die. Throughout the literature of the New Testament, including Matthew's Gospel, these two facets of Jesus' way are inseparable. They are also inseparable in the life of discipleship, which is discerned and embodied in the tensions between divine power and human suffering, in the constant movement back and forth between life in the presence of the heavenly, glorified Lord and the suffering, dying Son of Humanity. The Christian life is not lived solely in quest of the mountaintop, but in the movement from vision to witness, from glory to suffering, suffering to vision, and back again.

Moving Mountains in a Faithless and Perverse Generation

Matthew 17:14–23

Exploring the text

The transfiguration reveals Jesus' divine power. Now the story of a troubled child and his father reveals the disciples' powerlessness. While Mark's account of this episode focuses on the faith of the epileptic's father, Matthew keeps the spotlight on the disciples, emphasizing their "little faith" (17:20) and the resulting powerlessness to heal. Repeated references in the Greek to their powerlessness or inability (17:16, 19, 20) underline the main problem.

The man who begs Jesus to heal his son seems to have more faith than the disciples. He falls on his knees before Jesus, as if in prayer, hails Jesus as "Lord," and appeals for mercy. His "moonstruck" son falls often into fire or water. Many translations describe the disorder as epilepsy, but Matthew suggests that its roots lie in demonic possession (17:18). Regardless of the diagnosis, yet again Jesus meets and vanquishes the powers arrayed against God, which seek to destroy humankind. As the man finishes describing his son's symptoms, he also names the disciples' inability to heal the child. Jesus' harsh rebuke (17:17) echoes both Moses' complaint about the people of Israel (Deut. 32:5) and God's assessment of them: "a perverse generation, children in whom there is no faithfulness" (Deut. 32:20; cf. Matt. 17:20). "This generation" refers not only to those living at the moment, but to all those who throughout Israel's history–and all of human history–have turned away from God's glory and proven themselves faithless (cf. 11:16; 12:39–42; 16:4; and 23:36). The disciples demonstrate, as they will again after Jesus' arrest in Jerusalem, that they still belong at least as much to the ranks of fallen, faithless humankind as they do to **God's empire**.

After he has healed the child, the disciples ask him privately why they were unable to cast out the demon. The answer is their "little faith." But immediately after identifying "little faith" as the problem, Jesus affirms that faith even the size of a mustard seed (cf. 13:31–32) can move mountains. Indeed, "nothing will be impossible" ("unable," "powerless"). The disciples' faith must be even smaller than the smallest of all seeds, since it came nowhere near to moving any mountains. Jesus' response, which encompasses both rebuke and encouragement, names the erratic, moonstruck tension in which the disciples seem to live. They worship Jesus and confess that he is Christ (14:33; 16:16; cf. 28:17) even while they misunderstand, resist, and betray him.

Jesus wonders aloud how long he will be with them and how long he will bear them, echoing God's anger over Israel's complaining (Num. 14:27). His lament suggests not only his exasperation over the disciples' powerlessness, but his concern over how little time is left to be with them. The second prediction of his death and resurrection in Jerusalem (17:22–23) thus follows immediately after the account of the disciples' failure to heal the moonstruck child. The reference to "gathering in Galilee" (17:22) reminds the audience about where Jesus has been conducting his ministry of healing, inclusion, and restoration (cf. 4:15–16, 23–25). Jesus' ministry in marginal Galilee is drawing to a close, and his fate at the center of power in Israel already looms on the horizon. Jesus' first prediction (16:21) focused on the elders, chief priests, and scribes as those who will put him to death. Here Matthew uses a more generic designation: "The Son of Man will be betrayed [or handed over] into human hands." Not only Israel's leaders, but humankind more generally, including Jesus' own disciples, will have a hand in his fate. Whereas in 16:22 Peter openly rejected Jesus' prediction, now Matthew reports that the disciples are "deeply distressed." Their reaction suggests that they are coming to terms with the imminence of his death, but they apparently still fail to make any sense of his claim that on the third day he will rise from the dead. Their imagination is still limited by the power of death, which they cannot see past. Their all too human perceptions also help to explain their failure to exorcise the demon that possessed the moonstruck boy. This "faithless and perverse generation"–the generation of "little-faiths"–fails to discern God's power already at work in the midst of the death-dealing world.

Preaching and teaching the Word

Matthew's portrayal of the disciples in this section of the Gospel is both sobering and hopeful: sobering because of their painful incapacity to discern and fully embrace the power of God, not only at work in Jesus but available to them as well, and hope-filled not because of any innate capacity on the part of the disciples themselves, but because Jesus keeps affirming just how much power is available, even to those with mustard-seed faith. Within this tension we can easily see ourselves. Jesus' rebuke to the disciples for their "little faith" is a rebuke to Matthew's Christian community, and to the **church** today. But to each audience comes the promise of power to move mountains, and the claim that through faith nothing is impossible. Matthew is not working toward a church that swings from impotence to grandiosity and back again, but one that knows the grace to live in both places at the same time. Can we learn how to be honest about ourselves, about our less than mustard-seed faith, and at the same time move forward into the power of God's new creation all around us? Christian preaching should make space for moonstruck disciples, while pointing them toward the power of the cross.

We have grown accustomed, especially in "mainstream" churches, to rationalizing the claims of gospel faith upon our imagination and practice. "God doesn't really want us to move mountains, nor even to heal epileptics. We should temper our expectations with a healthy dose of realism." But Matthew never pulls punches. At every turn Matthew invites us to explore the dimensions of God's power, to baptize our imaginations in the extravagant, extraordinary claims of gospel faith. "Go on and try it," the evangelist seems to say. "Go ahead and move that mountain. Walk on that water!" Faith that is content to abide in the world as it is is really no faith at all. Faith that does not beseech God to demonstrate extravagant power in this world, that does not even test the boundaries of what is "possible," is but the powerless and godless religion of a "faithless and perverse generation." How long will Jesus put up with such "little-faiths"?

Perhaps the problem in many congregations today is that we live, like the disciples, still seeking to make sense of Jesus through eyes that do not yet embrace the power of the cross and resurrection. Jesus' warnings of the fate that awaits him at the "hands of humans" is always accompanied by the reminder that on the third day the Human One will be raised from the dead. The church always struggles to keep the reality of the cross and resurrection in sight, and to shape its life around this world-shattering truth: the power of death has been swallowed up, and with it all the forces that could keep us from God's presence and power (28:18–20; cf. 1 Cor. 15:54–55; Rom. 8:38–39). We live in the **time** of resurrection. If the boundary of death itself has been breached, why not epilepsy, or mountains? Too often we live as if we are moonstruck, casting ourselves from fire to water. Like the disciples, we may sometimes fail to exorcise the demons, but, like them, we ought to keep trying, for resurrection faith knows no wall that God's power cannot overwhelm. Even a little faith, even the tiniest shred of faith, even faith that sometimes fails, is sufficient for God to use.

The Tax Revolt

Matthew 17:24–27

Exploring the text

The conversation between Jesus and Peter concerning the payment of the *didrachma* (or "half-shekel") tax is unique to Matthew. During Jesus' day, free male Israelites paid this tax annually to support the expenses of the temple. By Matthew's time, the Jerusalem temple had been destroyed, but the Romans continued to collect the tax in support of the temple of Jupiter Capitolinus in Rome. When pressed by the tax collectors about whether Jesus pays the tax, Peter affirms that he does (17:24–25). In the subsequent conversation, however, Jesus asserts that the "children" are free not to pay the tax (17:26).

A key question is who are these "children"? In 17:25 they are literally the offspring of "the kings of the earth" and thus exempt from the tolls and taxes that "others" must pay. But in 17:26, Jesus seems to use "children" in a way that might refer to Israel, to Jesus and his disciples, or even to the church. If the children of earthly kings are not required to pay taxes, then by analogy "God's children" are also freed from such obligations. Even though God's children are free, Jesus sends Peter fishing to secure the necessary coin for the tax payment anyway, so as not to "give offense to them" (17:27). If read in this way, the story follows the general principle set forth by Paul in Romans 13, for example, that Christians, who are free, should nonetheless submit to the authorities and pay every obligation and tax, even those that are unfair, so that their acts of love might stand clear (Rom. 13:1–8; cf. also 1 Pet. 2:13–17; Tit. 3:1). Alternatively, when Jesus speaks of "the children" in 17:26, he may simply be naming the reality that obtains for elites and their families, and for no one else. Jesus, Peter, Matthew, and members of the church knew full well from their experience of oppressive taxation across the span of the first century that they all had to continue paying taxes, not only the temple tax, in order to avoid offending their earthly rulers.[1]

Perhaps even more important than the identification of "the children" is the phrase "kings of the earth," which recalls Psalm 2, where God holds in derision the kings of the earth who set themselves against God's anointed. Judgment comes against these rulers when God "set[s] my king on Zion, my holy hill" (Ps. 2:2–6). In light of the passion prediction that immediately precedes this story, for Matthew "the kings of the earth" include Herod and his sons, and Caesar himself, who oppose God's anointed, the Messiah (cf. 17:22–23). Just as Jesus, God's anointed, will be turned over to "human hands"–these very rulers–and killed, the followers of Jesus must also submit to the authority of human rulers. But the allusion to Psalm 2 affirms that God's Son will prevail and the nations will be his heritage (Ps. 2:7–9).

Jesus recognizes the need not to offend the rulers, but he does not reach into his own pocket to pay the tax. Instead he sends Peter to the sea to do a little fishing. Here, as elsewhere in Matthew, the fish is associated with God's surprising, extravagant provision (cf. 7:10; 14:17–19; 15:36). God supplies enough to pay the tax for both Peter and Jesus. For the moment, the human rulers are satisfied, and God's power has again manifested itself in a surprising way. The story affirms God's provision and power in the face of the demands of human rulers. Disciples of Jesus will pay taxes and tribute, whether fair and right or not, but they do so knowing that the power of human rulers is empty, able to deprive and kill, to be sure, but powerless to overcome God's anointed and his followers.

Preaching and teaching the Word

This unusual story raises questions for us about the nature of discipleship in a world dominated by the interests of kings, governors, and coercive powers. How do Christians best give witness to God's power and provision in the midst of human expressions of dominion and sovereignty? God does not give us all fish with coins in their mouths, but God does supply those who trust with what they need. God also uses the community of disciples to restore those who are victims of the political and economic systems of the world, to gather God's faithful, and to unmask the charades of human power. Preaching that attends to these realities will prepare disciples both for the "real world" and for God's surprising provision.

While the story comes nowhere near to presenting a definitive teaching on the payment of taxes by Christians, it does suggest that when Christians do pay taxes—and they usually must—they should remember that human rulers and systems are only that. When leaders rule by deceit, when they deprive people of what is needed to live, when they depend on violence and domination, and especially when they wrap themselves in the rhetoric of religion and manifest destiny, it is the obligation of Christian preaching to unmask their deceits and to continue to point to God's sovereignty and provision. And in all realms of life, even when paying taxes, Christians should bear witness to God's power, grace, and care.

Christians approach their dealings with governmental powers with a clear sense that we are citizens of a different, heavenly realm (cf. Phil. 3:20). Whether or not the story affirms the essential freedom of Christ's followers with regard to the payment of the temple tax, it is nonetheless true that Jesus' disciples are members of **God's empire**, not Caesar's. That does not mean that Christians can ignore secular obligations, but rather that Christians are free to act in ways that surprise oppressors and opponents by turning the other cheek, for example, or by going the extra mile (cf. 5:39–41), or even by paying onerous taxes. How might the community of disciples best support such subversions of the status quo, and how might we bear witness to God's transforming and reconciling power amidst the trappings of nation-states.

PART EIGHT

An Empire of "Little Ones"
18:1–35

Preliminary Remarks

The fourth of Jesus' five great speeches in Matthew, chapter 18, focuses on relationships among the members of the community called into being through the ministry of Jesus. Even though Matthew uses the seemingly anachronistic term *ekklēsia*, usually translated "**church**," in 18:17 (cf. 16:18), in Matthew's day the church was not yet the developed institutional structure it would later become. In the first century *ekklēsia* designated a decision-making body, the "assembly" or "congregation" of free men who were entitled to vote. Matthew thus uses the term *ekklēsia*, both here and in Matthew 16, in conjunction with language of "binding" and "loosing" (18:18; 16:19). Jesus' focus here is on the assembly of disciples as a body charged with authority and responsibility in representing the **heavenly empire** on earth, especially by the exercise of solidarity as "children," making certain that others are not caused to stumble, in practices aimed at restoration, and in the shocking, unlimited practice of forgiveness. Matthew intends this discourse to be heard as a single whole, but for convenience the discussion is divided into two segments (18:1–20; 18:21–35), the first introduced by the disciples' question about greatness in the empire of heaven (18:1) and the second by Peter's question regarding the limits of forgiveness (18:21).

Stumbling, Binding, and Loosing

Matthew 18:1–20*

Exploring the text

Matthew's opening phrase, "At that time," links this discourse with the preceding episode, in which Jesus articulated the principle of "not giving offense," using the catchword "scandalize," or "offend" (17:27; 18:6, 7, 8,

---

*The Revised Common Lectionary uses this in Year A, The 23rd Sunday in Ordinary Time: Matthew 18:15–20.

9). This theme is prominent throughout the discourse. In 17:24–27 Jesus is concerned about not offending the ruling elites as they collect taxes, but now the focus shifts to offenses among the members of the community. Matthew employs the phrase "these little ones" repetitively (18:6, 10, 14) to designate those who are the primary focus of concern. The catchphrase "among them" (18:2, 20) forms an inclusion around the material in this section. In the first instance it refers to the child Jesus places among the disciples as a model of greatness in God's empire, and in the second instance to Jesus' own presence among the disciples wherever "two or three are gathered in my name." Matthew thus uses this portion of the discourse to develop the claim with which the whole Gospel begins and ends, that Jesus is Emmanuel, God with us (1:23; 28:20).

Jesus' discourse is prompted by the disciples' question in 18:1: "Who is the greatest in the kingdom of heaven?" If the disciples were expecting a conventional answer to their question, they are disappointed. Jesus forcefully undermines conventional wisdom of any sort with regard to "greatness." Their question is a "stumbling block" to Christian community; Jesus replies with an illustration that would have caused them to stumble. He calls a small child (*paidion*, cf. on 8:5–13) into their midst. Ancient Mediterranean cultures associated greatness with social status, **honor**, wealth, nobility, **patronage**, and the exercise of power over others. Children, on the other hand, were regarded as less than fully human, as possessions of the patron of a household, and as representing weakness and dependency. Jesus' initial response to the disciples in 18:2–4 is, therefore, paradoxical and parabolic, a stumbling block to those who prefer conventional wisdom. Paul declares that God has chosen what is weak in the world, what is low and despised, in order to shame those who think they are strong (1 Cor. 1:18–31). Jesus' declaration of children as "greatest" unmasks the world's powers as pretentious puppets.

Jesus' response compels disciples to look at themselves critically. Those who enter the kingdom of heaven must turn and become like children (18:3). What does this mean? We are not invited here to sentimentalize childlikeness. Jesus associates the child with humility, which refers not to personal modesty but to social location among the humiliated ones.[1] Like Jesus himself, those who practice humility live in solidarity with the humiliated ones of this world, in vulnerability and dependence on God. In 19:10–12, Jesus develops a similar image when he associates discipleship with "eunuchs for the sake of the empire of heaven." In 20:25–28 he will connect greatness in the kingdom of heaven with servanthood.

The next portion of the "sermon" takes up the relational dimensions of life in a community of children. The sayings in 18:5; 18:10; and 18:18–20 all deal with "representative identification," in which one party represents or stands for another. In 18:5, Jesus explicitly makes a representative identification with children: "Whoever welcomes one such child in my name welcomes me" (cf. 25:31–46, esp. v. 40 and v. 45, and 10:14, 40–41). In 18:10 Jesus asserts that "the little ones" have angels in heaven who continually see the face of the Father. And in 18:18–20 he will claim that the decisions the disciples make on earth have power not only on earth but in heaven as well. These sayings all make representative links between children, disciples who turn and become like children, and Jesus himself.

The sayings in 18:5 and 18:10 frame the warnings in 18:6–9 about the extreme danger of causing the "little ones" to stumble or "despising" them (18:10). Matthew has used "despise" in the first sermon in contrast to "love" (6:24). To despise or to cause the little ones to stumble is to treat other members of the community as less than oneself, or even as less than human, as children, slaves, and women were treated in the larger society. Such behavior aggrandizes oneself and thereby denies God's common mercy and grace toward all. The danger is particularly acute for those who would be leaders of the community, for leadership that replicates worldly patterns of domination and subordination leads to the same voracious, devouring destructiveness that Jesus associates with the Gentiles (cf. 20:25–28) and with the **scribes** and **Pharisees** (cf. 23:1–36). Such leadership inevitably destroys rather than preserves life and community.

Causing another to stumble not only destroys the lives of "little ones," but puts the offender at risk of eternal **judgment**. Better to be drowned in the depth of the sea than to face such consequences (18:6). Jesus admits in 18:7 that the world is full of stumbling blocks, but he holds those who cause the stumbling no less accountable. The focus shifts from those who cause others to stumble in 18:6–7 to what causes "you" to stumble in 18:8–9. Causing others to stumble causes also one's own stumbling. The sayings in 18:8–9 replicate the warnings about adultery and lust in 5:29–30: removing the cause of stumbling, whether one's hand or foot or eye, is better than landing in the fires of hell. The world's empires bring constant stumbling; in contrast stands a community of children and little ones, who exercise mutual care for one another, mutual dependence on God, and mutual welcoming in the name of Jesus. In this community, weakness is strength, and vulnerability and dependence lead to inclusion and greatness. These are the foundations not only for a new community, but a radically different kind of community.

Jesus' teaching shifts in 18:12–14 to the image of a shepherd looking for one lost sheep. The reference to shepherds and sheep recalls earlier discussions of leadership among God's people (cf. 9:36; 10:6; 15:24; cf.

Ps. 100; Ezek. 34). The sheep who goes astray may be either one who has stumbled (18:6–9) or even the one who has caused the stumbling (cf. 18:15–17). The primary task of the shepherd is to recover the one that is lost, even if this requires leaving ninety-nine alone on the mountains. Finding the lost one is the cause of great rejoicing (cf. 13:44–45). The summary statement in 18:14 (cf. 18:4, 5, 10) asserts a foundational claim upon the community's identity and practice: "Your Father, the heavenly one," wills that not even one of the little ones should perish. Jesus here calls the community and its leaders to relentless pursuit of such little ones.

The following section lays out a process for dealing with those members of the community who have "sinned" against another member. The offenders may be the same people who cause little ones to stumble in the preceding discussion (18:6–9), but here they are treated essentially as lost sheep (18:12–13) and become the focus of repeated attempts at reconciliation, like the little ones God wills not to lose (18:14). Even when the process of reconciliation fails, the wrongdoer becomes like "a Gentile and a tax collector," an epithet that locates them as outsiders, but also places them back among those who are primary objects of Jesus' mission of restoration (18:17). The process of reconciliation and restoration (18:15–17) begins with the one offended naming the offense between the two parties alone. If this works, the one who was wronged "regains" the offender, just as the one lost sheep was found. If the initial attempt is not successful, more witnesses join in the process, then finally the whole assembly of leaders (the "church"). The fact that the process starts with the victim is crucial, for in seeking to "regain" the offender the victim no longer remains in the role of victim, but, like those who turn the other cheek or go the extra mile (cf. 5:38–42), reclaims his or her own authority and dignity. Here both victim and victimizer are effectively "little ones," who receive the care of other members of the community. The community does not take sides so much as it seeks true justice, the reconciliation and restoration of both parties.

The sayings in 18:18 about "binding " and "loosing" are often understood as warrants for the church's authority to make decisions about its boundaries. They more clearly serve as warnings to the community to recognize and exercise carefully its representative authority. It is not entirely clear what "binding" and "loosing" refer to, but the context would suggest actions that concern especially the severing or restoration of relationships. The representative character of the community's actions is expressed in the assertion that what is bound or loosed on earth is also bound or loosed in heaven. This not only grants to the members of the community tremendous earthly (and heavenly) authority, but also extraordinary responsibility. This responsibility must be exercised only with clear awareness of God's will that none of the "little ones" be lost (18:12–14, 15–17), that causes of stumbling be avoided at all costs (18:5–10), and that all disciples are called to turn away from worldly power and status and become like children (18:2–4).

With responsibility, however, comes a promise, again using the catchwords "earth" and "heaven": "If two of you agree upon earth concerning any matter you ask, it will be done for you by my Father, who is in heaven" (18:19). Jesus grants remarkable power to the members of the community, power even to represent the heavenly Father on earth. God's action requires the agreement of at least two persons, the smallest possible unit where reconciliation and unity may be embodied. In the midst of this embodiment of God's empire, where even two or three are gathered in Jesus' name, there Jesus himself, "God with us," will be found (18:20; 1:23; 28:20). In 25:31–46 Jesus is found among the "least ones," the hungry and thirsty, strangers, the naked, sick, and imprisoned, just as he also is represented in the weakness and dependence of children and disciples. The community that exercises divine power, that binds and looses on earth and in heaven, and that experiences the presence of Jesus himself is also the community of children and little ones who seek the lost, guard against stumbling blocks, and reach out to reclaim even the victimizer. Jesus will affirm in the next portion of this discourse that this is also a community of unrelenting forgiveness.

Preaching and teaching the Word

The "community discourse" calls leaders to childlike weakness and dependence, to loving care for the little ones, to relentless pursuit of those who have gone away, and to the responsible, reconciling exercise of heavenly power on earth. This is the essence of pastoral leadership. What kind of community would accept, affirm, and nourish such leadership? What kind of community would such leadership in turn generate?

The disciples' question, "Who is greatest in the kingdom of heaven?" is itself a "stumbling block" in the life of Christian communities. The quest for greatness in worldly terms breeds division, rends the fabric of community, and impairs the church's witness. The church that is defined by mutual servanthood, compassion, care for the little ones, and childlike humility will provide fertile soil for faith and prove a stumbling block for the world. Leadership in the church thus consists not in the exercise of power over others but in practices aimed at restoring and reclaiming those who have stumbled or wandered off. The model here is Jesus' own ministry to restore the lost sheep of Israel (9:36; 10:6). There will always be wandering sheep, even some sheep we might wish would wander away to another flock. The effort to reclaim and restore precisely these is what makes the church a disciplined, organically connected body of diverse parts, rather than a mere voluntary aggregate of like-minded individuals.

The church's practices of "binding" and "loosing" are not concerned so much with determining who is "in" and who is "out" as with the work of reconciliation and restoration. These tasks are best accomplished not by authoritative edicts or position statements, but in the inefficient, messy, frustrating, and joyous work of building relationships of solidarity and trust—relationships that fulfill the calling to become like children, the greatest in the empire of heaven.

Full Forgiveness

Matthew 18:21–35*

Exploring the text

Jesus' call to care for offenders and offended alike provokes an immediate response from Peter, who wonders how many times someone may sin against him and yet be forgiven. Peter's question focuses less on his own capacities to forgive than on those who disregard the offer and implications of forgiveness. Peter's willingness to forgive "seven times" signifies that he is entertaining the prospect of full, complete forgiveness on his own part. But what about those who take advantage of or refuse the call to forgiveness? Hearing Peter's question in this way helps to clarify the function of the parable that follows moments later.

But first Jesus explodes Peter's paradigm of perfection. Jesus could have just said, "Yes, perfect, complete forgiveness is required." But while Peter was being perfectly magnanimous, Jesus envisions a quantum leap to boundless, over the top, absurd, unimaginable levels of forgiveness. Jesus' call to forgive "seventy-seven" times counters the pronouncement of murderous revenge by Cain's descendant Lamech (Gen. 4:24). God's empire does not trade in such terror, nor find "justice" in revenge, but

*The Revised Common Lectionary uses this in Year A, The 24th Sunday in Ordinary Time.

stands in contrast to the bloody violence and retribution that stain human experience to this day. Jesus' answer also suggests that disciples should not anticipate an end to the sin or violence of the world around them, nor even the end of sin in the community of disciples. But to retaliate, to act in kind, is not permitted. Jesus' call to enduring, relentless forgiveness makes the disciples a new "generation," the first since the generation of Cain to trust themselves wholly to the power of forgiveness—not only when it seems reasonable or possible, but when it is unthinkable.

The parable of a servant who fails to forgive a small debt after having been forgiven an impossible debt (18:23–35) illustrates what happens when the fragile thread of forgiveness is broken. The story offers a caricature of economic life in the first-century world of **patronage**. While we are tempted to understand the king as an allegorical figure for God, his actions fit more closely the paradigm of someone like Herod. The king uses the "settling of accounts" to exercise discipline over his slaves. The slave who becomes the focus of this accounting is probably a highly placed "farmer" of taxes and tributes, for the sum he owes the king is astronomical, equivalent to what Rome extracted as tribute from all of Judea during a decade (Josephus, *Antiquities*, 14.78). When the servant is unable to pay, the king threatens to sell him and his family into the lowest form of slavery until the debt is repaid (which would never happen!). Repayment is probably not the real goal, but rather the king's assertion of power over those who are subservient to him, even at the highest levels. Thus, the king is satisfied when the servant falls prostrate before him (an action that elsewhere in Matthew is directed only toward Jesus) and promises payment. Remarkably, the king not only releases him but forgives the whole debt (18:27). This is the first moment of crisis in the story, the shock no one was expecting. Forgiving the whole debt effectively releases the servant from his legal and economic obligations to the king, making the servant a genuinely free man. But the king's largesse might also be expected to engender a deeper, more heartfelt, perhaps even more onerous sense of obligation on the part of the servant. What will the servant do with his newfound, albeit ambiguous, freedom? The answer comes immediately.

The freshly forgiven servant comes upon one who owes him a much smaller sum, about one six-hundred-thousandth part of what the forgiven servant had owed the king, and demands immediate payment. He acts as the king first had toward him, albeit with greater violence, for he seizes his "fellow servant" (a social equal) by the throat (18:28). Still more important, he turns a deaf ear to this fellow servant's plea for time to repay and has him tossed into the prison he himself had narrowly avoided. The astounding forgiveness shown the first servant, which might have been expected to ripple down through the system, has instead short-circuited. The forgiven servant proves unable to pass on to others the gift he has been given, and instead reverts to the patterns of domination and violence from which he had escaped only moments earlier. When other servants report his actions to the king, he is once again called to account (18:31–34). This time the king hands him over to "be tortured" until his debt (once forgiven) is fully repaid. He is judged according to the standards with which he has judged others (cf. 7:1–2), a victim of the system in which he has chosen to function.

Preaching and teaching the Word

Forgiveness is the defining discipline of the community of disciples. Unlimited forgiveness bears continued witness to the distinctive nature of God's reign and offers a true alternative, perhaps the only alternative, to the cycles of exploitation, violence, and revenge that plague the world. A church that dedicates itself to the practice of unlimited forgiveness is necessarily diverse, resilient, schooled in dealing with conflict, patient, and supportive. Limitless forgiveness cannot be sustained by individuals alone, nor even by a collection of individuals, but requires the sustained attention of a disciplined community that will not gloss over conflicts and differences or settle for words rather than transformed relationships.

Jesus' **parable** provokes questions and tensions. In what sense is "the **empire of the heavens**" comparable to this troubling story? The parable does not present us with a positive image of God's reign so much as it demonstrates what happens among humans when the habits of violence and domination disrupt the possibility of mutual forgiveness. Neither the first servant nor the king demonstrates unlimited forgiveness, which Jesus has just set forth as a requirement for his disciples. The threat with which the parable concludes, "So my heavenly Father will also do to every one of you, if you do not forgive your brother or sister from your heart" (18:35), makes it clear that God's forgiveness also has its limits. Matthew's tendency to set the threat of **judgment** right next to calls for mercy and forgiveness leaves us to sort out the paradox. How does Jesus' ministry embody at once both **salvation** and judgment? Why is the practice of forgiveness so crucial to Jesus' way, and the hinge on which salvation and judgment here turn?

The consequences of the failure to forgive–and to "forgive from the heart"–are enormous. The servant's refusal to practice toward another the kind of mercy the king has exercised toward him places him directly back into a world of punishment, vengeance, anger, and impossible debts. He chooses the measure by which he will be judged (cf. 7:2). Apparently we cannot make the practice of forgiveness an occasional matter, or something we do only when it seems reasonable or expedient. The world's alternatives to disciplined, unending forgiveness are always close at hand, always posing as the rational, necessary course of action. God's grace and mercy may in fact be so unsettling, may so deeply disrupt our lives and dislocate us from the patterns of relationship to which we are accustomed, that we flee in terror. We need not look far in our own world to recognize that real forgiveness would fundamentally undermine the patterns of domination and exploitation, of terror and vengeance, of suffered injustice and "righteous" retribution that constitute our way of life. We more easily trust in violence and retributive justice to resolve our conflicts than we do in the offer of God's forgiveness. Do the transformed relationships that forgiveness may generate frighten us? What indeed will God do with those people—with us—who refuse to accept the reality of forgiveness?

Sometimes what we call forgiveness disguises power dynamics that are anything but salutary. In one reading of this parable, for example, the king's offer to forgive the servant's enormous debt is a means to inscribe still more deeply the servant's sense of obligation. In this scenario, the servant has no good options, for both of the paths before him lead to his deeper enslavement and to greater honor and domination for the king. The offer to forgive another often serves primarily as a way to reverse the power dynamics, so that the victim can regard himself or herself as a bigger, better person than the one who did the original wrong. In this form of faux forgiveness, the relationship may suffer further alienation rather than genuine restoration. Real forgiveness does not merely reverse the power dynamics, but gives up claims to power for the sake of transformed relationships, rooted in recognition of our common humanity before God.

In 18:15–20, Jesus focused primarily on forgiveness in interpersonal relationships, whereas the forgiveness described in the parable has more to do with financial debt. The Gospel holds together what we tend to separate: sins or interpersonal transgressions, on the one hand, and economic debt, on the other. Economic obligations alter relationships, as those who loan to or borrow from friends often discover. Jesus' ministry inaugurates a time when the forgiveness of debts and sins makes possible new, transformed relationships. How do our financial obligations shape our relationships with others? Do our relationships embody good news, in both interpersonal and economic realms?

PART NINE

Training the Disciples for Jerusalem
19:1–20:34

Preliminary Remarks

As soon as Jesus has finished his sermon on life together in the community of disciples, he leaves Galilee for the last time and crosses into Judea, on his way toward Jerusalem (19:1).The sermon on community (Matt. 18) focused on care for "the little ones," restoring sinful members, dealing with conflicts, and forgiveness. The stories in Matthew 19–20 continue to display Jesus' concern for oppressed and vulnerable people (19:3–15) alongside illustrations of the resistance posed by the religious elites (19:3–9) and the dangers of worldly riches (19:16–30). But the primary focus of these two chapters is Jesus' preparation of the disciples for what is coming in Jerusalem and for their mission after he is gone. Each encounter (e.g., 19:3–9, 16–22; 20:20–23) generates stupefied, aggressive, or indignant responses from the disciples (e.g., 19:10, 13, 25; 20:24), to whom Jesus offers additional instruction (19:11–12, 23–30; 20:1–16, 25–28). The leitmotif throughout these stories is power, especially the distinctive nature and effects of divine power in contrast to human power.

Jesus' Family Values

Matthew 19:1–15

Exploring the text

As Jesus leaves Galilee for the last time, he is still healing the crowds that follow him. **Pharisees** come to test him, again with hostile intent (19:3; cf. 16:1; 22:15; 22:34–35). This is a border skirmish. Jesus aims to enter the capital, take possession of the temple, and lay claim to **God's empire**. Along the way to his coronation on the cross, a variety of opponents will challenge him in verbal contests (see "**Controversy stories**"), seeking to win victories that will end his campaign and reestablish their own authority. The Pharisees' test concerning divorce law (19:3–9) is the first of seven such contests (cf. 21:14–22:46) set between the entry into Judea and Jesus' arrest in Jerusalem.

Rabbinic debates over the interpretation of Deuteronomy 24:1, which speaks of men divorcing wives who are not pleasing or who do "something objectionable," lie behind the Pharisees' question. The focus of Deuteronomy 24:1–4, however, is not divorce per se, but remarrying a woman after she has married another and then been divorced or widowed by her second husband. The Pharisees are not interested in Jesus' opinion in any case, except as it might provide an opportunity to entrap and discredit him. They presume that Jesus does not possess sufficient skill in the interpretation of the Law to resolve an issue their own teachers have been unable to settle. Embroiling him in a controversy might incite popular reaction and distract him from his vocation. They pose the question casuistically, with the emphasis falling on the last three words: "Is it lawful for a man to divorce his wife *for any cause?*" The Pharisees, following Deuteronomy 24, presume the legality and legitimacy of divorce, as well as male cultural dominance and prerogative in initiating divorce. Jesus will challenge each of these assumptions.

Jesus typically responds to such challenges with a question of his own, here posed in a way that mocks his opponents' presumed superiority in matters of interpretation of the Law: "Have you not read . . ." (Matt. 19:4; cf. 12:3, 5; 21:16; 21:42; 22:31). The Pharisees appeal to the Law, but Jesus appeals to God's original intention for male and female in the creation (19:4–5; cf. Gen. 1:27; 2:24). A man and a woman are to join together and become one flesh (19:5–6). God's will is for unity, for joining into one flesh what had been two, separate beings. When humans divide what God has joined, they defy God's will. The Pharisees' rejoinder (19:7) seeks to pose a fundamental conflict between this creation principle and the Law of Moses, but Jesus rebuts their challenge with the reminder that Moses did not permit divorce because it was God's will, but because of "your hard-heartedness" (19:8). The Mosaic divorce laws were, in fact, an exigency meant primarily to protect the females when relationships ended. The Law does not condone the rupture of relationships that are meant to bear witness to God's will for reconciliation, unity, and fruitfulness. For Jesus, God's intention for the creation is not in conflict with the Mosaic commandment, for the Law addresses only what to do when human sinfulness and callousness reign in place of God's will.

Jesus' final statement in 19:9 is usually taken as a piece of Christian case law that defines an exception–"unchastity"–to the otherwise clear denial of divorce among Jesus' followers. As case law, it has not proven very helpful, for it is not clear precisely what constitutes "unchastity," just as it was not clear to the Pharisees what Deuteronomy 24:1 meant by "unpleasant" or doing "something objectionable." While Jesus contends

against the casuistry of the Pharisees here, the vagaries of his own saying have invited similar casuistic wrangling and disputation among later
generations of his followers. By turning this verse into a Christian doctrine on marriage and divorce, we overlook the fact that Jesus addresses
this saying very clearly to his opponents, not to the disciples. "But I say
to you . . ." (19:9a) recalls the "antitheses" of the Sermon on the Mount
(5:21–48), where Jesus radicalizes the tenets of Israelite Law and tradition
(cf. especially 5:32, almost the exact equivalent of the saying here). Jesus'
statement in 19:9 radicalizes the whole of Deuteronomy 24:1–4, so as to
condemn not only men who remarry wives they had earlier divorced, but
all men who divorce and remarry, especially when the woman has not
been unfaithful.

Putting aside for the moment whatever this might imply for the marital
practices of the Christian community that is listening in, Jesus' teaching
here is directed to the Pharisees as an allegory of their relationship with
God. Jesus is not the first to use images of marriage, unfaithfulness, and
divorce as analogies to Israel's relationship with God. Hosea 3 is perhaps
the most famous such instance, but the language Jesus uses in this story
evokes especially Malachi 2:14–16 ("you have been faithless to the wife of
your youth" and "'I hate divorce,' says the LORD, the God of Israel") and,
still more prominently, the allegory on Deuteronomy 24:1–4 in Jeremiah
3:1–5. For Jesus, the Pharisees represent unfaithful Israel of old, "playing
the whore with many lovers" (Jer. 3:1) and then calling shamelessly to
God, "the friend of my youth" (Jer. 3:4). We hear then, once again, Jesus'
claim that the Pharisees' actions are not yoked to their words (e.g., 12:33–
37; 15:1–9; 23:2–36). They have used the Law to justify their own status
and power, even their own divorces, perhaps even when unfaithfulness
was not a factor. But more than this, they have divorced themselves from
God, who has remained faithful, and married themselves to the powers
of this world (cf. Deut. 32:4–5). They are, as Jesus has already said, "an
evil and adulterous generation" (Matt. 12:39; 16:4), guilty themselves of
infidelity before God (cf. the "Song of Moses," Deut. 32:1–21).

The disciples miss the analogical implications of Jesus' statement. They
wonder aloud if, given the strictness of Jesus' teaching, it might be better
not to marry at all (19:10). Jesus' response to the Pharisees effectively
denies men—whether Pharisees or disciples—the advantageous personal
and property rights that they presume the Law grants them. Jesus treats
marriage as a relationship of mutual commitment and obligation, rather
than as a hierarchy designed to enhance the honor, privilege, and well-
being of the male. Jesus' response to his disciples does not address their
question about marriage directly, but makes his teaching on relationships

even more radical. He admits that "only those to whom this teaching is given can receive it" (19:11; cf. 13:10–17), then gives them another analogy to "receive" (19:12d): eunuchs. Eunuchs have no family, no right of access to the temple, and no honor in the society of men. They stood next to women on the lowest rungs of the religious cultus and society. Jesus speaks of eunuchs born so or made so by others, and finally of those who have "made themselves eunuchs for the sake of the **kingdom of heaven**" (19:12). Jesus is apparently calling his disciples to "receive" the status of eunuchs for the sake of God's empire—set aside for service, marginal and estranged from their families, without rights or status in the world, choosing to renounce their cultural prerogatives of power.[1] Those who look at the world from this perspective will not find it so hard to receive Jesus' teaching about divorce.

The fact that power and status are the underlying issues in this section is confirmed in the next episode, where Jesus lifts up children as those to whom the empire of heaven belongs (19:14). Both his actions—welcoming them and laying his hands on them (19:14–15)–and his words confirm that children have a central place in the community of disciples. The story also sets the children in contrast to the disciples, revealing the latters' lack of progress toward realization of their "eunuch calling." They have forgotten Jesus' admonitions to become like children, to welcome children, and to attend to the needs of the "little ones" (18:2–5, 6, 10). Earlier they had been unable to rebuke the demon that possessed a child (17:16, 18; cf. 16:22, where Peter rebukes Jesus), but now they rebuke the children. Perhaps they are thinking of themselves as the gatekeepers holding back the forces of Hades (16:18–19), but if so they have wildly misidentified their adversaries. The story thus represents another missed opportunity, a failed exam, for the disciples (cf. 17:14–21). They have understanding and power, but the leaven of the Pharisees, specifically the human love of honor and status, seems still to permeate their consciousness and actions.

Preaching and teaching the Word

The community of disciples includes the married, the celibate, and children. Jesus honors all three callings as opportunities to manifest the ideal of unity in God's reign. The institution of marriage expresses God's desire for reconciliation, unity amidst diversity, and for covenant faithfulness. Marriage is the human correlate for God's own intended relationship with Israel and with the community of disciples, who represent Israel restored, bearing witness to the nations. Jesus' stress on the importance of marriage in God's original intention for the creation suggests why some regard marriage as a "sacrament," i.e., a relationship in which God and humans act in concert. Nonetheless, this does not justify the modern tendency to sacralize social institutions such as marriage. It is God's presence and, in turn, the way the marriage relationship bears witness to who God is that renders marriage sacred, not anything inherent in the institution of marriage itself. By analogy, churches are not "sacred space" because we hang a name on the building that says "church," but because of what happens in such spaces that names and bears witness to God's presence and power. Marriage is sacred when it is a locus of faithfulness and justice. Modern, essentialist discussions of marriage and the family turn these "institutions" into idols, and where idolatry rules, relationships will be broken. Jesus does not here call us to defend the institution of marriage, but to work for relationships in every sphere of life that bear witness to God's love and faithfulness.

Why does Jesus appeal to the creation story in his initial response to the Pharisees? After the fall, alienation, hardheartedness, greed, and covetousness distort and break our relationships. Jesus' demand for faithfulness in marriage and his prohibition of divorce are marks of the coming full restoration of relationships with God and the creation. In marriage and in other relationships marked by covenant faithfulness, we have the opportunity to learn to love and be loved fully, as God also loves us.[2] But as long as we also live in the world of human power, lust, and hardheartedness, we must also expect to find brokenness, even in ourselves. So we aim for the marks of God's empire, but humbly, with the patience and forgiveness that Jesus shows toward his disciples.

It is sad irony that Jesus' teachings on marriage and divorce have so persistently generated among Christian interpreters a kind of legalistic, case-law-oriented, ecclesial nit-picking that resembles more than anything else the Pharisees' fondness for casuistry. The leaven of the Pharisees works powerfully. We so easily overlook the fact that Jesus directs his teaching on marriage and divorce to the Pharisees as a critique of hardheartedness and faithlessness. At the same time, we largely ignore what Jesus says to his disciples about becoming eunuchs for the kingdom of heaven, and learning about the kingdom from our children. We are condemned by what we have done and left undone with these stories. Who benefits and who loses from our interpretations and pronouncements on marriage and divorce? Who is justified and granted power, or pilloried and excluded, by our pronouncements? Do our assumptions inscribe the same sexism and classism that lay beneath the Pharisees' question?

What can we learn from the "eunuchs made so for the kingdom of heaven" and from our children, both of which groups embody social vulnerability and weakness? The juxtaposition of marriage, asceticism, and childlikeness in these stories suggests that the community of disciples embodies diverse expressions of covenant faithfulness. There is no hierarchy among these vocations and offices, although Jesus does "ordain" the children (19:15). Jesus' interactions in these episodes also suggest that disciples will learn the most about God's kingdom in the presence of those who practice faithfulness at the margins of power and status. Yet these are the very people most often ignored or excluded from communities of the righteous. On his way to Jerusalem and the cross, Jesus takes time to pray for and lay hands on the children. He makes room for the eunuchs and the children alongside his arrogant disciples. Only in communities like this is it possible to bear the weight of the cross.

Wealth and Wholeness

Matthew 19:16–30

Exploring the text

In the preceding stories Jesus has identified a variety of social settings and practices in which disciples bear witness to God's presence and power, including faithful marriage, the renunciation of male status and power, and childlikeness. The story of a man who comes to Jesus seeking to acquire eternal life adds another element to this list. Christians bear witness to the power of God by divesting themselves of the world's things. To those who leave behind the attachments and baggage of this world Jesus offers abundance, glory, and eternal life "at the renewal of all things" (19:27–29).

The man, who for good reasons is not yet identified as "young" (19:20) or rich (19:22), asks Jesus to name the "one good thing" he might do to secure eternal life. Jesus' initial answer conveys frustration (19:17). It was common knowledge among the people of Israel that the Law, whose source is God, expresses what is "good," so those who "want to enter life" should keep the commandments. When pressed to identify which commandments he has in mind. Jesus points the man toward the Ten Commandments, especially those which focus on human relationships, which he underlines by adding to the list the commandment to love your neighbor as yourself (19:19; cf. 22:39; Lev 19:18).

The man is not satisfied, either with Jesus' answer or, apparently, with his own life. He claims that he has kept all the commandments. He must be "perfect." Matthew has saved until this moment the information that this is a "young man" (19:20), in order to highlight what Jesus says next: if the man really wants to be "perfect," he must sell his possessions, give the money to the poor, and then follow Jesus (19:21). The word translated "perfect" in the NRSV (*teleios*; cf. 5:48) may also mean "whole," "complete," or "mature." So perhaps what the young man really lacks is maturity or wholeness. Jesus asks him, in effect, to become like the pearl merchant who sells all that he has to buy the one pearl that surpasses all others (13:45–46). But this the young man will not do. It turns out he is not only perfect and young, but rich too (19:22). He goes away grieving, apparently unwilling to divest himself of his possessions in order to follow Jesus. The way to "heavenly treasure" (19:21; cf. 6:19–21; 13:22) is clear, but the earthly costs are too high.

After this exchange Jesus warns his disciples that riches make it virtually impossible for people to enter the **empire of heaven** (19:23–24). The image of a camel trying to get through the eye of a needle is a graphic illustration of just how absurdly impossible this would be—like getting an ocean liner through a straw, or putting the Grand Canyon into your pocket. The disciples are shocked. They thought the rich, perfect young man had his ticket punched, but in fact he doesn't stand the tiniest chance of entry into God's empire. Like many of their Jewish and Gentile contemporaries and many people today, the disciples apparently consider wealth a sign of blessing from God. The man who has come to Jesus in quest of "eternal life" would seem to possess all that is needed, but it's all his possessions that are keeping him out. We have to let go of our things in order to learn to trust God, and we have to trust God in order to let go of our things. Trust is what the rich man lacks. If it's impossible for a man like this to enter the kingdom, they ask, could anyone (19:25)?

Jesus' statement that only God, not humans, can make this happen is not meant as reassurance to the rich that God will find a way to get them in despite their baggage. He means, rather, that **salvation** is dependent on God, not on the things humans accumulate—whether possessions, power, honor, or security—in order to justify themselves and, they suppose, complete and perfect their lives. The prophets persistently warn against the corrosive power of wealth and its uselessness in the face of divine judgment (e.g., Amos 6:4–8; Ezek. 7:19–20). While God promises to bless faithful Israel with wealth (Deut. 28:1–14), God does not bless those who build up wealth at the expense of others. Human wealth, unless shared as Jesus tells the young man to do, ruptures community, effaces our humanity, and marks us for judgment (James 5:1–5). Why would those who trust God for their life care about human wealth in any case (Matt. 6:19–34)?

Peter observes that the disciples have, in fact, done what Jesus asked the rich young man to do: they have left everything to follow him (19:27; cf. 4:18–22; 9:9). What then will they receive: wealth? eternal life? power and status (cf. 18:1; 20:20–22)? entry into the heavenly empire? Jesus announces that "at the new beginning" (NRSV, 19:28: "renewal of all things") they will sit as "judges of the tribes of Israel," an image that conveys their vindication and honor, not the power actually to judge others, which remains with God. Jesus is not thinking only of the Twelve, but of all those who for the sake of Jesus leave their houses, families, and fields (19:29). They will receive a hundredfold reward (cf. 13:8, 23), as well as "eternal life." The story ends with the announcement of prophetic reversal–the first will be last and the last first–which is the focus of the following parable (19:30; cf. 20:16).

Preaching and teaching the Word

Like the rich man and the disciples, we easily turn the sense of well-being that wealth and possessions provide into the conviction that God has blessed us, as individuals or as a nation. But that very conviction then threatens our trust in God and one another. Americans have a historical tendency to despise poor people as "lazy" and undeserving, or even criminal. So Jesus is warning us of the cancer we call wealth. He does not mean to leave us much wiggle room, for there is too much at stake, too much potential for self-deception, and too much risk of being consumed by what we consume. Possessions insulate us from suffering and numb us to the reality of death. Jesus, who is leading his disciples to Jerusalem, the center of Jewish wealth and pride, to embrace suffering and overwhelm death, will not permit his disciples the delusion of confusing wealth with blessing.

The church in North America has largely grown blind to the fundamental tensions between the pursuit of wealth and the call to enter the kingdom of heaven. In our world, money means power. Because money rules the world, those who follow Jesus into God's heavenly empire necessarily are engaged in protest against this human form of governance.[1] The way we deal with money and possessions is thus inescapably a matter of faith, not only for individual Christians, but for the church itself. Wealth is a communal and ecclesial issue in part because so many churches have themselves become wealthy landowners. Wealth affects the integrity of our proclamation: as long as the church treats money and possessions as incidental to faith and salvation, individual Christians will not hear or understand Jesus' call to give up our possessions and follow him. It is also impossible for those who do respond to this call to sustain this kind of witness without the intentional support of the larger Christian community.

The call to poverty for the sake of Christ is thus the vocation of the church, not just of unusual individuals.

It might be easier to fulfill the intention of Jesus' teachings in this section if we were children as yet unscathed by the habits of gluttony, or "eunuchs" who could focus single-mindedly on devotion to God. Most of us cannot responsibly leave our homes, "fields," or families to follow Jesus as his disciples have. Jesus and his disciples themselves needed the support of extended communities, including children (18:3–5; 19:13–15). For some, then, the call to leave behind home, family, career, and possessions to follow Jesus is an opportunity to engage in a powerful means of witness to God's abundance and care (cf. 6:19–34; 10:8–10). They become teachers for those whose primary means of responding to this call, for the moment, is to offer support and sustenance. But note well, wealth remains an enormous risk for those on the support team. Most important, the church must never forget or disdain the witness of poverty for the sake of Christ. Where this awareness is lacking, the church's witness is choked and corroded.

Jesus calls us to share our resources and gifts—of every kind—freely with others. In a society beset by increasing economic insecurity, how can the church put this kind of witness into meaningful practice? How can we nurture radical dependence on God? How in a society of gluttony and unparalleled consumption do we unveil the risks, emptiness, and destructiveness of the pursuit of things, and bear public witness to God's abundance and care for the world?

The Problem with Justice

Matthew 20:1–16*

Exploring the text

The sense of **justice** set forth in this **parable** is likely to offend modern audiences, even Christians, just as much as it did the workers first sent to the vineyard by the householder. We encounter here a radical expres-

---

*The Revised Common Lectionary uses this in Year A, The 25th Sunday in Ordinary Time.

sion of the **gospel**, which proves more disruptive than comfortable. If Matthew means for us to understand the householder's actions toward the workers who come last to the vineyard as an analogy for the kind of grace and justice God wills, then we are brought face-to-face with a grace that undermines all human pursuits of personal merit and that subverts the world's most basic economic and social constructions.

The parable explicates the statements of reversal that frame it (19:30; 20:16). The "For" with which 20:1 begins also links the parable to what has preceded, where Jesus has lifted up eunuchs and children as models of those who belong in the kingdom of heaven (19:12; 19:14), and challenged the disciples' notion that the rich and pious are guaranteed salvation before all others (19:16–26). The disciples have left everything to follow Jesus (19:27–29). Yet Jesus is also aware that his disciples' spiritual pride can yield a form of self-righteousness that imperils their participation in **God's empire** no less than does the rich man's riches. The parable, then, forms part of Jesus' response to Peter's claims about the disciples' faithfulness to him (19:27). The parable also unveils the arbitrary, exploitive, and oppressive character of agrarian life in the Roman Empire and Israel in the first century, when day laborers of the kind depicted in this story were little more than fuel–bodies to be consumed–for the economic engines of the elites. The landowner acts, however, in a way that ultimately threatens the identities of everyone who participates in the system.

The "vineyard" is a stock metaphor for the people of Israel (cf. Isa. 5:1–7); the landowner's call to work in the vineyard thus reminds us of Jesus' call for workers to join him in his mission to the lost sheep of the house of Israel (cf. 9:36–38; 10:6). Matthew uses the temporal marker "evening" (20:8) in conjunction with moments of decision or great portent (cf. 14:15; 14:23; 26:20; 27:57). More generally, the phrase "when it was evening" may carry eschatological weight, suggesting the end of the day or the twelfth hour, when the final judgment arrives. The owner's repeated visits to the marketplace to hire more workers may reflect the eschatological scenario Jesus paints in 9:37–38: "The harvest is plentiful, but the laborers are few; therefore ask the Lord of the harvest to send out laborers into his harvest."

The story focuses, however, on the peculiar sense of justice demonstrated by the landowner. At the beginning of the day, he hires some laborers to work in his vineyard for a denarius, the typical wage of a day laborer, which did not permit the workers to support themselves or their families at more than the most primitive level. He returns again to the marketplace at nine ("the third hour") and discovers others standing idle. He sends them into his vineyard with the promise that he will pay them what is "just" (20:4). He returns again to the marketplace at noon and at three, and again sends workers to the vineyard, apparently under the same circumstances as before. Finally he returns "at the eleventh hour" (an hour before sunset). This time the householder asks why these workers have been "standing idle" all day. Their response, "Because no one has hired us," sounds lame, but hints of the dependence of such workers. The householder commands these last ones to go into the vineyard, like the other workers before them (20:7//20:4), but there is no record of a conversation about what they will be paid. Even the reassurance that he will pay "whatever is just" is missing now.

When it is evening (the moment of **judgment**), the landowner gives careful instructions about the procedures for paying the various workers. Rather than pay the laborers in the same order in which they were hired, the vineyard owner commands that those hired last be paid first (20:8), which sets up the conflict with those who have worked all day (and conforms the story's plot with the summary statement in 20:16). The reversal of the expected order of payment together with the equal payments creates the primary tension in the story. When those who were hired at the end of the day receive a full daily wage, those who worked the full day expect more. The latter (who are the "first" in the story's classification system) have "borne the burden of the day and the scorching heat." As they see it, if those who work just an hour receive a full denarius, those who worked all day should justly receive more. Most of us would agree with them. Does not real justice require proportional recompense? Shouldn't the wages fit the work, as the punishment fits the crime? Thus, when "the first" receive only the promised denarius, they grumble against the landowner, who has treated "these last ones" just like those who worked all day. Their words are ironic: "You have made them equal to us!" (20:12).

The last portion of the story records the landowner's rationale in three parts. First, he claims that he is doing the first workers no wrong, since he is paying them exactly what they had agreed to be paid (20:13). From his perspective, all the workers have received what "belongs to them." The landowner's statement to the grumblers, "Take what belongs to you and go," conveys a sense of rupture and judgment. These workers are now estranged from the owner of the vineyard. Second, he claims the right to dispose of his property as he sees fit (20:14b-15a). Finally, the landowner draws on the tradition of the "evil eye," which signifies envy and malice: "Or is your eye evil because I am good?" In the Gospel story, God's graciousness toward humankind, especially the last and the least, is the cause of jealousy and violence on the part of the elites. Here, too, the owner's sense of justice creates a level playing field economically, but mocks the first workers' sense of entitlement, thereby bringing division and estrangement.

Preaching and teaching the Word

Lest we think this story presents a scenario far removed from our reality, we should remember that "labor pools" are an everyday fact of life all around us, in cities and in the farmlands, burning up the bodies of the vulnerable to supply inexpensive produce and flood the markets with cheap goods produced by people paid less than a living wage. If nothing else, the parable uncovers the hidden realities of our economic systems, no less in the twenty-first century than in Jesus' day.

The parable threatens our foundational notions of justice. What happens when reward is distributed, not according to systems of "just recompense," but freely and equitably, without any regard for the merits of the workers? The trouble in the parable arises not because the owner does not keep his contract with those who worked all day, nor because he is particularly generous toward anyone, but because he pays everyone the same. His actions mock those who work all day, as well as the systems of fairness and "justice" by which we order our world. While we may think of justice as equality, in practice our economic, political, religious, social, and legal systems all aim to preserve a sense of order based on hierarchy, status distinctions, and difference. Does the landowner represent God's way of dealing with the world? Is God's justice like this?

God's justice reaches out to include the least, the last, the little ones, the children, the poor, the weak, and the suffering. God's justice consists of forgiving debts, restoring relationships, and making the creation whole. Justice ordered around "merit" or differentiation of status, on the other hand, preserves a world of division and alienation. If God does act as the landowner has, then the parable points to the radical, disruptive, even offensive character of God's free and unmerited grace toward humankind. The problem with such grace is that it "makes them equal to us," whoever "they" might be in our various systems of differentiation. Throughout its history, the **church** has often functioned in ways that confirm and preserve differences, whether economic, social, spiritual, or racial. This is precisely what the parable subverts.

The statements that frame the parable (19:30; 20:16) have often been allegorized so as to refer to law (="the first" now become last) and gospel (="the last" now become first), from which the step to anti-Semitic readings, or anti-Catholic readings among Protestants, is but a small one. But these readings twist the parable into a story that merely reinscribes the patterns of difference by which we order our worlds. In Matthew's day the story could indeed be used to challenge the sense of entitlement of the Jewish elites, but the goal of the story is not to attack Judaism and replace it with Christianity. There is room in God's grace and justice for both the first and the last, however these might be defined functionally. But the parable subverts any criteria by which we might represent ourselves before God as "the first ones." In the end, there is no first and last, righteous and unrighteous, Jew or Gentile, Protestant or Catholic in God's empire, for all stand before God on the basis of the same grace, all called to work in the same vineyard, together producing its fruit (cf. 3:10; 7:18–20; 13:8; 21:43).

The Cup of Suffering and the Gift of Sight

Matthew 20:17–34

Exploring the text

Have the disciples understood the kind of **justice** set forth in the preceding parable and what it requires of them? Are they ready for what will happen in Jerusalem? The stories in this section suggest that envy, competition, self-interest, and blindness are still problems that Jesus must address as he prepares his disciples for their entry into the city. For the final time before he enters Jerusalem, Jesus warns the disciples of his impending passion. The new information supplied in 20:19 makes this the most detailed prediction yet (cf. 16:21; 17:12; 17:22–23): he will be mocked and beaten, and his death will be by crucifixion. For the first time "the Gentiles" also enter the picture as participants in Jesus' death. When Jesus had first predicted his death (16:21), Peter had openly rebuked him. The second time (17:22–23) the disciples were "greatly distressed." This time Matthew records no reaction of the disciples, but instead tells about the request of the mother of the "sons of Zebedee" and the conflict it generates. Mediterranean mothers are expected to advocate for their sons' advancement (see, e.g., Bathsheba's manipulations on behalf of her son, Solomon: 1 Kgs. 1:11–31). Like King David's sons, the disciples are now positioning themselves for the succession. But they still misunderstand the nature of Jesus' kingship. The succession to power in this empire will be through suffering. So Jesus asks whether they are able to drink from the same cup–a dual image associated both with the suffering imposed as **judgment** on Israel by imperial powers (e.g., Ezek. 23:31–34; Jer. 49:12; cf. Jer. 25:15–29; 51:7; Isa. 51:17, 22) and with **salvation** (e.g., Pss. 16:5; 116:13).[1] When they pledge glibly that they are able to drink this cup, he confirms that they will indeed encounter suffering. But he also reminds them that he is not the kind of executive they think he is. Only God has the power to grant seats of honor (Matt. 20:23).

The exchange between Jesus and the sons of Zebedee inflames the indignation of the other disciples toward the brothers. The ten don't want to be left out, but they too do not know what they are asking (cf. 20:22). Jesus' explanation about the nature of power in the community of disciples is a commentary on his own relationship with the Father (20:23). Even if he is God's chosen messiah and king, Jesus' authority and power are expressed in service, which means he is nothing like an oriental potentate. The tyranny the disciples see exercised by rulers such as Herod or Caesar is radically different in nature and effect from the kind of power that enlivens the community of disciples (20:25).

The three sayings in 20:26–28 recall preceding episodes. "Whoever wishes to be great among you must be your servant" answers directly the question the disciples asked in 18:1. "Whoever wishes to be first among you must be your slave" returns to the images of "first" and "last" of 19:30 and 20:16. Finally, the claim that "the **Son of Man** came not to be served but to serve, and to give his life a ransom for many" ties Jesus' model of power–servanthood–directly to his predictions of suffering and death in Jerusalem (20:17–19; 16:21; 17:22–23). In 19:28 Jesus had described the Son of Humanity sitting on his throne of glory. In 20:18–19 the Son of Humanity is delivered up to death, crucified, and vindicated by resurrection from the dead. Now, in 20:28, the Son of Humanity is portrayed as a servant whose death ransoms many (cf. Exod. 21:30; Isa. 53:10–12). Jesus' identity as a servant has its fullest expression in his crucifixion, which redeems "many" by breaking the enslaving bonds of death itself.

Just as Jesus leaves Jericho for Jerusalem, two blind men call out to him for mercy, naming Jesus as "Lord" and "**Son of David**," the same titles used by the Canaanite woman in 15:22. Although they are blind, they can see what the crowds, who try to silence them, cannot (20:31). Like the Canaanite woman, they are doggedly persistent. Their specific request, which Matthew delays until Jesus asks them what they want, is a prayer that would fit well on the lips of Jesus' disciples and the whole of Israel: "Lord, let our eyes be opened" (20:33). When Jesus touches them and they regain their sight (lit., "look up"), they also follow him. Sight leads to discipleship.

Preaching and teaching the Word

Why does Jesus persist in warning his disciples of his impending death, including now the specifics of mocking, beating, and crucifixion? As he has brought them along step-by-step, now to the moment just before they enter Jerusalem, he has made space for them to adjust their perceptions of his messiahship. Nothing that takes place in Jerusalem will be a surprise to them, except perhaps their own participation in the events that lead up to his arrest and death. Jesus' detailed foreknowledge of what will happen also suggests that he will be an active participant, not a passive victim, in all that takes place. Finally, the form of Jesus' death, the public shame and suffering of Roman crucifixion, is consistent with Jesus' true identity as the Son of David, the servant king.

The disciples may finally be coming to grips with the possibility of Jesus' death, but despite four clear warnings (16:21; 17:12; 17:22–23; 20:18–19) they still do not understand that the route to the **empire of heaven** runs through suffering and death, their own as well as Jesus'. Nor do they seem to have any inkling of what he is talking about when he speaks of being raised after three days. Matthew provides a case study in the ways humans deny bad news. The disciples still cannot comprehend that the power to overcome death comes through engaging rather than avoiding it. Couldn't Jesus just stop the process that is leading to his death, demonstrate his divine power openly, and establish his rule without the necessity of the cross? This was essentially the content of Satan's last temptation of Jesus (4:8–9), as well as Peter's rebuke (16:22–23). As long as death still is the dominant reality that confronts humankind, the world will go on as it has, regardless of who rules. Only the defeat of death itself will establish the rule of the empire of heaven.

Jesus, the Son of David, rules in service and suffering. To the world, this kind of leadership is upside down. This kind of leadership means that in the community of disciples there are no rulers, masters, rabbis, kings, or Caesars (cf. 23:8–12). How is leadership expressed in our congregations and ecclesiastical structures? What models of power does the leadership we see in the church draw upon? To what reality does it bear witness? In the stories in Matthew 19–20, Jesus has already taught his disciples that marriage, celibacy, childlikeness, and poverty are forms of witness to God's rule and power. Now he names service and death as a slave for the sake of others as crucial forms of that same witness. This means that the **church's** vocation also necessarily entails suffering and death, because precisely this form of witness is required to reveal that the powers of violence and death are impotent, and to display the true nature and reach of God's presence, mercy, and power. Is this a cup the church today is willing to drink? Will we drink the cup of suffering only when, or if, it is forced on us? Or will we do so knowing the true nature of our calling as disciples of Jesus and trusting God's power to redeem and vindicate?

Jesus the Son of David is both healer and the source of sight. The first time Jesus had healed two blind men he warned them not to tell anyone, but they went away and told the news throughout the region (9:30–31). This time, when the blind gain their sight they follow him toward Jerusalem (20:34). Do they anticipate a triumphant entry? Do they expect Jesus will reclaim the temple? Does their sight enable them to discern what remains obscure to the disciples, that the rule of God comes through the defeat of death? What would this kind of sight mean in today's world? Would we turn our eyes in awe toward spectacles of human triumph? Would we look for the restoration of the temples of the nation-state? Where would we look in order to see the Son of David?

PART TEN

The Possession of the Temple
21:1–22:46

Preliminary Remarks

Jesus enters Jerusalem for the Passover, hailed as the **Son of David**, riding the animals of kings and farmers. His entry mocks the triumphant parades of military conquerors and sets the city astir. He then stages a series of prophetic actions aimed at reclaiming the temple as a center of prayer and healing. He continues his occupation of the temple with his disciples and the crowds through the next day, while the Jewish leaders stage a series verbal assaults and challenges meant to undermine his honor and his authority. Outmaneuvered and beaten at every turn, the leaders will resort to judicial murder to remove the Son of David from power.

The Victory Parade

Matthew 21:1–11*

Exploring the text

Many of us may remember old images of Soviet-era "May Day" parades, in which Red Army soldiers, tanks, missiles, and other military hardware would parade past the leaders of the nation and gathered citizenry. Closer to home, the inauguration of a President is a political ritual accompanied by pomp and ceremony, speeches, military flyovers, and other symbols of national pride and power. Ancient "entrance processions" were of similar character: an emperor, governor, or victorious military commander would enter a city amidst fanfare and singing, accompanied by soldiers and even prisoners of war, to be met by the leading figures of the city, who would offer speeches of welcome and gifts of tribute, hailing the conqueror's justice and power. The religious ceremonies and sacrifices that usually accompanied these events, as they

---

*The Revised Common Lectionary uses this in Year A, Passion/Palm Sunday, The 6th Sunday in Lent, Liturgy of the Palms.

still do today, lent the experience an aura of divine majesty and approba-
tion. Such events were called a "parousia," the same term used in the New
Testament to refer to the "coming" of Christ at the end of the age.

The story of Jesus' entrance into Jerusalem recalls such grand processions, but with some provocative twists: no prisoners of war, no military
accompaniment, and no leaders from the city coming out to meet their
king. What if none of the important dignitaries showed up for the inauguration of the President? Jesus has been a king in exile; he has chosen
to conduct his mission among the marginal people, in the hinterlands,
away from Israel's capital. It is not clear that the crowds that hail Jesus as
"Son of David" (21:9) are residents of the city itself, for Matthew reports
that Jesus' entry first sets the city in "turmoil" (21:10). God's anointed is
certainly not acknowledged by the leadership of the city, who will prove
murderous.

Jesus' entry sets in motion the events that will realize the prophecies
that Jesus has set before his disciples concerning his fate in Jerusalem (cf.
16:21; 17:22–23; 20:17–19). Jesus is fully in charge of these events! He
not only knows where to send his disciples to find the donkey and colt
he will use for his entry, but also anticipates objections (21:2–3). Jesus
surveys and choreographs the events in Jerusalem from a perspective
that no one else in the story shares. He acts both with foresight into how
the Jerusalem authorities will respond and according to what he knows
to be God's will.

His entry into Jerusalem is a **"prophetic-symbolic" action**, a form of
"street theater," in which he will use the generic signals associated with
the "parousias" of emperors and military conquerors in conjunction with
signs that point to the character of his rule. By twisting the political rituals associated with Roman and Jewish elite power to his own ends, he
puts the powers into his parody parade. Jesus' "triumphal entry" signals
the triumph of God's identification with the weak, the lowly, and the
marginal–those who will come to him for healing and to praise him in
the temple in the next episode (21:14–16). Jesus' actions implicitly make
the source and character of his power the central issue (cf. 21:23). On the
world's terms, this scene is not really triumphal at all, but an affirmation
of the kind of power Jesus has displayed all during his ministry in Galilee,
and simultaneously a mockery of what ordinarily passes for power among
the Jerusalem elite. The "triumphal entry" tears the facade from the scaf-
folding that holds the Jerusalem "establishment" together.

Throughout this story Matthew carefully foreshadows events, images,
and themes that will be developed in the subsequent narrative (e.g.,
Mount of Olives, Matt. 24:3; 26:30; Jesus as king, 27:11, 29, 37, 42; Son

of David, 21:15; 22:42–44; prophet, 21:46; 26:68; Jerusalem shaken, 27:51, 54). The evangelist also continues to exhibit a penchant for "twos": two citations of Scripture around which the passage is structured (21:5 = Isaiah 62:11 and Zechariah 9:9; 21:9 = Psalm 118:25–26); two disciples who go to secure the animals for Jesus' entry; and not one, but two animals upon which Jesus rides. Both of the citations focus on God's victory over the nations on Israel's behalf, and establish a clear messianic frame for Jesus' entrance. The reference to Psalm 118, which will be featured again later in the chapter (21:42), suggests the fate that awaits him at the hands of Israel's leaders and Rome's imperial order, but also affirms God's steadfast love and vindication of the psalmist before his enemies. The acclamation of Jesus as Son of David according to this psalm is one of many ironic references in this story.

Matthew's care in presenting this episode should also be considered in our interpretation of the curious scene in which Jesus apparently enters Jerusalem simultaneously riding both a donkey and a colt (21:2, 5, 7). This image is sometimes regarded as Matthew's clumsy, literalistic misreading of the Hebrew parallelism in Zechariah 9:9. It is, rather, a deliberate literary device—the kind that works best in oral presentations. It signals: (a) Jesus' royal, messianic identity as Son of David (the donkey is associated with coronations of kings, cf. 1 Kgs. 1:33–48); (b) Jesus' identification with what is meek or humble (Matt. 21:5; cf. 5:5; 11:29), i.e., "the colt of a pack animal"; (c) Matthew's identification of Jesus with Moses (Moses rides a donkey in Exod. 4:19–20; cf. Matt. 2:19–21); and (d) a strong affirmation of Jesus' fulfillment of the messianic vision of Zechariah 9–14 (cf. Matt. 21:12–13; 26:15–16; 26:26–29; 26:30–35; 27:3–10; 27:51–53), where the messiah not only restores Israel and shatters her enemies, but brings peace to the nations and sets prisoners free (Zech. 9:9–11). Matthew has also replaced the words "Rejoice greatly, O daughter Zion!" (Zech. 9:9) with "Tell the daughter of Zion" (Isa. 62:11), perhaps to reflect the fact that Jesus' entry must be explained to the people of Jerusalem and does not, in fact, elicit rejoicing.

The question and answer with which the passage ends (21:10–11), in which the crowds announce to the people of Jerusalem that "This is the prophet Jesus from Nazareth in Galilee," drips with irony. On one level, the crowds have it right: Jesus is a prophet and he has just acted in a decidedly prophetic way, by twisting an imperial ritual of power to his own purposes and holding the authorities up for mockery. On the other hand, while Jesus acts as and will meet the fate of a prophet, he is more. Moreover, within the span of a few days, the crowds themselves, at the instigation of the authorities, will turn decisively against Jesus, acting as

Israel always has toward the prophets (cf. 23:29–39). The crowds also identify Jesus as "from Nazareth in Galilee" (cf. 2:22–23), that is, both rural "NowheresVille" (where the king grew up in exile) and "Galilee of the Gentiles," where light has dawned for those who sit in darkness (cf. 4:15–16). Light will once again dawn from darkness, even in Jerusalem (cf. 27:45). Each major element in 21:10 and 11–Jerusalem, crowds, prophet, Galilee–carries mixed valences. By this means, Matthew signals that up will be down and down will be up. Everyone stands on ground that will be shaken.

Preaching and teaching the Word

This passage invites us to look critically and creatively at the rituals by which rulers paint their empires in divine hues. Symbolic, public demonstrations of political power are often saturated in religious imagery. In our own context, even "secular" spectacles, such as football's "Super Bowl," now juxtapose political and religious imagery with power. Jesus' entry into Jerusalem shows us the power of ritual, the importance of engaging such rituals critically, and the risks of challenging conventional symbols of power. Preaching, itself a form of ritualized speech, is one of the primary tools by which Christians speak truth to power. Proclamation joined with prophetic-symbolic action can be transformative.

Palm Sunday celebrations of the triumphal entry often miss the sense of irony that pervades this story. Do our commemorations capture Jesus' parody of the worldly powers? Do we sense what the story means for our own exercise of authority? Jesus' prophetic-symbolic entry into Jerusalem signals that the way before him will be a struggle over the nature and character of God's power. The church embodies this power where it also stands with the weak and lowly, with those on the margins, where it strips away the pretensions of human rulers and unmasks the facades upon which systems of domination and exploitation are built. This passage calls the church not to triumphalism, but to identification with a king who comes to town, comically, on a coronation donkey and a beast of burden. God triumphs in weakness. God triumphs in the scandal and shame of the cross.

The Occupation of the Temple

Matthew 21:12–17

Exploring the text

Jesus completes his entry into Jerusalem without being properly recognized by the authorities. He now proceeds to the temple, the center of religious, economic, and political power among the Jewish people and the focus of Israel's cultic activity. Entrance processions and "Parousias" often included cultic acts such as sacrifices in temples. Jesus' actions foreshadow Rome's destruction of the temple in 70 CE, shortly before Matthew was written. At the level of the narrative itself, Jesus' actions symbolize God's judgment on the corruption and exploitation of the temple by Israel's leaders. Jesus does not direct his polemic against the temple per se, but against its use to exploit and divide God's people, rather than to heal and restore. Jesus first disrupts the economic systems associated with the temple (21:12–13). Then he takes possession of the temple and welcomes and heals those who were ordinarily excluded (21:14). Finally, the temple becomes the setting of his first direct encounter with the authorities in Jerusalem (21:15–16). Jesus is greater than the temple (12:6), and his body will eventually displace the temple as the locus of **salvation**, but for the moment Jesus reclaims the temple as a symbol of God's saving presence.

Jesus first drives out "all who were selling and buying in the temple" (21:12). Matthew uses the word here translated "drive out" (lit., "cast out") in stories of exorcism. He is fighting demonic forces. The temple is possessed by those who use it for their own interests rather than for access to God's presence. "Selling and buying" refers to those who were involved in the commerce required to support the temple apparatus. Jesus then overturns the tables of those who exchange currencies for pilgrims to pay their temple taxes and offerings and of the merchants who sell sacrificial animals to those who are too poor to bring their own. The sacrifice of doves was associated especially with the poor, with women, and with lepers.

In 21:13 Jesus announces the rationale for his actions: God's house of prayer (Isa. 56:7) has become a "den of robbers" (Jer. 7:11). Prayer is a primary human response to God's presence, which in Jewish thought was located in the temple. Sacrifice is a form of prayer. But the temple had become a place of theft and exploitation. For Jesus, the leaders both rob those who come to the temple and usurp God's authority, depriving people—especially aliens, orphans, and widows (cf. Jer. 7:6)—of God's presence and healing. Jeremiah 7 promises that God is present where there is **justice**, not oppression, and where the blood of the innocent is not shed. The prophet also challenges those who steal, murder, commit adultery, swear falsely, and make offerings to Baal and then stand before God "in this house" and say, "We are safe" (Jer. 7:5–10). Jesus' identification of the temple as a den of robbers is a prophetic word of **judgment** against the leaders who use the temple to justify and sanction their practices of injustice and exploitation.

Jesus' actions disrupt the operation of the temple system, but do not transform it. That will happen with his death and resurrection (cf. 27:51). For now, the most disruptive action yet takes place: the "blind and the lame" come to him in the temple and he heals them (21:14). The "blind and lame" stand for all who were excluded from the temple, including the children who hail Jesus as **Son of David** in 21:15 (again citing Ps. 118; cf. Matt. 21:9). These are the people among whom the Son of David has conducted his ministry (cf. 9:27–28; 11:5; 12:22; 15:30–31; 18:1–6; 19:13–15; 20:29–34). Now they join him in his occupation of the temple. This action turns the temple into a space of inclusion and thus fundamentally threatens the power of the **chief priests** and **scribes** (21:15). Their power and place in Jewish society, as well as their wealth, depend on the use of the temple to mark the boundaries and distinctions that secure their authority. If even the blind, the lame, and the children have access to the temple, then it no longer can serve to preserve social and religious divisions and hierarchies or to delimit access to God's power. This explains why now, after all that has already transpired, the chief priests and scribes finally show up, outraged. Jesus' actions to this point have been annoying but manageable threats. The merchants' tables will be righted again. But his occupation of the temple with the blind, the lame, and the children has the potential to ruin the whole system. Now the leaders must act.

Their indignant question, "Do you hear what these are saying?" offers a sharp contrast to the praise of the children. Jesus' answer indicates that he accepts the appropriateness of the children's appellation. The phrase "have you never read" is a well-established rebuke in Matthew (12:3–7; 19:4; cf. also 21:42). Jesus does not become servile or apologetic in the face of the authorities' indignation. His citation of Psalm 8:2 affirms that the children read Scripture with more accuracy and authority than the chief priests and scribes. Just as Jesus' triumphal entry parodied the public rituals of the powerful, so too his affirmation of the children's praise mocks the status and authority of Israel's leaders.

Jesus then "leaves them" and departs the city. He still holds possession of the temple, for the chief priests and scribes have not yet discredited and dislodged him, nor will they. He will return to the temple and skirmish again with them the next day (21:23–22:46). Only after he has delivered a final, stinging rebuke of the religious elites (chap. 23) will he finally relinquish of his own accord his claim on the temple, at which time he will also prophesy its destruction (24:1–2).

Preaching and teaching the Word

Jesus demonstrates great skill in the use of **prophetic-symbolic actions**. He challenges the temple-based authority of the religious leaders at its heart. He seeks to restore the temple itself to its proper function in **God's rule**. He reclaims sacred space for healing and restoration of the weak and vulnerable. Jesus' radical challenge to the religious leaders teaches us that all human systems of power, even those at work in the church and religious institutions, are subject to manipulation and exploitation. The temple itself is not the focus of Jesus' polemic in these verses, but rather the leaders' use of the temple to serve their interests and to offer them "safety" from being held accountable for injustice, exploitation, and violence. What are the "temples" within which leaders today hide? Have our religious traditions and institutions been co-opted to serve merely human interests? Are we able to hear the voices of prophets, or of the children and the vulnerable?

This story also points to the importance of the temple in the creation and maintenance of Jewish social, political, economic, and religious relationships. The temple was understood as the physical and religious center of Israelite society. Its various precincts defined both social status and access to God. Over time, the temple also became the center of Jewish economic life. In all these ways the temple defined and represented ways of understanding who God is, how God relates to the world, and how humans are to order their relationships. Sometimes this meant that domination and exploitation were confirmed as expressions of what is "normal," or even divinely ordained. For most of us, temples and church buildings no longer serve these same functions. Our views of the world, ourselves, and God are more often shaped by media (the new priests) and by economic and political institutions. Our modern temples are shopping malls and stadiums. Discipleship requires the cultivation of a critical eye that discerns the spaces where reality is "constructed" and imposed on us. Faithful witness may require us to contest the construction of reality that is held up as normative for us in such spaces.

Eventually Jesus will leave the temple behind, effectively returning it to the Jerusalem authorities and its ultimate fate. But already Jesus has been preparing his disciples for an alternative "space," for the empire of heaven, embodied especially in the inclusive settings of table fellowship that constitute his "body." Early Christians understood the "body of Christ" as an alternative to the Jerusalem temple, even before the destruction of the temple itself (cf. 1 Cor. 3:16–17; 6:19). Since the crucifixion and resurrection of Jesus, Christians confess that God no longer dwells in spaces constructed by human beings, but is loose in the world, present in power wherever even two or three are gathered in Jesus' name (18:20; cf. also 28:16–20). The challenge for the church is always to follow God faithfully into the world, to the places where God is making space for the blind and the lame. Every denomination and every congregation lives at constant risk of becoming another temple. The body of Christ exists neither to be self-perpetuating nor to serve merely human interests, but to give itself up for the sake of others, as Jesus himself does.

The Fruitless Fig Tree

Matthew 21:18–22

Exploring the text

Contemporary audiences find Jesus' cursing of the fig tree baffling, if not offensive. His reaction to the absence of fruit on the tree seems harsh and arbitrary, and the story seems to bear little apparent connection, at least at a superficial level, to its context. But the surprising, hyperbolic, and even abrasive character of this action should help us identify it as a **prophetic sign-act**, delivered not in response to Jesus' hunger but for the sake of Jesus' disciples and directed against the "fruitlessness" of the Jerusalem leaders. The story interrupts the flow of Jesus' conflicts with the Jewish authorities in the temple (cf. 21:14–16 and 21:23–27) precisely in order to comment upon them.

Jesus returns in the morning to Jerusalem from the night he has spent in Bethany. The note that Jesus is hungry recalls his hunger following the temptation (4:2), his defense of the disciples when they pluck grain to satisfy their hunger on the Sabbath (12:1–8), as well as his ongoing ministry to the hungry crowds that followed him during his ministry in Galilee (14:13–21; 15:32–39). God satisfies both physical hunger and the hunger of those who yearn for the taste of justice (5:6). The fig tree, however, is not doing its part in supplying provisions for the **empire of heaven**. Even though it has leaves, which would ordinarily be preceded by the appearance of fruit, there is no fruit to be found.

Throughout Matthew fruit symbolizes appropriate responses to the proclamation of God's reign; it signifies human actions that are commensurate with God's mercy, presence, and healing power (cf. 3:8; 3:10; 7:16–20; 12:33), and with the harvest that Jesus is gathering (cf. 21:41, 43). The sweet fruit of a fig tree is a symbol of God's blessing (Num. 29:5; Deut. 8:7–8). Like the Jerusalem authorities, however, the appearance of this tree belies another reality. Like them, it has not produced fruit fit for the reign of God. Jesus' "curse" articulates God's judgment not only against the tree, but against those leaders who have failed to produce the kind of fruit God requires. The fact that the tree immediately withers and dies symbolizes the destruction that will soon visit those who now oppose Jesus' ministry. A withered fig tree was itself a common prophetic sign of judgment (cf. Isa. 34:4; Jer. 8:13; 29:17; Hos. 2:12; 9:10; 9:16). Jesus' action both announces God's impending judgment and gives notice of its cause.

The disciples express astonishment at how quickly the tree withers (Matt. 21:20), which leads Jesus to offer another teaching on the power of faith, which the disciples should well know by now. His teaching is carefully crafted to fit into the larger context that frames this episode. He asserts that those who have faith can command mountains to be thrown into the sea and it will be done. There is no limit to God's power at work among Jesus and the disciples. Jesus then promises that the disciples will receive whatever they ask for in prayer with faith (21:22; cf. 18:18–20). "Prayer" recalls Jesus' designation of the temple as God's house of prayer (21:13), as well as his teaching on the centrality of humble, honest prayer in the realization of God's empire (6:5–15). Prayer coupled with "faith" creates a social space in which God's power is manifest, thereby providing an alternative to the temple, which has been controlled by those who produce no fruit. Prayer and faith are at the heart of God's alternative temple; they are the locus of God's presence and power, the means by which God will produce fruit in the disciples.

Preaching and teaching the Word

In contemporary spirituality prayer is often the focus of one's personal relationship with God; in Matthew, prayer is a practice that lies at the heart of the community Jesus has called into being. Jesus promises that whatever "you" (plural) ask for in prayer with faith, you will receive. All the verbs in 21:21–22, in fact, are plural, which suggests that Jesus is speaking not to the individual, nor even to a collective of individuals, but to the community of disciples, where even two or three are gathered together in Jesus' name (18:20). The community is both constituted and nourished by such prayer in faith, which yields the fruit God desires. Prayer in faith among the disciples generates and sustains the body that will take the place of the temple and its leaders, and that the resurrected Jesus will commission with power and presence to take the gospel into all the world (28:16–20). With this teaching, then, Jesus continues to form a people who will produce the fruits of God's vineyard (21:43). By these same practices, the living Jesus continues to create that community today.

The Power Crisis

Matthew 21:23–32*

Exploring the text

After spending the night in Bethany (21:17) and cursing the fig tree (21:18–22), Jesus returns to Jerusalem and resumes his occupation of the temple. The **chief priests** and **elders** of the people confront him. Matthew persistently names the chief priests at the head of the alliance of figures who oppose Jesus, which includes the **scribes**, **Pharisees**, and elders alternately at the chief priests' side. The elders represent the wealthy elite, whose interests often did coincide with those of the chief priests. Their designation as "elders of the people" is ironic, for later it will become clear that they fear rather than represent the crowds (21:26; 21:46). Because Jesus has mocked the leaders' authority and taken possession of the temple, they now attempt to dislodge him by challenging the nature and source of his authority. The whole story includes the challenge (21:23), Jesus' initial response and the ensuing exchange (21:24–27), and three parables (21:28–32; 21:33–46; and 22:1–14). This **controversy story** is the first of five challenges (see 22:15–22; 22:23–33; 22:34–40; 22:41–46) aimed at undermining Jesus' authority. Any successful attempt to defeat Jesus in verbal riposte would allow the authorities to reclaim the temple and reestablish their own authority. Their failure will require them to resort to violence.

*The Revised Common Lectionary uses this in Year A, The 26th Sunday in Ordinary Time.

The chief priests and elders raise two related, but distinct, questions: "By what authority [or what kind of authority] are you doing these things?" and "Who gave you this authority?" (21:23). The first question focuses on the nature of Jesus' authority and implies that the leaders are looking for legal authority for Jesus' actions. The audience knows that Jesus, the **Son of David**, has this authority, but the leaders do not recognize or accept this identification. The question about the source of Jesus' power is not new; the Pharisees have already accused Jesus of casting out demons by Beelzebul (9:34; 12:24). These two questions together pose the fundamental terms of Jesus' struggle with the Jewish leaders and articulate the nature of the conflict that will lead to his crucifixion.

As the one holding the upper hand, Jesus first refuses a direct answer to the questions. Instead he challenges them with a question of his own about the origins of John's baptism. Was it heavenly or human? His question puts them in a bind. If they affirm that John's baptism represented God's call, as the crowds believe, he will ask why they did not submit to John's baptism. If they deny that John was a prophet sent from heaven, they will alienate themselves from the crowds, whom they fear (21:26). They break their huddle and punt: "We do not know." We may imagine this answer, only two words long in the Greek, being delivered almost inaudibly, under their breath. With this exchange, the controversy proper has already reached its resolution. The leaders' failure to answer Jesus' question leaves his authority intact and diminishes their own. Jesus, however, is not done with the chief priests and elders. He employs the "political capital" he has just confirmed to launch a series of parables that demonstrate the justice of God's **judgment** against these leaders. He will invite them to offer their own judgment of the characters in his **parables**, thereby drawing them out of their strategic silence, ultimately to pronounce judgment upon themselves (21:31–32, 40–41).[1]

The first of the three parables that comprise Jesus' extended dialogue with the chief priests and elders is a cousin of Luke's account of the prodigal son and his older brother (Luke 15:11–32). The "two sons" (lit., "children") tradition is deeply embedded in the story of God's people, most prominently in the stories of Cain and Abel, Jacob and Esau, Joseph and his brothers, Aaron and Moses, and even David and his brothers. Other elements in this parable also draw from the biblical tradition. The people of Israel are often called God's "children," sometimes rebellious children (e.g., Isa. 1:2–4; Deut. 32:5–6). The vineyard is a common biblical symbol for Israel (cf. on 20:2; 21:33; Isa. 5; Isa. 27:2–6; Ps. 80:8–16; Jer. 2:21). This apparently simple story thus resonates deeply with the old stories about fathers, vineyards, alienated sons, and disobedient children. This richness also lends the story ambivalence. How will the audience, especially the religious leaders, read themselves into the story?

A man who owns a vineyard asks his two children in turn to go and work in the vineyard. The first refuses, rudely and without explanation, but later "changes his mind" and goes as requested. Jesus does not use the word "repent" to describe this turnabout, which might tip his hand too soon. The second son offers lip service: his two-word answer, literally "I, Lord," emphasizes this child's seeming willingness and certainty, in contrast to the first. He even adopts a respectful tone of address, calling his father "Lord" (NRSV: "sir"). But then he does not go. Jesus' question to the Jerusalem leaders focuses on which son "does" the will of the father. They correctly affirm that the son who goes to tend the vineyard, even though he initially refused, is the one who does the father's will. Their reply is clear and unambiguous, but they have not noticed how it might apply to themselves.

The parable clearly emphasizes the importance of "doing" over mere speech. On this Jesus and his adversaries agree. Beyond this, the parable would also admit diverse allegorical associations. With which of the children might the leaders identify themselves? As those who control the temple and preserve the traditions of the Law, they would typically identify with the child who has done what is required. They surely would not see themselves as the one who disobeys, although that is precisely where Jesus will locate them. Jesus' reading of the story, in contrast, is tied integrally to the immediate context of his dispute with the leaders. His own application of the parable turns on two details: First, Jesus links the parable with the preceding discussion about John's baptism (21:25–27). For him, doing the father's will corresponds to believing John, who "came to you in the way of righteousness," and bearing the fruit of repentance (21:32a; cf. 3:2, 8). By this definition of "doing" what the father asks, all would agree that the leaders have failed. The second important detail concerns the matter of repentance. Jesus says that while John's proclamation prompted belief among the tax collectors and sinners, "you did not change your minds and believe him" (21:32). Here Jesus uses the same word for "change your mind" as he had for the first child's turnabout after refusing to go (21:29). Because the tax collectors and sinners did change their minds (which Jesus here equates with repentance) and bore the fruit of righteousness (e.g., joining at table with Jesus and his disciples, cf. 9:10–11), they will go into God's kingdom ahead of the leaders, who did not change their minds and go into the vineyard (Israel) to work (bear fruit) (21:31).

Preaching and teaching the Word

All the controversy stories in chapters 21 and 22 will demonstrate Jesus' mastery of the Jerusalem leaders in debate. The religious leaders are reduced to mumbling under their breath in the face of Jesus' authority. In contrast, the leaders' authority depends on the manipulation of the crowds, intimidation, and the exercise of "sanctioned" violence against troublemakers like Jesus. Matthew is unmasking the bluster, insecurity, and impotence of the Jewish authorities before the Galilean teacher. Jesus' God-given authority, on the other hand, is manifested in truth that speaks to (human) power and unmasks its hypocrisy and hollowness. The Jewish leaders do not understand this kind of power because it is of a fundamentally different kind from their own, and from a different source. It does not matter that Jesus refuses to tell the leaders "by what authority I am doing these things" (21:27), for they could not and would not comprehend it if he did tell them. To the extent that the **church** bears witness to the nature and consequences of God's power, it will also unmask the pretensions of human power.

In these stories faith consists of accepting authority that claims to represent God, whether that of the religious leaders, John, or Jesus. Only Jesus and John manifest power that requires a "change of mind" about the nature of power itself. Still more important, their power produces "fruit" in the form of gathering and restoration, forgiveness, table fellowship with tax collectors and sinners, release from demonic powers, sight, and understanding. Can Jesus' adversaries claim as much? If faith entails discerning power, then faith is also utterly "political" in nature, in that it critically challenges whatever political commonplaces rule the day. The church today often seems content to occupy a comfortable, albeit shrinking, niche within a diverse religious landscape. It thus renders itself effectively irrelevant except as one option among many in the marketplace of ideas. The faith that Jesus represents and draws forth, on the other hand, cannot be ignored by either the religious or the political authorities, for he renders the politics of Pharisees, **Sadducees**, **Herodians**, zealots, and Romans obsolete. For the followers of Jesus, a fusion of Christian faith and human politics—a "Christian Democratic" party, for example, or an "evangelical caucus"—would be hard to imagine, for the **empire of heaven** challenges all human constructions of power. How, then, does the church engage the politics of the day without becoming captive to it? How does it embody and bear witness to God's presence that unmasks self-serving human politics?

"Yes" does not always mean "yes." "No" may not be the final word. As so often in the Gospel, Jesus focuses here on the fruit of our actions, which speak louder than and expose the emptiness of words (cf. 5:33–37; 7:21–23; 23:16–22). The power of words to mask and distort reality, even to create and sustain false realities, should be evident to those of us who live in a world of advertising and mass media. Yet we are still easily seduced. This may be a problem especially for religious leaders, whose main tools are words. The performance of the gospel–its embodiment in individuals and communities–is the most important form of proclamation we have. One of the preacher's primary tasks is to provide language to help people make sense of the signs of God's power they see around them but cannot yet name. A second is to evoke the imagination–the sight–that makes this discernment possible. A third task, perhaps the most important, is to call forth the practices that incarnate the good news of God's empire.

The Wicked Tenant Farmers

Matthew 21:33–46*

Exploring the text

Many interpreters see in this story a distilled account of Matthew's understanding of **salvation** history, focusing especially on the place of Israel and the **church** in God's plan of redemption. The **parable** includes numerous elements that lend themselves to allegorization, especially in light of Jesus' passion in Jerusalem. But this parable, like so many others in Matthew, presents more than one face. The parable turns on the fact that Jesus and the Jewish leaders each identify its characters in a distinctive way. The parable's many faces make it a riddle for Matthew's audience no less than for the chief priests and elders. Matthew invites the audience to grapple especially with the question of who God is and how God fulfills the covenant with Israel. The parable thus poses interpretive questions that are crucial for the whole Gospel. It is the questions more than the apparent answers that make this a signature story for Matthew.

In brief, a landowner establishes a vineyard that he then leases to tenant farmers. When it is time for the landowner to collect the portion of the

*The Revised Common Lectionary uses this in Year A, The 27th Sunday in Ordinary Time.

harvest due to him, he sends various emissaries whom the tenants abuse in turn, culminating in the murder of the landowner's son. The tenant farmers believe that if they kill the heir, they will secure their claim to the vineyard itself. After recounting the story, Jesus turns to the **chief priests**, the **elders** of the people, and the **Pharisees** (21:23, 45) to ask what the landowner will do with such evil tenant farmers. Without hesitation they affirm that he will "put those wretches to a miserable death" and lease the vineyard to other tenants who will give him the produce when the harvest comes (21:41). Jesus answers with a quotation from Psalm 118, which states that the stone rejected by the builders in fact becomes the cornerstone (or keystone). He then affirms that the **empire of God** will be taken from "you" (i.e., the Jerusalem authorities) and given to another people who will produce its fruits.

In the church's allegorical readings of the parable, the landowner is identified as God, the tenants are the Jerusalem authorities or perhaps all of Israel, the son is Jesus, the servants sent before him are the law and the prophets (or John?), the fruits are works pleasing to God, and the "other tenants" (21:41) or "people" (21:43), to whom the vineyard is finally given, are the (Gentile) church. In Matthew's version alone, the tenants remove the son from the vineyard before they kill him, a detail that aligns the son's murder with Jesus' crucifixion outside the walls of Jerusalem. Does that mean that the vineyard stands for Jerusalem? Jewish tradition commonly identifies the vineyard with Israel, as in Isaiah 5, from which Matthew's account draws the opening description of the vineyard (21:33; Isa. 5:1–2). But in 21:43 Jesus himself identifies the vineyard as the kingdom of God. How can we be sure which allegorical reading is right?

When the parable is allegorized as the church traditionally has done, it clearly signals the end of the leaders' reign over Israel, which will be set under the care of another people (the church? Rome?). If the vineyard is understood primarily as God's empire and the tenants as all of Israel, not just its leaders, then the allegory suggests that God is abandoning the covenant with Israel in favor of the church. In this case, the story signals not just a prophetic critique of Israel's leadership, but a decisive shift in salvation history that carries profound theological implications: the God who offers and expects unlimited forgiveness (cf. 18:21–35) has run out of patience with Israel, the covenant people. Is this the way Jesus understood the parable? or Matthew? Allegory is notoriously difficult to control. Because the parable admits so many diverse allegorical associations, it becomes a mirror, revealing mostly the assumptions and convictions of its diverse audiences. The judgments we pronounce on the characters in the story become the judgments we pronounce on ourselves.

Matthew notes in 21:45 that the chief priests and Pharisees understand, at least by the end, that Jesus sees them in the role of the tenant farmers. But how would they have seen themselves? Jesus depends on the Jewish leaders to read themselves into the story in such a way that they are prepared to offer an answer when he asks them for their judgment on the tenants. Jesus knows well what answer they are likely to render. They identify with the landowner, for the chief priests and elders were themselves wealthy landowners in the first century. They would regard the tenants' behavior as an attack upon their authority, their families, and their property. Because of their identification with the landowner, they readily slip the noose Jesus gives them around the tenants' necks, only to discover it drawing tight around their own.

Like the chief priests and elders, every audience seeks a point of entry into the story that works to their own advantage. Modern readers have read themselves into the story as those who will receive the vineyard/kingdom. The church thus easily hears an affirmation of its place in salvation history at the expense of Israel. Matthew, however, clearly names the chief priests, elders, and Pharisees as the target (21:45–46; cf. 21:23–27, 31–32). The parable stands within the deep and broad stream of prophetic critique aimed at Israel's leadership, as in Isaiah 5:1–7, the portion of Isaiah's critique of the Jerusalem leadership from which Matthew draws the opening imagery for the parable (21:33; cf. Isa. 5:1–2; cf. also Jer. 2:21). The parable does not wrest salvation from all of Israel, but announces judgment upon those who fail to produce the fruit of the vineyard at the harvest (cf. 9:37–38; 10:5–8) or who seek to make the vineyard their own rather than tend it as faithful stewards. The church's supersessionist readings of the story have yielded anti-Semitic violence and triumphalism, rather than the fruit of repentance: mercy, forgiveness, healing, and reconciliation.

This parable thus invites its audience to confront what it means to be stewards of the vineyard. The most important question it poses, however, is theological: when the chief priests and elders name what the landowner would do to the wicked tenants, do they also accurately name what God would do? In announcing that the landowner will deal mercilessly with the tenants, the chief priests and elders name their own judgment. God will deal with them as the landowner would deal with the tenants: "The measure you give will be the measure you get" (7:2). Is God really who the Jewish leaders think God is? Our answer to this question will determine how we read not only this story but Matthew's whole Gospel. With this parable, then, Matthew poses the definitive interpretive riddle of the Gospel.

Preaching and teaching the Word

This parable trades in implausibility. The tenant farmers repeatedly abuse the owner's servants, and even think that by killing the son they will somehow claim his inheritance (21:38–39). The landowner, for his part, thinks the tenants will respect his son, even after they have met the earlier emissaries with violence and murder. Both perspectives appear on the surface to be utterly implausible, yet they accurately depict the reality that the Gospel as a whole describes: at its heart, the **Gospel** is the story of God's implausible mercy in the face of implacable rebellion.

Preachers must be careful in dealing with this story not to replicate the anti-Semitism that it has so often bred in the history of the church. The foundation of this anti-Semitism is the tendency to read the Gospel stories through the lenses of ethnic and religious generalizations, looking for clear insiders and outsiders, and finally locating ourselves within the stories in such a way that God is on our side. This is the very mechanism by which the authorities in this story pronounce their own judgment. This story does not announce the triumph of the church. It issues a call and a warning to the church, especially its leaders, to join the harvest and produce the fruit of repentance (cf. 3:8; 3:10; 7:15–20; 12:33; 18:8, 22, 23; 21:19). Judgment will not be based on ethnic identity or institutional affiliation, but on the **eschatological** fruit we bear for God's harvest. This is not a form of "works righteousness," but a matter of faithful response to the presence of the crucified and risen **Son of God** in our midst. The fruit of repentance is forgiveness, restoration, and reconciliation. Is this harvest evident and abundant in our assemblies?

The parable implicitly affirms Jesus' awareness of the fate that awaits him at the hands of the Jerusalem authorities. He unveils the seemingly inexplicable violence of the tenants/leaders toward the son, and even the violent nature of their God. Like the chief priests and elders, who make the landowner/God in their own image, we too reveal much about ourselves and our understandings of God by the notions of **judgment** that we affirm. Those who are rejected by God in Matthew's Gospel are those whose theological convictions lead them to deny God's power and mercy. They are judged with the very judgment with which they judge (7:1–2). And they are judged because by standing in judgment over others they usurp God's power and deny God's goodness.

Like the other parables that make up Jesus' response to the chief priests' and elders' questions about authority, this story focuses on the nature of power. The leaders' power lies not in mercy, but in their control over land and temple. They have sought to claim as their own what they were given as stewards. Their position is tenuous; Matthew notes that they seek to take hold of Jesus, but they fear the crowds (21:46; as Herod also feared the people, cf. 14:5), whom they will eventually manipulate to their own will. With these images Matthew paints a picture of illegitimate power, power that is exercised in denial of God's will and mercy. Every day the church faces questions about how it will respond to such power in the world. And every day the church must respond by asking itself hard questions about its own exercise of power. What kind of power is this? And whose power is it?

A Banquet for the Worthy

Matthew 22:1–14*

Exploring the text

The final element in Jesus' response to the chief priests and elders (cf. 21:23–27) is a **parable** in two parts (22:2–10, 11–13) that explores a world of dishonored kings, destroyed cities, wedding banquets filled with street people, and dress codes. Interpreters rightly conclude that Jesus means this story to be read as allegory, but the move to allegory admits a wide array of possible associations that need to stay in play for the parable to work. The parable works, in other words, by means of its ambiguity and multivalence. Is this, like the two preceding parables, an allegory for the continuing story of Israel and her leaders? Is God like the king in the story? Who is the man who fails to dress appropriately and is thrown into the outer darkness?

Matthew's reminder at the beginning of the story is important: "Jesus, answering, again spoke to them [i.e., the **chief priests**, **elders**, and **Pharisees**, 21:23, 45] in parables." Most English translations drop the term "answering" as a redundancy, but for Matthew it signals that this parable is a reply to the leaders' hostile responses in the preceding parable (21:41, 45–46). The primary interpretive task, then, is to discern what this story says to "them." The theme that runs consistently through the story is "worthiness," i.e., behavior appropriate to the king's invitation and the

---

*The Revised Common Lectionary uses this in Year A, The 28th Sunday in Ordinary Time.

time. The king will have a wedding banquet for his son, it will be full, and all the guests will be properly attired. Marriage is a metaphor for the relationship between God and Israel (e.g., Hos. 2:16–20; Isa. 54:5–6; 62:5). The banquet is associated with celebration of the covenant (e.g., Prov. 9:1–2; Isa. 55:1–3; Isa. 25:6–10). Matthew has also tied banqueting with Jesus' ministry of inclusion and reconciliation (9:10–13) and with messianic promise (8:11–12). What kind of behavior is appropriate to the covenant relationship between God and Israel, especially her leaders?

The king who is having a wedding banquet for his son is widely perceived to represent God and his son, Jesus. But this king is a demanding and venomous fellow, cast in the mold of oriental potentates like Herod. The king may also be losing his grip on power. The people he invites to the banquet "make light of it" and go about their business (22:5–6). Some of them even mistreat and kill the king's slaves, which elicits a response in kind from the king. He sends troops, destroys the murderers, and burns their city (22:7). This is widely perceived by interpreters as an allusion to the destruction of Jerusalem by the Romans in 70 CE, but more generally it represents Middle Eastern customs of retributive justice. It may also allude to Israel's history of killing God's messengers (cf. 23:34–35).

With the first guest list wiped clean, the king sends his slaves to invite everyone they can find. The phrase translated "main streets" (NRSV) or highways actually refers to the places where roads begin or end, that is, the borders of the region.[1] This time the slaves succeed in their mission, filling the banquet hall with "both good and bad" (22:10; cf. 13:24–30, 36–43, 47–50). When the king inspects the guests, he notices someone who is not wearing a wedding robe, which makes the man out of place. The king addresses the man as "Friend" (22:12), but in Matthew this is an ironic, even hostile greeting (cf. 20:13; 26:50). When called to account for his presence in the hall without the proper attire, the man is "speechless," as Jesus' adversaries later will be (22:34; cf. also 22:46). The banquet motifs, the inappropriate attire, silence, and judgment all echo Zephaniah's condemnation of Judah's religious and political leaders (Zeph. 1, esp. 1:7–9). Like the original invitees, the man is not worthy (cf. 22:8), and so is bound hand and foot and tossed out. "Outer darkness" and "weeping and gnashing of teeth" recall earlier pronouncements of **judgment** (8:12; 13:42; 13:50; also 24:51; 25:30) and lift the scene into an **eschatological** realm.

Do the king's fury and the penalty match the crime? Is this story, as often supposed, an allegory of the Jewish leaders' dealings with Jesus (22:5–6) and of God's dealings with the Jewish leaders (22:7)? Does it envision the supplanting of Israel (the first invitees) by the Gentile church (the street people)? Or is it meant to contrast Israel's rich, landowning leaders with the poor, common people from the border regions, like Galilee? Because this is a parable and not just an allegory, it defies simplistic decoding and invites reflection from various angles.

How might Jesus' adversaries have heard this story? The ambiguity of the images leaves room for the leaders in multiple places. They are indeed like the original invitees, who make light of the king's invitation and eventually turn murderous. They are also like the man whose unworthiness is revealed in the absence of garments that fit the occasion. Perhaps they could even identify with a king who behaves like this one. But whichever figure they see in the mirror, the image is not flattering. At its simplest, the parable—in both parts—challenges its hearers to respond appropriately to the invitation to join the banquet of the **empire of heaven**, which Israel's leaders have resolutely scorned. In the context of Jesus' ongoing engagement with these leaders, the most important motifs in both portions of the story concern response to call, worthiness, actions that match calling, reversals of expectation, and judgment.

Preaching and teaching the Word

Because the parable has often been read by Christians as a general indictment of Israel, now supposed to have been replaced by the Gentile church (called from the streets and boundary roads), it has been used to support anti-Semitism and Christian triumphalism. Jesus is not speaking here to Israel as a whole, however, but to her leaders, as had Israel's prophets in earlier days. Throughout the parable the focus is on "worthiness," which is not defined in terms of ethnic identity or religious affiliation, but in images of gathering, inclusion, and celebration. Good and bad alike can come to the banquet (22:10), but they must respond to the invitation and come wearing the right clothes—repentance, faithfulness, humility, and forgiveness. Is the **church** a place for this kind of celebration? What clothes do we wear?

Those who spurn the king's initial invitations are arrogant, busy, and violent. Does our discipleship include time to listen to God's call? What form does God's invitation to us take? Are we too busy to respond? Are we willing to listen to the servants in our midst, inviting us to leave behind our arrogance and self-sufficiency? When we get to the banquet, will we be carrying the old world with us?

Some preachers, including Martin Luther, have been reluctant to preach from this passage because of misgivings about the capricious, violent image allegorically ascribed to God through the character of the king. Many readers are put off by the tone of judgment, destruction, and exclusion that pervades many of Matthew's parables, including this one.

But the harsh, exaggerated images of this parable are typical of prophetic critique in the Bible. Matthew's intention is not to describe God, but to employ a shocking, worldly story to warn those whose behavior does not conform to the time. This is a message the church, like Israel's leaders in Jesus' day, persistently needs to hear.

The Tax Trap

Matthew 22:15–22*

Exploring the text

The **Pharisees** are the first group to engage Jesus in another contest following his long response to the **chief priests'** and **elders'** challenge (21:23–22:14). This time their plot requires them to become temporary bedfellows with the **Herodians**. Supporters of Herodian rule would ordinarily have stood opposed to the Pharisees on most issues, including the question they now set before Jesus, "Is it lawful to pay taxes to Caesar, or not?" (22:17). Perhaps there is even some hostility between the Pharisees and Herodians, because the Pharisees decide to send their interns in their stead (22:16). The plan is to force Jesus into the open on a divisive issue. If Jesus affirms that the tax should be paid to Caesar, they will report this to the people, who find the tax onerous and religiously offensive. If, on the other hand, Jesus says that the tax should not be paid, he would effectively be challenging Caesar's authority, which the Herodians would surely report as sedition.

The Pharisees' disciples have been well coached. They flatter him with effusive, fulsome praise, emphasizing his integrity and impartiality. In fact, the success of their plot depends on Jesus' integrity and lack of deference to the powerful (22:16). A simple, politically naive answer–either yes or no–best accomplishes their purpose. But Jesus is not the country bumpkin they think he is. They claim to know a lot about his character (22:16), but he knows the evil in their hearts (22:18; cf. 9:4; 12:24–25). He tells them he is aware of their hypocrisy (22:18), and then asks for the

---

*The Revised Common Lectionary uses this in Year A, The 29th Sunday in Ordinary Time.

coin used to pay the tax, which they readily supply. The tribute was both a source of Rome's wealth and an assertion of authority.[1] It was paid in Roman coinage that, in Jesus' time, named Tiberius as emperor, son of the divine Augustus and "high priest."[2] Their admission that the coin bears the emperor's image and inscription sets up Jesus' resolution of their question: "Then give to Caesar what is Caesar's, and to God the things that are God's" (22:21).

Jesus' answer is on one hand an artful dodge. They have asked him to publicly declare himself either for or against the tax. He declares himself both for and against the tax. His answer also effectively poses for his opponents another, more important question: "In whose 'economy' [or empire] do you live?"[3] Caesar's coin asserts imperial authority; they have the coin, so they must rightfully pay the tax. Jesus, who died to such obligations at his baptism (cf. on 3:13–17), but has also willingly offered the resources to pay such taxes (cf. on 17:24–27), affirms the propriety of paying the tribute where it is due. One cannot participate in the economy of the empire without paying tribute to its authority. But he also reminds his adversaries of their obligations to God's economy and the **empire of heaven**, presumably the "fruit" of repentance for which John and Jesus have repeatedly called (e.g., 3:8; 21:41, 43). Upon hearing this answer, the Pharisees' disciples depart (as had Satan in 4:11) in amazement, as if having witnessed a miracle (22:22; cf. 8:27; 9:33; 15:31; 21:20).

Preaching and teaching the Word

This story has traditionally been read (often in conjunction with Rom. 13:1–7) with an eye toward formulating a perspective on Christian relationships to the state. Catholics, joined more recently by Protestant interpreters, have asserted that only the coin belongs to Caesar, while the whole person belongs to God. Obedience to God therefore trumps allegiance to the state. Older, traditional Protestant interpretation focused on the doctrine of the "two kingdoms." Tributes to God and the state stand side by side. Fulfillment of obligations to the state also fulfills the demand for obedience to God. This story, however, offers no direct support for any of these perspectives, even if it invites us to raise these kinds of questions. Jesus is not offering an implicit affirmation of Roman rule, or any other form of human rule. He is not establishing a pecking order of religious and political obligations, nor even distinguishing between the two. He invites his hearers to be honest about whose empire they serve, whose economy they trade in, whose benevolence they depend on, and whose salvation they seek.

Those who place their allegiance with the God of Jesus Christ subsequently have to make decisions about when, how, and to what end they also pay tribute to nations, states, or other human authorities. The question before Christians, then, is always "Whose world is it?" Then we sort carefully and critically through our responses to the obligations set before us by the world. Who is Lord? Whom do we serve? Can we offer allegiance to both God and nation? Can we pay tribute to both the God of Jesus Christ and the gods of commerce, consumption, comfort, and control?

The God of the Living

Matthew 22:23–33

Exploring the text

Each of Jesus' responses to the challenges (see **controversy stories**) set before him in Jerusalem have focused ultimately on his claims about who God is and what God calls Israel to do. The mocking question the **Sadducees** now pose about the resurrection will prompt another strong theological declaration from Jesus: "[God] is God not of the dead, but of the living" (22:32; cf. 16:16; 26:63).

The Sadducees represent the Jewish ruling class, who would have been skeptical or even hostile toward popular **eschatological** hope–including the idea of resurrection–that imagined the end of existing social and economic structures. Their open declaration that they do not believe in the resurrection (22:23) puts them at odds with popular belief and makes their question a subterfuge that mocks both the notion of resurrection and Jesus himself. The question they set before Jesus is a case study based on Deuteronomy 25:5–6, which concerns passing on one's seed by means of offspring, through whom one's life is blessed and perpetuated generation after generation. The commandment and belief in the resurrection each focuses, albeit in different ways, on the same underlying issue: the perpetuation of life after death. The Sadducees' challenge highlights the alternatives by playing on the word "raising up": if a man dies childless, his brother should marry the widow and "raise up" (*anastesei*) children for his deceased brother (22:24). After recounting their case study about the woman who marries seven brothers in turn without bearing any children, they ask, "In the resurrection [*anastasei*], whose wife will she be?"

The Sadducees' argument, however, actually shifts the topic from the means of perpetuating life to a matter of property rights: "Whose wife will she be?" This question, as Jesus will note, is entirely a concern of the present age. Jesus first announces that they are "wrong," a judgment that denotes not just intellectual error, but failure to obtain a goal in knowledge, speech, or action. The roots of their failure lie in the fact that they "know neither the scriptures nor the power of God" (22:29). Jesus' first proof for this assertion highlights their reduction of the issue of life after death to the mundane, this-worldly perspective of marriage and property rights. They have looked into the resurrection life with the eyes of this world, and thus have failed to reach the goal. In the **time** of resurrection, there is no marrying at all, for the people of the resurrection are "like angels in heaven" (22:30).

Since the Sadducees have based their case on the law of Moses, Jesus next appeals directly to the word of the living God to Moses himself. His scriptural argument is built on the theophany of Exodus 3, where "the angel of the LORD" announces God's name to Moses from the burning bush and promises to deliver the people from slavery in Egypt. The most important element of this theophany for Jesus is the repeated affirmation of God's identity: "I am the God of your father, the God of Abraham, the God of Isaac, and the God of Jacob" (Exod. 3:6, 15, 16). Jesus identifies this claim as a word not only to Moses but "to you from God" (22:31), which the Sadducees have failed to "read" (cf. 12:3, 5; 19:4; 21:16; 21:42). This God is the One through whom Abraham, Isaac, and Jacob—that is, Israel—continue to live. This God has promised "to be with you" (Exod. 3:12; cf. Matt. 1:23; 28:20). The God of Israel is thus the God of the living, not of the dead (22:32). The resurrection of the dead (22:31) expresses God's power (22:29) both to preserve Israel and, especially, to defeat the power of death itself. The story thus reconfirms Jesus' authority over the Jerusalem authorities and affirms the foundational theological argument that will drive the rest of the Gospel story: God is the God of the living. The resurrection of the crucified Jesus will be the ultimate proof.

Preaching and teaching the Word

Since Peter's confession that Jesus is "the Messiah, the **Son of the Living God**" (16:16), Jesus has been warning his disciples that he will suffer and die in Jerusalem at the hands of the leaders with whom he now debates, and promising that he will be raised from the dead after three days (16:21; 17:12; 17:22–23; 20:18–19). This story roots his claim about the resurrection in the foundational theological conviction that God is God of the living. Jesus knows what will happen in Jerusalem because he knows his adversaries, but also because he knows who God is. Jesus' crucifixion is not merely a story of tragic human disobedience, but the story of God's defeat of death and of those whose power is rooted in death. For Jesus, the resurrection is neither an artifact of popular belief nor merely an assertion that God will make things right in the end. The resurrection is the defining and crowning revelation of the nature and effect of God's power. The crucifixion and resurrection are thus the bedrock theological convictions that call forth and sustain all Christian proclamation and practice.

The Sadducees set out to mock Jesus by mocking the idea of the resurrection. Jesus' crucifixion and resurrection represent God's mockery of death. The implications of resurrection lie not only in the future, as if this power could be constrained by human notions of time or contained within some distant world always beyond our reach, but in the world inhabited by imperial powers, religious leaders, and the disciples of Jesus. The defeat of death exposes all human economic, political, social, and religious constructs built upon the presumption of death–in other words, all human constructs–as facades for a reality whose time has passed. The Christian community lives in the time of resurrection. Is the resurrection the defining feature of our calendars and clocks? Is it the bearing to which our moral compasses point?

Resurrection is the cornerstone of the life of disciples here and now. Matthew, in fact, will make clear that Jesus is not the only one raised from the dead (27:52–53). Those who are baptized in the name of Jesus take on the form of his dying and his resurrected life, which means that we are called to live as if we are no more constrained by the powers of this world than Jesus is. When we live in the conviction of the resurrection, we bear witness to the claims that Jesus "saves his people from their sins" (1:21) and is "God with us" (1:23; 28:20; cf. Exod. 3:12). How do our congregations, by both word and deed, make known the power of the God of the living, the God who liberates us from slavery? Where are the spaces around us in which death seems most powerful? These are the spaces where the power of God is being revealed, the spaces where Christians are called to discern and name the power that others cannot see.

The Final Challenges

Matthew 22:34–46*

Exploring the text

Matthew's note that the **Pharisees** "gather" together again in opposition to Jesus (22:34, 41) recalls Psalm 2:2, where earthly rulers "gather together against the Lord and his **Christ**." In Jesus' last encounter, he "silenced" the **Sadducees** (and "overwhelmed" the crowd, 22:33). But his answer now raises another potential line of attack for his adversaries. Because Jesus apparently places a higher priority on God's word of self-identification to Moses than on the Law of Moses itself (22:31–32), he might also recognize gradations of importance or authority among God's commandments, a position the Pharisees could use against him. Does he believe, as the Pharisees would have insisted, that all the commandments of the Torah are of equal importance? In order to press this attack, a legal expert from among the Pharisees steps forward. His professional expertise makes him a formidable opponent and shapes the character of his question. He invites Jesus to classify and rank the commandments of the law: "What kind of commandment is great in the Law?" Were Jesus to identify one great commandment, it would imply that the rest are of lesser importance.

Jesus' response is straightforward, yet more subtle than it appears. He first identifies Deuteronomy 6:5, the lead sentence of the Shema, which the faithful recite twice daily, as both the "greatest" and the "first" commandment (22:38, only in Matthew). So Jesus has answered the lawyer's question directly. The Shema is the greatest commandment. But he does not stop there. A second commandment, drawn from the Holiness Code, is "like" it, that is, another "great" and "first" commandment. The first of these great and first commandments focuses on loving God, the second on loving the neighbor (22:39; cf. Lev. 19:18). Together the two commandments express the "vertical" and "horizontal" dimensions of the Law. But do these two "great" commandments, which are central to Israel's identity and vocation, overshadow the rest? Jesus is still not finished answering. He adds that "all the law and the prophets hang on these two commandments" (22:40). To "hang on" means to "depend on" or "be tied together

*The Revised Common Lectionary uses this in Year A, The 30th Sunday in Ordinary Time.

by," as a door hangs on hinges. Without the hinges the door doesn't work, and without the door the hinges are useless. This answer allows Jesus to affirm the two commandments as "great" and "first" without suggesting that they trump or diminish the rest. There is not one great commandment, nor even two, and then many subordinate commandments, but an integral whole that encompasses the law and the prophets. The greatness of these two commandments lies not in their distinction from the others, but in their capacity to articulate the root and foundation of the whole tradition.

Matthew does not record any response from the lawyer or the Pharisees, who, like the Sadducees before them, have apparently been silenced. But while they are still "gathered together" (22:41)–they have not yet abandoned their attempt to oust him from the temple–Jesus turns the tables and asks them a challenging question. What about the Messiah? Whose son is he? He probes their understanding of the Messiah in order to draw them into the open. The Pharisees have heard supplicants and the crowds repeatedly hail Jesus as "Lord, **Son of David**" (15:22; 20:30–31; cf. 9:27; 12:23; 21:9, 15), but have rejected this designation in favor of the claim that his power is from Beelzebul (9:34; 12:24). Jesus and the Pharisees both know that the Scriptures affirm that the messiah is the Son of David. If the Pharisees confirm this, it will lead by implication to the conclusion that Jesus the Son of David is also God's messiah. If they deny it, they risk the wrath of the crowds, whom they fear (21:46). Jesus is thus inviting his opponents either to accept publicly his authority as the Son of David and messiah, or once again to claim that his power is from Beelzebul. Either way they face dishonor. The former would require them to give account for their continuing opposition to Jesus, while the latter would be an admission that Beelzebul's son has persistently defeated them in public debates.

The Pharisees really have no choice as to what they will answer. They can't even say, "We don't know," as the **chief priests** and **elders** had done earlier in the day (cf. 21:27), for everyone knows the messiah is David's Son. We might imagine that they mumble the answer under their breath. With their reply in hand, Jesus proceeds to a riddle based on Psalm 110:1, where David calls the messiah "Lord." How can David, under the inspiration of the Spirit, call his son "Lord" (22:43, 45)? How can the messiah be both David's son and David's Lord? The answer has to do with authority, the issue that has been contested in every story since the chief priests and elders first challenged Jesus to name the source and nature of his power (21:23–27). Psalm 110:1 speaks of "the Lord" sitting at the right hand of David, a position of authority, until "I [David] put all your enemies beneath your feet." David here adopts the role of a servant, while asserting the dominion of the Lord over all enemies. The rest of Psalm 110 goes on to affirm that the Lord's anointed will rule in the midst of his enemies (Ps. 110:2), shatter kings, and execute judgment among the nations (110:5–6). David the psalmist can call his son, the messiah, "Lord" because David recognizes an authority equal to or surpassing his own. The Pharisees are prepared to say that the messiah is David's son, but not to grant Jesus the Son of David authority as "Lord." So "none of them is able to give him an answer." They are unable to answer because they have no will to admit Jesus' authority over them. After this day no one will dare to ask him any more questions (22:46). Jesus' successful defenses of his authority in the temple in Jerusalem mean that those who challenge his God-given power must now turn to violence.

Preaching and teaching the Word

Why do the powers in Jerusalem resist Jesus? Because the divine power he manifests surpasses and subverts their own. If he were just another oriental despot, at least the same kind of power they know would be in play and they could sidle up to it as they have to Caesar and his minions. Nor is Jesus willing to enter into political power-sharing arrangements with them or come to mutually agreeable terms. God's power will subdue all enemies (22:44) and bring kings to ruin. What does this messianic promise say to the relationship of modern Christians with the powers of this world? Where will the church be standing when the Lord shatters the powers of this world? How do the cross and resurrection bring an end to the rule of these powers?

Matthew's persistent warnings to religious people are audible here again. The quest to hang on to power in its human forms is a key factor in the refusal of the Jerusalem leaders to admit the divine nature of Jesus' authority. All of the Jerusalem authorities have now seen Jesus' power firsthand and been silenced by it. They are nonetheless unable and unwilling to grant the reality the Canaanite woman, the crowds, the blind, and the children in the temple have named. Jesus has said that it is nearly impossible for a rich person to enter the **empire of heaven**. Apparently it is also nearly impossible for a person who wields human power, especially religious power, to enter the heavenly empire.

Matthew consistently associates the title "Son of David" with healing and the restoration of sight. This power fulfills the intention of the great and first commandments, to love God and love neighbor, as well as all the rest of the Law and the Prophets. How is the love of God connected in the experience of the **church** with love of neighbor? Who is the neighbor in whom God's presence and power may be found? How does loving one's neighbor bring about healing and the restoration of sight?

PART ELEVEN

The Jerusalem Sermons
23:1–25:46

Preliminary Remarks

Matthew sets the last of Jesus' five great discourses (chaps. 5–7; 10; 13; 18; 23–25) first in the temple itself (23) and then on the Mount of Olives (24–25), a site associated with the revelation of God's glory in both **judgment** and **salvation** (Ezek. 10, esp. 10:18; 11:22–24; Zech. 14, esp. 14:4). The differing settings and content of chapters 23 and 24–25 should not lead us to drive too sharp a wedge between them. Jesus' final warning of the judgment to fall upon Jerusalem for rejecting God's messiah (chap. 23) triggers the **apocalyptic** warnings and **parables** of 24–25. Modern readers may find Jesus' rhetoric in chapter 23 unduly harsh, but it is typical of prophetic diatribes among both Jews and Greeks. His scathing depiction of the **scribes** and **Pharisees**, who here represent the religious leaders of Jerusalem, is not meant as objective historical description, but as caricature, and should not be used, as it too often has been, to vilify Judaism or the Jewish people. It is meant, rather, as a warning to the disciples and crowds, whom Matthew identifies as the audience (23:1–12).

Jesus' blistering condemnation of the Jewish leaders in the temple (23:13–36) gives way to predictions of judgment and desolation (23:37–39). Then Jesus abandons the temple. As he leads his disciples away, he prophesies its destruction (24:1–2). This pronouncement unsettles the disciples, who then ask about the timing of the destruction of the temple and the signs that will signal "the end of the age" (24:3). Jesus' answer describes **times** of upheaval, danger, and intense suffering, but he also offers the reassurance of his presence and the hope of vindication (24:4–35). Because God alone knows the time of the end, disciples must live in a state of constant watchfulness, ready with the fruit of repentance for the **Son of Man**'s return (24:36–44). Jesus ends his final teachings with a series of parables that explore what it means to be ready and awake (24:45–25:46).

The Signs of Greatness

Matthew 23:1–12*

Exploring the text

Jesus' defeat of all those who have challenged him (21:23–22:40) since he entered Jerusalem and began his occupation of the temple (21:1–17) leaves him still in possession of the temple. He now speaks to the disciples and crowds (23:1), who will be required to choose between Jesus and the Jerusalem authorities. The harsh rhetoric of this chapter is both a final pronouncement of **judgment** against the **Jewish leaders** and a warning to the disciples and crowds to avoid their ways. Jesus' hostile caricature of the **"scribes** and **Pharisees"** is meant to help the crowds (and the disciples) see clearly the differences between leadership that bears witness to God's power and leadership that seeks power for its own ends.

The "scribes and Pharisees sit on Moses' seat," a position of authority as interpreters of the law (23:2). Jesus tells his audience to "follow what they teach you, but don't do what they do" (23:3). This saying may sound strange in light of what Jesus has said before about the "leaven of the Pharisees" (cf. 15:14; 16:5, 11) and what he will now say about them (23:4–7, 13–36). Jesus wants to affirm the importance of preserving and teaching the tradition, but train his audience to be discriminating students. Israel needs interpreters of the tradition—Jesus himself is one—in order for it to remain a living, life-breathing witness. But the current occupants of "Moses' seat" do not conform their actions to the traditions they teach (23:3). The scribes and Pharisees fail the test of consistency of word and deed (23:2–3). They lay burdens on others, while doing nothing themselves (23:4; cf. 11:28–30). Even the good deeds they do are done so as to be seen by others (23:5; cf. 6:1–7, 16–18), thereby to gain public honor and privilege (23:6–7). The disciples and the crowds must pay careful attention to the "fruit" that falls from the tree (cf. 7:15–20; 12:33–37).

In 23:8–12, Jesus offers the contrasting vision of a community without "teachers," "fathers," or "guides," which here represent titles associated with status and authority. Teaching and guiding in themselves are not the problem, but the threat to the integrity of the community that accompanies attaching offices, titles, and personal power to such functions.

*The Revised Common Lectionary uses this in Year A, The 31st Sunday in Ordinary Time.

Wherever "leaders" are distinguished from "followers," or "the powerful" from those "subordinate" to them, human power is likely to overshadow the power of God. There is but one teacher (23:8), one Father ("the one in heaven," 23:9), and one instructor or guide, the Messiah himself (23:10). The alternative to organization around status and hierarchy is a community of equality and solidarity. The **church** is thus a community of students, brothers and sisters, and servants. The final sayings in the section reiterate prior teachings regarding service and humility (23:11–12; cf. 18:1–4; 19:10–15; 19:30; 20:16; 20:25–28). The reversals of status–the greatest is the servant, the exalted will be humbled, the humiliated will be exalted–carry an **eschatological** tone that will be developed in chapters 24–25. It is God who will do the humbling and exalting.

Preaching and teaching the Word

Performance is the most important form of interpretation. Matthew's Jesus has repeatedly emphasized what we do as the true expression of our beliefs and values. When our actions, both as individuals and as communities, are at odds with our espoused beliefs, our theology itself is called into question. What is the most important thing that distinguishes the "scribes and Pharisees" from Jesus and the community of disciples? Not beliefs and confessions, but the integrity of profession and practice. "Faith without works is dead" (Jas. 2:14–26), and faith in conflict with one's actions is a lie. What do we really believe? The answer is revealed in what we do.

One important aspect of what Christians "do" concerns the way we organize and recognize authority in our communities. A community that calls itself Christian but enshrines hierarchies of status and authority, or distinctions of race, class, gender, or wealth, betrays the power of God revealed in the cross, just as surely as Peter, Judas, and the other disciples will betray Jesus. If we are to serve Christ, we must learn to become servants of one another. This requires that our congregations become places where it is difficult to avoid learning humility with mutual servanthood. How do we facilitate recognition of the differences between worldly power and the divine power that marks the community of disciples? How do we make our congregations places that foster mutual servanthood? How can we nurture the relationships of mutual care and solidarity that are necessary to make the address "brothers and sisters" more than a polite platitude?

Jesus' teaching here poses a particularly sharp warning to ministers, teachers, and professors of the church for whom robes with bars are a mark of distinction. The real authority of leaders within the Christian community is earned in service and solidarity with the humiliated ones, not in classrooms or boardrooms. The pastor's task is to remind the members of congregations, who may be as enamored of ornamentation as leaders themselves, that there is but one teacher, master, and professor in the church–the Messiah who was crucified.

The Judgment of "This Generation"

Matthew 23:13–24:2

Exploring the text

The "woes" Jesus now pronounces against the **scribes** and **Pharisees** echo the language and develop a form of invective distinctive to the prophetic tradition (e.g., Isa. 5:8–14; 10:1–11; Hab. 2:6–20; 1 Enoch 94–99; cf. also Rev. 9:12; 11:14; 19:10, 16, 19). Although he addresses the scribes and Pharisees directly ("Woe to you . . ."), Jesus' primary audience is still the disciples and the crowds (Matt. 23:1). Jesus builds an elaborate, sevenfold case that calls for **judgment** (23:13–36), then pronounces a single lament for and judgment upon Jerusalem (23:37–38). Then he leads his disciples from the temple, abandoning it to destruction (24:1–2).

The list of woes builds toward a climax that focuses on the violence that "this generation"–the offspring of Cain (23:35)–has always directed against God's emissaries (23:29–36). The first woe condemns the scribes and Pharisees for shutting out those who seek to enter the **empire of heaven** (23:13). This image contrasts the scribes and Pharisees with Peter and the disciples, to whom Jesus has given the keys to the kingdom and the task of keeping the door open (16:18–19). To be sure, the scribes and Pharisees go to enormous effort to make converts, only to turn them into "twice as much the child of hell" as themselves (23:15). The longest accusation, the third (23:16–22), criticizes the legal minutiae that developed in the attempt to regulate the oaths and vows by which people in the oral culture of the first century secured their word. The fine distinctions they developed came to resemble the often incomprehensible "fine print" found in legal contracts, credit card offers, and the end of television, radio, and print advertisements today. Jesus highlights the absurdity of allowing people to swear by the gold in the temple or the gift on the altar, but not by the temple and the altar themselves (23:16–19). In the end, there is but one true authority, God who sits on the throne of heaven, and God is not bound by any human oath. Jesus' accusation here recalls his prohibition against oaths in the Sermon on the Mount (5:33–37). The next three woes develop more images of the Pharisees' and scribes' disproportionate focus on matters of minutiae at the expense of what really matters. The scribes and Pharisees pay careful attention to the details of tithing regulations ("mint, dill, and cumin") while neglecting **justice**, **mercy**, and faith (23:23–24; cf. 5:43–48; 9:13; 12:7; 22:34–40; Mic. 6:8; Hos. 2:19; 12:6; Jer. 22:3; Zech. 7:9–10). They attend to the scrupulous cleanliness of the plate and cup, while ignoring the fact that what they eat and drink has been taken from others through greed and self-indulgence (23:25–26). They create the appearance of **righteousness**, while inside they are dead, defiling, and lawless (23:27–28).

The seventh and climactic woe picks up from the sixth woe the imagery of tombs and the polemic against appearances that mask reality. But here the accusation is even more scathing and poignant. The scribes and Pharisees build tombs for the prophets and decorate the graves of the righteous. They make speeches that express regret for the actions of their ancestors, yet insist that, had they lived in the days of the prophets, they would not have participated in shedding blood (23:29–30). Their public actions and words make a pious display that conveys an aura of **honor** and respect. But all of these public rituals and speeches mask the truth. Jesus knows that the leaders have been plotting his death (cf. 12:14, 21:46). Their recognition and public condemnation of the sins of their ancestors thus serves as testimony against them. They are guilty not only because they are descendants of those who murdered the prophets, but because they, too, at this moment, are plotting an act that will "fill up . . . the measure of [their] ancestors" (23:31–32; cf. 7:2).

The accusations in 23:33–36 mingle allusions to the violence perpetrated against God's prophets in the days of the ancestors with references to what will befall Jesus and his disciples, including crucifixion, beating, and persecution (23:34; cf. 10:17–23; 16:21; 17:22–23; 20:18–19). For Jesus, these instances of violence disclose a pattern of behavior—an ancient curse—that runs all the way back to the story of Cain and Abel (Gen. 4:1–16) and before that to the serpent's lies in the garden (Gen. 3). This curse, freely chosen by "this generation," accounts for "all the righteous blood shed on earth" (23:35). Those who murder God's agents declare themselves members of the generation of Cain and children of the serpent.[1] The leaders who will crucify Jesus are "snakes" and "the offspring of vipers" (23:33), whose destiny is "Gehenna," the smoldering refuse dump in the southern part of Jerusalem that was a symbol of eternal torment for the godless. Ironically, Jesus' death and resurrection is the only power sufficient to break the primeval curses of Adam and Eve and Cain.

As Jesus concludes his accusations against "this generation" (23:36), his tone shifts from condemnation to a lament for Jerusalem. Jerusalem is both the ultimate focus of Jesus' ministry to gather and restore Israel and the city that kills the prophets and stones those sent to it (23:37). Jesus' ministry is the culmination of God's enduring attempt to gather Israel under the wings of God's presence (Pss. 36:7; 57:1; 61:4; Isa. 31:5). But Israel's leaders have, for the moment, frustrated this attempt. Their fruit—division and violence—will prevail in the short term. As a consequence, their "house," which probably refers to both the temple and the city, is left "desolate" (forsaken) (23:38). Yet, as so often in prophetic declarations of judgment, there is also a seed of hope. Jesus cites Psalm 118:26, which the crowds had chanted at his entry into Jerusalem (21:9). Psalm 118 celebrates God's "steadfast love" and deliverance of the psalmist from mortal enemies (118:6–7), nations (118:10–14), and death itself (118:17–19). When Israel can sing this song, they will see Jesus again (23:39), bearing God's **salvation** (cf. 1:21). When Jerusalem is able to welcome and bless the prophets sent by God, the humbled city will once again be exalted and blessed.[2]

When Jesus ends his announcement of judgment against Jerusalem and its leaders, he departs from the temple with his disciples. He has possessed it since his entry into Jerusalem the day before (21:12–14). He has withstood the leaders' attacks on his authority and demonstrated the integrity of his word and deed (21:23–22:46). Now he leaves the temple of his own accord (24:1; cf. 23:38). But as they depart with him, Jesus' disciples draw his attention to the temple building. Are they still impressed by its grandeur? Are they still in thrall of powers that are passing away? Jesus issues an authoritative response: "Truly I tell you, not one stone will be left here upon another; all will be thrown down" (24:2). What seems so stable, magnificent, and impregnable will be turned to rubble—and not merely the buildings themselves, but the way of life, the religious system, the economic order, and the social power that developed in conjunction with the temple. All will be thrown down.

Preaching and teaching the Word

The task of the preacher and teacher in dealing with this passage is to keep the church's own feet to the fire. Jesus does not target particular scribes and Pharisees, nor all scribes and Pharisees, nor Jews and Judaism. His target is really all those of "this generation" who have set themselves in opposition to God's rule and restoration of the people of Israel. His stinging rhetoric stands in line with the vivid condemnations of Israel's leaders offered by Amos, Hosea, Isaiah, Jeremiah, Ezekiel, and Zechariah. He unveils the myopia, hypocrisy, destruction of relationships, and violence that accompany religious and political systems in which self-interest and devotion to rules replace devotion to God and care for people. Moreover, while Jesus' polemic focuses on Israel's leaders, he directs his comments as a warning to the disciples and crowds (23:1). Later generations of Christians who employ this passage to condemn others, especially Jewish people, in fact are guilty themselves of the hypocrisy Jesus here condemns. Jesus clearly warns his disciples not to judge others. The criteria we employ when we judge others become the measure by which we in turn will be judged (cf. 7:1–5). When this passage is turned on others rather than used to unveil our own hypocrisy, it becomes a weapon even more dangerous to the one holding it than to the one against whom it is aimed.

Most of us can easily identify with the faults Jesus uncovers in the scribes and Pharisees. We too squabble over the decorations while neglecting justice, mercy, and faith. We too pursue converts to our churches, but neither invite them into God's kingdom nor go in ourselves. We too use the Bible as a rule book to judge and exclude others, while representing ourselves as the righteous ones. And we too are likely to remain committed members of the generation of Cain, sanctifying our violence in the name of God, while proclaiming that we know better than did our predecessors. Self-deception and blindness afflict us all, but especially when we turn away from God's presence toward human honors, power, and institutions. The sixth and seventh woes (23:27–32) disclose with particular clarity the capacity of religious ritual and institution building to mask reality by baptizing merely human power and self-interest with the aura of divinity.

The woes should be read in conjunction with the "blessings" or "beatitudes" of Matthew 5:3–12, with which they form an illuminating contrast. The "religion" of Jesus' followers consists in poverty, mourning, gentleness, mercy, purity of heart, peacemaking, and suffering for the sake of righteousness. These are the true marks of God's rule, the experiences and practices through which Christ's disciples discern and respond faithfully to God's presence and power.

The Christian communities in which Matthew's Gospel was performed (and lived) probably understood the destruction of the temple by the Romans in 70 CE as the fulfillment of Jesus' words in 24:1–2. Yet his words resonate beyond that tragic event. Humans persistently seek to secure our own way in the world. Our cities, shopping malls, stadiums, tall buildings, and other grand structures create the illusion that we are in control of our world. In some people's view, the earth is simply a rough and unfinished resource, waiting to be "developed" and perfected for human use. As testaments to human pride and arrogance, structures like the temple—even structures purportedly built to "glorify God"—are bound for destruction. Jesus' words to the disciples as they leave the temple are a warning against placing our trust in the idols we make, the grand structures we think will last forever. When the disciples look back at the temple, they remind us of Israel in the wilderness, yearning for their flesh-pots back in Egypt (Exod. 16:2–3; 14:11–12), or Lot's wife turning back to look at the sulfur and fire that God rains down on Sodom and Gomorrah (Gen. 19:24–26).[3] Following Jesus will always seem risky, dangerous, and uncertain, and the dangers will be real. In times of crisis and transition, the church must learn to follow God's lead without looking back and without grasping for crumbling securities. The way of Jesus leads toward the cross, not back to the temple. But doom, gloom, and danger are not the final words. What appears as divine judgment also bears the seeds of hope. The cross leads to resurrection. Jesus promises a day when Jerusalem will again say, "Blessed is he who comes in the name of the Lord" (23:39).

PRELIMINARY REMARKS ON THE APOCALYPTIC VISION OF MATTHEW 24

Jesus' announcement of the coming destruction of the temple (24:1–2) may have shocked his disciples. For the people of Israel, the temple was an important, if ambiguous, symbol of power, much as "Washington" or "Congress" is today. Even if we have mixed feelings about what goes on in such places, we nonetheless cherish the institutions themselves, which represent the venerability, security and stability, and noble ideals of the American people. When they are alone with Jesus on the Mount of Olives, the disciples thus seek clarity and reassurance (24:3; cf. 17:19, where their insecurity also prompts a closed-door meeting). Their questions focus first on the timing of the destruction of the temple and then on the signs accompanying the "coming" or "presence" (Parousia) of the **Son of Humanity** and "the end of the age" (24:3). Although Jesus' answer in Matthew 24 may first strike readers as episodic and disorganized, its arrangement is relatively straightforward. In 24:4–35 Matthew describes a variety of visions of danger and suffering (24:4–12, 15–21, 23–26, 29), which then give way to statements of reassurance (24:8, 13–14, 22, 27–28, 30–31, 32–35). Jesus tells the disciples that even he does not know when the end will come, so they must always be ready (24:36–44). The parables that bring the discourse to its close examine the nature of this readiness (24:45–25:46).

Like many present-day "apocalyptists," the disciples may imagine that there are signs and fixed dates for the end of the age. They may also presume direct connections between the destruction of the temple, the coming of the Son of Man, and the "end of the age." Their questions suggest that they want to be apocalyptic insider traders. Jesus responds in the language and imagery of Israel's prophetic and **apocalyptic** traditions, but in ways that subvert the disciples' expectations. He tells the disciples that (1) they will observe many traditional apocalyptic signs and events, most of which are not, in fact, signs of the end (24:6–8, 9–12, 15–21, 29–30); (2) they will encounter periods of internal conflict (24:9–12) and intense suffering (24:15–21), which also may not signal the end; (3) these crises will give rise to "false prophets" and messianic pretenders, who prey on the burdened and vulnerable (24:4–5; 11:23–26); (4) awareness of the true nature of events and of the promised presence of the Son of Humanity enables the elect to endure to the end (e.g., 24:6–8, 13); (5) the end is not fixed, but will follow the proclamation of the gospel to the whole world (24:14; cf. 28:18–20); (6) Jesus himself does not know the day or hour of the end—only God knows (24:36); and so, (7) as they suffer for his name, the disciples must stay awake, ready at all times for the coming of the Son of Man, whose revelation generates both dread and hope (24:42–51, esp. 24:44).

Apocalyptic revelations like those collected in this chapter (or John's Revelation) often do not describe events in linear sequence. Instead they are kaleidoscopic, multivalent, and difficult to locate with certainty in chronological time. This makes Jesus' teaching deeply frustrating to modern readers hoping to connect the dots in a straight line. Some of Jesus' teachings here seem at home in the experience of Matthew's church after the destruction of the temple in 70 CE (24:9–13, 15–22). The statements about the coming of the Son of Man seem to refer to events at the end of history, but might also refer to Jesus' death and resurrection (e.g., 24:29–31). Little of what Jesus says refers unambiguously to a single event, and all of it anticipates what is about to unfold before Jesus and the disciples. The destruction and rebuilding of "the temple" will begin within hours.

The Suffering of the Elect and the Coming of the Son of Humanity

Matthew 24:4–35

Exploring the text

"THE BIRTHPANGS" (24:4–8)

The first portion of Jesus' response to the disciples is a warning against being deceived. There will be messianic pretenders who "will lead many astray." False messiahs apparently arise in conjunction with crises, such as reports and rumors of wars, famines, and earthquakes. The disciples are not to be alarmed or frightened by these reports, which are inevitable among human nations and empires. These are cataclysms, to be sure, but they are not signs of the end, only the "beginning of the birthpangs" (24:8). **Judgment** is the beginning of **salvation**.

ENDURANCE AMIDST CONFLICT (24:9–14)

During the time when human powers dominate our imagination, disciples can expect to be "betrayed" (or "handed over") for torture and be put to death (24:9). Jesus has already warned his disciples of this in the Sermon on the Mount (cf. 5:10–12) and again in the Mission Discourse (10:16–25, 34–39). He goes on to speak of betrayals, hatred, false prophets, deception, lawlessness, and love that grows cold—all of which threaten the community of disciples and their witness. The language Jesus uses to describe these threats also resonates with the events now leading toward the cross. Judas will "betray" Jesus. The disciples' love is growing cold; they are already bickering (20:20–28) and will soon splinter, scatter (26:31; 26:21–22, 56), and desert Jesus, who will be handed over, tortured, and executed. The "end," or goal, of which Jesus speaks in 24:13 may refer first to Jesus' death and resurrection, and then to the disciples' subsequent proclamation of the "good news" to the nations (24:14; 28:18–20). The proclamation of the gospel, not the wars of humans or earthly disasters (24:6–7), will bring about the "end" (24:14), whether that is understood as the fulfillment of God's will, the end of the current imperial age (24:3), or the physical end of this world.

"THE DESOLATING SACRILEGE" (24:15–22)

Jesus develops his admonition to "endure to the end" (24:13) with an image from Daniel 9:27 (cf. also Dan. 8:9–14, esp. 8:13), the "desolating sacrilege standing in the holy place." Matthew's aside, "let the reader understand," is an engraved invitation to reread Daniel, which reminds us of the persistence of both imperial oppression, whether at the hand of foreign princes or Israel's own faithless leaders, and God's faithful judgment of them. The disciples are more likely to "endure" if they know that God always brings the rule of "nations" and "empires" (24:7) to an "end." In Daniel, the desolating sacrilege refers to the desecration of the temple in 167 BCE by Antiochus IV Epiphanes, the "prince" whose troops were sent to destroy the city and the "sanctuary" (Dan. 9:26). Daniel's prophecy found fresh fulfillment in the razing of the temple by Rome in 70 CE. Another fulfillment of Daniel's "desolating sacrilege" may lie even closer at hand: Jesus has already declared that the temple is defiled (21:12–14) and now "desolate" (23:38). The Jerusalem leaders' persecution and murder of Jesus and his followers will result in the flight of Christians from Jerusalem (24:20; cf. Acts 4–9). However we identify the "sacrilege," it shatters the world and threatens life, like the flood in Noah's day (24:37–39). The response should be immediate flight, leaving behind all possessions (24:17–18). Jesus describes this as a **time** of intense, unsurpassed suffering that poses a particularly strong risk to the most vulnerable (24:19–21). God's mercy "cuts short" these days for the sake of "the elect" (24:22).

"THE COMING OF THE SON OF HUMANITY" (24:23–31)

The "elect" are still the focus of Jesus' concern in this section. He reiterates his earlier warning that the crises facing the disciples will give rise to false prophets and messiahs (24:23–26; cf. 24:4–5), who may produce impressive signs and wonders that mislead even the elect. Whether the disciples are in the wilderness or the prayer room, the only sign that should impress them is the cross (cf. 24:30). What will be the "sign" of his coming (24:24; cf. 24:3)? Jesus' answer, in effect, is that they will know it when they see it—and everyone will see it. The Parousia of the **Son of Man** will not be limited to a particular location, not even the Mount of Olives, but will fill the horizon—completely, suddenly, and unambiguously—like lightning (24:27). In modern theological discussion, Parousia is virtually a synonym for Jesus' second coming. But in Jesus' day it commonly meant simply "presence" or "appearing." It was used to designate the epiphanies of gods and goddesses and as a technical term for the official visits of Caesar or other powerful conquerors (cf. on 21:1–11). The Parousia may indeed refer to Jesus' coming as judge and savior at the end of human history. But the foremost "appearance" of Jesus in power is his cross and resurrection. This epiphany changes the world for all to see, though few will admit it.

The saying about corpses and vultures (lit., "eagles," 24:28) is also multivalent. Just as certainly as garbage attracts flies and as vultures "gather" around a corpse, false prophets are drawn to suffering (24:23–26). The saying may also suggest that the coming of the Son of Man is as certain as these natural phenomena. The sight of vultures signals from afar the presence of death. So too the coming of the Son of Humanity will make plain to all that the **empire of heaven** has defeated the dark forces of this world. The eagle was also a symbol of the Roman Empire, whose "gathering" against Jerusalem and the temple may be hinted at here. Finally, the leaders of Jerusalem also "gather" repeatedly as they plot against, condemn, and exult in Jesus' death (cf. 26:3, 57; 27:17, 27, 62; 28:12), like vultures circling before they devour their prey.

The reprise in 24:29–31 again offers the disciples reassurance amidst signs of chaos and judgment. Jesus draws upon Isaiah 13 (24:29), where God calls nations and kingdoms against Babylon (Isa. 13:4; cf. Matt. 24:7) on the "day of the Lord." The darkening of the luminaries is a well-known prophetic image used in association with God's judgment against imperial powers (cf. Ezek. 32:7–8, against Egypt; Joel 2:2, against Zion itself). God's judgment is a cosmic cataclysm: the stars and constellations give no light, nor the moon, nor the sun at its rising (Isa. 13:10). God's wrath shakes, snuffs, and subdues even the astral powers. Like the lightning against the dark sky (24:27), the "sign" of the Son of Man—perhaps the cross, or the crucified and resurrected Messiah himself—then appears, also "in heaven" (24:30).

All the images of the Son of Humanity in 24:27–31 locate his appearance in the heavenly realm, where all will see him. But on earth this heavenly vision provokes mourning (cf. Zech. 12:10–14), for he comes as judge (à la Dan. 7:13–14) to destroy the empires humans have made (cf. Matt. 26:64, where a very similar saying conveys the threat of judgment against the Jewish leaders). For the disciples, on the other hand, the coming of the Son of Man is the realization of their hope for God's rule and salvation (cf. 16:27–28). The Son of Humanity sends his angels out to "gather" the elect from the "four winds, from one end of heaven to the other" (24:31; cf. Isa. 43:5–6; Zech. 2:6). Jesus' adversaries "gather" against him repeatedly during the passion account, but here it is the elect who are gathered to be with God (cf. 8:11; 13:30; 23:37).

"THE LESSON OF THE FIG TREE" (24:32–35)

The fig tree put on leaves in late April, a sure sign that summer was at hand.[1] Seeing "all these things" is an even more certain indication that he is near (24:33) (and that the harvest will follow). But what are "all these things" that will happen before "this generation passes away" (24:34)? Does the phrase refer to all the afflictions (24:29) that precede the end, as described in 24:4–31, or more narrowly to the appearance of the Son of Man himself? Does it also refer to what the disciples will witness in the next few days in Jerusalem? Equally ambiguous is the term "this genera-tion," which could designate the disciples, the people living at that time, "this [evil] generation" (of Cain, 23:31–36) that now is preparing to kill Jesus, or the new generation consisting of those who follow Jesus on the way to the cross. Elsewhere in Matthew "this generation" persistently refers to Jesus' opponents (cf. 11:16; 12:41, 42, 45; 16:4; 23:36), except in 17:17, where Jesus calls his disciples a "faithless and perverse generation." If the saying in fact refers to the evil, faithless, and perverse generation that stands opposed to Jesus, then it is, contrary to popular perception, not an affirmation of the imminence of the Parousia, but a reminder of the violent, chaotic reality that awaits those who reject Jesus' way. How certain is this teaching? Heaven and earth will pass away, but not Jesus' word (24:35). In Isaiah 65:17, from which Matthew draws this image, and Revelation 21:1, the vision of heaven and earth passing away also reveals the glory of the new creation that follows God's judgment of the world's empires.

Preaching and teaching the Word

Humans build empires. Emperors fill holy spaces with monuments to themselves. Empires preserve themselves through violence, draining life from others to preserve their own. And empires always fall. The suffer-ing and affliction caused by failing empires is a sign of their end, but not necessarily the end of the world. Again and again in this chapter Jesus reminds the disciples of coming violence, directed first against him, then against the elect. These are the death throes of the old world and the birth pangs of the empire of heaven. God always judges empires.

As the American empire draws to a close, disciples should know what to expect: violence, persecution, and death, the shattering of seemingly stable institutions, false prophets, and sometimes the need for sudden flight, leaving everything behind. But after all this comes the **Son of**

Humanity, judge and savior (24:29–31, 45–51; 16:27–28; 26:64). The promise of **salvation** does not mean, however, that Jesus' disciples are "raptured" or rescued from suffering. Suffering for his name (24:9–12, 15–21) is the means by which disciples take up the cross and bear witness to God's redeeming power (24:13–14). The age before the end is thus, as Jesus says, the most dangerous time ever for the elect (24:21). They endure because they know that the "birth pangs" (24:8) presage their redemption.

Who are the "false messiahs" and "false prophets" about whom Jesus warns his disciples (24:4–5, 11, 23–26)? They display an uncanny ability to show up just when there are rumors of war (24:6), when the community itself is under duress (24:9–12), or in the wake of intense suffering (24:15–28). They may come in Jesus' name (24:5) and demonstrate great powers (24:24), which seem to promise relief or success. But in the end the false prophets are like vultures (24:28), preying on the community rather than bearing witness to the power of the cross. False prophets are a more common feature of the landscape of Christian community than we might imagine. The only way to distinguish true from false prophets may be to observe the fruit they bear and the cruciform character of their lives. Judgment of false prophets, however, is God's business, not ours (13:40; cf. 13:29–30, 36–43, 47–50).

Jesus envisions a time when disciples might suddenly be required to flee the world's violence (24:15–21). This may refer first to events surrounding the destruction of Jerusalem in the decade or two before Matthew was written. In any case, when worlds are being torn apart, there may be no time to collect possessions or even grab a coat. Disciples must live light on their feet. The desecration of holy space signals the end of a way of life. Americans have some sense of this, perhaps, in the wake of the 9/11 attacks on New York and Washington, when American temples were suddenly devastated. We have tried to return to business as usual, but the world we knew has ended. The destruction of Jerusalem by the Romans brought an end to the world of "temple Judaism." The coming of the Son of Humanity ends the world as we have known it. Jesus tells his disciples not to turn back for the things of a dissolving world. The church may be one of those dissolving elements, or it may be a community of refuge for those who flee violence, war, and the catastrophic failure of our temples. At its best, the **church** is the community with roots in heaven, bearing witness to God's mercy for a world that is passing away.

Watching for the Son of Man

Matthew 24:36–51*

Exploring the text

When the disciples heard Jesus foretell the destruction of the temple (24:1–2) they asked him when this would happen and what signs would herald his advent and the end of the age (24:3). He has answered their questions by pointing to the suffering and trauma that accompany the passing of worlds. He also has pointed to the certainty of the return of the **Son of Man** as judge (24:3–35). But he has given the disciples very little information that would help them know precisely where they are on a time line. Now he tells them clearly that neither he nor the angels have this knowledge, but only God (24:36). What he can tell them is that lives will be suddenly disrupted. He compares the coming of the Son of Humanity to the days of Noah, when people conducted their lives normally–eating, drinking, and marrying–right up to the moment when the floods came (24:38).

The images in 24:40–41 are often read today in support of dispensational theories of a "rapture," in which the elect are suddenly lifted from the earth, "leaving behind" loved ones, friends, and coworkers. Matthew does not develop any clear notion of this kind of "rapture" (nor does Paul or any other New Testament writer). Jesus makes no distinctions regarding the relative righteousness of those taken and those left behind. Nor does the rest of the Gospel present a consistent picture of whether the righteous or the wicked are taken first at the judgment (cf. 24:31; 13:40–42, 49–50). Jesus' teaching indicates only that the coming of the Son of Humanity brings sudden, surprising division.

Given the sudden, certain, and disruptive, but unknown, unexpected, and unplottable nature of the Son of Man's coming, Jesus calls his disciples to adopt a posture of wakefulness and readiness (24:42–44). Watching patiently for signs of Jesus' presence is one of the foundational disciplines of the **church**. The fact that no one knows the day on which the Lord comes (24:42) should engender neither complacent business as usual nor feverish attempts to figure out what Jesus himself does not know. Jesus uses the analogy of a person whose house has been broken into to suggest

*The Revised Common Lectionary uses this in Year A, Advent 1: Matthew 24:36–44.

that readiness, not precise foreknowledge, is the important thing. Yes, it would be great if thieves called ahead to say they were on their way. But because the thief's coming is unannounced, the householder must be ready at all times. The people of Noah's day were inattentive and unprepared (24:38–39), as are the people of "this generation" (11:16; 12:41–45; 16:4; 23:36). The disciples will not know—cannot know—the **time** of the Lord's coming, but they must be watchful and ready nonetheless.

What might "readiness" for the Lord's coming look like in practice? Jesus now offers the first of four **parables** that address this question (24:45 to 25:46). He contrasts two slaves who are put in charge of a household and given the responsibility of providing food for the other slaves at the right time. When the master arrives unexpectedly, he blesses the slave whom he finds working and puts him in charge of all his possessions. On the other hand, the slave who uses the master's delay as an opportunity to abuse the other slaves and carouse with drunkards will face a violent end when the master comes (24:50–51). These two scenarios recall Jesus' contrast between those who produce the fruit of the kingdom in its time (cf. 3:8; 7:15–20; 12:33–35; 21:43) and the hypocrites who use the time to serve their own self-interest (cf. 21:33–39; 23:13–36). At one level, the comparison distinguishes disciples from the **Pharisees**, **chief priests**, and **elders**. But it is also a warning to the disciples, and to the church listening over their shoulders, not to adopt the same perspective that characterizes Jesus' adversaries. Whether we attune our vision to worldly progress and prosperity or look into the apparently bottomless cup of suffering and injustice, we may be tempted to make ourselves comfortable for the long haul. Disciples who no longer watch for the Lord's coming and are not found working and providing food for the other slaves (cf. 14:13–21; 15:32–38) are liable to drift toward the abuse of power the wicked slave manifests.

Preaching and teaching the Word

Jesus disavows knowledge of apocalyptic timetables and signs that mark historical dispensations, except in the most general terms. If we seek to discern in Jesus' teaching a code that will reveal a definitive timetable for the end times, we completely miss Jesus' point. The danger in plotting the chronological moment when the Son of Man will come is that we risk locating his advent and rule somewhere in the future and, thus, grant ourselves permission to live within the regimes of human time. The homeowner does not and cannot know when the thief is coming (24:43) and so must live in a constant state of readiness. Readiness means doing the work of discipleship, especially caring for the vulnerable (24:45–46; cf. 25:31–46). Matthew's **"eschatology"** thus has a decidedly ethical cast.

Knowing what time it is affects the fruit we produce. In turn, the "fruit" we bear in forgiveness, reconciliation, and care for those in need signals the temporal regime under which we live. Jesus is training his disciples to live until further notice in the time of the **empire of heaven**. When the church gathers, we should leave our watches at home. Are we ready? Are we living, even after two thousand years, as if the Lord is near, at the very gates (24:33)?

It is in the very nature of Christian discipleship to be those who "stay awake," "watching" for the Lord's coming and their neighbor's need (24:42–43; Mark 13:33–37; Luke 12:35–40; 21:34–36; Rom. 13:11–13; 1 Thess. 5:2–8; Col. 4:2; 1 Pet. 5:8; Rev. 3:2). This discipline requires active resistance to the world's distractions and worries, senses sharply tuned to the cross, and practice in locating the places where the risen Jesus is present in power in the world. Disciples are not just watching for the lightninglike advent of the Son of Man, which will be apparent to all, but for the dark places of suffering where God's power is not yet named. Disciples will also watch for signs of abuse, betrayal, and the cooling of love that deny the power of the cross within the community (24:10–12). Watching is a communal discipline that is sustained and nurtured through story, prayer, and faithful listening to the voices of the hungry, naked, sick, and imprisoned (cf. 25:31–46). Christian insomniacs stay awake by remembering the story to which they have been joined, which trains them to notice the irruptions of divine power that promise the full presence of the empire of heaven.

The Oil Crisis[1]

Matthew 25:1–13*

Engaging the text

Matthew again calls his disciples to watchfulness, for no one knows the day or hour (25:13; cf. 24:3, 36, 42–44, 50). This **parable** concerns the fate of five foolish young women, who together with five wise young

*The Revised Common Lectionary uses this in Year A, The 32nd Sunday in Ordinary Time.

women await the coming of the bridegroom. Many readers presume that the foolish run short of fuel because their lanterns were burning while they awaited the groom, even when they slept. But Matthew states that the maidens brought torches (not lamps or lanterns), presumably made of oil-soaked rags, which would have been used during the wedding procession. While they wait the torches are not lit. Once the torches are lit, the oil in the rags would last but a few minutes. Jesus says that the foolish brought their torches, but no oil at all (25:3). At one level, the groom's delay is irrelevant; they are not ready even if he is on time. His delay, then, is not the cause of their problem, but an opportunity missed. They are doubly foolish: rather than use the delay to get the oil they need, they fall asleep with the wise.

The situation described in 25:2–6 provides a prologue to the main action of the parable, which focuses on two dialogues, first between the wise and foolish women, after the coming of the bridegroom is announced (25:6–9), and then between the groom and the foolish when they return and find the door shut (25:10–12). Each dialogue pursues a possible way out for the foolish maidens, but in each case a happy ending remains beyond reach: the wise maidens do not have enough oil to share, and the bridegroom refuses to open the door to the foolish latecomers. Modern audiences, especially, might expect a different resolution, some satisfying twist that would rescue the foolish at the last moment. The closed door and the groom's refusal to recognize and admit the foolish maidens thus provides the final shock in this story. Rather than a "Hollywood ending," the audience must grapple with a tragic image of exclusion and **judgment**. The time of repentance has passed.

No allegorization is necessary in order to make sense of the story in its context. Yet several details suggest that Matthew does invite the audience to make associations between the parable and the life of the community as they await the coming of the **Son of Humanity**. The parable is full of links to earlier events and teachings. The contrast between the wise and foolish maidens recalls the parable of the wise and foolish builders at the end of the Sermon on the Mount (7:24–27). Jesus has already referred to himself as a bridegroom in 9:15. The bridegroom image also recalls the parable of the king's wedding feast, to which many (all) are called but few are chosen (22:1–14). Among the early Christians, the wedding banquet signified the time of salvation, for which one must be dressed right (22:11–13). "Going out to meet the groom" suggests the "Parousia" processions by which emperors or conquerors were welcomed into cities (cf. on 21:1–11). Many commentators see in the delay of the bridegroom (25:5) a reference to the delay of Jesus' second coming. The groom's midnight advent is the moment of judgment, with the groom himself in the role of judge. The foolish maidens' plea of "Lord, Lord," and the groom's reply, "I do not know you," both recall 7:21–23, where Jesus warns that only those who "do the will of my Father who is in heaven" will enter the **kingdom of heaven**. The links between this story and the rest of the Gospel show us that wisdom and readiness consist of actions congruent with the advent of God's empire.

Preaching and teaching the Word

How is the empire of heaven like the events in this story? It comes suddenly and decisively and brings division between those who are ready and those who squander the time they have. Jesus tells this story in order to clarify for his audience the kind of **time** in which they live. For Matthew the bridegroom's delay, when the disciples watch in readiness, is an opportunity more than a problem. Because Christians know neither the day nor the hour of his coming, they live in a perpetual state of watchfulness, reading the signs of the times, ready to hear the shout, and prepared to go in to the wedding feast with the bridegroom. Even if they should fall asleep, their preparations (e.g., mercy, forgiveness, restored relationships) leave them ready. They are ready for this time (*kairos*), regardless of its chronological duration.

Jesus' call to watchful waiting and readiness seems to stand in tension with Matthew's claim that the risen Jesus is already with us in mission in the world (18:20; 28:18–20), but the warning to watchfulness and the promise of presence work together toward the same end: a community of disciples living on the edge of history, no longer captive to the times of this world. The followers of Jesus live in the certitude of Christ's coming and presence, not in angst over his absence or delay. What does this certainty mean in the lives of congregations? How can we cultivate greater awareness of the time in which we live? What disciplines do we need in order to be ready?

All of us live somewhere between readiness and foolishness, caught between human perspectives and the vision of God's rule. Does the parable guarantee a place at the banquet for those who, on the world's terms, appear to be ready and secure, like the foolish maidens? The wise and the foolish wait and drowse together, even while some lack the resources they need to join the celebration when the groom arrives. How does the promise of God's rule and the specter of God's **judgment** interrupt business as usual? Which of our daily practices and perspectives prepare us for Christ's coming, and which for the continuation of this world?

The Investment Crisis

Matthew 25:14–30*

Exploring the text

Readers usually approach the **parable** of the talents as an allegory for what Jesus (the absent Lord, cf. 25:15, 25:5) expects of his disciples (the slaves) while he is away (i.e., the delay of the Parousia), namely, the investment of talents–not just financial resources, but gifts and skills–for the sake of the **kingdom**. The story, however, presumes a real practice in the ancient **patronage**-based economy. Slaves were given money to use for trading in land and commodities, with the understanding that both the money and the profit belonged to the master.[1] A "talent" was a sum of money (not individual skills or gifts) equivalent to roughly twenty years of wages for a day laborer. In today's currency, the sums granted to each servant would thus range in value from at least a half million to several million dollars. When the master returns (the final judgment), he rewards the first two slaves, who have doubled the money they were given, with additional opportunities and responsibilities (25:21, 23). The third slave, however, has hidden his grant in the ground, an action he attributes to fear. He hands the money back to the master, who condemns him and has him "cast into outer darkness" (25:30).

A full two thirds of this parable focuses on the final reckoning. The long, repetitive lists of accomplishments and rewards, delivered in sonorous tones, make the scene sound like a graduation ceremony. The master's words convey an almost "religious" tone: "Well done, good and trustworthy slave . . . enter into the joy of your master." All of this builds narrative tension as the audience waits to hear what will happen to the last slave. Surprisingly, this servant is neither servile nor apologetic. He interrupts the ceremony by naming aloud a truth the ritual is meant to obscure. The master is not the kindly benefactor he seems, but a "harsh man," a thief who "gathers where he has not sown seed" (25:24).

Interpretation of the parable turns on the audience's assessment of the third slave's actions and words. Is his accusation against the master an outrageous, insulting lie, or the truth? Is he a "wicked and lazy" slave (25:26) who blames the master for his own sloth? Does he represent the

---

*The Revised Common Lectionary uses this in Year A, The 33rd Sunday in Ordinary Time.

Jewish leaders, who, in some interpretations, have buried the gifts given them, including the law, the temple, the word of the prophets, and now the gift of God's presence in Jesus? Or is he a courageous whistle-blower, who refuses to play the game, publicly unveils the dark reality of the patronage system, and pays the price for naming the hollow, corrupt heart of the system?[2] In this way, is he like Jesus himself, who has just exposed the corruption of the temple system and denounced Israel's rich masters, who will soon condemn and kill him?

Regardless of who we think the third slave represents in an allegorical reading of the parable, we should not dismiss his accusations too quickly. His report to the master has the character of a **prophetic-symbolic action** that threatens the whole system by naming how it works. The master does use people to serve his interests. His first and second servants have successfully sown and reaped, but their reward does not include being set free from obligation or bondage. They remain caught within the system. The third slave's outspoken assertion makes one wonder how "fearful" he really is. But he rightly names fear as the central motivation of the economic system from which he now effectively declares independence. The master himself, ironically, voices a double-edged proverb that affirms the rapacious character of the patronage economy: to those who have, more will be given, and they will have in abundance; from those who have nothing, even what they have will be taken away (25:29). Jesus had already used this saying in 13:12 with reference to the "secrets of the kingdom" given to the disciples and the understanding that would be taken from those who oppose God's way. Poor and vulnerable people would have employed this proverb to name their all-too-common fate. The master uses it to sanction his greed, announcing, in effect, "This is the way the world is."

Preaching and teaching the Word

At their best, allegorical readings of this parable have called the church to use its gifts and resources for the sake of God's empire, bearing the fruit of the cross. At its worst, allegory has reduced the parable either to a baseless condemnation of the Jewish people or to a banal warning to individuals to make the most of their opportunities and gifts, with little or no regard for the christological frame or ethical implications of their actions. Could Caesar or the **chief priests** have just as well told this story? When we hear this parable, do we hear Jesus speaking?

The third slave rightly names the basis of the ancient economy: fear. Fear motivates not only the third slave, but all three of them. Even those who succeed in this economy remain enslaved. The story does not describe the economy of the empire of heaven, but Caesar's economy, which depends ultimately on obligation, intimidation, violence, exploitation, and alienation. It's all too easy for modern readers to hear in this story an implicit affirmation of venture capitalism. We do well to recognize, rather, the ways this parable exposes the dark sides of the ancient economy, and of all economies that wink at exploitation and greed as "normal" or necessary occurrences. Will Jesus, or God, really act like the master in this story? What do our readings of the story reveal about our economic assumptions? What do they reveal about our images of God?

Which way of reading the story is right? Matthew is content to leave us to wrestle with the parable's ambivalence. This is, after all, a parable, not merely an analogy to be decoded and domesticated. As with so many parables in Matthew, this story suspends us between alternative readings and worlds. One approach affirms the successful slaves as models of discipleship, but leaves their world of injustice and violence intact. The other discloses the greed and fear of that world, but offers no alternative except the fate that awaits one who has defied the powers. Matthew's aim may not be to force a choice between these alternative readings and worlds, but to leave us, with the disciples, grappling for our lives between a familiar, but hostile, landscape and a hope-filled horizon littered with deadly perils.

The Sheep and the Goats

Matthew 25:31–46*

Exploring the text

Jesus' **parable** of the sheep and the goats has functioned, like the Sermon on the Mount, as a charter text for many intentional Christian communities, including Latin American "base communities" and Catholic Worker Houses. Audiences hear in this story a foundational articulation of the Christian calling and a clarion warning of the consequences of not attending to the relational dimensions of discipleship. At the final judgment, the **Son of Humanity** (25:31), or King (25:34), divides the

---

*The Revised Common Lectionary uses this in Year A, Christ the King (or Reign of Christ).

righteous from the unrighteous on the basis of ministry to "the least of these my sisters and brother." This image has generated a long quest to determine precisely who Jesus has in mind when he speaks of "the least of these" (25:40, 45), a quest that turns out to be rather goatlike. Contrary to first impressions, Matthew does not intend by means of this story to provide the righteous with the means to distinguish themselves from the unrighteous, but affirms those who serve the least ones without any distinction or expectation of reward.

Matthew's setting for the story, which is unique to this Gospel, confirms its importance. This is the final element in the last of Jesus' great speeches (chapters 5–7; 10; 13; 18; 23–25). It brings to a close the eschatological discourse, with its focus on watchfulness and readiness, and prepares for the story of Jesus' death. The Son of Humanity, about to be judged and condemned by the world's powers, here describes the final judgment of all the nations, over which he will himself preside. In Matthew's overarching structure, the parable of the sheep and the goats also stands in correspondence with the beginning of Jesus' first speech. Like the Beatitudes, the parable describes the vision and practices that define the subjects of the **empire of heaven**.

Many scholars argue that this story is an "apocalyptic prediction" rather than a "parable." The question has to do with whether it points to the nature of God's reign and subverts the audience's way of looking at the world, as in most of Jesus' parables, or merely depicts in a straightforward way Jesus' vision of the final judgment. If the story catches its readers in the quest to identify the "least ones," it is a parable—a sting aimed at Matthew's audience. In order to understand how it works, we have to set aside two common ways of understanding the story. First, this story is not a digital snapshot of the final judgment. Second, while the story sets forth the basis for the final judgment, this also is not the only or most important thing it reveals. Matthew may be more interested in the hidden presence of the Son of Man/king among the least ones, which is the real issue upon which the distinction between the sheep and the goats is drawn. The parable explores the nature of divine presence as much as it describes the practices of the just.

The story begins with an **apocalyptic** image: the Son of Humanity comes in glory, and all the angels with him, and sits on his glorious throne. Later (25:34, 40) Matthew identifies this figure as "king"; both the sheep and the goats address him as "Lord." All of the nations are gathered before him, and he divides them to his right and left. The Son of Man then explains his judgment, first to the sheep on his right. The criteria of **judgment** are stated four times in the parable (35–36, 37–39,

42–43, and 44), as if to drive home the point by repetition: "I was hungry and you gave me food. I was thirsty and you gave me something to drink. I was a stranger and you welcomed me. I was naked and you took care of me. I was in prison and you visited me." When speaking to the goats (25:41–43), the king states each of the criteria in the negative. If the point of the story was to set forth these criteria, Matthew could stop now. But the king reveals a secret: he was himself present among "the least of these my brothers and sisters" (25:40, 45).

Both the sheep and the goats express surprise. In fact, they each ask the king the exact same question: "Lord, when did we see *you* . . .?" The question carries different force in each case, however. Coming from the sheep, who had served the least ones, the question indicates that they had not acted out of awareness of his presence or with expectation of any reward they might receive. Coming from the goats, however, the question suggests that, had they only known that the king was among those in need, they too would surely have acted to meet their need. The hidden presence of the judge, the failure of both the righteous and the unrighteous to recognize him, and the consequences of this for their actions toward the least ones provide the twists that make this story a parable.

Much scholarship has been devoted to making sure that later audiences are not left as visually impaired as the sheep and the goats, by determining exactly whom Jesus has in mind as "the least of these my brothers and sisters." Some interpreters identify "the least ones" as Christians in general, while others regard them as anyone in need, whether Christian or not. Much recent scholarship identifies the least ones with Christian missionaries in Jesus' (cf. 10:5–42) or Matthew's own day, on the ground that Matthew has already used the designation "least ones" (the superlative form of the term *mikros*, "the small" or "little ones") to refer to members of the community of disciples (10:42; 18:6, 10, 14). However one decides this question, the quest to identify the "least ones" itself places one in the position of the goats. The goats are unrighteous not because they are godless or unethical, but because they are motivated by self-interest, by what the king can ultimately do for them. They too would have liked to know who the least ones are and where the Son of Man is among them, so that they could offer appropriate service and gain eternal reward. The church's quest to identify the least ones traps it within the same perspectives and motives that prove to be the goats' undoing.

It seems not to matter to the righteous if the king, the Son of Humanity, the apocalyptic judge, or even God is anywhere in the picture when they see people in need. They simply respond to those in need around them, without counting the cost or anticipating possible reward. Their actions toward the least ones, whoever they might be, run directly counter to the patterns of giving and care that were normative in the ancient **patronage** economy (and modern capitalism), where one gave gifts not to the least, but to the mighty, always calculating potential rewards. Thus, like many of Jesus' parables, this story lifts up "crazy," countercultural behavior as the model for Jesus' disciples to follow. It also turns would-be insiders–the well-informed and well-intentioned righteous ones–into goats. Ultimately, it undermines the whole system of arrangements by which Christians have for twenty centuries sought to divide the world into the righteous (themselves) and the unrighteous, even as it unveils for us where the Lord of all nations is to be found.

Preaching and teaching the Word

The parable of the sheep and the goats provides preachers first of all with an opportunity to describe those practices of hospitality, presence, and relationship that characterize Christian discipleship. The practices that Jesus here sets forth as criteria for judgment–feeding the hungry, giving drink to the thirsty, welcoming the stranger, clothing the naked, and visiting the sick and the prisoners–reflect Jesus' own ministry among the "little ones" and the "least ones." The parable of the sheep and the goats offers examples of the way Jesus' disciples will continue his mission "to all nations" (25:32; 28:19). Christian practice is fundamentally about making space for others, especially the most vulnerable, just as God has come to make space for us. How and for whom do we make room today? How do the spaces where we gather as the **church** testify to the sacrificial and restorative power of God's presence among us?

A disciple's relationship with Jesus is integrally related to his or her relationship with real people, especially with the "least ones." Some might describe these relationships in terms of "social justice," others in terms of "evangelization." Both tend to turn people into abstractions, whereas Jesus calls us into the dangers, risks, opportunities, and possibilities of real relationships. There are no extrinsic rewards to be gained, in this world or the next, by means of these relationships–only the possibility of discovering, together with the least ones, the presence and power of God. These relationships do not make sense at all on the worldly level, perhaps not even in terms of the church's need to count "giving units." Such relationships are neither practical nor an efficient use of time. These relationships are, nonetheless, the heart and soul of God's mission in the world.

Jesus' presence among the least ones does not mean that Matthew romanticizes the poor or those who suffer. It does confirm that "Christ comes in the stranger's guise." The Son of Humanity, the heavenly Caesar, is present among those whose lives seem least to embody the world's notions of power and glory. Here again Matthew juxtaposes divine power with worldly weakness and vulnerability. Without speaking directly of the impending passion, the parable nevertheless speaks christologically, in anticipation of the events about to unfold. Jesus is portrayed simultaneously as the highest divine power and the most scorned form of humanity, the Lord of all nations and the Son of Humanity. He will perfectly embody these same dimensions of his identity when he is nailed to the cross.

The parable ultimately subverts all our attempts to render the world into categories of good and bad, righteous and unrighteous, weak and powerful. Disciples who engage this story honestly are likely to find themselves caught somewhere between the sheep and the goats. This parable is not meant to grant certainty to any of Jesus' disciples, but to make us watchful, attending carefully, faithfully, and creatively to Christ's presence among the least of our brothers and sisters. Anything other than this ambivalent, risky, and uncertain existence is likely to yield something other than the full realization of God's empire of the heavens. God's empire belongs not to the self-proclaimed righteous ones, but to those who continually hunger and thirst for God's righteousness, which leads not to certainty but to the cross.

PART TWELVE

The Revelation of the Son of God in Power

26:1–28:20

Preparing the King for Coronation

Matthew 26:1–13

Exploring the text

The **eschatological** warnings of chapter 24 and the **parables** of chapter 25 complete Jesus' formal "classroom" training of the disciples, but each event that now follows on the way toward Jesus' crucifixion is an intensive exercise in "field education." The deadly conspiracies and violence of Jesus' adversaries will test the disciples' discernment, understanding, faith, courage, and readiness to follow Jesus in the way of the cross. The formula "When Jesus had finished saying all these things . . ." (26:1) is by now a familiar marker at the end of Jesus' long discourses (7:28; 11:1; 13:53; 19:1). In each case, the material immediately following the formula has signaled the content and themes of the subsequent narrative. Here, Jesus warns his disciples once again that the Passover is coming, when "the **Son of Humanity** will be handed over to be crucified" (26:2). When Jesus has spoken in the past to his disciples about being "handed over to be crucified," he has also spoken of being raised on the third day (16:21; 17:22–23; 20:18–19), but here this note of vindication is missing. For the moment at least, Jesus focuses his disciples' attention solely on his looming crucifixion. Matthew links the crucifixion of Jesus with the Passover, or Feast of Unleavened Bread, when Israel's memory and hope of redemption from bondage were renewed (Exod. 12–13).

At the same time, the "**chief priests** and **elders** of the people" (16:21; 21:23; cf. 20:18; 21:15) "gather" in the residence of the high priest, Caiaphas, a location that ensures "stealth" (or "evil intent"), and "conspire" to arrest and kill Jesus (26:3–4). Their conspiracy makes the killing a crime punishable by execution (Exod. 21:14). Jesus' mission has entailed "gathering" (12:30; 13:2; 18:20; cf. 22:10) and he has spoken of the final judgment as a "gathering" (13:29–30, 40–43, 47; 25:31–32). In Jerusalem, Jesus' actions and teaching persistently generate gatherings of his adversaries (26:3; cf. 22:34, 41; 26:57; 27:17, 27, 62; 28:12) to conspire against him (26:4; 22:15; 27:1, 7; 28:12; cf. 12:14). The presence in the city of large numbers of Passover pilgrims, many of whom are sympathetic to Jesus, poses the main obstacle Israel's leaders must overcome in order

264

to kill Jesus (26:5). They prefer not to arrest and kill Jesus during "the feast" (26:5), but the timing of Jesus' death lies in his hands, not theirs. In order for their plot to succeed during the Passover festival, they will have to control and manipulate the people, a task at which they will succeed (27:20–26). At the moment the leaders fear a "riot," but later they will incite a riot, in order to induce Pilate to execute Jesus (27:24).

Matthew then shifts the focus back to Jesus, but in a new setting, the home of Simon the leper in Bethany. This location provides an ironic contrast to the palace of Caiaphas, where the leaders conspire to kill Jesus. Simon's uncleanness bars him from the temple and defiles those who come into contact with him. This also makes his home an ideal "safe house" for Jesus, whose purity is contagious anyway (8:2–4). The rough-and-tumble character of the setting intensifies when an unnamed woman enters and anoints Jesus' head with expensive perfume (26:7). This is a lavish and multivalent **symbolic action**, which should not be reduced to any single meaning. Anointing the head could be a simple act of hospitality, but it is also associated with commissioning for divine service, especially of priests and kings (e.g., Exod. 29:7; Lev. 21:10; 1 Sam. 10:1; 16:6; 24:6).

Matthew does not tell us what the woman understands or intends by her action, only what Jesus understands by it: she is preparing him for burial (26:12). The disciples, however, are angered by the "wastefulness" of her action (26:8–9). They have learned well their responsibility to care for those in need (14:15–21; 15:32–38; 25:31–46). They are apparently oblivious, however, to what **time** it is and the implications of her action. The continued presence of "the poor" is a primary symptom of imperial economics. Jesus' death and resurrection–his coronation, as it were–will break the power that leads peoples to generate and condone disparities of wealth and class. The disciples are still called to embrace their own poverty (cf. 10:8–10) as they proclaim and embody their dependence on God and share the resources God gives them with those in need. But the woman's action is nevertheless the right action for this moment, for it focuses attention on the meaning of events about to transpire and reminds the disciples what time they are living in. The anointing of Jesus signifies both who he is and what he will accomplish through his death, and thus will be remembered wherever "good news"–the announcement of the king's deeds–is proclaimed in the whole world (26:13).

Preaching and teaching the Word

Does Caiaphas's palace make it harder for him to discern what God wills? Does the fact that Simon is a leper also make room for an unnamed woman to act extravagantly? How do the spaces in which Christians gather hinder or enable our sight? For whom do they make room? What kinds of interactions do they invite or suppress?

While the religious leaders seek to avoid acting against Jesus during Passover, they do not control the pace or timing of this drama. During the course of Jesus' ministry, he has been operating on **Empire of Heaven** time—the time of gathering, healing, restoring, and finally the time when death is defeated. Not even his disciples seem to recognize this. They are operating on social justice time, fighting the symptoms of the old order. The woman's actions reset the clock. The new king is anointed and about to be crowned. Like Saul hunting David, old King Death will seek to extend the time of his rule. But after the crucifixion and resurrection of Jesus, death will rule only by illusion and trickery.

The leaders gathered in the home of Caiaphas engage in the rituals of empire. They plan; they weigh pros and cons; they choose stealth, deceit, manipulation, and murder. In the home of Simon the rituals focus on table fellowship and acts of kindness and honor. The disciples, however, are engaged in the ritual of criticism, by which they mean to stake a claim to power. The woman's ritual action may mean more than she knows, but by her action she redefines the moment, focuses attention on Jesus, and reveals what time it really is. With her actions she preaches the ultimate sermon, the one everyone will remember. What stories do our rituals proclaim, and what vistas do they reveal? Which clock do they follow, and whose time do they tell?

Disciples rightly hear God's call to fight poverty and injustice. The world does not realize that fear of death is the source of injustice and poverty, and death is about to be defeated. We will have the poor with us as long as the empire of death rules our imagination and practice. In the death of Jesus is the miracle the poor need: the revelation of the empire of mercy and abundance. How does the peculiar calling of the **church** as a community of sharing and forgiveness—forgiveness of debts!—come to fruition in our life together? How is God's abundance revealed to a world that presumes scarcity and makes a god of greed?

Betrayal and Promise: Jesus' Last Meal with His Disciples

Matthew 26:14–35*

Exploring the text

Matthew tells the story of Jesus' last meal with his disciples, the Passover supper, in three scenes. The first (26:14–25) focuses on the disciples' preparations, including Judas' contract with the **chief priests**, Jesus' predictions of betrayal, and the breakdown of trust and integrity in the community of disciples. The second scene describes Jesus' words and actions at the Supper itself (26:26–30). Finally, Jesus reiterates his awareness that the disciples will desert and deny him, to which they offer repeated demurrals (26:31–35). Matthew thus frames the Last Supper between notices of impending betrayal.

JUDAS OFFERS HIS SERVICES TO THE CHIEF PRIESTS
(26:14–16)

Peter has represented the disciples as a group; now so does Judas, "one of the twelve" (26:14). He carries on, in a twisted way, the disciples' interest in money, displayed prominently in the previous story (26: 8–9). The leaders of Israel do not really need him in order to arrest Jesus, sway the crowds, and execute Jesus. Nor is the money he seeks–the value of an injured slave (Exod. 21:32)–a significant sum. Zechariah 11:12–13 names this sum as the pay offered to God's faux-shepherd who tends the doomed flocks named "Favor" and "Unity," a **prophetic-symbolic act** associated with judgment against Israel's corrupt leaders. Whatever his motives, Judas begins watching for an opportunity to "hand Jesus over" (26:16; 27:2; cf. 4:12; 10:4, 17, 19, 21; 17:22; 20:18–19; 26:2).

THE PASSOVER MEAL WITH BETRAYERS
(26:17–25)

Passover celebrates the renewal of the covenant between God and Israel, beginning when God freed the people from slavery in Egypt (cf.

*The Revised Common Lectionary uses this in Year A, Passion/Palm Sunday, The 6th Sunday in Lent: Matthew 26:14–27:66.

Exod. 12–13). Jesus' mission itself is yet another sign of God's faithfulness to Israel. When Israel celebrates Passover, it remembers God's demands and faithfulness as well as its own liberation and resistance to God. All of this history is represented in the mission of Jesus and the responses it has generated.[1] Jesus' last meal with his disciples itself embodies these same dynamics. Jesus celebrates the Passover with his betrayers. Jesus will "keep the Passover" with his disciples because his "**time** is near" (26:18). Israel's liturgical calendar thus becomes integrally, intimately tied with Jesus' calling.

At table, Jesus' disciples probably expected to hear the traditional story of how the people put the blood of the unblemished lamb on their doors so that God would pass over their houses while destroying the Egyptians' firstborn children and animals (Exod. 12:1–13). But instead Matthew records Jesus' announcement that "one of you will betray me" (26:21). While Judas is clearly identified as "the betrayer," all of them, in fact, will betray Jesus. The betrayals begin with their individual demurrals, "Surely not I, Lord" (26:22). Each of them personally promises his loyalty, but these individual responses signal that their community is splintering. They will support neither Jesus nor one another.

Jesus identifies the betrayer as the one who has dipped his hand into the bowl with him (26:23), which includes both one of them and all of them. Jesus' knowledge of this reality conveys both his insight and his control of the unfolding events: "The **Son of Humanity** goes as it is written of him" (26:24). "Woe to that one who betrays the Son of Humanity" classifies the betrayer among the **scribes** and **Pharisees**–"this generation" (23:35–36)–whose judgment Jesus has earlier announced. Like the other disciples, Judas protests, "Surely not I, Rabbi?" The others had identified Jesus as "Lord" (26:22), but Judas calls him "Rabbi" (26:25), a title Jesus had warned the disciples against (23:8), the same title Judas will use at the moment of betrayal (26:49).

Jesus' enigmatic response to Judas, "You have said it" (26:25), links this passage to answers Jesus supplies in his trials before the high priest and council (26:64) and before Pilate (27:11). In each case, Jesus implicitly affirms the other's statement, but with a note of distance, as if he is putting final resolution back into his adversaries' hands, saying, "Yes, the answer is what you make of it." Judas holds the true answer to his question in his own hands. Judas is not the betrayer because Jesus has identified him as such, nor because it is Judas's destiny, although both are true at some level, but primarily because Judas is making it so.

THE EMBODIMENT OF PROMISE (26:26–29)

Jesus lifts up both loaf and cup as symbols that unveil the meaning of the events about to take place. The bread Jesus blesses, breaks, and eats with his disciples is a multivalent symbol, evoking associations with the unleavened bread of the Passover, which recalls Israel's flight from Egypt, the common bread of fellowship shared every day at meals in antiquity, and the abundant bread that God has supplied on the two occasions when Jesus and his disciples fed the crowds in the wilderness (14:13–21; 15:32–38, esp. 14:19 and 15:36). The bread reminds us of Israel's liberation, generates fellowship, and promises the sufficiency and abundance of God's provision.[2] Jesus' assertion, "This is my body" (26:26), adds yet more meaning and ambiguity to the symbol of bread. The debates across church history about the precise meaning of this statement have often reduced it to divisive abstractions, whereas Jesus' words are intentionally generative and rich. The word "this" may refer not only to the bread itself (in Greek, "this" does not agree in gender with "bread"), but to the whole process of blessing, breaking, sharing, taking, eating, remembering, and hoping.[3] Christian tradition has also understood the broken bread as a symbol for the suffering and death that Jesus will endure, and his disciples after him. Above all, taking and eating the bread signals solidarity with Jesus in the way of the cross. This solidarity in suffering is the key to preserving the community of disciples even in the midst of betrayal (26:14–16, 21–25) and desertion (26:31–35).

The cup that Jesus then gives them signifies the promise of covenant relationship and the forgiveness of sins for many (26:27–28). In both Testaments, the cup is used symbolically in association with both **judgment** and promise.[4] Jesus identifies the cup as his "blood of the covenant" (26:28). Blood is life. Blood "poured out" signifies both violence–the blood of the righteous poured out on the earth (cf. 23:35)–and sacrifice (e.g., Lev. 4:7, 18, 25, 30, 34). Blood evokes the Passover event itself, when Israel is protected from the judgments that fall upon the Egyptians. The language Jesus uses also recalls the covenant between God and Israel that Moses enacts in Exodus 24:1–8 in connection with the giving of the Law and the promise of the land. Finally, Matthew's Jesus has already spoken of the cup in association with suffering (20:22–23).

Together the bread and cup point back to Israel's story of liberation, covenant, violence, judgment, and renewal, and forward toward Jesus' death and resurrection and the promise of **salvation** and abundance. The statement that Jesus will not drink the fruit of the vine again until he drinks it new with the disciples in his father's empire (26:29) is a word of promise. The **empire of heaven** coincides with the fruition of Jesus' fellowship with his followers (cf. 1:23; 28:20). Sharing the bread and cup with Jesus generates a community bound together with Jesus in suffering, in covenant, and in forgiveness (cf. 9:1–9; 18:21–22, 23–35). Memory, experience, and hope thus commingle, ferment, and leaven one another in the meal Jesus shares with his disciples. Past and future are joined in the present experience of the community.

JESUS AS STUMBLING BLOCK (26:30–35)

Jesus and the disciples end their last meal together with a hymn (perhaps Pss. 115–118 or a hymn of thanksgiving),[5] then go out toward the Mount of Olives (26:30), where Jesus had delivered his final discourse to the disciples (cf. 24:3). The Mount of Olives is associated with the glory of God and the promise of restoration (cf. Ezek. 11:22–24; Zech. 14:3–5), but their conversation on the way there is consumed with desertion and denial. Matthew often uses the word the NSRV here translates as "desert" or "deserters" (*skandalizo*, 26:31, 33) in reference to Jesus as a source of stumbling, scandal, or offense (11:6; 13:57; 15:12; 17:27).

The events that will happen that very night, as Jesus proceeds on the way to the cross, will cause the disciples to stumble and desert him (cf. 26:56). Jesus asserts that this stumbling fulfills Zechariah 13:7: "I will strike the shepherd, and the sheep of the flock will be scattered." It is God who speaks in this verse, and God who strikes the shepherd. The scattering is thus both a human response to the terror of the striking and an expression of God's will. The larger context of the citation in Zechariah indicates that the scattering is part of the "refining" and "testing" that leads to the reconstitution of God's people (Zech. 13:7–9). Jesus himself promises that he will be "raised up"–the passive voice indicates that God, who has struck the shepherd and scattered the sheep, also does the raising–and go ahead of them to Galilee (26:32; cf. 28:7, 10, 16). But the disciples already are stumbling. As before, they resist Jesus' predictions and ignore his promise of resurrection (cf. 16:21–23; 17:22–23). Peter boasts that even if all the rest stumble because of Jesus, he will never do so (26:33). Rather than preserving the solidarity Jesus had celebrated at the supper moments before (26:26–29), the community of disciples once again begins splintering into individual fragments (cf. 26:22). Jesus assures Peter that before morning Peter will deny Jesus three times (26:34; cf. 26:69–75). The rest of the disciples join Peter in asserting their loyalty to Jesus, thereby denying both Jesus' word and God's own voice in scripture.

Preaching and teaching the Word

Many Christian communities, misunderstanding Paul's warnings about sharing the table in an unworthy manner (1 Cor. 11:27), have made moral rectitude a requirement for access to the Lord's Table. But Jesus shares the supper with his disciples even knowing that they will betray and desert him. The Last Supper thus continues Jesus' tradition of sharing table with outcasts, sinners, even the unrepentant (cf. 9:10–13). The disciples' persistent assertions of loyalty to Jesus reveal more clearly their pride than their commitment, yet Jesus offers them God's mercy and forgiveness. The forgiveness proclaimed and embodied at the table is "for all" ("for many" in 26:28 has an unrestricted reference), even for betrayers. God's grace always precedes our repentance and understanding.

Jesus' last supper with the disciples is also a **prophetic-symbolic action**, a preemptive response to the violence and betrayal just on the horizon. While much of the Christian tradition has focused on what really happens to the bread and wine and how they are related to the body and blood of Jesus, Jesus speaks clearly of what is most important: the establishment of covenant (cf. Exod. 24:8 and Jer. 31:31–34) and the pouring out of blood (cf. Isa. 53:12) for the forgiveness of sins (26:28). Our tendency to hear these claims in personal, individual terms is not misfounded, but it may cause us to miss the systemic and communal dimensions of the Table. Sharing table with Jesus, Israel's crucified and resurrected Messiah, ends the hegemony of the generation of Cain (cf. 23:35–36), for whom the shedding of human blood is the greatest sacrifice, the holiest act one can imagine (Gen. 4:1–16). The covenant in Jesus' blood, poured out for the forgiveness of all, renders obsolete all systems of sacrifice, from those offered in the Jerusalem temple to the blood sacrifices of war, which we typically sanctify. The Lord's Table is a "counterritual" to the liturgies of violence, war, and terror that continue to beset the world.[6]

The disciples have challenged and questioned Jesus' announcements of his own suffering and death (16:21–23; 17:22–23), so we are not surprised by their responses when he predicts their betrayals and desertions. Their boastful, individualistic replies (26:22, 25, 33–35) signal that they are not yet ready to carry on his mission, even after he has bound them together at the table with him in the way of the cross. Pride destroys the community of disciples, splintering the body when its members most need to be in solidarity with one another. Humility, honesty, and service are the keys to enduring the crises of faith. The experience of forgiveness and the redemptive power of the Lord's Table are rooted in recognition of our common humanity and sinfulness before God. Faith is not bravado and boasting in the face of the powers of this world. Faith is humble service that crosses the world's boundaries on the way to the cross.

The disciples' desertion of Jesus is really about the scandal of the cross. Despite Jesus' repeated warnings, the image of the crucified Messiah remains beyond the disciples' grasp, and so too for us. Over time, the disciples have ceased to resist this notion openly, but it is still a stumbling block. For us it has become a commonplace. Our stumbling over the cross may be less evident than the betrayals and desertions of the disciples, but is no less real. Our investments in the securities of this world and our pursuit of the salvation offered by nation-states and the marketplace betray our own stumbling faith. Like Peter, we can use an occasional dose of cold water. For the moment, Peter will not hear the warning that he will deny Jesus three times before morning, but later Peter will look back, grieve, and remember (26:75). Jesus' word will be vindicated, and thus convict Peter. Beyond this conviction lies hope. The truth of Jesus' words to Peter implies that all his other words are true as well. Betrayals come. The cross is coming. And then the resurrection also comes. God is coming in power to redeem the world.

Sheep Asleep and Scattered

Matthew 26:36–56*

Exploring the text

Jesus goes "with them" (the disciples, 26:36) to Gethsemane. Jesus, who has been "with" the disciples (26:18, 20; cf. 1:23; 18:20; 26:29; 28:20), now asks them to be with him in preparation for the completion of his mission. But despite their bluster about not stumbling, deserting, or denying Jesus (26:31–35), the disciples will lose energy and then take flight. Jesus spends the last hours before his arrest in prayer, distress, and lament. His distress concerns both his own fate and the disciples' lack of readiness for what is coming. He distances himself from most of the disciples ("You sit here, while I go over there to pray," cf. Gen. 22:5), but takes with

---

*The Revised Common Lectionary uses this in Year A, Passion/Palm Sunday, The 6th Sunday in Lent: Matthew 26:14–27:66.

him Peter, James, and John, the same three disciples who had witnessed his transfiguration (17:1–8). Then Jesus had told them not to share their vision with anyone "until the **Son of Humanity** is raised from the dead" (17:9). Now he calls upon them to be "watchers" (26:38, 40–41; cf. 24:42; 25:13), to stay awake and pray, as he does.

Jesus' prayers (26:39, 42, 44) are genuine human expressions of "grief" and "distress" (26:38), but we should understand his prayers more as disciplined preparation than as expressions of fear or a lack of resolve. His deep grief (26:38: lit., "my soul is exceedingly sorrowful") echoes two psalms that appeal for deliverance but also express hope and trust in God (Pss. 42:5, 11; 43:5). Throwing himself on the ground (26:39) follows the pattern of Abraham's prayers before God (Gen. 17:3, 17; cf. Num. 22:31; 1 Kgs. 18:39; Dan. 8:17). What is "possible" (26:39, 42) belongs to the will of God (cf. 19:26; 6:9–10), which Jesus repeatedly affirms, the second time in language that quotes the "Lord's Prayer" (26:39, 42; cf. 6:10). The "cup" could refer to the prophetic cup of God's wrath, but Matthew's audience would recall most immediately the cup that is Jesus' redemptive suffering and death (20:22–23; 26:27–29). Jesus prays three times, the biblical quotient for faithful, powerful prayer. Amidst his despair, he confirms his trust in God.

Jesus' powerful, disciplined prayer stands in sharp contrast to the disciples' sleepiness. Each time Jesus prays, he returns to find the disciples sleeping (26:40, 43, 45). The first time he chides Peter, who only moments before promised to stay with him to the death. Peter's resistance to the **"time** of trial" (26:41; cf. 6:13) depends on his staying awake and praying. But Jesus also recognizes the frailty of "the flesh"—now abundant in the disciples—contesting the "eagerness" of the spirit (26:41; cf. 26:33, 35; Rom. 7:14–25). Jesus wants the disciples to prepare themselves as he does for what is "at hand" (26:46), to be ready to drink the cup that he drinks, and to confirm God's will as he has, but they are not yet ready. His "hour" and the "betrayer" are "at hand" (26:45, 46; cf. 26:18; 3:2; 4:17; 10:7); he mocks them for napping at the edge of the **apocalypse**. It is time to "arise and go" (26:46), first to meet those who will "hand him over" (26:45, 46), then to meet death, and then the day of resurrection and renewed mission (28:19).

Before Jesus has finished speaking, Judas arrives with a vast crowd, armed with swords and clubs, sent by the **chief priests** and **elders** (26:47). The latter have apparently succeeded in winning over the crowds, whom they earlier feared (26:5). Matthew again describes Judas as "one of the twelve" (26:47; cf. 26:14), in order to identify him as a representative figure for them and to heighten the irony of the scene. Jesus will be "seized" or "handed over" repeatedly during the hours that follow, first by Judas to the accompanying mob (26:50), then by the mob to the chief priests and elders (26:57), then by the chief priests and elders to Pilate (27:2, 18), and finally by Pilate to the executioners (27:26). The string of seizures and betrayals begins with Judas's ironic, aggressive kiss. He greets Jesus as "Rabbi" (cf. 26:25), a title only he uses in Matthew. Jesus greets him in turn as "friend," which in this Gospel conveys tension, even rebuke (cf. 20:13; 22:12).

As the crowd surges forward to seize Jesus, "one of those with Jesus"–presumably a suddenly aroused disciple–"extends his hand" (as Jesus had, to heal a leper, 8:3, and to save sinking Peter, 14:31), draws his sword, and cuts off the ear of the high priest's slave (26:51). Jesus disarms the disciple with the command to return the sword "to its place" (26:52), which is not this place. The disciple has not learned the lesson of disciplined, creative nonretaliation (5:38–42), nor is he in line with Jesus' repeated instructions about the "cup" he must drink. Jesus is not just concerned with the futility of resistance in the midst of a heavily armed mob. Taking up the sword, whether of aggression or of retaliation, commits the user to that power, that life, and that fate (26:52). The **kingdom of heaven** does not come with military power. Moreover, if Jesus' goal were to escape this posse, or the cross, he could call on God to send more than twelve legions of angels–more than enough for all of Israel (26:53). Jesus confirms in a general reference to Scripture that God's plan is being realized even in the events of this moment (26:54).

Jesus then turns from the disciple to the crowds, the same crowds that had observed and hailed his actions and attended his proclamations during the occupation of the temple (21:12–23:39). Now they have come to him as if he were a bandit or thief, rather than the one who had cleansed the temple of bandits (21:12–13). Jesus' words distance him from both the elites who run the temple and the brigands and terrorists who resisted the temple establishment through violent means. Jesus' mission is not about popular revolt, but is the realization of God's will and way as announced in the prophetic writings (26:56; cf. 26:54; 23:34–37). Jesus' refusal of violence and his announcement that the events unfolding fulfill God's intention strike terror in the hearts of his disciples, who desert him and flee (26:56).

Preaching and teaching the Word

Why is Judas's betrayal necessary? The chief priests and elders would presumably have no trouble locating and arresting Jesus at their will. They would prefer, in fact, to wait until after the Passover festival has ended and the volatile crowds have gone home (26:5). But Judas's betrayal forces their hand. God controls the time, not they. The betrayal sets in motion the events that will lead rapidly to Jesus' public execution, prior to the end of Passover. Throughout the passion story, as the other human actors, such as Judas and the Jerusalem leaders, pursue their agendas, it is Jesus and, through him, God who exercise sovereignty over all that happens. The betrayal fulfills the Scriptures, perhaps specifically Isaiah 53:6, 12 (LXX), where God's servant is "handed over to death" for our sins. Humans play their roles, scheming and manipulating events, all the time unaware that they are fulfilling a larger design they cannot or will not discern. The Gospel is God's story.

Matthew does not tell us how it has happened, but these stories reveal that the crowds have gone over to the leaders' side. Perhaps it is necessary for Judas to lead the crowd to Jesus and identify him by the "sign" of a kiss, even though the crowds have watched Jesus daily in the temple, because the crowds, like their leaders, are now blind (cf. 15:14; 23:16–22). The leaders know that the crowds are dangerous (21:46; 26:5), but also that they can be turned into a tool for violence (27:20–26). Although Jesus has lost his battle for the crowds, he will nonetheless die for their transgressions (Isa. 53:12). The cross embodies the love of enemies. Jesus' death is at once both a sign of **judgment** and the realization of **salvation**.

During its long watch, the **church** has often been drowsy, bewildered, or even asleep. We are lulled by the passage of time, distracted by the attractions and worries of this world, and content just to keep the church going. But the time is still at hand and the need for watchfulness more acute than ever (cf. 24:42–25:13). The first disciplines of the church are to watch and pray, from which follow the rest of our peculiar practices. But wakefulness remains one of the hardest tasks for Christians. It takes less than an hour for the disciples to fall asleep (26:40). Like parents trying to rouse napping children, Jesus must make repeated visits to waken them. There is some painful humor in Matthew's account. One of the last things the earthly Jesus says directly to his disciples is a sarcastic zinger: "Are you still sleeping and taking your rest?" (26:45). It remains a viable question.

The Gethsemane episodes juxtapose two story lines: Jesus preparing for death and the betrayers arriving to seize him. Matthew thus continues to portray the clash of two empires, one still determined by violence and the other determined to receive that same violence. Israel's true king does not inflict violence, but embraces and transforms it. The battle lines are being drawn, but one side refuses to pick up the traditional weapons. The empire of heaven will use the enemy's very own device to defeat it. The chief weapon of imperial control will provide the means of redemption. Will the church, like the disciples, also flee this reality, or wake up and go with Jesus to the cross?

Trials and Oaths

Matthew 26:57–27:10*

Exploring the text

At the palace of Caiaphas, both Jesus and Peter face trials in which oaths play a central role. Soon after this, Judas will announce to the **chief priests** and **elders** his guilt for "betraying innocent blood" (27:4) and then proceed to hang himself. The trials of Jesus and Judas end effectively in death sentences; Peter's trial will leave him physically unscathed, but scarred with the guilt of also having betrayed Jesus. These stories also put on trial the Jewish justice system, which is more concerned with power and appearances than with people or truth. These stories portray the diverse ways the various characters–Judas, Peter, the religious authorities–deal with their guilt for betraying, deserting, and condemning Jesus to death.

JESUS' TRIAL BEFORE THE JEWISH AUTHORITIES
(26:59–68)

The Gethsemane mob carries Jesus to Caiaphas, where again Jesus provokes a "gathering" (cf. 26:3), this time including legal scholars (26:57). Peter follows at a safe distance to the high priest's house, or perhaps the courtyard of the house, the same place where the chief priests and elders had first drafted their plot to kill Jesus (26:3–5). He then enters and takes a seat inside with the guards, "to see the end," just as the prophet Jonah had once "sat" outside Nineveh "to see" what would happen (Jonah 4:5).

Matthew portrays the chief priests and the council going through the motions of a trial, probably aimed at satisfying public opinion or, perhaps, their own sense of propriety. This is a hanging jury, just looking for reasonable, or even unreasonable, cause. The many "false witnesses" who testify are apparently unable to produce a coherent or compelling case, until two of them agree that Jesus had talked of being able to destroy the temple and in three days to build it again. Jesus has never said this in Matthew, but something like it is attributed to him in John 2:19. The false witnesses do not represent this as a statement of intent, but as Jesus' affirmation of power. Josephus, the first-century Jewish historian and apologist, reports

*The Revised Common Lectionary uses this in Year A, Passion/Palm Sunday, The 6th Sunday in Lent: Matthew 26:14–27:66.

that prophets who spoke of the fall of the city or temple were punished or killed (*Jewish Antiquities* 18.169–70; *Jewish War* 6.300–309). The high priest asks for a defense, but Jesus remains silent, like Isaiah's suffering servant (Isa. 53:7; cf. Pss. 38:13–15; 39:9). His silence suggests that he does not recognize the authority of this court; Jesus answers only to the Father. Ironically, Caiaphas then puts Jesus under oath to "the living God," and asks him whether he is the **Messiah**, the **Son of God** (26:63). Caiaphas's question echoes what Peter, who is listening, had earlier confessed (16:16). Jesus has consistently warned his followers against oaths (5:33–37; 23:16–22), but Caiaphas at least names the one true power who might—and will—validate Jesus' identity.

Jesus' enigmatic reply (26:64) echoes his response to Judas (26:25) and foreshadows what he will say to Pilate (27:11). "You have said it" implies affirmation of the preceding statement, but with the sense that the questioners will make of it what they will. Yes, Jesus is the Messiah, the Son of God, but not for Caiaphas and not in a way that Caiaphas would understand. Caiaphas hears in these words a threat, not the promise of God's **salvation**. Jesus' next statement amplifies the first part of his answer and corrects one aspect of Caiaphas's misunderstanding. For the first time Jesus declares beyond the circle of his disciples—and with a clear tone of authority—that he is "the **Son of Man**" according to the terms of Daniel 7:13–14, who comes on the clouds to rule and to judge (cf. 24:30–31). "Seated at the right hand of power" recalls Psalm 110 (esp. 110:1, 5), another passage that speaks of the king's authority and judgment of the nations (cf. 25:31). The one about to be condemned, mocked, beaten, and crucified will also be the final judge who sits at the right hand of God. When Jesus had spoken to his disciples about the coming of the Son of Humanity, his statements offered reassurance (16:27–28; 24:30–31; 25:31–33), but to Caiaphas and the elders this identification conveys only **judgment**.

For Caiaphas, Jesus' claim also constitutes clear blasphemy (a mocking or usurping of God's role), which he names both verbally and symbolically, tearing his clothes (cf. 2 Kgs. 19:1). The false witnesses are no longer needed. The question Caiaphas puts before the council recalls Jesus' earlier challenges to his adversaries: "How does it seem to you?" or "What do you think?" (26:66; cf. 21:28, 40). The council's answer is clear: "He deserves death" (cf. Lev. 24:13–16). Immediately after delivering this sonorous judgment, which was never in doubt, the trial disintegrates into a mob scene. The council members spit on, slap, and strike Jesus (26:67; cf. Isa. 50:6). They mockingly call him "Messiah" and invite him to name who it is that strikes him. They miss the irony of their joke. Jesus and the

Gospel audience already know that it is God who strikes the shepherd (26:31; cf. Zech. 13:7). Everything that is happening, even the council's mockery, conforms to God's will, which remains hidden from all the participants but the Son of the living God.

PETER'S "TRIAL" (26:69–75)

Peter has remained outside in the courtyard. Three times he is accused of being one of Jesus' accomplices (26:69, 71, 73), and three times he denies any knowledge of Jesus (26:70, 72, 74; cf. 26:34–35). Twice he is noticed by observant servant girls, and finally by people who recognize his Galilean accent. As his denials continue, they grow more vehement and coarse. With the second denial he includes an oath, and with the third both cursing and another oath. The denials are bad enough, but the oaths intensify his trouble. Jesus has clearly taught his disciples not to swear oaths, but to rely on God's judgment alone (5:33–37; 23:16–22). Peter saves his skin by reverting to the world's way of securing truth. As the cock crows, at the moment of Peter's third denial, Peter remembers Jesus' warning (26:34), which has now been fulfilled. This is Peter's darkest moment, but it also contains the seed of his redemption. Jesus' word about Peter is true. His word about the cross and resurrection will also be true. For the moment, however, Peter knows only grief and shame (26:75).

FINAL ADJUDICATIONS FOR JUDAS (27:1–10)

Again the scene shifts, now to the chief priests and elders, who as morning breaks are again gathered and conspiring to kill Jesus (27:1; cf. 26:4). They "hand him over" ("betray") to Pilate, who is named for the first time in Matthew. Their conspiracy in this moment concerns persuading Pilate to execute Jesus. They have no authority to carry out an execution themselves, and Pilate will be rightly suspicious of their motives (27:18). The success of their plan again hinges on manipulation of the crowds (27:20).

When the leaders hand Jesus over to Pilate, Judas enters the story for the final time. Only Matthew includes the story of Judas's suicide and the leaders' fretting over what to do with the silver. Many regard this material as an unnecessary interruption of the larger story, but Matthew uses it to intensify the prophetic critique of the leaders' callousness and blindness, drawing especially on Zechariah 11 and Jeremiah 18–19. Why did Judas betray Jesus? Had he hoped to compel a miraculous display of power from Jesus? Did he expect that Jesus would elude judgment, as he had earlier outwitted his adversaries (21:23–22:46), or call down twelve legions of angels to rescue him (26:53)? When he sees that Jesus is now condemned, he "changes his mind" (27:3; cf. 21:29) and returns to the chief priests and elders with the thirty pieces of silver (cf. 26:14–16). He confesses that he has "betrayed innocent blood," a crime worthy of a curse (Deut. 27:25) and judgment (2 Kgs. 21:16; 24:3–4). But they are unconcerned. Confronted with a true crime in which they are complicit, they leave the matter to Judas himself to resolve: "What is that to us? You see to it" (27:4). The first phrase denies their complicity in betraying innocent blood. Their very words–"You see to it"–will echo back to them when Pilate, too, washes his hands of guilt for Jesus' death (27:24). Judas "sees to it" by throwing the silver down in the temple, then "withdraws" (or "retreats," 27:5; cf. 2:12–14, 22; 4:12; 12:15; 14:13; 15:21) and hangs himself. The chief priests and elders undoubtedly appealed to Leviticus 24:13–16 as the basis for the death penalty in their judgment of blasphemy against Jesus. Judas may know the very next verse in Leviticus, which calls for death for anyone who kills another human (Lev. 24:17). He carries out the penalty for taking Jesus' life by taking his own (cf. also 2 Sam 17:23).

When Judas throws down the thirty pieces of silver in the temple (27:5), his action draws a connection with Zechariah 11:13 (cf. 26:9–10), where the prophet/pseudo shepherd throws the thirty pieces of silver he had been paid before "the potter" (cf. Matt. 27:7–9) in the temple, as a sign of the rupture between Judah and Israel. If Judas threw his pay into the inner sanctuary, he defiled the temple with blood money.[1] The chief priests apparently realize this when they discover the money. Their twisted sense of propriety kicks in (cf. 23:23). They recognize that this "blood money" cannot be put in the temple treasury (27:6); instead they use it to buy a "potter's field" where foreigners can be buried. For a moment Matthew steps out of the story to supply an etiology for the place name "Field of Blood," and then offers the last fulfillment quotation in the Gospel (27:9–10). Matthew attributes the citation to Jeremiah, but it comes mostly, again, from Zechariah 11:13. The reference to Jeremiah is not a Matthean error, but a way of inducing the audience to hear Zechariah together with Jeremiah 18–19 and 32:6–15, which recount Jeremiah's **prophetic-symbolic actions** and proclamations of **judgment** against the "elders of the people and the senior priests" (Jer. 19:1). These actions include the symbolic shattering of pottery (19:1, 10), a protest against the shedding of "innocent blood" (Jer. 19:4), the voiding of "the plans of Judah and Jerusalem" (19:7), warnings of impending death and destruction of the city (19:8–9), the renaming of a place for burial (19:6, 11), and purchasing a field with silver (32:6–9). In Jeremiah, the chief priests and elders witness the prophet's enactment of judgment. In Matthew, the chief priests and elders themselves reenact the events that foreshadow their doom.

Preaching and teaching the Word

In the midst of the leaders' attempts to pin something meaningful on Jesus, Jesus identifies himself with the image of Daniel's **Son of Humanity**, sitting at the right hand of God and coming on the clouds (26:64). In this moment, it becomes clear that the only one at this trial with any real authority is the accused. Those who sit in judgment of him are the true criminals. The reversal of roles and status is one of the most common prophetic motifs adopted by the evangelists. God overturns the powers of this world. The weak will be restored, the humiliated will be exalted, the poor will inherit the earth. The capacity to discern God's transformative power already at work in the world requires eyes trained on the cross, where the world is turned upside down.

Matthew's account of the trial of Jesus intensifies the sense of hypocrisy, evil, and violence of the religious leaders as they seek Jesus' death. This portrayal has motivated and condoned centuries of Christian violence against Jews. For Matthew, however, this portrayal is an intramural extension of the critique of Israel's unfaithful leadership that runs so deeply throughout the pages of the Bible. Matthew's interest, like that of the prophets before him, is the identification and announcement of judgment against corrupted leaders, whether Jewish, Roman, or Christian, not the vilification of the Jewish people or Judaism. In these stories, the leaders demonstrate their callousness and blindness. If they feel any guilt concerning their actions toward Jesus, it is not evident. They dismiss Judas, but fixate on what to do with the blood money. Their fixation on the minutiae covers over the enormity of their violence, and perhaps covers over any damage to their sense of righteousness. Things are already getting back to normal. They are unaware that their actions already pronounce their own judgment. Where Christian leaders exercise power destructively or for their own interests, or foment exclusion and violence against others, they fall under the same judgment Matthew here levels against the chief priests and elders of Jerusalem. Power, especially religious power, is always a dangerous and potentially corrupting force that must constantly be held up to the judgment of the cross.

Peter and Judas each desert and betray Jesus, and each eventually repents. What is the difference between them? Peter's experience reminds him of the truth of Jesus' words, which carry the seeds of redemption. Judas acts more decisively than Peter to carry out upon himself the judgment he thinks is due. There is no room in Judas for the experience of being forgiven. When he seeks to fix things, he turns to the leaders with whom he has schemed, rather than to the one he has offended. In his isolation and refusal of the paths of reconciliation he becomes the more tragic figure. Christian ministry often entails identifying the pathways to forgiveness and redemption and keeping them open. The church should be a sticky web of such pathways, a place to constantly bump into disciples fully aware of their own desertions and betrayals, and of God's endless mercy.

Again in these stories we see God's sovereign control of the events that lead to Jesus' death and resurrection. The human actors—from Peter to Judas, to the chief priests and elders, to the servant girls in the palace of Caiaphas—all play their roles of their own volition, seeking their own ends and fully responsible for the choices they make. And yet God is at work in all these choices and actions, in ways the human actors cannot perceive, often producing results the human actors neither foresee nor intend. God's power and sovereignty do not exclude or overwhelm human agency and accountability. God's sovereignty does ensure that justice and salvation come, despite and through our actions of betrayal.

Pilate's Hands

Matthew 27:11–26*

Exploring the text

The leaders' scheme to execute Jesus now moves into its final phases. He is presented to Pilate for interrogation and judgment. Pilate wants to release Jesus, but the leaders incite the crowds to call for his crucifixion. The governor finally agrees, under protest. While Pilate is nonetheless responsible for Jesus' execution, Matthew continues to emphasize the central role of the **chief priests** and **elders**, and finally of the people themselves. All are guilty of bringing Jesus to the cross, including those for whom his death and resurrection will win **salvation**.

---

*The Revised Common Lectionary uses this in Year A, Passion/Palm Sunday, The 6th Sunday in Lent: Matthew 26:14–27:66 or Matthew 27:11–54.

Jesus "is stood" before the governor (27:11). The passive voice, muffled in the NRSV, signals God's continuing agency, as well as the fact that, for the moment, Jesus is not the master of his body. Caiaphas had wanted to know if Jesus is the **Christ**, the **Son of God** (26:63). Pilate wants to know if Jesus really claims to be the "King of the Jews," as the chief priests and elders have apparently charged. If so, Jesus would represent a threat to Pilate's authority and to the sovereignty of the Roman Empire. Again, Jesus' enigmatic response, "You say it" (27:11; cf. 26:25; 26:64), conveys an ambiguous affirmation of the preceding statement, with the sense that the interlocutor will make of it what he will. Jesus is the king of the Jews, but not in a way that Pilate would understand. The chief priests and elders try to tighten their case by offering additional accusations, none of which Jesus bothers to answer (27:12–14; cf. 26:62; Isa. 53:7; Pss. 38:13–15; 39:9). Pilate asks, "Do you not hear how many accusations they make against you?" But Jesus does not need another chance to answer. His silence turns the accusations into mere background noise. Pilate is "amazed," which in Matthew suggests a positive impression in response to a demonstration of power (cf. 8:27; 9:33; 15:31). Pilate seems to like this "king," whose silence renders his accusers fools. He discerns that the leaders are acting from "jealousy" (or "envy," 27:18).

Pilate effectively decides not to decide about Jesus. He too can be a manipulative schemer. He will use the custom of releasing a prisoner during Passover as the means to resolve the case. He may hope that, given the choice between Jesus called Messiah and Jesus called Barabbas ("his father's son"), a "famous" prisoner, the crowds will call for the release of the "so-called Messiah" (27:17). The crowds, who now "gather" (27:17), will decide the fate of the two prisoners, thus avoiding any political consequences for Pilate himself. As he takes his place on the "judgment seat," where the **Son of Man** will soon sit (25:31; 26:64), Pilate's wife sends word that she has suffered intensely because of a dream about "that innocent man." The dream is a divine intervention (cf. 1:20; 2:12–13; 2:19; 2:22), not to save Jesus, but to proclaim again his innocence (27:19; cf. 27:4). Pilate has all the more reason, then, to release Jesus, but nonetheless proceeds with the plan to which he has committed himself.

Matthew reports the bare fact that the chief priests and elders persuade the crowds to ask for Barabbas's release and the execution of Jesus (27:20). When Pilate asks which of the two to release, the crowds give their leaders' answer: Barabbas. If Barabbas is to be released, then how should Jesus be dealt with? "Let him be crucified!" they all answer. There is no middle way. Only death. Only crucifixion. Pilate defends Jesus: "Why? What evil has he done?" They have no rationale to offer, only more shouting: "Let him be crucified!" Pilate realizes that he has no options, and that the crowd is on the edge of riot (27:24). The riotous crowds the chief priests and elders had first feared (26:5) have now become their tool. Pilate makes a public show of his distaste for this judgment by washing his hands (27:24; cf. Deut. 21:1–9), but he is fully complicit in Jesus' death, even if an unwilling participant. He sits in the seat of judgment and he has the power to carry out his own will, but he has ceded this authority to the crowds and, through them, to the Jewish leaders.

Judas had announced his guilt for betraying "innocent blood." Pilate now declares himself innocent (27:24) and then adds, "See to it yourselves," just what the chief priests and elders had said to Judas when he announced his guilt (27:4). Judas saw to it by hanging himself. The crowds now "see to it" by making a sweeping, unprompted assertion of their guilt: "His blood be on us and on our children!" (27:25). With this statement Matthew's whole Gospel reaches a turning point. Everything from the beginning of the Gospel has been building toward this moment. Three times the crowds—now identified as "the people as a whole," i.e., God's own people, Israel—have announced their will. This time they declare their full awareness and acceptance of the implications. The chief priests and elders had probably supplied the crowd's earlier answers, but this statement seems unrehearsed and spontaneous. The crowd is no longer the puppet of the leaders, but also fully complicit in Jesus' death. With Judas, only the crowds openly claim responsibility for Jesus' death. Pilate accedes. Barabbas is released. Jesus is beaten and "handed over" to be crucified (27:26; cf. 27:2).

Preaching and teaching the Word

The final verses of this passage have had terrifying consequences for the relations between Christians and Jews. Matthew seems to go out of his way to absolve Pilate from guilt and to locate the responsibility for Jesus' death not only with the Jewish leaders, and not only with the crowds assembled that day, but with all of Israel for all time. We can only understand this judgment in light of Matthew's larger theological perspective. The Jewish people are not singled out here as the only ones guilty of Jesus' blood—they simply join an ever-growing list. Judas is guilty. Peter and the other disciples are guilty. Pilate, despite his disclaimers, is guilty. The Roman Empire is guilty. The chief priests and elders are guilty. The scribes and Pharisees are guilty, as are the Sadducees and Herodians. And ultimately it is God, the one who strikes the shepherd (26:31), who is guilty. It is not Matthew's intention to place the guilt for Jesus' crucifixion on any single party, group, nation, or religion, but rather to make clear that all are complicit in his death—even us. It does not matter whether one is Jew or Gentile, leader or follower, chief priest or slave girl, Judas or Peter. No one emerges from this story less guilty of Jesus' blood than any other. This is the bad news. The **good news** to which Matthew's audience can lay claim is that Jesus' death and resurrection wipes away the effect of this blood guilt—for all (26:28)—and cancels the power of death itself. We do not come before God demanding salvation because our **righteousness** surpasses that of others, or because we would not have made the same decisions as Peter, or Judas, or the leaders, or Pilate, or the people (cf. 23:30). We come before God to receive the gift of salvation because it is freely offered to all. This is the wonder and the scandal of the gospel.

The Rituals of Torture

Matthew 27:27–44*

Exploring the text

Torture and terror are the steady companions of war and domination, even in modern societies that consider themselves above such actions, or where torture is usually veiled from public view. Torture has a long and persistent presence across history and cultures; it is operative wherever human power becomes unbalanced. Torture is also a form of ritualized violence, a "liturgy"[1] that expresses the conquest of one person, power, or worldview by another. Torture is meant to dehumanize its victims and destroy their communities. The cross is a form of torture. Rome used crucifixion as a public liturgy to restore order and remind witnesses that Roman rule represents divine power over life and death.

Unlike some modern cinematic representations, Matthew's account of the beatings and humiliations directed against Jesus shows little interest in providing graphic details for their own sake. Matthew focuses, instead, on the ironies that attend Jesus' torture. The Jewish leaders had mocked and abused Jesus as "the Christ" (26:63, 67–68). Because the trial before Pilate focused on whether Jesus was "king of the Jews" (27:11), this charge determines the form the Roman degradations take. The torture begins

---

*The Revised Common Lectionary uses this in Year A, Passion/Palm Sunday, The 6th Sunday in Lent: Matthew 26:14–27:66 or Matthew 27:11–54.

with the beating given to Jesus the moment Pilate's decision is rendered (27:26). It then moves to the governor's administrative center (the "praetorium"), where the whole cohort of Pilate's soldiers (five to six hundred men) "gathers" (27:27; cf., e.g., 26:3, 57; 27:17, 62; 28:12) around Jesus.

The cohort strips Jesus, which itself is a form of public humiliation, but only the first step in this part of their liturgy. When modern prisoners first enter jail or prison, they are stripped of their clothing and given clothes that identify them as a prisoner. This ritual marks the transition between the prisoner's old identity and his or her new one, often a number rather than a name. After stripping Jesus, the cohort provides him not with jailhouse clothes, however, but with a fool's costume that mimics and mocks his identity as king. The scarlet robe is probably one of the soldier's own; it signifies authority, albeit that of a commoner. A crown of thorns is placed on his head. The sharp points both bring pain and mimic the "rays of sun" that symbolize divinity on real crowns.[2] The reed is his royal scepter, but in a moment they use it to beat him on his head (27:30). The soldiers kneel before him, exclaiming, "Hail, King of the Jews!" (27:29; an imitation of "Hail, Caesar"). They end their ritual of mockery where the Jewish leaders had begun, spitting on him (27:30; cf. 26:67).

Jesus is then reclothed in his own clothing (27:31), which would bear the marks of his earlier beatings (26:67; 27:26). Then the parade begins, which customarily proceeded along the most crowded roads. Both the parade and the execution itself remind the onlookers of what happens to those who oppose the divinely ordered empire of Rome. Usually the condemned would carry the member of the cross on which they were to be affixed. In this case, however, one of the onlookers, Simon from Cyrene (a city in what is now Libya), is conscripted (27:32; cf. 5:41) for this task. His name reminds us of the absence of Simon Peter, who promised never to desert Jesus and to accompany him to death (26:33, 35).[3]

Matthew mentions the crucifixion itself almost in passing (27:35). The focus turns, instead, to a series of vignettes that link the story to the Psalms and to Isaiah 52–53, which supply interpretive cues that help the audience understand the meaning of Jesus' crucifixion. The mocking and the offer of wine mixed with gall evoke Psalm 69:19–21, a lament and prayer for **salvation** (27:34; cf. also 27:48). The casting of lots for his clothing draws on Psalm 22:18 (cf. also 27:46=Ps. 22:1), which catalogs the psalmist's torments but also celebrates God's deliverance of the righteous sufferer. The sign the soldiers affix above his head, "This is Jesus, the King of the Jews," ironically turns the cross into Jesus' throne. Jesus' rule will extend beyond Israel to the nations (cf. 25:31), over the whole of heaven and earth (28:18), even over the guards now seated (a position of authority) at his feet. Jesus is then joined in crucifixion by two terrorists. The term "bandits" probably refers to those who took up arms against the rule of Rome and Jerusalem's leaders. Jesus is "numbered with the transgressors" (Isa. 53:12). Their location on his right and left recalls James's and John's requests for these "seats" in 20:21. Like Peter, they had thought they could "drink the cup" that Jesus drinks, but they, too, have fled, their places taken by strangers.[4]

Now that Jesus is crucified, the parade of mockers comes to him. They "shake their heads" (Ps. 22:7) and resume their lampoons based on the themes of his trials. The new element in their taunts is a persistent invitation to Jesus to "save himself" and "come down from the cross" (27:40, 42). They presume that salvation lies in escape from the cross. If Jesus has the power to destroy and rebuild the temple (cf. 26:61), why can he not save himself? If he is **God's Son** (echoing the temptation, 4:6), why not come down from the cross? The **chief priests**, **scribes**, and **elders** also reappear to mock Jesus' saving power (27:41–42): "If he is the King of Israel, let him come down from the cross." They claim that if he did so, they would then believe him. They misunderstand his mission and the meaning of the cross. Twice in the Gospel Jesus has offered the Jewish authorities the sign of Jonah (12:38–42; 16:1–4), but they have not understood it. The real king of Israel will not flee death, but defeat it. The cross and resurrection are the sign of power the authorities seek, but not in the terms they would accept. They also taunt Jesus, who has claimed to be God's Son, for "trusting God." They invite God to "deliver him now" (i.e., from the cross), if God wants to. But Jesus' identity as Israel's king and God's Son is expressed perfectly in the conquest of death, not in escape from it, which would leave its power intact. The leaders of Israel, it turns out, trust the power of death more than they trust God. Finally, the bandit terrorists being crucified to his right and left add their taunts (27:44). They join the disciples, the leaders, and the crowds in stumbling over the cross.

Preaching and teaching the Word

The rituals of abuse, mockery, and torture that accompany Jesus' crucifixion display the inhumanity and the insecurity of Jesus' adversaries. Murder in any form is dehumanizing for the perpetrators. Murdering the innocent requires that the victim also be dehumanized. The acts Matthew describes in this section lay bare the ugliness of Jesus' adversaries, but not just theirs, for they act as representatives of all of humankind. Turning God's Son into an object of ridicule and mockery is inevitable for any people who trust death more than the offer of salvation. The prevalence of torture, bullying, abuse, and mockery—now common in our political discourse and practices—means that the good news of Christ's conquest of death has not been clearly heard and believed.

At the Last Supper, Jesus told his disciples that his blood was a covenant, poured out for many for the forgiveness of sins (26:28). The celebration of the Lord's Supper is thus a counter-ritual to the world's liturgies of torture and death.[5] At table with strangers and enemies, we embody the light of truth that melts the power of community-destroying violence. The Lord's Supper is the place where we learn the story and the disciplines that make an alternative world possible, a world where the violent not only do not have the last word, but where they may be embraced and loved and learn for themselves the power of the cross.

The echoes of the Psalms and Isaiah, especially the servant song of Isaiah 52–53, now begin to ring more clearly in Matthew's account, not as "proof texts," but as interpretive cues that guide our sense of what Jesus' death means. The laments to which Matthew appeals persistently affirm God's deliverance and salvation. If Matthew's description of Jesus' crucifixion only kindles our sense of outrage or righteous anger, we merely locate ourselves among those who misunderstand and mock the power of the cross. Matthew reminds us that God saves by means of, not despite, the cross. God still controls the events of this story, even and especially in the moments when the world seems to have gained the upper hand.

The chief priests' and elders' string of taunts places in ironic relief Matthew's understanding of the cross and salvation: (1) the destruction and rebuilding of the temple concerns his death and resurrection (and, secondarily, the destruction of the temple a generation later); (2) Jesus has not come to save himself, but to save others; (3) Jesus displays the divine character of his power as King and Son of God, especially in the defeat of death; and (4) the cross makes a public display of the conquest of death. There is truly no salvation outside the cross, and no transformation of the world that leaves death's power still intact. The mocking and torture of Jesus shows humanity at its worst, but also reveals that the promise of God's salvation is drawing near.

The Apocalyptic Moment:
The Death of Jesus

Matthew 27:45–56*

Exploring the text

Matthew's story of Jesus' death is riddled with **apocalyptic** images and references. This moment marks the decisive turn of the ages. Jesus has been announcing and embodying the **empire of God**, but now, with his death, the good news is realized with definitive power and clarity. Matthew fuses the death of Jesus with the release of the Spirit and other apocalyptic signs. All that is solid now shakes. Even death itself, the primary power by which Rome and the Jerusalem elites have sought to suppress the power of God revealed in Jesus, is swept aside. The **eschatological** floodgates now open wide.

As Jesus' death approaches, Matthew notes that darkness falls over the whole land from noon until three o'clock, ordinarily the brightest part of the day. The darkness seems to signal the triumph of death, but it is really an apocalyptic sign of the end of this world and of the coming of **God's Son** in power. Jesus has taught his disciples that the darkening of the sun will accompany his "coming" and the end of the age (24:29–30). With the darkness comes the **Son of Man**'s judgment of this world (cf. Amos 8:9; Zeph. 1:15). Then, God's light will dawn in the darkness (cf. 4:14–16).

Matthew repeats the reference to "three o'clock" (one of the times of daily prayer in Jewish tradition) in the next verse, when Jesus cries out his sense of abandonment, citing the opening lines of Psalm 22, which provides the primary interpretive lens for the whole passion story (cf. 27:35; 27:39–40; 27:42–44). Matthew is interested not only in the cry of abandonment itself, but in the whole psalm, which affirms God's redemption and vindication of the righteous sufferer, as well as the turning of all the ends of the earth toward the Lord, who will rule the nations (Ps. 22:27–29; cf. Matt. 28:18–20). The mission of Jesus' disciples to the ends of the earth has its genesis in God's redemption of the forsaken one.

---

*The Revised Common Lectionary uses this in Year A, Passion/Palm Sunday (The 6th Sunday in Lent), Liturgy of the Passion: Matthew 26:14–27:66 or Matthew 27:11–54.

The bystanders misunderstand Jesus' cry. They think he is calling Elijah. One of them runs to get a sponge, soaked in sour wine, for Jesus to drink. Here Matthew alludes to Psalm 69, which culminates in judgment against those who torment the righteous sufferer (69:21–28) and in the promise of **salvation** for Zion (69:35). Other bystanders wait to see whether Elijah will come to save Jesus. If Elijah did come now it would be in **judgment** of those witnessing Jesus' death. The Gospel audience knows that "Elijah" has already come, as John the Baptizer, who, like Jesus himself, was rejected and murdered by the authorities (cf. 3:11–17; 14:1–12; 17:10–13). Those who mock and crucify Jesus have already given their answer to the forerunner. They do not yet perceive or accept that the messianic age is already dawning. They misunderstand to whom Jesus is calling and what he seeks when he cries out in the words of Psalm 22. They look for Elijah to save him from death, but Jesus is looking for God to bring salvation through his death.

A second time Jesus "cries out in a loud voice" (27:50; cf. Ps. 22:2, 5, 24), but this time the cry is left unarticulated. Jesus' cries frame his citation of Psalm 22:1 and the subsequent confusion of the bystanders. The confusion is about to be swept away in a whirl of apocalyptic portents, all set in motion by Jesus' death. Matthew uses three Greek words to mark the moment, literally, "[he] released the spirit." Every major English translation supplies the pronoun "his" to modify "spirit," and then renders the phrase as an idiom for Jesus' "expiration": e.g., "breathed his last" (NRSV, TEV), "yielded up his spirit" (RSV), "gave up his spirit" (NIV, NAB, NET). These translations rightly convey the sense that this is the moment of death. By adding the pronoun "his," however, they also obscure Matthew's double meaning: Jesus not only gives up his spirit, he also releases the Spirit. The apocalyptic moment, the turn of the ages, has arrived, signaled first by the release of the Spirit into the world.

Matthew immediately recounts, in rapid-fire sequence, four other eschatological events that occur in association with Jesus' death and the release of the Spirit. The temple veil is torn in two from top to bottom. The passive verb "was torn" and the direction of the tear, from top to bottom, unmistakably indicate divine agency. The tearing of the veil may signify God's judgment against the temple and its leaders, or the fact that God's presence will no longer be contained in the temple, or both. God is now present wherever two or three are gathered in the name of Jesus (18:20) and where the risen Jesus accompanies the disciples in mission to the ends of the earth (28:18–20). The torn veil marks the effective end of the sacrificial system and the temple, as well as the movement of God's presence and power into the world. The turn of the ages has begun.

The shaking of the earth and the splitting of rocks (27:51b; cf. 24:7, 29; again, the passive voice suggests divine agency) are classic images associated with judgment (cf. 1 Kgs. 19:11–12; Isa. 2:19; 29:6; Ezek. 38:19; Pss. 68:8; 104:32; 114:7) and, in apocalyptic literature, with the end of one age and the beginning of another (cf. 4 Ezra 6:13–16; 9:2–3; 2 Bar. 27:7; 70:8; Zech. 14:4–5; Ezek. 37:1–14, esp. 37:12). Again the transformation is spatial: what was solid is no longer so. God is shaking the whole creation (cf. Heb. 12:26; Hag. 2:6, 21–22, where the shaking of earth and heaven accompanies the overthrow of earthly empires).

The final eschatological sign Matthew identifies is the resurrection. Only Matthew records that at the death of Jesus the tombs were opened and the bodies of the saints were raised. If it was not yet clear that Matthew is working hard to convey the apocalyptic character of the death of Jesus, the resurrection of the saints seals the case. The resurrection of the dead, the restoration of Israel, the pouring out of the Spirit, and the expectation of divine judgment were pillars in popular Jewish eschatological expectation. By recording the resurrection of the saints here, Matthew links the resurrection integrally with the death of Jesus. He also effectively democratizes the resurrection: not only will Jesus be raised, but the more general resurrection has begun. But Matthew also creates a problem, which must be resolved by literary/temporal sleight of hand. Jesus himself has not yet been raised, so the resurrection of the saints is out of sequence. Matthew addresses the problem with the clarification in 27:53 that the saints really didn't appear until after Jesus was raised, even though the account suggests that their resurrection coincides with his death. Neither God nor the evangelist is bound to our modern, linear conceptions of time. Matthew's literary tactic serves to indicate the true nature and significance of Jesus' death.

"The holy city" (27:53) at first glance appears to be merely another way to name historical, earthly "Jerusalem." But Matthew may be working within an early Christian tradition, reflected most clearly in John's Apocalypse (cf. Rev. 11:2; 21:2; 21:10; 22:19), that associated "holy city" not with earthly Jerusalem but with its heavenly, eschatological counterpart. Matthew has already used this expression in the story of Jesus' temptation, when the devil takes Jesus to the holy city (4:5) and places him on the pinnacle of the temple. "Holy city" is thus associated with visionary experience. Elsewhere Matthew persistently uses the name "Jerusalem" to designate the city where Jesus suffers and dies. The "saints" who "appeared to many in the holy city" after Jesus' resurrection may thus be eschatological beings making their appearance in an eschatological city. In any case, Matthew's choice of the term "holy city" rather than "Jerusalem" again signals the eschatological dimensions of the account.

The centurion who witnesses Jesus' death concludes that "Truly this was the [or "a"] **Son of God**" (27:54). It is possible his words are in fact another expression of mockery or of imperial triumph ("This really *was* a son of god, and we took him out"). His words, however, follow the eschatological signs in 27:51–53 and are accompanied by the experience of fear (cf. 17:5–6; 28:8–9, where "fear" signals the perception of divine presence), which suggest that they may indeed represent the first Gentile confession of Jesus as Son of God. The title used by the passersby (27:40) and the Jewish authorities (27:41–43) to mock Jesus now rings ironically on the centurion's lips. Roman emperors were often designated as "sons of god." Is the centurion reconsidering what this title means and whom it fits? The mission to the nations (cf. 28:18–20), yet another manifestation of eschatological reality, has already begun. The centurion's words also represent the fulfillment of the final vision of Psalm 22, where the psalmist envisions the time when "all the ends of the earth shall remember and turn to the LORD; and all the families of the nations shall worship before him. For dominion belongs to the LORD, and he rules over the nations" (Ps. 22:27–28).

"Many women" are also present, observing from afar all that happens. These "followers" from Galilee include Mary Magdalene, Mary the mother of James and Joseph, and the mother of the sons of Zebedee (cf. 20:20–21). Two of these women will be the first witnesses of the empty tomb and the resurrected Jesus (28:1–10). The claim that women were the first witnesses of the resurrection is consistent across the Gospel tradition. The witness of such women was, perhaps, the crucial element in the spread of the Christian faith in the early centuries of the church's existence.

Preaching and teaching the Word

For Matthew, the death of Jesus is the decisive moment of apocalyptic transformation, the moment when God's Son is fully revealed and the power of God's Spirit is loosed into the world. Time and space are shaken and transformed in this eschatological scene. From this moment forth, the world needs no longer to be centered around the temple and sacrificial systems, bound by the power of death, or beset by human dominion and violence. The death of Jesus redeems and restores the whole of creation. Christians are not still waiting for the eschaton to begin. For Matthew, as for the other New Testament writers, the last days commence with the death of Jesus. God is already transforming and redeeming this broken world. This is the reality to which Christian preaching must return again and again, the foundation from which all Christian witness springs.

Jesus' cry of dereliction, citing Psalm 22, expresses both his sense of abandonment by God and the world and his trust in God to redeem and vindicate him. The resurrection and the other eschatological signs that accompany his crucifixion attest that Jesus' death is not a tragic mistake to be erased, but the definitive embodiment of God's power. The cross and resurrection are the culmination of Jesus' mission, the full revelation of what it means to be **Messiah**, Son of Man, and the Son of God. Discipleship takes its primary cues from this revelation; like Jesus, disciples are called to give up their lives for the sake of others. Cruciform life is still the primary way in which the **church** bears witness to God's power and presence in the world.

Tomb Robbers

Matthew 27:57–66[*]

Exploring the text

Victims of crucifixion were sometimes left unburied, to be picked apart as carrion. A new character, Joseph of Arimathea, now steps forward to make sure this does not happen. He is unusual, both a rich man and a disciple of Jesus. He uses his wealth to honor a poor man who has been crucified; he risks his own life by appearing publicly before Pilate to ask for the body.[1] Pilate may have sympathized with Jesus (cf. 27:14); he does not hesitate to honor this request. Joseph's gesture is all the more personal for the fact that he places Jesus in his own new tomb, one that Joseph himself had hewn in the rock (27:60). In Jewish tradition, the most important preparation for burial is washing the body, which is not mentioned here at all. Perhaps Joseph is not burying Jesus, but safeguarding his body. He wraps Jesus' body in clean linen, seals the tomb with a large rock, and departs. Joseph of Arimathea is like Israel's (Jacob's) son Joseph (Gen. 37–45) and Jesus' adoptive father, Joseph (Matt. 1–2), both of whom remain faithful to God in the face of imperial power. Mary Magdalene and "the other Mary" are also present, and sit down opposite the tomb.

---

[*]The Revised Common Lectionary uses this in Year A, Passion/Palm Sunday, The 6th Sunday in Lent: Matthew 26:14–27:66.

Why? They are fulfilling Jesus' command to "watch" (24:42; 25:13). They are looking for him (cf. 28:1–10, esp. 28:5).

The burial of Jesus in the rich man's tomb provides another link between Jesus' story and Isaiah's last song about Israel's Suffering Servant (cf. Isa. 53:9). Joseph's act reminds us that God redeems God's righteous, suffering servant. Matthew has already told us that the rocks and earth that now entomb Jesus are shattering (27:51–52). Securing Jesus' body in a tomb sets the stage for the chief priests' and Pharisees' efforts to make the tomb even more secure (27:62–66). They remember that Jesus had spoken of rising again after three days (27:63; cf. 26:61; 27:40). So again they "gather" (27:62; cf. 26:3, 57; 27:17, 27; 28:12) before Pilate, whom they address as "Lord" (27:63, NRSV: "sir") on the day "after the day of Preparation" (27:62, i.e., on Saturday, the Passover Sabbath, the "second day" in their reckoning). They request that the tomb be secured "until the third day" (i.e., the next day, Sunday). They fear that "the last deception would be worse than the first" (27:64). What is the first deception? Their words are double-edged. For them the deception is the claim that Jesus is the **Son of God**, the **Messiah**, and the coming **Son of Humanity**. They may also have in mind his warning about the destruction of the temple. But the leaders themselves have also been guilty of deception, which Jesus' resurrection would reveal for all to see. An empty tomb, their "last deception," undoes everything they have fought so hard to accomplish. Even the rumor of his resurrection would constitute a threat to their power. Pilate leaves it to them: "You have a guard of soldiers; go, make it as secure as you can." If anything should happen, Pilate cannot be blamed. Responsibility for securing the tomb thus falls to those who have the most to lose from its being found empty. They take their guard to the tomb and seal the stone (27:66).

Preaching and teaching the Word

No human power can withstand God's power to vindicate and redeem the one who dies on the cross. Ironically, after the chief priests' and Pharisees' efforts to secure the tomb, the events that follow should provide them with incontrovertible proof of the resurrection. But to no avail. Their next "gathering" will be to bribe the guards and invent a story of deception (28:11–15).

The actions of Joseph of Arimathea and the two Marys are at one level inexplicable. Quietly, yet publicly and with some risk to themselves, they honor Jesus and prepare for his resurrection. Is Joseph's act a farewell, or does he know that the rocks are already splitting and will not hold Jesus? Are the women merely grieving, or are they "watching for the end" (not the end Peter mistakenly watched for in 26:58). Those who bear witness to the reality of the resurrection do not necessarily do so with great fanfare. They do so with simple gestures that run against the grain of reason, but position them to see what God is doing. These are the practices of hope.

The Resurrection

Matthew 28:1–15*

Exploring the text

Many women who had followed Jesus from Galilee had been watching from afar at the moment of his death (27:55), three of whom Matthew had identified in particular: Mary Magdalene, Mary the mother of James and Joseph, and the mother of the sons of Zebedee (27:56). At the tomb where Joseph of Arimathea laid the body of Jesus (27:57–61), Mary Magdalene and Mary the mother of James and Joseph were also present, again at a distance (Ms. Zebedee has gone missing). Now, just as the Sabbath is ending and the first day of the week is dawning, these two women come again to the tomb. Mark and Luke both indicate that they bring spices to anoint Jesus' body. In Mark 16:3 they even wonder aloud who will roll the stone away. Matthew, however, says nothing about spices or an intention to anoint Jesus. Instead they come to observe, just as they had observed his death and entombment (28:1; cf. 27:55–56). The word Matthew uses to describe their intent (*theoreomai*) indicates that they are not just "having a look around," but intentionally observing or watching for something unusual. As they had followed Jesus from Galilee, these two women apparently had been watching and listening carefully to Jesus' announcements of his suffering, death, and resurrection. So far, events have unfolded just as he said they would. They have come, now at the earliest possible moment of the "third day," when Jesus had said he would be raised from the dead (16:21; 17:22–23; 20:17–19), to see what will happen. They are not disappointed.

Jesus' death has shaken a lot of things loose (cf. 27:51–54). He had listed earthquakes, a classic apocalyptic portent, as a sign of the "birth-

*The Revised Common Lectionary uses this in Year A, Easter Vigil 1, Resurrection of the Lord/Easter: Matthew 28:1–10.

pangs" (24:8). Now, for the second time since his death, the earth itself trembles (cf. 27:51). This time it is a "great earthquake"–a cosmic, tectonic shift. At that same moment, an angel of the Lord descends from heaven, rolls away the stone, and sits down on it. Again the boundaries between heaven and earth are breached and blurred (cf., e.g., on 9:1–8; 14:22–33). Angels have appeared in dreams earlier in the Gospel (1:20, 24; 2:13, 19), but this is not a dream. The angel's clothing resembles Jesus' appearance at the transfiguration (17:2; cf. Dan. 7:9), while the mention of lightning recalls Jesus' description of the coming of the **Son of Humanity** (24:27). The guards suffer their own personal earthquakes from fear of the angel and then "become as dead men." It is not clear whether they hear the divine messenger's words. They will not understand or bear faithful witness to what they experience (28:4; cf. 28:11–15).

The angel first offers a word of reassurance, directed specifically to the women alone, the same expression Jesus himself has offered in association with manifestations of divine presence and power (14:27; 17:7; 28:10; cf. 1:20, Gen. 15:1). The angel confirms why the women have come to the tomb: "You are looking for Jesus who was crucified." The announcement that Jesus "has been raised, as he said" affirms that it is God who has raised him (implied by the passive voice) and that the resurrection fulfills and vindicates Jesus' word. The claim that "he is not here" indicates that when the angel rolls away the stone he is not freeing Jesus, who is no longer bound by the constraints of human space, but is opening the tomb for the women to see (28:6a,c). He then commissions the women to tell the disciples that Jesus has been raised from the dead. They are to follow him to Galilee where they will see him, exactly as he had told them in 26:32.

Filled with "fear and great joy," they run to do as they have been commanded. In Mark 16:8, fear motivates the women's (initial) silence in response to the empty tomb. In Matthew's account, however, the fear is a natural human response–best rendered as "awe" or "reverence"–to divine epiphanies (e.g., 14:27; 17:7). Fear and great joy here go together as differing dimensions of a singular and wholly appropriate response. Their race to tell the disciples is suddenly interrupted, however, by the appearance of Jesus himself. Matthew shows no interest in the location or details of this "meeting," except to note that the women approach him worshipfully and take hold of his feet. Again, this is just the right response to the presence of the risen Christ in power. He reassures them, using the same words as the angel (28:10; cf. 28:5), and reiterates the command to tell the disciples–here designated "my brothers"–to go to Galilee, where he promises they will see him.

Meanwhile, some of the guards also leave the tomb and go "into the city" to report to the **chief priests** "everything that had happened." Matthew has told us that when the tombs were opened and the saints were raised at the moment of Jesus' death, the saints went into the holy city after his resurrection and appeared to many (27:52–53). So there may be three bands of witnesses loose in Jerusalem on Sunday morning: the women (and presumably the disciples), the risen saints, and the "dead men" (28:4) who report to the chief priests. For the final time in Matthew, the chief priests and elders "gather" to "take counsel" (cf. 26:3–4; 27:1; cf. 12:14; 22:15; 27:7), this time to devise a plan to undermine the credibility of the reports of the resurrection. The guards are to say that Jesus' disciples stole the body while they were sleeping (28:13). The council offers them a "substantial amount of silver" (perhaps more than Judas was given to betray Jesus) and promises protection if Pilate hears of their dereliction (28:14).

This episode is the counterpart to the leaders' now failed preemptive strike against the possibility of a "last deception greater than the first" (27:62–66). It is for Matthew a final demonstration of where the real deception lies, as well as a way of accounting for resistance to the gospel "among the Jews to this day" (28:15). Everyone–the guards, the chief priests, and the women–agrees that the tomb is empty, but they have widely divergent ways of accounting for it. Matthew subtly mocks the chief priests' account: How would sleeping guards know who stole the body? Is the official version of events any more reasonable than the conviction that Jesus the Messiah has been raised from the dead?

Preaching and teaching the Word

Modern audiences often come to the resurrection looking for historical evidence and detailed information subject to corroboration or denial. None of the Gospels describes the resurrection itself, however, which by its nature stands always beyond the realm of human verification. What we see, instead, are the expanding circles of its ripples and traces: first the empty tomb, then the fear, stupor, and joy of its first witnesses, then the growth of a community of witnesses. The only meaningful argument for the reality of the resurrection is embodied in the community of the baptized, who have declared their allegiance to the crucified one and together constitute his body re-membered at Table. The community of disciples is commissioned to watch for and name the ripples that become waves of transformation. These waves move most powerfully in the presence of suffering and death.

The resurrection is a new beginning for Israel, the disciples, and for humankind, but Matthew also carefully presents it as the continuation of the passion story. The same women witness both events. The same Jewish leaders play their role. Most important, the Jesus who is crucified now speaks encouragement, can be touched, and makes preparations for the continuation of his mission. The resurrection does not set right a divine plan that was sidetracked by the crucifixion. It completes God's conquest of death and imperial power by vanquishing them at the point of their most powerful expression. Only the resurrection of this one–Israel's rejected Messiah, God's faithful Son, the one condemned by Israel's leaders and people, and the one crucified by the Romans–demonstrates the full extent of God's mercy, forgiveness, and power over all human dominions and death itself. The promise of resurrection is not that we will be rescued from death or transported to another, heavenly world, but that God's heavenly rule has reclaimed and now is transforming the whole of creation. We face death, bearing our crosses for his sake (16:24), with the certainty that it has no real power over us. Only in realization that Jesus has conquered death is true life possible.

We should not be unduly surprised that the primary "watchers" and witnesses of Jesus' death and resurrection are two women. All the Gospels agree that women are the first witnesses of the resurrection. From the earliest days of the church, women have stood at the front lines of God's martyrs (or "witnesses"), testifying in both word and deed to God's faithfulness. These two witnesses also illustrate the importance of being wakeful watchers (cf. 24:42–44). They make the risky trek to the tomb to observe an event that has been promised, but to which only they and the Jewish leaders have been attending. Disciples may not be the only ones to observe the traces of God's presence, or to meet angels and discover empty tombs. Christian witness requires, however, that we faithfully locate ourselves where we can see most clearly, and that we are ready to name God's presence and power when it is revealed to us.

Throughout the Gospel, Jesus has engendered division. We have noticed repeatedly how his demonstrations of power and proclamation of the **empire of heaven** bear both **judgment** and **salvation**. In this story both the women and the guards respond to the angel's appearance with fear. The guards' fear induces a deathlike state and eventual denial, whereas the women's fear and awe mingle with and give way to joy and worship. These reports describe the primal human responses to encounter with God's presence and power. The way of courage and faith leads to worship, which has no real grounding apart from the recognition of God's power in the cross and resurrection. The other way leads to deceit upon deceit. Jerusalem's leaders might have imagined all along that they were acting against Jesus for the good of the temple or the nation, but the guards' testimony to the empty tomb renders any further deception a pure act of self-interest and defiance of God. This is necessarily so, not only for Israel and its leaders during the time of Jesus and Matthew, but for all people in every time who observe but deny the signs of God's presence, especially the disturbances of everyday time and relationships that come in the wake of the cross and resurrection.

The response of Israel's leaders to the empty tomb raises another important set of questions for Matthew and its audiences. Does the leader's response signal the end of their story with God? Does Jesus' commission to the disciples in Galilee to proclaim the gospel to the "nations" mean that God has abandoned Israel (28:16–20)? The way we answer this question will determine and reflect who we understand the God of Jesus Christ to be (cf. esp. on 21:33–46). Did Matthew see the rejection of Jesus as the end of the line for Israel, or is Jesus' death and resurrection the crowning expression of God's faithfulness and the foundation upon which the mission to the nations could proceed?

Whenever Christians preach and teach on the resurrection, we need to remind ourselves that the resurrection is not a Christian idea, nor a vindication of the Christian religion. Resurrection hope had long been embedded in Israel's faith (cf., e.g., Isa. 24–27; 52:13–53:12; Dan. 12:1–3)[1] and would remain strong among the rabbis who, in the wake of the destruction of the temple, led the transformation of the Jewish tradition toward the forms of Judaism we know today. Israel's resurrection hope focused on God's deliverance of the people of Israel from oppression and death and on the vindication of the faithful. Matthew sees this hope embodied in the figure of Jesus, who from the beginning of the Gospel has endured the faithlessness and sown the seeds of the redemption of God's people Israel. His resurrection has already borne fruit in the resurrection of the saints (27:52–53). For Matthew, Jesus' mission, crucifixion, and resurrection together are the fulfillment and renewal of Israel's story, a story of judgment and salvation for Israel and the nations.

God with Us in Power

Matthew 28:16–20*

Exploring the text

Each of the four Gospels ends in a distinctive way. What makes the "Great Commission" the right ending for Matthew's story? Is it merely an ending, or also the culmination and goal of Matthew's narrative? The commissioning of Jesus' disciples draws together the most significant motifs and themes of the Gospel. Some interpreters describe it as an "index," "key," or summary of the whole. The disciples' mission is not the end, but the continuation of the whole story.

Matthew sets the story in Galilee, where Jesus' own mission had begun (cf. 2:22–23; 4:12–16). Jesus has taught (5:1; 8:1), prayed (14:23), healed and fed the crowds (15:29–30), and been tempted (4:8) and transfigured (17:1–2, 9) on mountains. The setting thus prepares us for yet another manifestation of God's power. Leaving the mountain unnamed prevents subsequent generations from memorializing the spot; God's power and presence cannot be contained (cf. 17:1–9), but now move with the disciples into the whole world. Matthew's reminder that only the "eleven" are present lends a note of brokenness to a potentially triumphalistic scene. Jesus commissions the very people who days earlier had betrayed him and fled. Their initial response to the risen Christ on the mountain is a mixture of worship and doubt. The term Matthew uses for "doubt" (only in Matthew in the New Testament) is the same word Jesus used when chiding Peter for "standing in two places," or "being of two minds," when Peter had sunk after walking a few steps to Jesus on the storming sea (14:31). Now, in the presence of the resurrected one, the disciples again are of two minds, caught between two worlds.

Jesus "comes toward" his disciples as he speaks to them, as he had after the transfiguration (17:7), another divine revelation on a mountain. In both cases his gesture is meant to reassure the disciples. His words also convey reassurance, empowerment, and vocation. The risen Jesus announces to his disciples the reordering of the world. The commission itself (28:19–20a) is framed by two claims: first, that Jesus has been given all authority in heaven and on earth (28:18) and, second, that he will be

*The Revised Common Lectionary uses this in Year A, Trinity Sunday.

with them always until the end of the age (28:20). These statements are the warrants for the disciples' mission. Together they lift up once more the focus on power and presence that has dominated Matthew's narrative.

The claim that Jesus has received all power in heaven and on earth echoes Daniel 7:13–14, where the **"Son of Man"** comes to judge the imperial powers that have kept Israel in bondage. This warrant also recalls the moment when Satan takes Jesus to a mountaintop to offer him all the empires of the world (4:8–9). Now Jesus claims authority not only over worldly empires, but over all of creation. Matthew has used the language of "heaven and earth" again and again (5:18; 6:10; 6:19–20; 11:25; 16:19; 18:18; 18:19) to remind us of the ways Jesus blurs the boundaries between the divine and the human (cf. 9:1–8; 14:22–33; 18:18–20). The conviction that Jesus is Lord of both realms, heaven and earth, is at the heart of early Christian hymns and confessions of Jesus (cf. Eph. 1:20–23; Phil. 2:6–11; Col. 1:15–20; 1 Tim. 3:16; 1 Pet. 3:18–22). Throughout the Gospel, Matthew has carefully nurtured the audience's perception of this power—power that gathers and restores, that heals and sets free from bondage, that forgives and reconciles. This is the power that Jesus now embodies in full and that Christians confess to be the only true power in the world.

The reordering of heaven and earth under the lordship of Jesus Christ provides Matthew's basis ("therefore," 28:19) for the commission proper, which is delivered by means of supporting clauses surrounding the primary, central command: "make disciples of all nations." The supporting clauses delineate the means or circumstances under which the "discipling" takes place. Jesus' own training of his disciples is the model. They have been "going" throughout Galilee and Judea, back and forth into Gentile and Jewish territories, and finally to Jerusalem and the cross. Now the disciples are to begin again from Galilee, where Jesus' mission started, baptizing and leading others to discern, comprehend, and embrace God's rule. Does the mission to "all nations" suggest the end of the mission to Israel in favor of a predominantly or exclusively Gentile mission? There is no compelling evidence in the Gospel that God's covenant with Israel has ended. Despite the resistance of Israel's rulers and people, and even the desertion of his own disciples, Jesus' saving power embraces all. The mission to the nations depends on the realization that the cross and resurrection bring to fruition Jesus' mission to "save his people from their sins" (1:21). Jesus' comprehensive authority over all of heaven and earth includes Israel. God's mission of restoration and reconciliation now extends to the nations because Israel's true king is now enthroned.

The disciples realize their mission while "going" (28:19) and by means of baptizing and teaching (28:19–20). Discipleship takes place on the way, always moving and always pushing back the boundaries the world imposes on our imagination and practices. Jesus' "going" led him to the margins, to the wilderness and to Galilee, but finally into confrontation with the powers in Jerusalem. The "going" of Jesus' disciples implies similar movement, conflict, and effect. The disciples will baptize people of all nations ". . . in the name of the Father and of the Son and of the Holy Spirit." This baptism signals a turning away from the world, away from violent leaders, away from the economies of rich and poor, away from the religions of sacrifice and status, and away from the politics of exclusion and exploitation. Baptism in the name of the Father, the Son, and the Holy Spirit means the embrace of God's rule of healing and restoration, the power of Jesus' cross and resurrection, and the renewing force of the Spirit loose in the world (see discussion of 27:50, p. 289). The disciples are to "teach" as Jesus has taught them, in both word and deed, sharing divine power (cf. 10:1, 7–8), warning against worldly leaven, and preparing others to follow him to the cross. His teaching has nurtured their capacity to discern and bear witness to God's power and rule.

The commissioning ends with the promise that Jesus will be present with "you" (the disciples in mission) "always, to the end of the age" (28:20). This promise reprises Matthew's identification of Jesus as Emmanuel, "God with us," in the birth narrative (1:23). It recalls the promise that Jesus is present wherever even "two or three are gathered in my name" (18:20), as well as the notice that Jesus, the Son of Man, is present among "the least of these my sisters and brothers" who hunger and thirst, who are strangers, naked, sick, or in prison (25:31–46). Mission thus entails ongoing discernment of Jesus' presence and healing power. Jesus' presence continues the transformation begun during his ministry. Mission thus contests the world's constructions of space. The one who has received all power in heaven and on earth and who is present even to the end of the age cannot be contained within temples or churches, nor within nations or political structures or economic systems. Jesus' presence extends to "the end of the age," when God's harvest is complete (13:39). In the present **time**, earthly empires will continue to defy God, but for disciples this is a time of gathering, restoration, and resurrection, of watching and readiness. The risen Jesus is with us in power, shaking the foundations of the world.

Preaching and teaching the Word

Matthew recognizes that discipleship is lived between worship and doubt, between betrayal and brokenness and the reality of resurrection. Here, where heaven and earth are becoming one, hope answers despair.

The way of discipleship lies neither in utopian visions of another world, nor in "realistic" acceptance of "the way the world is." Hope is open-eyed and critically realistic about this world, but always watching for and naming the presence of the One who is transforming both heaven and earth.

The commissioning scene is often read as a triumphalist vision, which has supported colonizing models of mission. In Matthew's vision, however, Christian discipleship replicates Jesus' steps to the lost and the least, and to conflict and the cross, but never into domination, exploitation, or violence. The Great Commission invites disciples into practices that bear witness to God's kind of power in the world, attended by humility, mutual forgiveness, and worship that mingles the joy of resurrection with a sense of our continuing brokenness and "two-minded" living.

It is easier for people to resist the temptations of triumphalism and colonialism when they journey in mission with the "least ones." The way of discipleship requires us to leave behind the (false) certainties of our humanly constructed worlds and join with Jesus in the journey that leads through death to new life with God. On this way, in the presence of the risen Jesus, it is possible to see both God and the world differently, especially to discern that, despite the ways the world trains us to see otherwise, Jesus is already ruling over both earth and heaven. We need Jesus with us on the journey of discipleship through the whole world, for it is his power and presence that is remaking the world. But he also needs us, for only as we journey with him, naming his presence and power in the contested spaces, is God's empire made known to others, just as Matthew has made it known to us.

NOTES

MATTHEW 1:18–25

1. M. Eugene Boring, *The Gospel of Matthew,* The New Interpreter's Bible, vol. 8 (Nashville: Abingdon Press, 1995), 138.

MATTHEW 2:1–12

1. James C. Scott, *Domination and the Arts of Resistance* (New Haven, CT: Yale University Press, 1990), contends that surveillance and atomization of subordinate populations are key to imperial control of dominated peoples.
2. See further Richard Horsley, ed., *Christmas Unwrapped: Consumerism, Christ, and Culture* (Harrisburg, PA: Trinity Press International, 2001).

MATTHEW 4:1–11

1. Boring, *Matthew,* 165, citing Paul S. Minear, *New Testament Apocalyptic* (Nashville: Abingdon Press, 1981), 108. See also the series of books by Walter Wink, *Naming the Powers* (Philadelphia: Fortress Press, 1984); *Unmasking the Powers* (Philadelphia: Fortress Press, 1986); and *Engaging the Powers* (Minneapolis: Fortress Press, 1992); and the writings of William Stringfellow, including *An Ethic for Christians and Other Aliens in a Strange Land* (Waco, TX: Word Books, 1973).

PART TWO: PRELIMINARY REMARKS

1. Ulrich Luz, *Matthew 1–7*, trans. James E. Crouch (Minneapolis: Fortress Press, 2007), 173.

MATTHEW 5:21–37

1. On "restorative justice" see Howard Zehr, *The Little Book of Restorative Justice* (Intercourse, PA: Good Books, 2002); Christopher Marshall, *Beyond Retribution: A New Testament Vision for Justice, Crime, and Punishment* (Grand Rapids: Eerdmans, 2001). For a treatment of the relationship between theories of atonement and retributive justice, see Timothy Gorringe, *God's Just Vengeance* (Cambridge: Cambridge University Press, 1996).

2. L. William Countryman, *Dirt, Greed, and Sex* (Philadelphia: Fortress Press, 1988).

MATTHEW 5:38–48

1. Wink, *Engaging the Powers*, 175–184.
2. Cf. Michel de Certeau, "How Is Christianity Thinkable Today?" *Theology Digest* 19 (1971): 334–45, esp. 339–41.

MATTHEW 6:19–34

1. Douglas E. Oakman, "The Radical Jesus: You Cannot Serve God and Mammon," *Biblical Theology Bulletin* 34 (2004): 122–29.

MATTHEW 8:5–13

1. Warren Carter, *Matthew and the Margins* (Maryknoll, NY: Orbis Books, 2000), 127; J. P. Brown, "Techniques of Imperial Control: The Background of the Gospel Event," in *The Bible and Liberation: Political and Social Hermeneutics,* ed. Norman Gottwald (Maryknoll, NY: Orbis Books, 1983), 357–77.

MATTHEW 8:14–17

1. Donald A. Hagner, *Matthew 1–13*, Word Biblical Commentary 33A (Dallas: Word Books, 1993), 209.

MATTHEW 8:18–22

1. Hagner, *Matthew 1–13*, 218.

MATTHEW 10:5–15

1. On Isaiah's reading of the place of the Gentiles in God's mission, see Isa. 2:2–4; 42:1–4; 45; 55:3–5. Paul's formulation, "the Jew first and also the Greek" (cf. Rom. 2:9–10), has two simultaneous missions (cf. Gal. 2:7–10) conducted in the wake of Jesus' death and resurrection. Matthew preserves a strict focus on the mission to Israel during Jesus' lifetime, but with a persistent awareness that salvation is for the nations as well as Israel, and that the mission to the nations lies on the horizon following the fulfillment of the mission to Israel.
2. According to Ulrich Luz, *Matthew 8–20* (Minneapolis: Fortress Press, 2001), 78n58, *The Martyrdom of Isaiah* 2:10–11 illustrates the practice of poverty in the wilderness as a prophetic action against injustice. John the Baptizer also conducts his wilderness mission in poverty and defenselessness that manifest radical dependence on God (cf. on Matt. 3:4).

3. Dorothy Jean Weaver, *Matthew's Missionary Discourse: A Literary Critical Analysis* (JSNTS 38; Sheffield: JSOT Press, 1990), 88.

MATTHEW 10:16–23

1. Weaver, *Matthew's Missionary Discourse*, 92.
2. Ibid., 95.

MATTHEW 10:24–11:1

1. Stanley Hauerwas, *Matthew*, Brazos Theological Commentary on the Bible (Grand Rapids: Brazos Press, 2006), 110.

MATTHEW 12:1–21

1. J. Louis Martyn, *Galatians*, The Anchor Bible Commentary 33a (New York: Doubleday, 1997), 23.

MATTHEW 12:22–50

1. See Wink, *Unmasking the Powers*, 43–50; Ched Myers, *Binding the Strong Man* (Maryknoll, NY: Orbis, 1991), 190–94.
2. Luz, *Matthew 8–20*, 217.

MATTHEW 13:1–23

1. Hauerwas, *Matthew*, 130.

MATTHEW 13:24–43

1. Luz, *Matthew 8–20*, 255.

MATTHEW 13:44–52

1. Luz, *Matthew 8–20*, 278.

MATTHEW 14:1–12

1. See Luz, *Matthew 8–20*, 308–9; Howard Clarke, *The Gospel of Matthew and Its Readers* (Bloomington, IN: Indiana University Press, 2003), 129–31.

MATTHEW 15:1–20

1. Carter, *Matthew and the Margins*, 315.
2. Herman C. Waetjen, *The Origin and Destiny of Humanness* (San Rafael, CA: Crystal Press, 1976), 165.

MATTHEW 15:21–28

1. Waetjen, *The Origin and Destiny of Humanness*, 167.

MATTHEW 16:13–20

1. Carter, *Matthew and the Margins*, 332.
2. W. D. Davies and Dale C. Allison Jr., *The Gospel according to Saint Matthew*, vol. 2 (Edinburgh: T. & T. Clark, 1991), 623–24.
3. Ibid., 629.

MATTHEW 16:21–28

1. Paul S. Minear, *The Good News according to Matthew: A Training Manual for Prophets* (St. Louis: Chalice Press, 2000), 59.
2. Luz, *Matthew 8–20*, 382.
3. Boring, *Matthew*, 352.

MATTHEW 17:24–27

1. Warren Carter, *Matthew and Empire: Initial Explorations* (Harrisburg, PA: Trinity Press International, 2001), 130–44.

MATTHEW 18:1–20

1. Klaus Wengst, *Humility: Solidarity with the Humiliated*, trans. John Bowden (Philadelphia: Fortress Press, 1988).

MATTHEW 19:1–15

1. Carter, *Matthew and the Margins*, 383–84.
2. Hauerwas, *Matthew*, 169–70.

MATTHEW 19:16–30

1. Luz, *Matthew 8–20*, 522.

MATTHEW 20:17–34

1. Carter, *Matthew and the Margins*, 401–2; cf. Jon Berquist, *Ancient Wine, New Wineskins: The Lord's Supper in Old Testament Perspective* (St. Louis: Chalice Press, 1991), 51–67.

MATTHEW 21:23–32

1. Boring, *Matthew*, 412.

MATTHEW 22:1–14

1. Ulrich Luz, *Matthew 21–28*, trans. James E. Crouch (Minneapolis: Fortress Press, 2005), 55.

MATTHEW 22:15–22

1. Carter, *Matthew and the Margins*, 439.

2. Luz, *Matthew 21–28*, 65.
3. Klaus Wengst, *Pax Romana and the Peace of Jesus Christ* (Philadelphia: Fortress Press, 1987), 60.

MATTHEW 23:13–24:2

1. Paul S. Minear, *The Golgotha Earthquake: Three Witnesses* (Cleveland: Pilgrim Press, 1995), 80.
2. Ibid., 81.
3. Thomas G. Long, *Matthew*, Westminster Bible Companion (Louisville, KY: Westminster John Knox Press, 1997), 266.

MATTHEW 24:4–35

1. Luz, *Matthew 21–28*, 207–8.

MATTHEW 25:1–13

1. I am indebted to the Rev. Jane Fahey for this title.

MATTHEW 25:14–30

1. Luz, *Matthew 21–28*, 251.
2. William R. Herzog II, *Parables as Subversive Speech: Jesus as Pedagogue of the Oppressed* (Louisville, KY: Westminster John Knox Press, 1994), 150–68.

MATTHEW 26:14–35

1. Minear, *The Good News according to Matthew*, 85–86.
2. Berquist, *Ancient Wine, New Wineskins*, 41–50.
3. Luz, *Matthew 21–28*, 374–78.
4. Berquist, *Ancient Wine, New Wineskins*, 51–67.
5. Luz, *Matthew 21–28*, 387.
6. William T. Cavanaugh, *Torture and Eucharist: Theology, Politics, and the Body of Christ* (Malden, MA: Blackwell, 1998).

MATTHEW 26:57–27:10

1. W. D. Davies and Dale C. Allison Jr., *The Gospel according to Saint Matthew*, vol. 3 (Edinburgh: T. & T. Clark, 1997), 564–65.

MATTHEW 27:27–44

1. Cavanaugh, *Torture and Eucharist*, 21–71.
2. Boring, *Matthew*, 488.
3. Carter, *Matthew and the Margins*, 531.
4. Ibid., 532.
5. Cavanaugh, *Torture and Eucharist*, 203–81.

MATTHEW 27:57–66

1. Carter, *Matthew and the Margins*, 539.

MATTHEW 28:1–15

1. Among many recent volumes on resurrection belief among Jews and Christians, see especially Kevin J. Madigan and Jon D. Levenson, *Resurrection: The Power of God for Christians and Jews* (New Haven, CT: Yale University Press, 2008), as well as Levenson's earlier volume, *The Death and Resurrection of the Beloved Son: The Transformation of Child Sacrifice in Judaism and Christianity* (New Haven, CT: Yale University Press, 1993).

GLOSSARY

Apocalyptic/eschatology/eschatological. In New Testament studies, there are few terms more slippery than these, which are often used interchangeably or in conjunction with one another. Eschatology means, literally, the study of the last things, usually understood with reference, variously, to the end of the world (literally or metaphorically), the "last days," Jesus' second coming, the final judgment, or some combination of these. New Testament eschatology includes spatial (relational) as well as temporal dimensions (see **Time**). God's presence and power, the **empire of heaven**, the restoration of Israel, the resurrection, the pouring out of the Spirit, and the gathering of the nations are all manifestations of eschatological reality. Because Matthew focuses so much attention on the ways Jesus crosses the boundaries between the human and the divine and how the kingdom of heaven comes upon earth, Matthew's eschatology might better be called "acrology," i.e., the study of boundaries, edges, and margins.

Apocalyptic refers to what is disclosed or revealed. Ancient Jewish apocalyptic worldviews featured the expectation of divine intervention to restore creation and to gather and vindicate Israel. Apocalyptic literature typically includes visions, dreams, symbols, and sometimes bizarre images meant to dislocate the audience from familiar perspectives and assumptions, so as to reveal God's identity and will, or to disclose the true (fallen) character of the world. Apocalyptic literature often hides at the same time it reveals. Matthew's **parables**, which simultaneously reveal and conceal, are a form of apocalyptic speech concerned especially with **salvation** and **judgment**, particularly of Israel. Matthew's "eschatological discourse" (chaps. 23–25 or 24–25) contains materials that have both apocalyptic and eschatological flavor, which focus primarily on developing community disciplines of watchfulness and resistance to false prophets and messiahs.

Like other New Testament authors, Matthew uses apocalyptic and eschatological forms and imagery to divorce audiences from the assumptions and entanglements of the fallen world, to engender hope, and to nurture imagination focused on God's presence and transforming power. For Matthew, Jesus' crucifixion is the defining apocalyptic (revelatory) moment, which turns the course of history, vanquishes death, and manifests God's true presence and power.

Christological titles. The portrayal of Jesus in Matthew's narrative itself is more important than any title used to describe Jesus, who both fulfills and redefines the existing categories and expectations. Matthew employs a wide array of titles to designate Jesus and define his identity, because none of them adequately describe him. The most prominent titles employed by Matthew are Son of God, Son of Man, and Son of David, which together both describe his messianic identity and convey the ambiguity and misunderstanding he generates. Jesus' divine power and identity are clearest to demons and to people on the margins of Jewish social power, but threaten the Jewish authorities. Even for the disciples, Jesus is a puzzle they can't quite work out, until they witness his crucifixion and resurrection (but still they "doubt," 28:17). The most important names and titles for Jesus that Matthew develops include:

Jesus, a Greek version of "Joshua," who led the people of Israel into the promised land. Matthew defines "Jesus" as the one who "will save his people from their sins" (1:21). But whom does "his people" include?

Emmanuel, "God with us" (1:23; cf. 28:20; 18:20; see Isa. 7:14). The whole of Matthew's Gospel may be understood as an attempt to define what this claim (Isaiah calls it a "sign") means.

Christ or **Messiah**, God's anointed one, is the title Peter uses to confess who the disciples think Jesus is (16:16), but Peter immediately reveals that he misunderstands what this confession means. The Jewish leaders seize upon this title at Jesus' trial (26:63) and lift it up again as they later mock him (26:68), alongside their derision of him as **"King of the Jews"** or **"King of Israel"** (27:37, 42). The unnamed woman at Bethany who anoints Jesus' head (26:6–13) may recognize more clearly than anyone else that Jesus' rule as king comes about through his death.

The **Son of David** is both a political figure, Israel's king, and, for Matthew, a healer. Jesus fulfills God's promise to raise up an offspring who will rule from David's throne and bring salvation to Israel. Technically, Jesus is Son of David by means of his public adoption by Joseph (1:21, 25). Jesus the Son of David is a king in exile, forced to flee to Egypt as an infant and to grow up in "Galilee of the Gentiles." This king enters Jerusalem to the acclaim of the marginal and disreputable. Jesus' ministry redefines who the Son of David is and how his kingly rule is realized—for Matthew principally in healing and restoration. Son of David is for Matthew a title filled with paradox, for Israel's leaders reject the rule of Jesus, while the blind, distressed, and marginal hail him as the awaited king.

Son of Man (lit., "the son of the man"), or **Son of Humanity**, or the **Human One**, is the title Jesus uses to designate himself. The Son of Man title in Matthew works like many of Jesus' **parables**: it is used openly, but carries multiple valences, including both judgment and vindication, and invites misunderstanding. It never occurs as an address or as part of a confession, but always in association with what Jesus does (e.g., healing, gathering, forgiving sins, cf. 8:20; 9:6), his suffering and death (e.g., 17:22–23; 20:18–19; 19:28; 26:2), and his coming in power as judge and savior (10:23; 16:27–28; 24:30; 24:36; 25:31; 26:64). Jesus thus designates himself as the representative figure for all of humankind, as one whose power is expressed in healing, humility, service, and suffering, and as the one who will be vindicated by God and come as judge of the nations and human rulers.

Son of God is a title that was used outside the Christian tradition loosely to designate humans who possessed surpassing powers, including, for example, the power to read minds (cf., e.g., 9:2, 4). Caesar Augustus was called both "savior" and "son of God." Across the ancient Near East, including Israel, kings were often designated "son of God" (cf. Pss. 2:6–7; 89:26–27; 2 Sam. 7:14). Israel herself is called God's "Son" (Exod. 4:22–23; Jer. 31:9, 20; Hos. 11:1), expressing both Israel's status as God's chosen and her call to obedience and service to God. As Son of God, Jesus thus recapitulates Israel's story, bringing to fulfillment God's intentions for Israel and for Israel's witness to the nations. For Matthew, Jesus' obedience to God, especially in his crucifixion, is the crucial factor in his identity as God's Son (3:17; 17:5).

Church. Only in Matthew does Jesus use the word *ekklēsia* ("church," 16:18; 18:17 twice). Matthew's use of the term is widely regarded as an anachronism, but the term was widely used in Greco-Roman cultures to designate assemblies, especially legislative or decision-making bodies. Already in the Greek Old Testament (LXX), *ekklēsia* refers to the congregation of Israel (Deut. 31:30; Judg. 20:2; 1 Sam. 17:47; 1 Kgs. 8:14). Each occasion in which Matthew uses the term focuses on the "church" (or "assembly" or "congregation") as an entity that exercises representative power on earth on behalf of "heaven." The congregation "binds" and "looses" (16:19; 18:18–20), which seems to refer to actions aimed at resisting the powers of death (16:18) and facilitating reconciliation and restoration of errant disciples (18:15–17). This suggests that Matthew's use of "church" is consistent with prior usage of the term in Jewish tradition to refer to Israel as a decision-making and witness-bearing body, and may not presume later, more developed use of the term in the Christian tradition. By extension, the church in Matthew is also the body of disciples called to bear witness to God's power in the world, especially the power of Jesus' cross and resurrection, bringing healing, liberation, and reconciliation to a broken, bound, and alienated world. Mission, i.e., bearing witness to God's presence and power in Jesus, is not one thing among many others that the assembly of disciples does. Rather, "the church exists by mission, just as fire exists by burning" (Emil Brunner, cf. Carlos Cardoza-Orlandi, *Mission: An Essential Guide* [Nashville: Abingdon Press, 2002], 13). The mission of Jesus' disciples in Matthew includes practices of repentance, hospitality, forgiveness, healing, exorcism, proclamation, watching, praying, teaching, baptizing, and mercy toward the least ones, all without expectation of reward or earthly success, but with certainty that God will vindicate the faithful. The church is thus called to continue Jesus' mission of announcing God's presence and rule to the world and to bear witness to God's faithfulness and **justice/righteousness**, as Israel also has been called to do.

Controversy stories. Matthew's controversy stories (or conflict stories, or "challenge-riposte" stories) are contests for honor, focusing on Jesus' teaching and actions, or the actions of his disciples. Controversies usually signal formal opposition to Jesus and his ministry. In some instances, the challenges are "trick" questions, meant to pose a riddle that Jesus presumably will not be able to solve (e.g., 22:23–33) or to entrap him in an unpopular or dangerous controversy (e.g., 22:15–22). Jesus' challengers usually are attempting to diminish his honor and public status; the winner gains honor and esteem at the loser's expense. Matthew includes roughly fifteen controversy stories in the Gospel, most of them clustered in chapters 9 and 12, and especially in chapters 21 and 22, just before his arrest, where defeat in any controversy would bring to an end the threat Jesus poses to the Jerusalem leaders.

Fulfillment quotations. Matthew's story is deeply immersed in the Scriptures. The Gospel includes a rich and deep array of quotations, allusions, paraphrases, and scriptural allegories, including ten "fulfillment" or "formula quotations," all distinctive to this Gospel, that are introduced by a statement (e.g., 1:22) that identifies an event or element in the story as the fulfillment of Scripture (1:22–23; 2:15; 2:17–18; 2:23; 4:14–16; 8:17; 12:18–21; 13:35; 21:4–5; 27:9). While Matthew usually follows the

Septuagint when quoting Scripture, these ten citations differ from any known text type. Matthew typically uses these citations as a concluding or transitional summary following a narrative. The most obvious function of the quotations is to highlight important links between Jesus and the stories and hopes of Israel. Many of the quotations, however, are ambiguous prophecies, open to more than one interpretation, or to multiple "fulfillments." Matthew usually draws the quotations from rich, resonant historical and literary contexts that repay careful attention.

Gospel/good news. While this term is used only four times in Matthew, on three of those occasions it is used in conjunction with the term **empire** or **kingdom** (4:23; 9:35; 24:14; cf. 26:13). Like the messengers who made public announcements of the "good news" of Caesar's "kingdom," Jesus is the herald of God's rule in both word and deed. The early Christians used this term "gospel" in conscious imitation (and mockery) of the announcements of military victories and ascensions of rulers to power. The gospel is thus not merely good news about salvation to come in some distant future, but the proclamation and enactment of a new power and order, God's kingdom, among us here and now.

Honor. Honor was one of the central values of ancient Mediterranean peoples and a primary and limited "good" for which individuals and households competed. While people today associate honor with respect, integrity, and distinction, ancient people understood honor to have a close association with the accumulation of wealth, status, and social power. Public encounters between social equals were contests for honor, usually with clear winners and losers. The **controversy stories** are accounts of such public contests for honor. While most people considered crucifixion the ultimate expression of dishonor, for Christians the death of Jesus and his vindication by God constituted a foundational challenge to the world's reckoning of power and honor.

Jewish religious leaders. Throughout Matthew's Gospel, Jesus' primary opponents come from segments of first-century Jewish society that reflect the interests of wealth, political power, and religious status and distinction. In various ways, each of Jesus' adversaries–who often stood in opposition to each other in other matters–has something at stake in preserving the existing arrangements and in opposing the rule of God that Jesus announces and inaugurates. We should understand these character groups not as representatives of the Jewish people or of "Judaism," but as figures who represent and reveal the nature of human opposition to God's ways, across times, cultures, and religions. Jesus' opponents include the self-righteous, collaborators with Rome, and rich, exploitive landowners, but also intellectuals, bureaucrats, and ultimately even the crowds. Many of Jesus' opponents may have been motivated by sincere interest in preserving Israel's integrity in the midst of a complex and threatening world, by love of Israel's Scriptures, traditions, and religious institutions, or simply by their fear of what Rome might do in response to a messianic revolt. There were, and are, many sources of blindness and many reasons to fear and oppose God's coming rule, especially for those who are deeply invested in the preservation of the existing order.

The Pharisees were a broad-based, varied, and evolving movement of mostly laypeople who were concerned with the question of what it meant to be the true people of God. The Pharisees' roots may lie in the upheaval of the Babylonian exile, in concerns about "syncretism," and in questions about identity upon the exiles' return under the leadership of Ezra and Nehemiah. Over time, the Pharisaic movement took shape in the quest for separation and distinction based on careful observance of the law, Sabbath practice, and purity regulations (not hygiene, but rituals that distinguished "clean" from "unclean"). The Pharisees also preserved and advocated the "tradition of the elders" (15:2), which was the oral tradition of interpretation of the law handed down across the generations and later recorded in the Mishnah. Like Jesus, they affirmed the resurrection and upheld the importance of table fellowship. But for Jesus table fellowship was a site for discerning God's presence among sinners and outcasts, while for the Pharisees it was often a setting for marking distinctions (cf. 9:10–13).

Matthew persistently identifies the Pharisees as opponents of Jesus, both in Galilee and in Judea and Jerusalem. They are the identified targets of Jesus' harsh polemic against hypocrisy and violence in Matthew 23. Matthew's harsh depiction of the Pharisees is a literary caricature, which should not be taken to represent Judaism, nor even all of ancient Pharisaism. For Matthew, rather, this caricature represents human religiosity diverted from true devotion to God toward self-interest and grandiosity, which in turn breeds alienation and ruptures the trust and integrity of God's people, thus standing at odds with Jesus' campaign of inclusion and restoration.

Scribes represent the intellectual elite who were students of the Law and the Prophets. We might compare them, variously, with professors, lawyers, and bureaucrats. They often served as agents and representatives of the ruling authorities of Jerusalem, whose power they legitimated and articulated both there and in other cities of Israel. Their "learning" was usually exercised for the sake of the elites, and thus at the expense of smallholders and common people. In Matthew, the scribes are often allied with the Pharisees, with whom they worked to reestablish Judaism following the destruction of Jerusalem and the temple by the Romans.

Matthew usually mentions the **elders** of the people in association with the **chief priests**. The elders were probably people of wealth and status who represented the interests of Jerusalem's most distinguished families. The chief priests had official charge of the temple and its systems of sacrifice. They laid claim to identity with ancient priestly lineage, but usually served at the discretion of rulers like Herod the Great. Both the chief priests and the elders were, in Jesus' day, wealthy landowners–one might even call them land barons–who used their power and office to legitimize exploitation and land theft. In Matthew they are the primary figures involved in orchestrating Jesus' arrest, trial, and execution.

Sadducees, like the Pharisees, were concerned with the preservation of Jewish life and identity under foreign domination and cultural syncretism, but approached this through accommodation rather than through separation. During the Maccabean period, Sadducees established a hold on the high priesthood and, through it, both political power and wealth. They were the aristocrats of Jesus' day, seeking moderation and the preservation of the existing order. They emphasized God's transcendence and distance from daily human life and they rejected the more dynamic, oral "tradition of the elders" in favor of "conservative" interpretation of the law. Because they lacked popular support and were no longer needed after Rome reasserted its power following the Jewish revolt in 66–70 CE, they left no significant legacy. For Matthew, the Sadducees represent political stasis and corruption, characteristic of those who seek comity with the world's rulers. For the Sadducees, God is not the God of "the living" (22:32). The term **"Herodians"** (cf. 22:16) may also designate the Sadducees or their close allies, i.e., people who supported and benefited from the rule of the Herods, who served as Roman client kings and princes during the lifetime of Jesus.

Judgment/salvation/mercy. Matthew's Gospel features warnings and images of judgment more prominently and frequently than the other Gospels, especially in the **parables** and discourses, which typically end on a note of warning. At the same time, Matthew highlights God's mercy, forgiveness, and salvation. Modern readers may find Matthew's juxtaposition of judgment and salvation disconcerting or paradoxical, but for the evangelist the two are inextricably linked. God's presence and power that are announced and expressed in Jesus' ministry bring both judgment and salvation. Life in God's presence is salvation, just as life lived apart from God means judgment. Jesus' statements about the "coming" of the **Son of Humanity** (e.g., 16:27–28; 24:30–31; 25:31–46) typically include both references to judgment and, for Jesus' disciples, reassurances of vindication and salvation. Jesus thus envisions salvation and judgment in present human experience, as well as in God's actions to come. Judgment comes to those who reject Jesus and his ministry, as they had rejected the prophets before him, and on those who trust human forms of power–both political and religious–rather than the power of God manifested in Jesus. Matthew also focuses especially on the ethical and relational dimensions of human practice as the basis for judgment and salvation (or wholeness). Matthew's parable of the sheep and the goats (25:31–46) describes a time when all people, including Israel, the nations, and Jesus' own followers, will stand before the Son of Man as judge, who will divide them based on their practices of mercy and justice toward those who are most vulnerable. The story also affirms that the king/judge/Son of Humanity is present among the "least ones," but that neither the righteous nor the unrighteous have recognized him. This implies that doing good, even to those in need, may bring judgment if one does it only to earn God's reward. Salvation, rather, is discovered among those who care for one another without regard for what they might receive in return and among those who build genuine relationships of justice and wholeness with the most vulnerable people of this world.

Kingdom/empire of heaven/God's reign/God's rule/God's empire, heavenly empire. The empire of heaven is Matthew's designation for the irruption of God's power and rule in the human world. The Greek word *basileia* was used to designate the "empire of Rome." Matthew uses the same term to designate the "kingdom" or "empire," of heaven. Although English translations usually prefer the more archaic "kingdom" over "empire," in this commentary the two words are used interchangeably, with a mild preference for "empire," which more clearly highlights the alternative political, economic, and social dimensions of the rule of God in contrast to the empire of Rome and other human empires. Mark and Luke prefer the designation "empire/kingdom of God" (4 times in Matthew). Matthew may have preferred the modifier "heaven" (32 times in Matthew) in deference to Jewish sensitivities about uttering the divine name. "Heaven" also allows Matthew more clearly to set the spatial designations "heaven" and "earth" in play. For Matthew, the heavenly empire is not located in another space or time (e.g., the future), but is already present in the proclamation and ministry of Jesus and his disciples here in this world. Jesus crosses and blurs the boundaries between heaven and earth, demonstrates and shares divine power with his disciples, and grants to humans God's power to forgive debts and sin. Jesus' ministry of healing, forgiveness, feeding, restoration, gathering, exorcism, crossing of social boundaries, and community formation delineates the nature, effects, and dimensions of God's power and rule. Although the empire of the heavens is more real and powerful than the empires of this world, it remains invisible to many and constitutes a threat to those who hold human power and status. Jesus turns to **parables** to describe the empire of heaven because of their power to provoke the hearing, sight, and understanding necessary to discern God's presence and to turn (repent) toward God.

Parable. The parables are the definitive expression of Jesus' teaching for, not just about, the **empire of heaven**. Strange, explosive, enigmatic, and audacious, parables are an **"apocalyptic"** form of speech that simultaneously conceal and reveal God's empire. Parables are like Janus, the Roman god of gates, doorways, endings, and beginnings, who was usually depicted with two faces (or sometimes four). The parables have more than one face; they open doors for some while shutting others out. On the one hand, they reveal "what has been hidden from the foundation of the world" (Matt. 13:35), but Jesus tells them, on the other hand, so that his audience might "hear" but never "understand" (13:13; Isa. 6:9–10).

Matthew's Gospel includes roughly twenty parables, about half of which are unique to this Gospel alone. All but a handful are clustered together in four blocks: the parable discourse (13:3–52), the discourse on discipleship (18:12–14, 23–35), Jesus' response to the Jerusalem leaders' questions about his authority (21:23–22:14), and the "eschatological discourse" (24:42–25:46). Where the parables are delivered to the crowds or adversaries, they produce misunderstanding, division, and hostility. When the disciples are the primary audience, Jesus may include an extended explanation (e.g., 13:18–23, 36–43, 49–50) or concluding application (e.g., 18:35; 20:16). The disciples, whose understanding of the parables bears fruit, hear them as a revelation of God's will and rule. For others, especially for Jesus' adversaries who do not bear fruit fit for the kingdom, the parables both speak about and become the occasion for judgment. Parables are learned and understood not in the abstract, but in practice. Obedience–bearing fruit–is the most important hermeneutical requirement (see Luz, *Matthew 8–20*, 292–93).

Given the ambiguity and multivalence of Jesus' parables, their interpretation requires particular care by modern readers, who customarily try to find the single or primary meaning of Jesus' teaching, whether by the use of imaginative allegory or by reduction. C. H. Dodd's oft-repeated definition of parables is still a viable starting point today: "At its simplest the parable is a metaphor or simile drawn from nature or common life, arresting the hearer by its vividness or strangeness, and leaving the mind in sufficient doubt about its precise application to tease it into active thought" (Dodd, *The Parables of the Kingdom*, rev. ed. [London: Collins: 1961] 15–16). The elements juxtaposed in Jesus' parables may at first appear to be simple similes for the sake of direct comparison ("the kingdom of heaven is like . . ."), but upon closer examination the juxtapositions turn out to be more catalytic than comparative. The parables combust, producing both smoke and light. If we find that a parable raises nagging questions for us, resists precise application, refuses to fit neatly into a box, and makes us keep thinking about God's rule and the world we live in, then that parable is probably working as it should.

It is important to respect a parable's capacity to generate diverse meanings even where Jesus supplies an allegorical explanation or application (13:18–23, 36–43, 49–50). Jesus' explanations are not meant to diminish or tame the generative power of the parables, but to focus them for the disciples. The allegorical explanation Jesus provides is not the only possible or right interpretation of the parable, but the right interpretation for the disciples. Even in the cases where Matthew supplies extended allegorical interpretations, the evangelist effectively creates room for the generative energy of the parable to have full expression by separating the explanation from the parable.

Parables are meant to be performed—to be heard, understood, and to bear fruit—rather than merely interpreted. Interpretation is, of course, always a necessary first step, but if we understand interpretation as translating the parable into essential ideas or teachings, we inevitably reduce its power to engage the whole person. One creative approach to the parables is to recast their characters and plots into contemporary formats, while preserving as much of the original dynamics—conflict, surprise, risk—of the parable as possible. Another is to invite contemporary audiences to reflect critically on the characters they vilify or with whom they identify, and consider why.

The parables are meant to disturb the everyday rationality of their audience and, by means of dislocation and destabilization, lead those who will listen to a place where they may discern what God is doing. Those who are left blind and deaf by the world may respond to a word that exposes and breaks free of the limits of worldly expectation. Jesus' parables thus work to unveil the world as it is, to subvert prevailing worldviews, and to transform our relationships with God and the world.* Some of Jesus' parables are exposés that provide their audiences with the tools to critically examine the way their world really works. The laborers in the vineyard (20:1–16), for example, describes the vulnerability of the day laborers and the power of the landowners. The parable of the talents (25:14–30) pulls the cover from the workings of the ancient **patronage** economy. Telling stories that reveal the way the world works gives hearers critical distance and, potentially, the capacity to imagine another way (for an insightful approach to the parables informed by Paolo Freire's liberative pedagogy, see William Herzog II, *Parables as Subversive Speech: Jesus as Pedagogue of the Oppressed* [Louisville, KY: Westminster John Knox Press, 1994]). Some parables not only expose, but subvert the ways we see ourselves and the world. Matthew's version of the "wicked tenant farmers" (21:33–44) decodes the world of rich landowners and opportunistic and violent tenants, and then turns the tables on Jesus' adversaries, the **chief priests** and **elders**, who were themselves wealthy, exploitive landowners. Finally, the parables offer us visions and opportunities to transform the world. Amidst a variety of threats, some of the seeds in the parable of the sower (13:3–9) yield an abundant crop, thus inviting the audience to participate in the harvest Jesus is gathering. Even though it ends on a note of severe judgment, the parable of the unmerciful servant (18:23–35) invites its hearers to join Jesus in the way of forgiveness. Interpretation that attends to these kinds of dynamics at work within parables may in turn suggest ways we might retell the parables for our own times.

Patronage/patron. Patronage is the word used most often to describe the ancient economy. When modern people hear the word "economy," we typically think in terms of financial systems and means of acquiring wealth. Ancient people were clearer than we are today about the interrelationship of social, political, and financial dimensions of life, which together constituted the "economy" (lit., the law or order of the household). The patron (father or householder) was the central figure in the ancient household, which was the basic social unit of identity (not the individual), and the primary model for social life from the local to the cosmic levels. The whole empire was Caesar's household. Patrons and their households competed for **honor** and wealth, usually measured in terms of the number of "clients" (debtors) a patron had. Clients were expected to repay debts through cash or services and also to honor their patrons publicly. Virtually everyone was in debt to someone else or was considered to

---

*I am grateful to the Rev. Anne McKee for this typology of parables based on their capacity to expose, shatter, and create worlds.

be property of a patron (e.g., slaves, women, and children). In both public and private life, people attended constantly to debts and obligations, what they were owed and what they owed others, both financially and socially. At Jesus' baptism, he effectively declares himself free of obligation to anyone but God, his heavenly "Father." Jesus also calls on his disciples to forgive others' debts as they had themselves been forgiven. Jesus' understanding of forgiveness thus carried not merely religious implications, but financial, social, and political consequences of first importance.

Prophetic-symbolic action/prophetic sign-act. When Jesus heals someone or exorcises demons, his actions have an immediate effect on that person and usually impress observers as well. The meaning of his actions, however, reaches beyond the individuals healed or impressed. More often than not, Jesus' actions also challenge the assumptions and worldviews of his audience. Jesus' miracles, healings, exorcisms, and practices of table fellowship are signs that reveal God's presence and power at work in the world. The full meaning and consequences of Jesus' actions must be discerned in relation to the setting and symbolic order in which they occur. When Jesus enters Jerusalem to the acclaim of his followers (21:1–11), for example, he is enacting a well-known social script associated with the advent (or "Parousia") of military conquerors. His triumphal entry is thus a "prophetic-symbolic action" that announces to all of Jerusalem that its king has arrived. At the same time, Jesus is mocking the notions and conventions of power, status, and dominion associated with such triumphal entries in the Roman world. The full meaning of Jesus' entry lies in the questions it raises about power, kingship, and servanthood. Similarly, John the Baptizer's ministry of repentance in the wilderness around the Jordan River is both a sign of the inauguration of a new exodus and a repudiation of the sacrificial system's power to redeem. The crucial prophetic-symbolic action in Jesus' ministry is the crucifixion, which, more than just a means of execution, is a public "liturgy" or ritual action laden with meaning. Rome believes crucifixion reasserts its authority, restores social order, and demonstrates its divine power over life and death. The leaders of Israel see the crucifixion as a means to rid themselves of a messianic troubler and reestablish their control over the temple and the sacrificial system. For Jesus and the early Christians, however, the cross is the place where God vanquishes the power of death in its most extreme form, and thus demonstrates the true nature of divine power.

Righteousness/justice. Matthew emphasizes the importance of right relationships, between humans and God and between humans themselves. The word Matthew uses to designate these relationships is *dikaiosyne*, which has no precise English equivalent. Protestant interpreters have tended to prefer the English word "righteousness," which carries mostly religious and moral freight, while Catholic interpreters prefer the word "justice," which in English usage carries legal connotations. For Matthew, however, the term cannot be limited to either religious or legal spheres, but has more to do with relationships and actions that display or produce trust, equity, forgiveness, and reconciliation. Matthew uses the term "hypocrite" virtually as an antonym to "justice/righteousness": "hypocrites" may engage in behavior that meets the letter of the law or conveys the appearance of virtue and devotion, but in the end the hypocrite's actions serve his or her own self-interest by drawing attention and marking distinctions, rather than producing whole, reconciled relationships. For Matthew, righteousness/justice fulfills the true intention of the law and realizes God's will for humankind and the creation, which precedes the law. Jesus' adoptive father, Joseph, for example, is described as a "righteous" person (1:19) because he follows God's direction and will, even when doing so runs contrary to convention. Jesus himself, however, is Matthew's primary model of what it means to be just or righteous. Jesus' death on the cross is Matthew's defining expression of God's righteousness toward Israel and the nations, as well as humankind's righteous response to God and to one another.

Time. Human cultures have diverse ways of imagining and talking about the relationship of memory, experience, expectation, and hope to the stories in which they live. Modern, Western societies imagine time as a line that moves in one direction and that can be measured in precise increments. We also treat time as a commodity that can be bought and sold, and we have a strong orientation toward what we call the future. Our notions of time most resemble the ancient Greek notion of *chronos* time, time that could be measured or quantified. But Mediterranean people more commonly thought of time in terms of experience, relationship, and expectation, for which they used the word *kairos*. *Kairos* is a "kind of time," usually defined in association with particular experiences, behaviors, rulers, or seasons, e.g., the time of planting or harvest, festival times, Sabbath, the time of Caesar, war, messianic time, etc. *Kairos* time may or may not have clear chronological dimensions. Ancient people also had a much stronger orientation toward memory and the ancestors (what we call the "past") and toward present experience than toward the future. When we speak of "the end-time," we usually presume experience that lies at the end of, or beyond, the line of history, while New Testament era people would have considered the end-time as a *kairos*, a kind of time associated with such events as the gathering and restoration of Israel, resurrection of the dead, the outpouring of the Spirit, and the coming of the messiah, whether as savior, judge, or both. Knowing what time it is–the *kairos*–implies conforming one's behavior and expectations, as well as the community's practices, to the norms appropriate to that time. In Matthew, the announcement of the empire of heaven and God's presence and rule is a *kairos* associated with repentance, faith, the crossing of human and divine boundaries, divine power at work among humans, and ultimately Jesus' conquest of death. (See Bruce Malina, "Christ and Time: Swiss or Mediterranean?" *Catholic Biblical Quarterly* 51 [1989]: 1–31.)

SELECT BIBLIOGRAPHY

Twenty years ago there were but a handful of strong commentaries on Matthew's Gospel. Today many fine studies are available. Attentive readers will discover that in writing this volume I have turned most often to the commentaries by Warren Carter and Ulrich Luz. Carter's 2000 commentary, *Matthew and the Margins*, shifted attention to the Roman imperial context in which Matthew was written, drawing forth aspects of the Matthew narrative that had long been overlooked. Many of Carter's essays on Matthew and the Roman Empire have been collected in *Matthew and Empire: Initial Explorations* (Harrisburg, PA: Trinity Press International, 2001). International scholarship spurred by Carter's studies has been collected in John Riches and David C. Sim, *The Gospel of Matthew in Its Roman Imperial Context,* JSNT Supplement Series 276 (London and New York: T. & T. Clark International / Continuum, 2005). Over more than thirty years Ulrich Luz has been producing a series of outstanding studies devoted to Matthew, culminating in the three-volume commentary published in English as part of the Hermeneia Series (Minneapolis: Fortress Press): *Matthew 1–7* (new edition 2007), *Matthew 8–20* (2001), and *Matthew 21–28* (2005). Luz offers not only finely detailed and carefully argued theological expositions, but insight from the "reception history" of the Gospel, including, in the final volume, numerous photographs of Matthean stories in art. Other recommended volumes include:

Betz, Hans Dieter. *The Sermon on the Mount.* Hermeneia. Minneapolis: Fortress Press, 1995.

Boring, M. Eugene. *The Gospel of Matthew.* The New Interpreter's Bible, 8:87–505. Nashville: Abingdon Press, 1995.

Bruner, Frederick Dale. *Matthew,* vol. 1, *The Christbook: Matthew 1–12,* and *Matthew,* vol. 2, *The Churchbook: Matthew 13–28.* Dallas: Word Publishing, 1987 and 1990.

Byrne, Brendan, S.J. *Lifting the Burden: Reading Matthew's Gospel in the Church Today.* Collegeville, MN: Liturgical Press, 2004. An insightful survey from a Catholic perspective.

Carter, Warren. *Matthew and the Margins*. Maryknoll, NY: Orbis Books, 2000.

Clarke, Howard. *The Gospel of Matthew and Its Readers*. Bloomington, IN: Indiana University Press, 2003. A survey of readings of Matthew across the history of the church.

Crosby, Michael H. *House of Disciples: Church, Economics, and Justice in Matthew*. Maryknoll, NY: Orbis Books, 1988.

Davies, Margaret. *Matthew*. Sheffield: JSOT/Sheffield Academic Press, 1993. A brief, accessible, and solid resource.

Davies, W. D., and Dale C. Allison Jr. *The Gospel according to Saint Matthew*. International Critical Commentary. 3 vols. Edinburgh: T. & T. Clark, 1988, 1991, 1997. Careful, detailed, critical examination of the text and interpretive alternatives.

Garland, David. *Reading Matthew: A Literary and Theological Commentary on the First Gospel*. New York: Crossroad, 1993. An excellent study of Matthew as story.

Graves, Mike, and David M. May. *Preaching Matthew: Interpretation and Proclamation*. St. Louis: Chalice Press, 2007.

Guelich, Robert. *The Sermon on the Mount: A Foundation for Understanding*. Dallas: Word Publishing, 1982.

Hagner, Donald A. *Matthew 1–13* and *Matthew 14–28*. Word Biblical Commentary 33A and B. Dallas: Word Books, 1993 and 1995. A thorough, insightful commentary from an evangelical scholar.

Hare, Douglas R. A. *Matthew*. Interpretation. Louisville, KY: John Knox Press, 1993.

Harrington, Daniel J., S.J. *The Gospel of Matthew*. Sacra Pagina 1. Collegeville, MN: Michael Glazier / Liturgical Press, 1991. Fine readings in an accessible format.

Hauerwas, Stanley. *Matthew*. Brazos Theological Commentary on the Bible. Grand Rapids: Brazos Press, 2006. An insightful, thought-provoking commentary by a renowned ethicist.

Keener, Craig S. *Matthew*. IVP New Testament Commentary. Downers Grove, IL: InterVarsity Press, 1997.

———. *A Commentary on the Gospel of Matthew*. Grand Rapids: Wm. B. Eerdmans Publishing Co., 1999.

Kingsbury, Jack Dean. *Matthew as Story*. 2nd ed. Philadelphia: Fortress Press, 1988.

Levine, Amy-Jill. *The Social and Ethnic Dimensions of Matthean Salvation History: "Go Nowhere among the Gentiles . . ." (Matthew 10:5b)*. Lewiston, NY: Edwin Mellen Press, 1988.

Long, Thomas G. *Matthew*. Westminster Bible Companion. Louisville, KY: Westminster John Knox Press, 1997. An excellent resource for preachers and teachers of Matthew.